Signs in the Heavens

Biblical Prophecy and Astronomy

John Abent

© Copyright 1995 — John Abent

All rights reserved. This book is protected under the copyright laws of the United States of America. This book may not be copied or reprinted for commercial gain or profit. The use of short quotations or occasional page copying for personal or group study is permitted and encouraged. Permission will be granted upon request. Unless otherwise identified, Scripture quotations are from the King James Version of the Bible.

Take note that the name satan and related names are not capitalized. We choose not to acknowledge him, even to the point of violating grammatical rules.

Any emphasis within Scripture quotations is the author's own. Reference quotations also reflect occasional emphasis by the author and is noted accordingly.

Treasure House

An Imprint of

Destiny Image Publishers, Inc. ®

P.O. Box 310

Shippensburg, PA 17257-0310

"For where your treasure is
there will your heart be also." Matthew 6:21

ISBN 1-56043-828-2

For Worldwide Distribution
Printed in the U.S.A.

Treasure House books are available through these fine distributors outside the United States:

Christian Growth, Inc.
Jalan Kilang-Timor, Singapore 0315

Rhema Ministries Trading
Randburg, South Africa

Salvation Book Centre
Petaling, Jaya, Malaysia

Successful Christian Living
Capetown, Rep. of South Africa

Vine Christian Centre
Mid Glamorgan, Wales, United Kingdom

Vision Resources
Ponsonby, Auckland, New Zealand

WA Buchanan Company
Geebung, Queensland, Australia

Word Alive
Niverville, Manitoba, Canada

Inside the U.S., call toll free to order:
1-800-722-6774

Dedication

I would like to dedicate this work to a very special Christian, Bethany Pisanchyn. Her testimony allows us to view the Rapture, or the return of our Lord Jesus Christ, from a totally different perspective. Bethany is now 12 years old. At age ten she was diagnosed with a brain tumor. Removing the tumor, which was attached to her pituitary gland, required that both tumor and gland be removed. As a result of the operation, Bethany's entire glandular system has been affected and she has lost half her vision. She must take daily medications for the rest of her physical life.

However, we praise God for sparing Bethany and her sweet personality. She still goes to school, practices her piano, helps her mother, and is very determined to be an overcomer for Jesus Christ.

During her ordeal Bethany told her mom and dad, "I am glad that this happened to me and not to one of my brothers or sisters because that would be too much for me to handle." She obviously loves her younger brothers and sisters very much. After her operation she also stated that she was looking forward to the Second Coming of Christ more than ever before because then she would "have a new body."

Therefore, because of her testimony, her selfless, sacrificial love, and her overwhelming desire for Christ's return, I humbly dedicate *Signs in the Heavens* to Bethany Pisanchyn, one of the bravest and greatest Christians I know.

Acknowledgments

I would like to thank all those who have worked with me to make this book a reality. First, I would like to thank my wife, Laurene, who has endured many hours alone while I worked on the manuscript. She has given me her support and unfailing love throughout the years of study and research.

Second, I would like to thank all those who have assisted in the editing process. Dan Mahan, Bob Mahlstedt, Pastor Al Cremard, and Professor Steve Horine read the text and constructively directed me to make needed changes. I would also like to acknowledge the very fine editing staff of Treasure House for their high professional publishing standards.

I would also like to thank those who have helped to finance this project: Domnick and Nancy Brunori, Mark and Misty Abent, Bob and Lucille Mahlstedt, and Garfield and Lorraine Edmonds. I want to thank them for believing in my work and in the text of *Signs in the Heavens* enough to invest in its publication.

Other writers with whom I have had and still have very much in common with, theologically, are to be acknowledged for their time, effort, and courage.

Finally, I would like to thank all the members and friends of Faith Baptist Church, Berlin, Maryland, for their prayers, enthusiastic response, and support. Their response to the message contained within the pages of this book helped to assure me that God's Holy Spirit has been intimately involved in its development.

Contents

Foreword

This book is the end result of four years of study, contemplation, personal debate, information gathering, Scripture studies, prayer, and seeking the Lord's direction. Many times I attempted to abandon this study, only to have the Lord speak to my heart as He urged me to continue.

As a result, I have seen something in Scripture that I believe needs to be considered very carefully. I did not start out to write a book. I began my study with the sole purpose of gaining a better personal understanding of biblical prophecies. However, as I began to share the results of my study with others, they encouraged me to write this book.

My study of the Book of Revelation began with an intense interest and a desire to understand Revelation chapter 12, especially the visions that John saw in the beginning of the chapter and the explanations that follow. After reading hundreds of books on Revelation, I soon recognized, like Harry Ironside—a noted self-taught Bible expositor of the nineteenth century—that by reading a writer's interpretation of Revelation chapter 12, one can quickly determine the writer's position on eschatology. The writer's amillennial, premillennial, postmillennial, pretribulation, posttribulation, midtribulation, or other position can quickly be determined by the way the woman, the man-child, the child, and the dragon of Revelation chapter 12 are interpreted.

I have labored to reduce my biases to a minimum. From the very beginning I have declared that everything I believe about Revelation and prophecy is open to change or adjustment if the study of Scripture requires it. Truth was, and still is, my quest. I am guided by the truth that God is not the author of confusion.

I believe that God has given us a complete witness in prophecy. If we consider all of Scripture, which is saying a lot in itself, and seek a consistent and unified understanding of prophecy, which ties all of Scripture together from Genesis through the Gospels and the New Testament, then and only then can we begin to be certain that our understanding is correct. Truth always sheds light and often exposes other hidden facts.

This has been the case throughout this study. Scriptures that were once skimmed over and seemingly insignificant have burst forth with new insight and explanatory power. Truth explains and illuminates understanding. This fact has driven me to continue this study and write this book. Over and over I was led to pause, bow my head, and praise God for His perfect and complete Word as the Book of Revelation unfolded before me.

The process of learning should, and often does, produce a degree of caution in the academic mind. We are confronted with how much we do not know. I have exegeted many of the Scripture passages and compared my findings with other writers. I have decided, however, not to include the majority of my technical notes in this book. To include them would overburden the average reader, thus making this book appear as a technical commentary on the Book of Revelation. I do not wish to author a commentary on Revelation.

Technical commentaries usually have a narrow focus that exposes the smallest of potentially significant details. This is good and vital work for understanding the text. They usually list the possible interpretations and the positive and negatives of a referenced position. Therefore, the technical commentary is not written with the average reader in mind.

I have, instead, attempted to paint a picture by blending all the colors (pieces of information) together, while leaving the paints, palette, and brushes on my desk. I present this picture to the reader with a sense of great urgency and caution.

I feel *urgency* because there is no other book, that I know of, that blends together so many subject matters regarding prophecy and ties them to contemporary events. The subject matters of astronomy, science, history, contemporary characters/events, and Bible prophecy are all combined and considered as a comprehensive whole.

By considering all of these areas, I have come to an understanding of biblical prophecy that I believe validates the urgent warnings that have already gone out from many other authors—the *"Day of the Lord" is coming very soon.* The evidence that I present to the reader will complement many other pretribulation positions that are already circulating.

Because of this, I may not cover many selected topics in the study of prophecy with satisfactory detail for every reader. Instead, I will refer the curious reader to other sources for more detailed information. In addition, I will reveal some startling "new" evidence that seems to indicate that we are inescapably very near those final days that will, in fact, see the Rapture of the Church and the start of the tribulation period as prophesied by the prophet Daniel and the Lord Jesus Christ Himself.

I write with *caution* because I understand the seriousness of the material that I am releasing. I do not want this information to cause a panic or a mood of despair for fear of what may be coming upon the earth. On the other hand, I do want this book to wake professing Christians out of their sleep and guide non-Christians out of their darkness. We need to be about the King's business. The hour of His judgment may be fast approaching an unsuspecting, unrepentant "world" and "Laodicean Church."

It is my hope that this book will stir everyone who reads it to consider or reconsider the prophecies concerning the Second Coming of our Lord and Savior, Jesus Christ.

Preface

This book is primarily about prophecy. However, it is different from other prophecy books because it combines both the prophecies of the Old and New Testament Scriptures and the science of astronomy to produce one clear witness about the Second Coming of the Lord Jesus Christ.

The Church seems to have grown weary and confused over the debate between the premillennial, postmillennial, and amillennial positions. Premillennialists believe Christ will first return, then set up His 1,000-year Kingdom, while postmillennialists believe He will return after the Church has established the Kingdom of God; amillennialists do not believe in any specific 1,000-year reign. (See Chapter 3, "Theological and Eschatological Positions," for more on these positions.) These positions have been sparring for decades now, with no clear winner emerging from the ring. Each position has defended a claim of truth from the interpretation of books such as Daniel and Revelation, which are ultimately at the heart of understanding biblical prophecy.

Some positions depend on symbolic interpretation, while others take more of a literal position. Symbolic or allegorical interpretation has opened the door for a wide divergence of prophetic interpretations. As a result of the confusion, many pastors have shied away from teaching or preaching from the Book of Revelation. It is my belief that, while many pastors and Christian leaders are diligently teaching and watching for the Second Coming of Jesus Christ, many are not.

Some state that, "[they] are a pretribulationalist but [they] never preach on it." Rosenthal suggests that, because of this attitude, "...the prevailing views are, in fact, fatally flawed, and that a fresh new examination not only should be welcomed but warmly encouraged."[1]

I would agree with Paul S. Karleen, however, that for one to conclude that opposing positions are both wrong because they disagree is too restrictive and without good logic.[2] Still other groups are questioning the canonicity of Revelation itself.[3] Unanswered challenges arising from opposing positions have caused some (who held to the pretribulation position) to seek a kind of middle ground, which is precisely what the prewrath Rapture position of Marvin Rosenthal represents. As a result, some have left the pretribulationist position for Rosenthal's prewrath Rapture position.

This book is not a middle ground or a compromise with opposing positions. Instead, I seek to present the truth about the chronology of prophecy, specifically the Second Coming of the Lord Jesus Christ and the Rapture. In order to accomplish this I determined beforehand to explore every aspect of biblical prophecy previously held. "What if?" questions were asked.

What if the seven-year tribulation period, otherwise known as "Daniel's Seventieth Week," does not officially begin until the sixth or the seventh seal is opened? What would this do to the chronology of the visions of Revelation? What would this do to the placement of the two witnesses of Revelation chapter 11? When would satan be cast to the earth?

Why do most translators believe that the opening of the first seal starts the seven years of tribulation? Are there good exegetical reasons for this conclusion, or has it just been assumed?

I now believe the latter; however, it is just an assumption without good exegetical support. This book presents the position and the evidence to support that the Seventieth Week of Daniel and the seven years of tribulation begin with the opening of the seventh seal. With the seventh seal opened, the decrees of the scroll in the hands of Jesus Christ can be decreed and carried out.

This book is also different because it makes both logical and scriptural sense of *all* of the Book of Revelation. Passages that were skimmed over or problem passages previously unexplained are clarified and tied together. The visions as seen and presented to us by John, when properly understood, present one beautiful mosaic picture of the Church Age that leads up to the seven years of tribulation, followed by the millennial rule of Christ. This book presents a position that explains the gospel's account of Christ's Second Coming and clearly links these passages to the visions in Revelation.

The text that follows has challenged the dispensational pretribulation position, which I previously held, and will challenge those still holding it. The rewards of this challenge have not meant the "demise" of the pretribulation position, but instead have exposed the "certainty" of it. Many chronological changes will be presented and some previously held assumptions have been abandoned. In the past, these assumptions worked to support a pretribulation position, but have also been justifiably attacked for their thin foundation and biased reasoning. In essence, this book answers the criticism of the dispensational pretribulation position with a word of thanks. As a result of this challenge, the truth has been found and confusion dealt a deadly blow.

This challenge to dispensationalists was also sounded by David L. Turner when he said that, "...fresh studies are needed from a current evangelical perspective."[4] Turner also states, "It appears that the dispensationalist must come to terms with Matthew as a Gospel for the Church of all ages, not merely for the eschatological Jewish remnant. And since the similarity between Matthew 24 and Revelation 6 is often noted, it may be that dispensationalists should rethink their standard approach to this passage also."[5] I have come to terms with this challenge from David Turner.

God is not the author of confusion. This means that God's Word, when properly understood, will not be the seed of confusion. The confusion has arisen from errors in interpretation. By comparing Scripture with Scripture, truth will always be verified or nullified.

As Scripture is compared with Scripture, with the events of our contemporary history, the witness of the cosmos, and the signs that are coming in the heavens, no other conclusions are possible. *If I have properly interpreted the prophecies and the signs, then the year 1995 holds some rather ominous warnings that all will do well to at least consider.*

The evidence is overwhelming. So overwhelming, in fact, that despite great fear and reservations about pointing to any date as the potential season of God's judgment, I have been forced by the evidence *to sound the warning that the "Day of the Lord" and all that it encompasses may be soon upon us.*

Admittedly, this has not been an easy decision. However, in light of the evidence, to fail to do this poses an even greater weight of responsibility (Ezek. 33:7-9). Although many writers have rightfully objected to this, at the same time they themselves have pointed to the signs of our day and have indicated that the "Day of the Lord" is close.

The Lord has told us to watch and He has told us what to watch for—the signs of His coming in the earth, in the nations, and *in the heavens.* It is also believed that Revelation, along with Isaiah and Joel, give us a record of just what, where, and when the signs of Christ's "Second Coming" are to appear in the heavens. These signs involve constellations, cosmic collisions, and both solar and lunar eclipses, as well as signs in the earth.

To those professing Christians who are totally unaware of the prophetic implications, this book holds a rather stern warning. The Rapture may come as a "thief in the night" because they do not know and understand the *signs of our time.* For them, "it is time to wake up," lest that day come and reveal their nakedness and snare them with the rest of the world when the "Day of the Lord" commences with and after the Rapture of the Church.

The message to the Laodicean Church is filled with valuable information for those professing to be Christians, but who will be left behind when the Lord comes for the true members of the Body of Christ, those who have been truly born again and, therefore, indwelt by the Holy Spirit. However, the failure to escape the tribulation will reveal their shame and provide a last-chance opportunity to trust in the Lord Jesus Christ alone. This opportunity will come at a great physical cost.

This book is a must-read for every Christian. I have tried to write in such a way as to satisfy the careful but doubtful scholar's reasoning and the curiosity of the most average of readers.

The book stops at Revelation chapter 12 and only briefly touches chapters 13 through 22 (as they pertain to earlier chapters) because it is my belief that the message contained in the first half of Revelation needs to be shared as soon as possible. To delay the printing of this book while I complete the entire manuscript would be unwise. If time permits and a positive public response is forthcoming, then a second book will complete the study.

Now! It is time to begin.

End Notes

1. Marvin Rosenthal, *The Pre-Wrath Rapture of the Church*, (Nashville, TN: Thomas Nelson Publishers, 1990), p. 59.
2. Paul S. Karleen, *The Pre-Wrath Rapture of the Church, Is It Biblical?* (Langhorne, PA: BF Press, P.O. Box L-601, 1991), p. 93.
3. Jeffrey Sheler, "Cutting Loose the Holy Canon," *U.S. News and World Report*, (Nov. 8, 1993), p. 75.
4. David L. Turner, "The Structure and the Sequence of Matthew 24:1-41: Interaction With Evangelical Treatments," *Grace Theological Journal*, 10.1, (1989), p. 26.
5. Ibid., p. 27.

Figures

The following are figures that the text refers to at various places. They are provided to help you, the reader, understand the concepts presented in *Signs in the Heavens*.

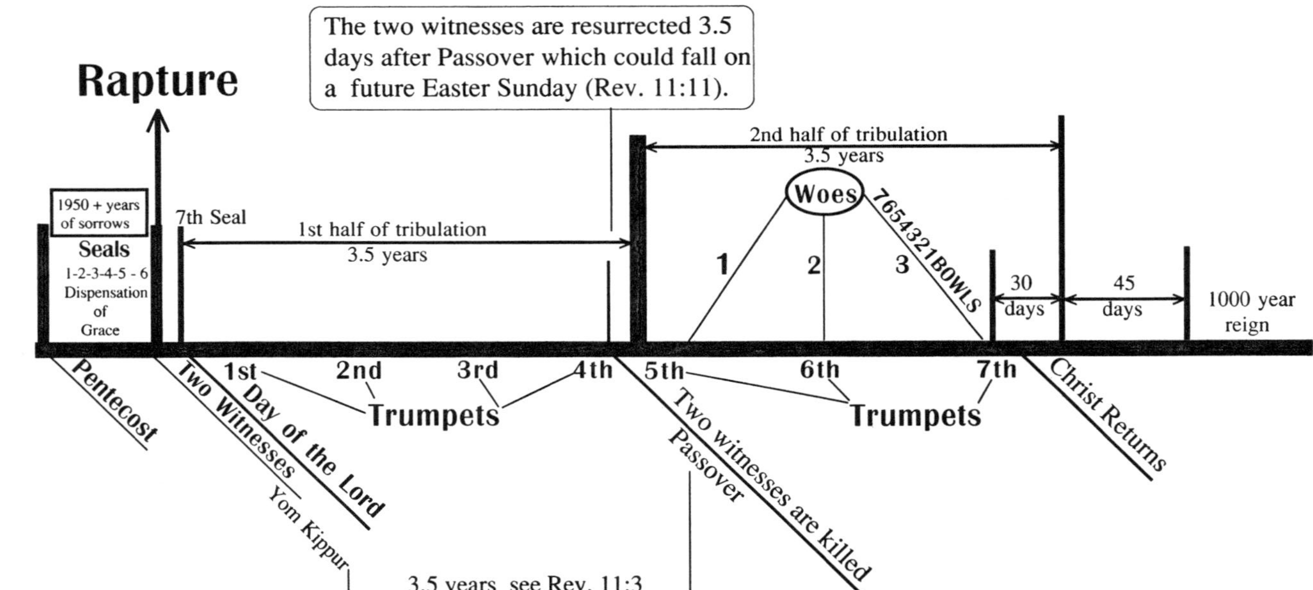

The ministry of the two witnesses begins before the seven year tribulation period starts (Mal. 4:5). Therefore, their ministry must end before the middle of the tribulation period. Antichrist will begin his 42 month rule just before the middle of the tribulation period with the death of the two witnesses. The sixth seal ends the church age with the fulfilling of the last half of Joel's prophecy (Joel 2:30-31). After a brief pause and the sealing of the 144,000, the seventh seal is opened and the Day of the Lord commences. The end of the church age is to end with great signs in the heavens taking place. The sixth seal includes the Rapture of the Church. The mighty wind that causes the heavens to depart as a rolled up scroll is the Holy Spirit departing with the Raptured saints of God.

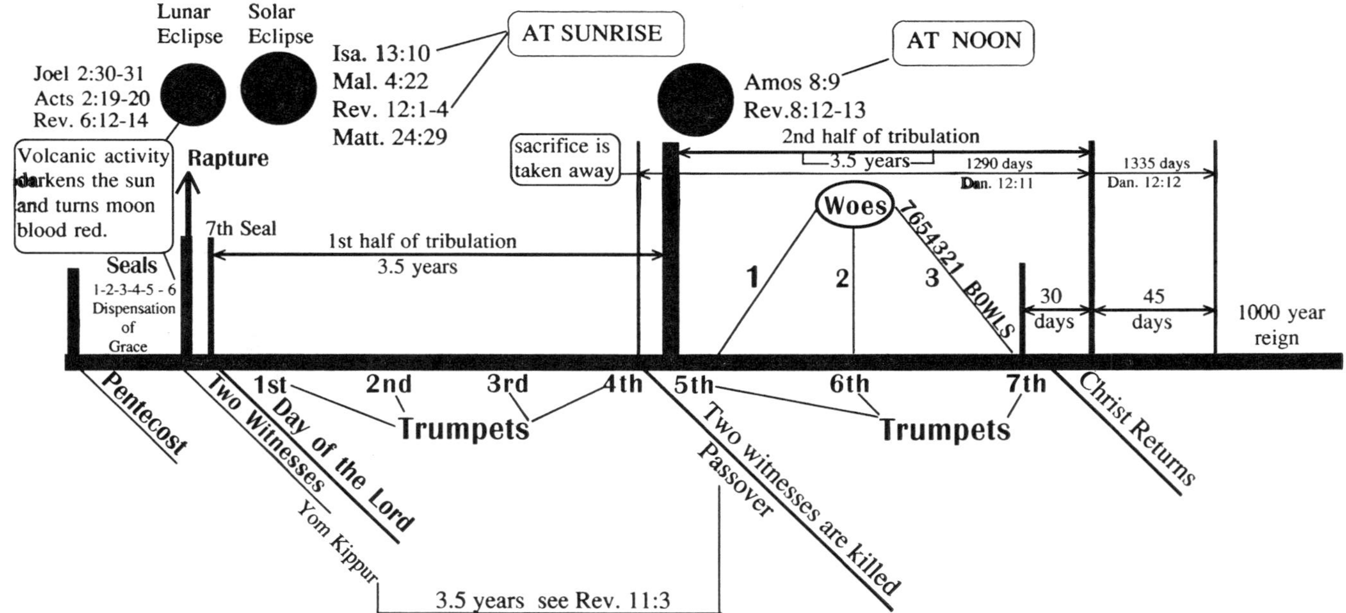

Some prophecies of the Bible, when literally interpreted, contain very specific astronomical data. When this data is correlated with the chronology of Daniel's 70th week and the Jewish feasts, the above chart shows how God can use very natural solar phenomena to fulfill His Word. The family of predicted events include:

1. A lunar eclipse that is turned to blood red BEFORE the coming of the Day of the Lord.

2. A sunrise solar eclipse that marks the beginning of the Day of the Lord.

3. A darkening of the sun at noon that could also be a solar eclipse.

4. The location of the sunrise solar eclipses must be in the constellation Virgo and specifically positioned under her feet.

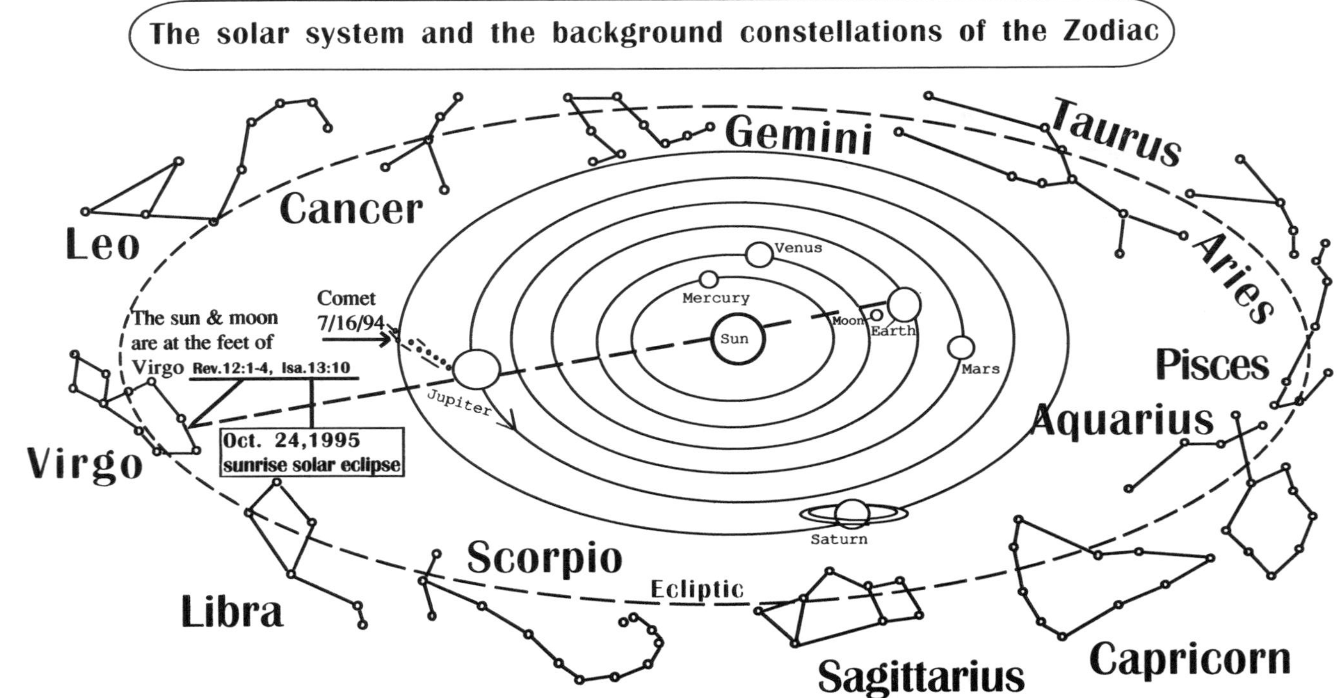

The above figure demonstrates how the moon could appear at the feet of Virgo during a solar eclipse. At the time of the new moon, both sun and moon are together. The woman (Virgo) is "clothed with the sun" in September/ October. Are these alignments the sign of the Son of man in heaven, the beginning of the tribulation period?

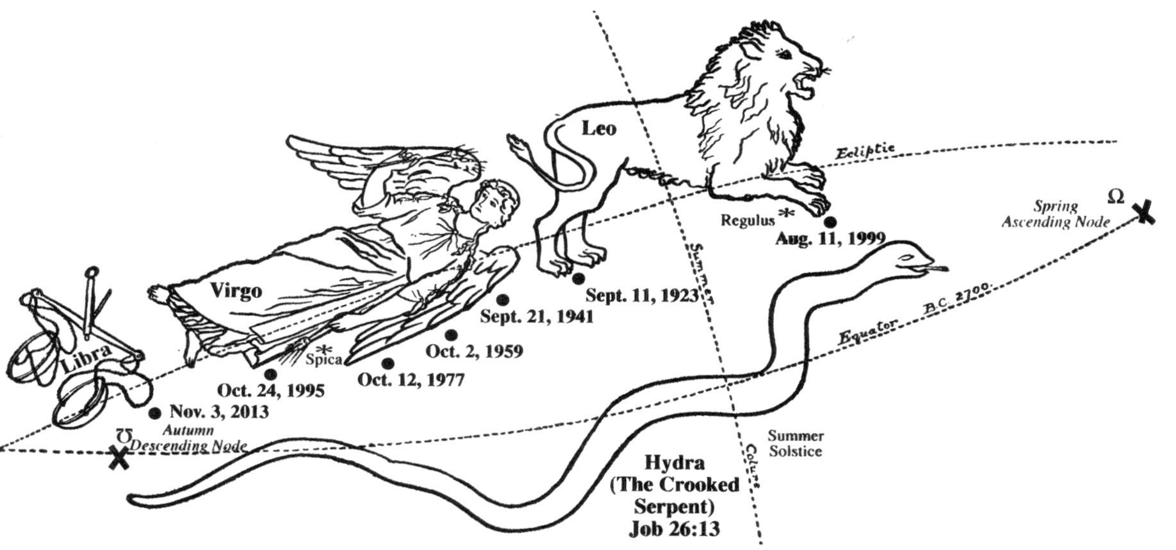

The above figure shows the passage of the sun along its ecliptic through the background constellations of the Zodiac. Eclipses that occurred near the tail or the head of Hydra, The Crooked Serpent, or The Dragon, appeared to the ancients as if the dragon was devouring the Sun. Thus, John's description in Revelation 12:1-4 of a dragon devouring the child is an ancient astronomical reference to a solar eclipse taking place in the tail of Hydra in the Fall.

The Assyrian "Ring with Wings", demonstrates the ancients' awareness of the "winged corona" that appears during some solar eclipses. They believed that solar eclipses were omens of God's wrath. The flaring solar corona revealed the glory of the god Helios. (Please note the image only holding a bow, cf. Rev. 6:1-2.) This imagery helps us to understand that Malachi is making reference to a solar eclipse accompanying the coming of the Day of the Lord, cf. Mal. 4:2, Isa. 13:10.

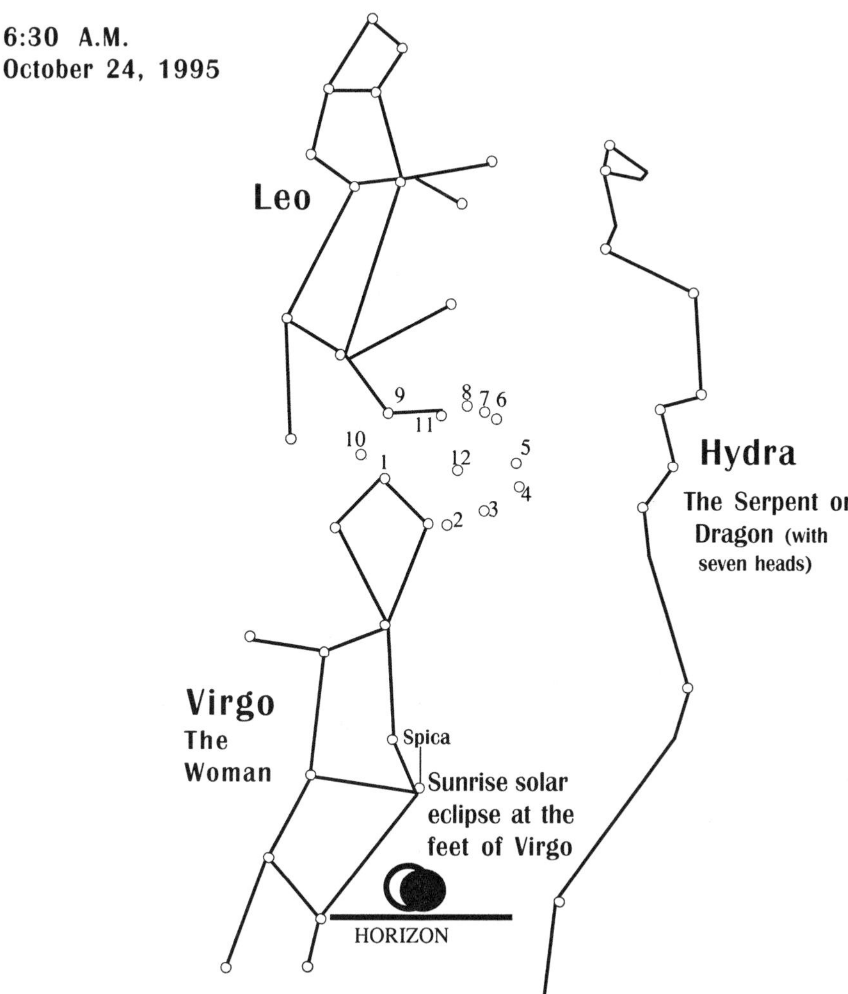

The above figure illustrates how the sunrise solar eclipse of October 24, 1995, can potentially fulfill the description in Rev. 12:1-4, and the prophecy of Isaiah 13:10. The dragon Hydra stands before the woman Virgo with the moon at her feet while being clothed with the sun. A crown of 12 stars ranging from a magnitude of 3.61 to 5 adorn her head. Are these heavenly alignments in conjunction with all the signs in the earth indicating that the coming of the Son of man is at hand? The return of Christ is near!

The ancient boundary stone depicts Draco at the top with
the stars Pollux and Castor and the moon
The bottom of the stone depicts Hydra, the other
celestial dragon. Hydra marks the celestial boundary
of the ecliptic of the ascending to descending nodes.

Introduction

Jesus told us that we are to watch for the *signs of the season* of His return. Remember, almost 1,900 years ago Jesus said that no man (living then) "knew" the day or the hour. However, He did not say that man would "never" know the times or the season of His coming and the end of the world. (See Matthew 24:36.)

If Jesus did not want believers to discern the signs of the times and the season of His coming, why did He admonish believers to watch for signs in the earth and in the heavens and to learn the parable of the fig tree? (See Matthew 24:32-35.) It would be out of character for God not to warn of terrible and impending judgment.

Therefore, as a watchman of the signs of the times in which we are living, I am sounding the warning that the "Day of the Lord" may be close at hand.

As someone who has always believed that the imminent return of Christ was always a part of early Christian belief, I am very aware of the potential folly in setting dates. It is often said that if someone sets a date for the coming of the Lord, that this will destroy the doctrine of imminence and that one cannot maintain the doctrine of hope, which the Rapture has been throughout centuries of Christian teaching.

I am not sure that this argument, in and of itself, is not without a fatal flaw. The argument usually goes like this: "If I set a date or look to a particular period of time, say 1995, as to when one should expect the Lord to return, then I will destroy the hope of the Rapture for Christians in Paul's day or during the days of the great Reformation and so on." This logic is built upon the assumption that what I can and do know to be potentially true about prophecy could have been known by earlier Christians also.

If these early Christians had been able to find out what I have discovered from biblical study and if they had come to the same conclusions, then the imminence and hope of the Rapture would have been destroyed. If Paul had known that the Lord was not coming back for another 1,950+ years, then how could he have encouraged believers with the teachings of the Rapture? "*Wherefore comfort one another with these words*" (1 Thess. 4:18). But the truth of the matter is that Paul did not know what you and I now know about prophecy and the "Day of the Lord," nor how it begins with the Rapture.

Revelation was not written until A.D. 92–93, well after Paul had finished his last epistle. Paul told the believers of Thessalonica that they had no need that he should write to them concerning the times and seasons, for their understanding was perfectly based on the knowledge that the coming of the Lord would be as "a thief in the night" only to the unsuspecting world living in darkness.

The Thessalonica believers, indwelt by the Holy Spirit, were not in darkness. *If* that day had come in their lifetime, they would have been aware of it. The Holy Spirit would have caused them to understand. If the world community had said, "peace and safety," and then sudden destruction came as the progressive pangs of a woman in childbirth, then they would have expected that the "Day of the Lord" was at hand.

We now know, however, that in addition to these signs, there are many other things that need to precede and/or parallel the events of a declared peace ("one world" government, unified global economics, universal religion, and the need to rebuild the temple). As a result of all the events that we see happening and of increased illumination, we can then expect to rightfully conclude that the "Day of the Lord" is at hand.

We desperately need to recognize the signs of the times and ask the same questions as the first disciples asked: "...[1] *Tell us, when shall these things be?* [2] *and what shall be the sign of Thy coming*, [3] *and of the end of the world?*" (Mt. 24:3). If it was right for the disciples to ask, is it not even more necessary for us to ask these same questions?

When we begin to see the things that Jesus and His Word have prophesied actually begin to happen, these questions are awakened in us. I believe these questions are even more natural for the times in which we live.

Daniel also asked the question, "*O my Lord, what shall be the end* [Hebrew *agariyth*, meaning last or future] *of these things*?" (Dan. 12:8b) But Daniel was told to go his way, "*...for the words are closed up and sealed till the time of the end*" (Dan. 12:9). They were sealed until the time of the end, which means that at the time of the end it would *no longer be necessary to conceal* the events that have been sealed for so long because at that time there would be a great need for the world to know the "Day of the Lord" was coming.

The truths of Scripture would be unlocked by the Spirit of God so that believers, those who are alive until the coming of the Lord, would know that their redemption is, in fact, drawing nigh. The doctrine of imminence is complemented by expectation and understanding, while hope is strengthened and not destroyed. Hope is magnified as it is about to be realized. In short, having an understanding of when the "Day of the Lord" might begin does not destroy the doctrine of imminence of past or future believers.

This is because the signs would be revealed very closely to the realization of the hope, therefore, being unable to adversely affect one's hope of rescue. In fact, signs of the Lord's coming should increase our hope of ratification. An ability to link together more and more prophetic signs is, of itself, the greatest indicator that the "Day of the Lord" and the Rapture are near. Therefore, for us to pick a day or a month or a year that the Lord could be coming back is very natural for one who studies the Word of God. But, no one can ever know with absolute certainty that any day, month, or year (labeled as a potential possibility), is in fact only "one possibility."

Certainty will arrive with the Rapture. The doctrine of imminence is not the formidable barrier that some profess it to be because imminence will remain intact and preserve hope until the day of the Rapture. However, as each day passes, we will have less and less doubt as each piece falls into its perfect place.

James L. Boyer makes a similar point while discussing chapters 2 and 3 of Revelation. Some object to a prophetic view of these chapters[1] because again it is believed that if these chapters speak of implicit long periods of time, before the Second Coming of Christ, and if the early Church understood these verses as indicating such periods, it would have shattered their own hopes for the Second Coming. This would have destroyed the doctrine of imminence.

However, Boyer rightfully states, "*It is the character of Bible prophecy to unfold as it is fulfilled.* OT messianic prophecy is an example. The OT did not say explicitly that there would be two separate comings separated by a long period of time. That time element was the specific aspect which the prophets themselves could not understand" (1 Pet. 1:11).[2] (Emphasis added.)

Therefore, because the prophecies of Christ's Second Coming are implicit long before their fulfillment rather than explicit, imminence is maintained until the time of the end. As time draws near the time of fulfillment, that which was implicit becomes more explicit. "But the implicit prophecy could not be understood until it was made clear by fulfillment, and by that time it could no longer be said, My Lord delays His coming (Mt. 24:48)."[3]

Walvoord also cites evidence for progressive understanding increasing as the time of Christ's return draws near. Although the references to the length of time periods of the first and second half of the tribulation in Daniel and Revelation are literal time periods, "they do not reveal the day or hour of Christ's return."[4] Walvoord goes on to illustrate the progressive understanding that the observer of Noah's family could gain. "Then as they observed Noah's family enter the ark and the door shutting, they could not know the day or the hour, but it was obvious that the flood could come at any time."[5]

Christ used this very illustration in describing how the Second Coming of Christ would occur (Mt. 24:38). "Using this OT illustration, Christ compares it to the events which will occur at the Second Coming of Christ. Like the flood, *the Second Coming will be preceded by specific signs* which indicate the approach but not the day or the hour of the coming of the Lord."[6] (Emphasis added.) It is of these signs that I see coming upon the earth and in the cosmos that I now write and ask you, dear reader, to carefully consider. For if the "Day of the Lord" comes upon you as a thief in the night, you will suffer the greatest of all losses, which is not only the loss of your own life, but even worse—the loss of your eternal soul.

> *And when He had called the people unto Him with His disciples also, He said unto them, Whosoever will come after Me, let him deny himself, and take up his cross, and follow Me. For whosoever will save his life shall lose it; but whosoever shall lose his life for My sake and the gospel's, the same shall save it. For what shall it profit a man, if he shall gain the whole world, and lose his own soul? Or what shall a man give in exchange for his soul? Whosoever therefore shall be ashamed of Me and of My words in this adulterous and sinful generation; of him also shall the Son of man be ashamed, when He cometh in the glory of His Father with the holy angels* (Mark 8:34-38).

What time is it for you? It is time for ***all*** to consider what God has told us to look for and recognize that it is all coming to pass.

End Notes

1. Robert L. Thomas, *Revelation 1–7: An Exegetical Commentary*, (Chicago, IL: Moody Press, 1992), pp. 511-512. All notes used by permission.

1. James L. Boyer, "Are the Seven Letters of Revelation 2–3 Prophetic?" *Grace Theological Journal*, 6.2, (1985), p. 269.

2. Ibid., p. 270.

3. John F. Walvoord, "Is a Pretribulational Rapture Revealed in Matthew," *Grace Theological Journal*, 6.2, (1985), p. 263.

4. Ibid., p. 263.

5. Ibid., p. 264.

Part I

Understanding Time

Chapter 1

Time

What Time Is It?

"What time is it?" Ask anyone this elementary question and generally you will receive a mannerly response. If the person is wearing a watch or near a clock, the answer will expectantly include the relevant hour and minutes before or after the hour. This is an easy enough question and, indeed, most grade school children are able to reply accurately.

However, if I should complicate this question with another inquiry, such as, "Can I trust your watch or clock to have the correct time?" you might respond, "Well! If you do not believe me, get your own watch!" This simple illustration is made to make the point that, even if we are wearing a watch, how do we know that the time is, in fact, correct?

The answer is that we do not! Unless, of course, we check with an authoritative outside source. The source may be our local television channel, radio station, or the Federal Weather Station, which is where most of our local television and radio stations get the correct time.

But how does the Federal Weather Service know that they have the correct time? They must check time against another acceptable authority, which is a precise atomic clock. This particular clock is regulated by astronomers. Astronomers maintain time in Universal Time (U.T.), which is essentially the time for the meridian of Greenwich, England. Universal Time is established and calculated by the slightly irregular rotation of the earth. Predictions are based on steady time unaffected by the earth's rotation, which is kept by atomic clocks.

> "The average of predictions of steady time services around the world is released as Coordinated Universal Time (U.T.C.). U.T.C. is kept aligned with U.T. by the occasional addition of leap seconds to U.T.C. at the end of December or June. They are publicly announced. The exact difference between the U.T. and U.T.C. can be calculated only after the fact, but is kept to less than one second."[1]

The point is, we are dependent upon a higher authority to make certain that we have the correct time of the day, month, and year. All of us, including the astronomers with their atomic clocks, observe the adjustment of time with calculations concerning the actual position of the earth relative to its journey around the sun. Ultimately, it is the sun and our earth's orbit around the sun that determines the exact time and, therefore, determines what day it is as well. Consequently, we as individuals really do not know what time it is unless we have someone to verify where we are in relationship to our journey around the sun. We are dependent upon God's wonderful creation of our solar system to give us time.

Before Jehovah God created the sun, moon, and stars, there was no such concept as time. In his book, *The Mind of God*, Paul Davis, a distinguished professor of Mathematical Physics at the University of Adelaide, makes this point, "The picture that we then obtain for the origin of the universe is a remarkable one. At some finite instant in the past the universe of space, time, and matter is bound by a space-time singularity. The coming-into-being of the universe is therefore represented not only by the abrupt appearance of matter, but of space and time as well."

Professor Davis goes on to say this, "The significance of this result cannot be over stressed. People often ask: Where did the big bang occur? The bang did not occur at a point in space at all. Space itself came into existence with the big bang. There is a similar difficulty over the question: What happened before the big bang? The answer is, there was no 'before.' Time itself began at the big bang. As we have seen, Saint Augustine long ago proclaimed that the world was made with time, not in time, and that is precisely the modern scientific position."[2]

Time, in this dimension of life, is forever correlated with respect to God's creation of the earth, sun, moon, and stars and the movement of the earth around the sun within our solar system. This is the way it is today and this is the way it has always been. Man, until modern history, has always looked to the heavens to determine times and seasons. As clearly stated in Genesis 1:14, God created the heavens by saying, "*Let there be lights in the firmament of the heaven to divide the day from the night; and let them be for signs, and for seasons, and for days, and years.*"

Astronomy, Astrology, and the Christian

Ancient astronomy was very vital to the survival of civilization. At the other extreme, ignorance and superstitions often changed the creative science into a perversion of worshiping planets. This practice evolved into the forbidden craft of astrology, which survives to this day as a dangerous multi-million dollar industry. Since Genesis, man has been fascinated by objects in the heavens. The solar system has been the subject for study and contemplation for millenniums. Astronomy is incomparably the oldest of the sciences.

> "Over 3,000 years ago, ancient Babylonian astronomers made careful records of their observations regarding the paths of the planets and the rising and setting of the sun, moon, and stars. [Their early records] have been discovered by archaeologists, and these Babylonian observations look very much like the tables found in a modern nautical almanac."[3]

> "Originally, the science of astronomy and astrology were one; in fact the term astrology etymologically describes this early science (and in fact our modern astronomy) better than the term now used for its current descendent. Only as astrology acquired its other meanings did the need for distinguishing between the original meaning of astrology (which astrologers designated as natural astrology) and those that it had gradually acquired through the ages (the latter group astrologers designated juridical astrology)."[4]

"Juridical astrology deals with the divinational aspects of astrology. The word astrology is derived from two Greek words, *astra* meaning 'star' and *logos* meaning 'word.' Thus, astrology is the word or science of the stars."[5]

Christianity, during the first four centuries, was strongly confronted with the problem of astrology. Such eclectic groups as Gnosticism, which adopted certain aspects of Christianity together with Oriental mysteries, Hellenistic philosophy, and Babylonian astrology, posed a great problem to early Christianity. Another problem was the fact that astrology was accepted by some within Christianity. For example, John Chrysostom noted in his *Homilies on First Corinthians* that there were many "in the multitude of our side 'who' fortify themselves with horoscope; many adhere to superstitious observances, and to omens, and auguries, and presages."

Christianity was required to provide an answer regarding the practice of astrology. At the Synod of Laodicea in A.D. 343–381 it was declared that "Astrologers are they who divine by the stars through the agency of demons, and place their faith in them."[6]

The person yielding to God is to refrain from having dependence upon astrological associations and predictions and to refrain from worshiping any of the heavenly objects. The Bible is very clear about this:

> *Hear ye the word which the Lord speaketh unto you, O house of Israel: Thus saith the Lord, Learn not the way of the heathen, and be not dismayed [confused or amazed] at the signs of heaven; for the heathen are dismayed at them*" (Jeremiah 10:1-2).

This passage in Jeremiah goes on to teach that it is the Lord God of heaven that men need to fear. "*Who would not fear Thee, O King of nations? For to Thee doth it appertain: forasmuch as among all the wise men of the nations, and in all their kingdoms, there is none like unto Thee*" (Jer. 10:7). (See also Isaiah 47:13; Daniel 1:20; 2:27; 4:7; and 5:7 for further listings about prohibitions against worshiping the sun, stars, moon, and planets with a misconception that they control or influence the circumstances in the lives of mankind upon the earth.)

Fortunately, there were legitimate reasons for the ancients to be observing the sun and the moon and the rising of the stars in the heavens. By careful observation and accurate record keeping, early perceptive men (who were part astronomer and part priest) were able to predict such events as lunar and solar eclipses. But more significant, they were able to track and predict when the Spring, Summer, Fall, and Winter solstices occurred. The ability to track new and full moons through the months helped them to determine when they should plant and harvest crops. It also helped ancient man to develop his first calendar. The skill of predicting solar and lunar eclipses helped provide a degree of security for the ruling kings. If an eclipse occurred, which was not predicted, it was envisioned as an omen or a sign of displeasure by the gods.

"Astounding as it seems, the ancient priests of Egypt could calculate the length of the year right down to the second." The priests were expected to predict the time when the Nile would overflow its banks and provide water and new enriched soil. "This ability gave the priest immense power and prestige (*when they were right*) as the Nile overflowed its banks soon after Midsummer Day."[7]

However, tracking, recording, and predicting the phases of the moon and the beginning of seasons took on greater significance for the Jew. Israel obeyed God by fulfilling the feast days given to them by God and these feasts were regulated by the lunar cycles of the new moon to full moon. Israel used the tracking of the moon to regulate its religious calendar.

The main point to consider is that, although God did forbid the sinful use of and warned against overemphasizing the significance of the heavenly bodies, as is the case of astrology, we can learn God's intended purpose for them from Scripture.

> *And God said, Let there be lights in the firmament of the heaven to divide the day from night; and let them be for* ***signs,*** *and for* ***seasons,*** *and for* ***days,*** *and* ***years*** (Genesis 1:14).

Most people will readily acknowledge that God created the sun and moon for the regulation of seasons, days, and years, but Genesis 1:14 also tells us that they are for ***signs***. Signs of what? The Hebrew word used here is *owth*, which means basically "a signal, as in the sense of appearing." It is also often used to indicate a flag, beacon, monument, omen, prodigy, or evidence.

> "There are approximately eighty occurrences concerning this in the Hebrew Old Testament and most of them have the flavor of the

> miraculous. Many of them are used in the same context with the Hebrew word *mowpheth* or 'wonder' (Ex. 7:3; Deut. 4:34; 6:22; 7:19; 26:8; Neh. 9:10; Is. 20:3). *Owth* is an indicator or a signal of something. A prophet may be known by the evidence [of a predicted sign], Deut. 13:1ff; Jer. 44:25,29. The Greek word *semeion* was the corresponding term... [*'And there appeared a great wonder in heaven...'* " Rev. 12:1-3]. *Owth* showed or confirmed anything in the past, present, or future. It excited attention or consideration. It distinguished one thing from another. It was an inducement to believe what was affirmed, professed, or promised. It was the acid test of prophecy."[8]

Yet today, the fact that God has also created the heavenly bodies for signs is often regarded as insignificant. This oversight and practice is especially true of contemporary conservative biblical scholars of prophecy. An understanding of astronomy can only help us in our study of prophecy as the two studies overlap.

The study of cosmology is a similar help. "To an astronomer, cosmology means the history and structure of the universe. Thus, for a Christian, cosmology is found in Genesis 1:1, '*In the beginning God created the heavens and the earth...;*' Hebrews 11:3 '*Through faith we understand that the worlds were framed by the Word of God, so that things which are seen were made of things which do appear;*' Jeremiah 51:15 '*He had made the earth by His power, He hath established the world by His wisdom, and He hath stretched out the heaven by His understanding,*' and other verses. But while the Bible gives a complete and simple history of the universe, it says very little about its structure. And at present, only the structure can be observed, the history being essentially invisible. Thus the *Bible and the astronomical observations taken together* should give a complete picture of cosmology."[9] (Emphasis added.)

As we arrange our study of prophecy, the references contain critical information for identifying the coming of the season identified as the "Great Day of the Lord." This data will be arranged, considered, supported by using accurate exegetical principles, and then clarified as the Holy Spirit directs. We will also validate our understanding with astronomical information *when applicable.*

Signs Given by God

The motion of our planet and its relationship to the sun not only regulates the seasons, days, and years, but is also used by God to indicate a confirming flag or signal. That confirmation provides information about what is or is about to happen concerning Him. One of the best illustrations of this is the rainbow.

God set His bow in the sky as a promise that He would never again destroy the earth with a flood. We know that the rainbow is caused by the prismatic effect of light from the sun passing through the atmosphere and residing moisture. The moisture or rain droplets in the air act as a prism and separate the white light in a spectrum of red, blue, green, and yellow bands of light. There is something miraculous about a rainbow in that it takes a complex atmosphere, with a perfect balance of moisture, gases, and sunlight, to produce it.

In addition to the appearance of this extraordinary rainbow, God has attached a significant message to this event in His complex created world—a promise not to destroy the world by water again. *"And it shall come to pass,* ***when I bring a cloud over the earth, that the bow shall be seen in the cloud: and I will remember My covenant...*** *"* (Gen. 9:14-15).

According to this passage, not every rain cloud is sent by God, but the rain clouds that are sent by God appear with a rainbow. According to the Bible then, God uses creation to remind man of His promises. However, God has promised to judge the world again, by fire. Therefore, from the rainbow and the star of Bethlehem we can conclude that it is not a precedent-setting event for God to use the heavenly bodies to speak to those wise enough to meditate upon the Holy Scriptures. To those who are wise, the meaning of the signs in the sun, moon, and stars should become very clear. After all, isn't that what the wise men did when they followed the star to Bethlehem?

Concerning His Second Coming, did not Jesus say: *"And then shall appear the sign* [*simieon*] *of the Son of man in heaven*" (Mt. 24:30a); *"And there shall be signs* [*simieon*] *in the sun, and in the moon, and in the stars...*" (Lk. 21:25). *Both of these passages are linked by the introductory phrase, "And then shall they see the Son of man coming in a cloud with power and great glory*" (Lk. 21:27). (See also Matthew 24:30b.)

It is when we *begin to see these things come to pass*, that we are to look up, for our redemption is drawing near, as suggested in Luke 21:28. The signs that we are to be looking for in the heavens as well as on the earth will be explored later after we study "the keeping of time" itself.

By keeping time, I mean counting minutes, hours, days, months, and years. Without any universal time system, ancient men marked time in recorded text, often by referencing the month and the day within the reign of ruling kings. "*And it came to pass in the month Nisan, in the twentieth year of Artaxerxes the king...*" (Neh. 2:1).

Men referenced years to ruling kings and days to the phases between the new moon and full moon. The counting of years was maintained in the Bible by recording the length of successive rulers as well as the length of succeeding generations (Gen. 5).

But does God keep time? We know that God has given the prophets visions of future events set for an appointed time and that at the end of time "*it* [the vision] *shall speak, and not lie*" (Hab. 2:3). Further, we are told to wait for the fulfillment of the vision because it will come. Therefore, if God has set a time for certain events to take place, He must also mark the passage of time. Could the cosmos and all that He has set in motion be God's "Cosmic Timepiece"? Is it a timepiece that will indicate to wise men that the appointed hour of God's judgment is about to begin? If the First Coming of Christ was marked by cosmic events, why not the Second Coming? What are the signs in the heavens telling us?

Contemporary man merely looks at his calendar and his watch, while never considering the rising and setting of the sun and the cycle of the moon through its phases. But there was a time when man was much more aware of the journey of the sun across the sky; actually, it is the journey of the earth around the sun and the rotation of the earth on its axis, but the results are basically the same for our discussion.

As early as 3000 B.C. we have indications that man was aware of the relative position of the earth to the sun in order to determine the Spring and Fall solstice—when the day and night are exactly 12 hours each.

Early Star Gazing

> "Archaeological surveys on the Golon Heights in 1967–1968 discovered strange mystery circles of stones at Rogem Hiri that archaeologists and astronomers, with joint calculations, now

> have determined must date back to at least 2500–3000 B.C. It was determined after a systematic study of astronomical and geological aspects of the complex, as well as associations between the architecture of the complex and celestial events, physical elements in the landscape and local ecology-related phenomena, by Professor Anthony Aveni of the Department of Physics and Astronomy, Colgate University, and by Yonathan Mizrachi, that the entry way of the structure was used to align and verify the June solstice sunrise. According to their analysis, 'If one were to stand at the center of the complex during the June solstice sunrise of 3000 B.C., the first gleam of sunrise would appear at the center of the northeast entryway in the outer wall.' "[10]

The landscape of the ancient world has revealed many other similar mystery circles, the most famous being Stonehenge. Stonehenge baffled archaeologists for many years. Despite evidence that may have indicated that Stonehenge was built to align with the solstices and lunar cycles, it was not until Professor Gerald Hawkins, a professional astronomer from the University of Boston, Massachusetts, "used a digital computer to document and compare the alignments with the rising and setting positions of the sun, moon, planets, and some bright stars in 1500 B.C. that his calculations discovered 10 alignments for the rising of the sun within 1 degree and 14 for the moon within 1.5 degrees. This evidence, coupled with some other features of Stonehenge, led him to believe that the complex was used to predict eclipses of the moon as well."[11]

During recent times man has lost interest in the observation of the heavens. He has replaced personal astronomical skills with modern, accurate clocks and the astronomical societies which scientifically provide information about the heavens apart from God. As a result, the activity and supposed understanding of the sun, moon, planets, and stars have been given over to the professional astronomer or the more threatening astrologers. It is precisely because of these two professions that most people, and especially biblically established Christians, have avoided the study of the heavens in relationship to biblical study and prophecy.

The general presupposition and belief among Bible-believing Christians, seems to be that astronomy is only for the atheistic physicist. That same physicist is also trying to prove that billions of years and the "Big

Bang" theory is the best "story" that reasonably explains our existence. The "Big Bang" theory needs to be refined into the belief of the "Big God" of the Bible.

New Agers and other misguided persons will underscore that the study of the heavens is for astrologers who "forecast" the future for individuals and nations. It is true that many Christians are sinning against the Lord in the practice of astrology, which is clearly forbidden in Scripture (Deut. 4:19). Therefore, fearful Christians erroneously conclude that they should not have any association with the stars because of the possible connection to astrology.

There are, however, many Bible-believing Christians who enthusiastically engage in astronomy. Why? Many of us believe that the heavens do, in fact, declare the glory of God. Dr. Joseph A. Seiss said that "[he had] not the slightest doubt or question on the subject [that the heavens proclaim the gospel message]. Taking the facts, figures, and names as our common, every-day astronomy gives them, [he] found such evident marks of connection and design, such thorough consistency in the elaboration of all details, such distinct and orderly progress of thought in the arrangements of beginning, continuity, and end, such a universal and multitudinous array of myths and legends founded on the constellations and running parallel with their meaning as thus interpreted, such a complete identity of images and terms with scriptural presentations of the same things, and such a self evidence and exhaustive outlining of all the great features of the Gospel story, along with such a profound and accurate penetration into the whole organization of the visible universe, that [he would] have to go against all laws of evidence and principles of logic not to accept it as very truth that these heavens do declare 'the glory of God' as embodied in the person, mission, work, and redemptive achievements of His Son Jesus Christ."[12] Someday all men will know the following statement to be true: "*The heavens declare the glory of God...*" (Ps. 19:1).

Constellations and the Origin of the Alphabet

The importance of the constellations to early man can be demonstrated in their impact on the formation of the alphabet. There are some scholars who believe that the constellations of the solar and lunar zodiac provided the source for the first alphabet.[13]

There is evidence that the constellations were the source for the origins of the alphabet.

> "If one ponders the far-flung and exacting demands for a satisfactory theory of the origin of the alphabet, there is no imaginable organizing principle except religion that is able to meet them. There were certain common religious ideas that were of great antiquity, that were distributed over the whole area concerned, and that were sufficiently cohesive to provide the necessary correlation and the constant order. These ideas were the cosmological concepts associated with ancient worship. They had to do with stars and crosses, circles and triangles, and segments of circles; with times and seasons, feast days, new moons, planting and harvest; with solstices and the spring equinox; with constellations, the sun and the moon, the planets and all the host of heaven….The ancient cultures of Egypt, Babylon, and Sinim were built upon these cosmological ideas of the star-gazers….In the capitals of each of these great empires the bull was the sacred animal through the period from the fourth to second millennium B.C., during which period Taurus the Bull reigned as the chief constellation of the zodiac, the circle of life. And at the spring equinox throughout this period and long after, while Aries the Ram was struggling to seize the ascendancy, the sacred bull was sacrificed on the royal altar."[14]

The shapes of the constellations determined the shape of the letters, while the name of the constellation provided the phonetic sounding and some meaning. It was God who placed the constellations and gave them their names. Therefore, language finds its origin in the names of the stars that God placed and named.

"It would seem then that further investigation is warranted because the first letter of the alphabet is the Greek *alpha.* The Hebrew *aleph*, 'a bull' is not the ordinary word for bull, but a special ancient word used for sacred cattle, corresponding to the Assyrian word *alphu*, 'a bull.' Scanning down through the other letters of the Hebrew alphabet having names and recognized meanings in the Hebrew, we find that they also deal with ideas in current astrology: a house, a hand, an eye, a fish, and a serpent; while strangely enough the last of all the Hebrew is *taw*, 'a mark or a sacred symbol;' the Aramaic *tor*, 'oryx' or 'ox;' the Arabic *thaur*; the Greek *tauros*; the Latin *taurus*; and the Germanic *thor*, 'the thunderer.' Two bulls? The first and last letters of the alphabet a bull? One is reminded of Alam and Alad, the two bulls of the Sumerians, one on the right hand, the other on the left of the gate of the temple; of *alpha* and *omega*, the beginning and the end, which is repeated with such impressive resonance in the Book of Revelation"[15] (Rev 1:8,11,17; 22:13). *"In the beginning was the Word, and the Word was with God, and the Word was God*" (Jn. 1:1). "In the beginning God created the heavens and the earth and placed and named every star in the heavens and by doing so wrote the Gospel message in the heavens."[16]

It is believed that the names of the stars tell the story of God's redemptive plan from the fall to complete the coming of the Kingdom of God (Gen. 3:15; Rev. 21:1-8). However, this story has been lost for millennia to the perversions of mythology and juridical astrology.

It is my belief, however, that Bible-believing, God-fearing Christians have surrendered the critical science of astronomy. "False assumptions of [natural] astrology [astronomy] have caused its neglect (*constellations*) as a field of study. This area, which is large, has been much overlooked as beneath contempt of scholars.... Modern material on the origin of the astrological signs is scarce and inadequate; original research is slow and arduous. However, [he] obtained sufficient information to outline its structure and to isolate some of the primitive astrological characters, many in early forms, which make the various astrological series."[17]

For example, a great number of Chinese characters are based upon astrological primitives, which represent dippers and other constellations. "The character for north (*pei*) is depicted by both the Big Dipper, or bushel measure, and the Little Dipper, which revolve about the North Pole. Two dippers side by side means 'to compare,' while two dippers opposed means 'back to back or opposed.' "[18]

"There are 22 letters in the Hebrew alphabet. Why 22? Possibly it was due to the fact that the first and twenty-second lunar constellations were *aleph and tau*, the bull and the ox, the *Alam and Alad*, the beginning and the end."[19]

The heavens declare the glory of God, but we are just too ignorant to see it and read it. Job was aware of the constellations, their names, and their message. Like the inspiration of the Word of God, the constellations were formed by the work of the Holy Spirit. "*By His spirit He hath garnished the heavens; His hand hath formed the crooked serpent*" (Job 26:13). This crooked serpent is the constellation Hydra.[20] (This is an important fact to note because the dragon of Revelation 12 is also the constellation Hydra.)

> "It is very significant that the word 'garnished' is employed here in its main sense of ornament, decoration, something added for embellishment; but it has the further meaning of 'summons and warning.' And by these adornings God hath summoned the heavens and filled them with proclamations and warnings of His great purposes. Perhaps it would be hard to find another word to fit the facts so closely or the original for which it stands. It falls in precisely with the whole idea of the celestial luminaries being used 'for signs,' of the gospel being written in the stars, and of the adornment and beaming of the heavens with this brightness of all sacred brightness."[21]

The theory of Hugh A. Moran and David Kelley is that writing developed from calendar stones and the keeping of records of harvest festivals, the equinoxes, the changes of the moon, lucky and unlucky days, and great portents like eclipses. Signs to represent the heavenly bodies like the sun, moon, and stars would be early and easily evolved, and from them would come derivative signs representing action, such as "rising and setting, being and becoming. But for growing science, philosophy, and religion, as well as for mathematical serial numbers and calculations, further symbolic ideographs would be necessary. The chief available source for such symbolic signs would be the already familiar forms and associated ideas representing the heavenly bodies and the process signs, which grew out of the primitive conception of creation and the movement of the heavens, such as the activities of the Dippers."[22]

We have ignorantly divested our interest of astronomy to the unbeliever in much the same way that psychology and psychiatry have taken over counseling. We have allowed biology and science to intimidate us with their theories, calculations, and irrefutable conclusions. The propaganda of evolution, for example, is taught as a fact in our classrooms even when some of the most educated and dedicated scientists in the field admit that it is a theory based on man's logic.

Michael Denton, one of those scientists, goes so far as to call the explanations offered by some evolutionists in defending Darwinism as being nothing more than "Tautology." A brochure distributed by the British Museum of Natural History stated that "the concept of evolution by natural selection is not, strictly speaking, scientific, because it has been established by logical deduction rather than empirical demonstration."[23]

The reason for the widespread acceptance of evolution is not because it makes sense or that it satisfies questions of scientific inquiry concerning man's beginnings, but because it allows creation without God. The concept justifies a life without accountability to a sovereign, omnipotent God. Evolution has a myriad of inconsistencies and many unresolved questions, requiring more faith than anything found in the Word of God.

We need not be intimidated by the science community. Truth is on our side. All we have to do is wait, and eventually the agnostic or atheistic scientist will self-destruct. Time will eventually shoot their godless theories full of holes.

Time and Our World

The initial question, "What time is it?" is really a question of relativity. It is only appropriate to ask the question because you have to be somewhere or need to do something at a certain time or at a certain place. Otherwise, the query is absolutely meaningless. Time means nothing without having space and matter. The maintenance, regulation, scheduling, and organizing of accurate time is important for all societies. The more complex the society, the more precise one must be in regulating the use of time. Depending upon your field of work, awareness of time will vary.

Time seems to go by faster when you are busy, and the converse is true as well. The question of time and of relativity to what a farmer must get done may be a good example. The farmer must milk the cows and feed the animals at regular intervals if he wants to maintain a high level of production on the farm. The farmer is equally concerned with the seasons. He must know when to plant and harvest the crops. If he miscalculates and sows too early or too late in the season, he could lose his crop to frost or other unfavorable weather conditions. The farmer will be attentive to the *Farmers Almanac* or the seasonal weather reports by a meteorologist. The determination by the outside source is usually determined by what is happening with the sun and seasonal patterns on the earth. Time is an important issue depending on each situation considered by the farmer.

Time is important to the study of prophecy as well because God has appointed a time for its fulfillment. If we do not learn to discern the signs of the times, then we will be overtaken by the "Day of the Lord" as a thief in the night (Rev. 3:3).

The ancient civilizations, like today's modern farmer, also depended on this same land, but without benefit of modern technology. They successfully relied upon the land as individuals and as a society. Their concept of time was important to their existence. It was life-threatening to ignore the signs. In contrast to the ancients, we now import and export our produce and grain at an incredible profit.

Today we simply go to the food store and pick up what we need. We depend on other economies throughout the world to supply our desires. We subconsciously ignore or have a weak concept of our need to tell time accurately relative to our day-to-day existence. By default then, we relegate a major portion of God's revelation as being unaccessible to man—the witness and the signs in the stars.

Israel and the Zodiac

Understanding how the ancients regarded time will be critical in order to understand Scriptures that describe objects in the cosmos. The men of the Bible had a unique perception and awareness of the heavens concerning God's intended purpose and plan. God gave Israel yearly feasts to be observed at specific times of the year. Israel needed to watch the heavenly objects and record observations for future reference with precision.

According to the Mosaic law, festivals were always celebrated on the same day of the month. Therefore, it was necessary to fix the commencement of the month with the appearance of the new moon. "The new moon was reckoned not by astronomical calculations but by actual personal observation [and recorded]. On the thirtieth day of the month *watchmen* were placed on commanding heights round Jerusalem to *watch the sky.* As soon as each of them detected the moon he hastened to a house in the city, which was kept for the purpose, and was examined by the president of the

Sanhedrin. When the evidence of the appearance was deemed satisfactory, the president rose up and formally announced it, uttering the words, 'It is consecrated.'

"The information was immediately sent throughout the land from the Mount of Olives by beacon fires on the tops of hills. The religious observance of the day of the new moon may plainly be regarded as the consecration of a natural division of time."[24]

The feasts of Israel were coordinated with the different phases of the moon, which is why Israel had a 354-day year, with 6 months of 30 days and 6 months of 29 days each. It has been determined that there are 365.2422 days in a year. Every fourth year, the modern calendar adds a day to the year, making up the difference by adding a second here and there, to synchronize our clocks with God's celestial clock.

It is believed that Israel did the same thing with their calendar every third year. They added an extra month to their calendar to make up the difference, but we have no clear biblical evidence for what was actually done to compensate for the extra 11.24 days of the year. All of these factors would cause the ancient Israelite and others to view the study of astronomy as an absolutely essential science. For God's chosen people, survival was at stake. Accurate accounting of the lunar cycles was necessary to maintain their relationship and covenants with the God of Israel. If Israel did not celebrate a feast that God had commanded, they could not expect His continued blessing. Instead they would reap His judgment.

The Jewish calendar is a lunar calendar based upon the cycles of the moon and had its beginnings with the implementation of the first Passover. "*This month shall be unto you the beginning of months: it shall be the first month of the year to you*" (Ex. 12:2). The new moon of each month marks the beginning of months for Israel. Israel was to hold a feast in which a burnt offering was offered up on the first day of every month. "*And in the beginnings of your months ye shall offer a burnt offering unto the Lord; ...this is the burnt offering of every month throughout the months of the year*" (Num. 28:11a,14).

It was on the occasion of keeping the feast associated with the first day of every month that was marked by the new moon that King Saul hoped to kill David. David knew that he was expected to be there, but he asked Jonathan to cover for him with an excuse (1 Sam. 20:5-6). David's empty place was duly noted by Saul, but it was not until the second day of the royal feast that David's absence was questioned by Saul.

> *So David hid himself in the field: and when the new moon was come, the king sat him down to eat meat. And the king sat upon his seat, as at other times, even upon a seat by the wall: and Jonathan arose, and Abner sat by Saul's side, and David's place was empty. Nevertheless Saul spake not any thing that day: for he thought, Something hath befallen him, he is not clean; surely he is not clean. And it came to pass on the morrow, which was the second day of the month, that David's place was empty: and Saul said unto Jonathan his son, Wherefore cometh not the son of Jesse to meat, neither yesterday, nor today?* (1 Samuel 20:24-27)

In Leviticus 25:1-22 the Lord told Israel to plant and harvest for six years, but on the seventh year they were not to plant the land; they were to give it rest. Israel had to number its years (Lev. 25:8-11), and when they reached the fiftieth year, the year of Jubilee, the year of liberty for Israel, nothing that grew in the land by itself was to be harvested or eaten. Israel's obedience to these commandments would result in God's blessing, while ignoring them would bring judgment.

For this reason Judah spent 70 years of captivity in Babylon. They failed to keep the sabbatical year for 490 years (2 Chron. 36:20-21). Ancient Israel was sufficiently motivated by God to keep accurate calendars. By following the phases of the new moon and the passage of the seasons, they increased their awareness of the sun's passage through the zodiac from month to month.

> *Canst thou bind the sweet influences of Pleiades, or loose the bands of Orion? Canst thou bring forth Mazzaroth in his season? Or canst thou guide Arcturus with his sons? Knowest thou the ordinances of heaven? Canst thou set the dominion thereof in the earth?* (Job 38:31-33)

From all of this it is evident that the ancient prophets of Israel had an in-depth understanding of astronomy and knew the location of the stars within the constellations because God's Word makes reference to them.

The word *mazzaroth* can be translated as "stars, planets, constellations, or zodiac." The reference to Arcturus and his sons in verse 32 is a clear reference to Taurus the Bull, which also contains the *Pleaides*, or what we currently call the "Seven Sisters." In conjunction to this passage in Job, consider the following passage from Psalm 19:1-6:

> *The heavens declare the glory of God; and the firmament sheweth His handywork. Day unto day uttereth speech, and night unto night sheweth knowledge. There is no speech nor language, where their voice is not heard. Their line is gone out through all the earth, and their words to the end of the world.* ***In them hath He set a tabernacle for the sun,*** *which is as a bridegroom coming out of his chamber, and rejoiceth as a strong man to run a race.* ***His going forth is from the end of the heaven, and his circuit unto the ends of it: and there is nothing hid from the heat thereof.***

Ancient Israel was acutely aware of moon phases, of the passage of the sun through the zodiac, and of using the stars in the heavens to accurately follow the passing of the year. This is one reason why God created the heavens the way He did (Gen. 1:14-16). According to Psalm 19:1-2 and Genesis 1:14 we "rediscover" the fact that God also created the heavens to declare His glory (which gives relative truth about the God of creation) and that the firmament, which is God's handiwork, speaks volumes concerning God. The language spoken is universal and is ever present.

The structure of Psalm 19:1-3 makes it clear that God has created the universe, in that it declares the redemption story. The word *declare* is *kaphar*, which generally means "to scribe, tell, number, or count"; but in the *piel*, an intensive stem, it means more specifically "to count something exactly or accurately."

The heavens, therefore, give an accurate account of God's glory and greatness. Yet, there is nothing that demonstrates the glory of God better than the truths of the gospel message. Before God began to create, He first determined how He was going to redeem man to Himself; then He created a universe and a world that reflected this glorious message. "*According as He hath chosen us in Him before the foundations of the world...*" (Eph. 1:4).

For the wrath of God is revealed from heaven against all ungodliness and unrighteousness of men, who hold the truth in unrighteousness; because that which may be known of God is manifest [made clear] *in them* [the heavens]; *for God hath shewed it unto them. For the invisible things of Him from the creation of the world are clearly seen, being understood by the things that are made, even His eternal power and Godhead; so that they are without excuse* (Romans 1:18-20).

God created a world surrounded by heavens that declare His glory and give evidence of His awesome power to create, regulate, and save. The crowing glory of God is His great work of salvation in Jesus Christ, and it is this message that the heavens and all of nature proclaims. That is why the apostle Paul was able to declare to the Romans that they were without excuse. Creation and the invisible things that hold creation together, testify to the truth of God, even the Godhead, His very divinity (Rom. 1:19-20).

Instead of bowing to the eternal God who created everything, man has chosen to manufacture artificial gods and deny God as Creator. They turn the truth that the heavens are declaring into the perversions of astrology, mythology, and idolatry.

Because that, when they knew God, they glorified Him not as God, neither were thankful; but became vain in their imaginations, and their foolish heart was darkened. Professing themselves to be wise, they became fools ... Who changed the truth of God into a lie, and worshipped and served the creature more than the Creator, who is blessed for ever. Amen (Romans 1:21-22,25).

These imaginative untruths are still propagated today and are growing in the stories of Naturalistic Evolutionary Biology. The devil is vigorously deceiving believers and nonbelievers by a spurious fraud.

The Heavens Declare the Truth of God

The message uttered, or that bubbles forth, in Psalm 19:1-3 is speech itself. The Hebrew word translated "speech" in the King James Version is *omer* and is used in this form only six times in the Old Testament (Job 22:28; Ps. 19:2-3; 68:11; 77:8; Hab. 3:9). In Job it is something decreed. In Psalm 68:1 and Habakkuk 3:9 it is the "Word" of God that is published. In Psalm 77:8 it is the "promises" of God.

In Psalm 19 we have God proclaiming the glorious truths of God's spoken Word long before He revealed Himself to man in His written Word. The witnesses of the heavens and the written Word were later confirmed in the incarnate Word, the Lord Jesus Christ, who proclaimed, "*Heaven and earth shall pass away* [God's testimony of truth in creation], *but My words will shall not pass away*" (Mt. 24:35).

It must be understood that if these heavens and earth pass away, so too will all the written copies of God's Word; but God's Word is safely secured in Heaven and in the Lord Jesus Himself, the incarnate Word of God. "*And the Word was made flesh, and dwelt among us…*" (Jn. 1:14).

We, as professing fundamental, Bible-believing Christians, must get our heads out of the proverbial sand and recognize once again that the heavens unconditionally declare and confirm the truth of God and His holy Word. Presently, we have a more sure Word of prophecy, as recorded in the written Word of God; but before the written Word, God had authored the gospel message throughout the heavens. "The earliest prophecies of the gospel were visually preserved by associating them with star patterns called signs or constellations."[25] (See Kenneth C. Fleming's book, *God's Voice in the Stars, Zodiac Signs and Bible Truth.*)

The heavens hold key signs identifying the season when the "Day of the Lord" will come. As Bible-believing Christians we do not require confirmation of the truths of God's Word. We accept it by faith. But in the Word of God we find the principle that in the testimony of two or three witnesses the truth is established (Mt. 18:16; 2 Cor. 13:1).

The world has heard the testimony of creation—the sun, stars, moon, and earth—as well as the witness of Jesus Christ and the witness of the Bible. Therefore, saying "I did not know" will not be an acceptable excuse for those who plead for mercy at the Great White Throne Judgment. The heavens do declare the glory of God.

By night the heavens declare the knowledge *(da'at)* of God (Ps. 19:2). The Hebrew word *da'at* is from the word *yada*. The feminine noun form means "to know." According to the *Theological Word Dictionary of the Old Testament*:

> "[*Da'at*] is a general term for knowledge, particularly that which is of a personal, experimental nature (Prov. 24:5). It is also used for technical knowledge or ability, such as that needed for building the tabernacle and temple (Ex. 31:3; 35:31; 1 Kings 7:14). *Da'at* is also used for discernment (Ps. 119:66). *Da'at* is possessed by God (Job 10:7; Ps. 139:6; Prov. 3:20), from whom nothing can be hidden (Ps. 139:1-18). He teaches it to man (Ps. 94:10; 119:66; Prov. 2:6).
>
> "It appears parallel with wisdom (*kokma*) and understanding (*te buna*), instruction (*musar*), and the law (*tora*). Wisdom is used in series with 'science' (*madda'* in Dan. 1:4) and is the opposite of 'folly' (*iwwelet* in Prov. 12:23; 13:16; 14:18; 15:2). Hence *da'at* is the contemplative perception of the wise man (Prov. 1:4; 2:6; 5:2; Eccles. 1:18)."

The Star of Bethlehem

The message that the heavens are proclaiming has been nearly lost to the wise men of the ancient world. Men like the three kings of the East saw the star of David and knew that it was the "sign" of the One who was promised by God. The promise is contained in Scripture, but the sign of His coming was also found in the stars of the heavens. What did these wise men of antiquity know about the stars and the signs in the heavens that revealed the coming of the Messiah? What did they know that we may be missing today?

It is believed that their familiarity with the names of the stars (contained in the circle of stars that marks the path of the sun) is what God used to confirm the time of the First Coming of God's Son to Israel (Mt. 2:6-10). This circle of stars is known today as the "constellations of the zodiac" (Virgo, Libra Taurus, Aries, Leo, Scorpio, etc.).

There is textual evidence to indicate that Israel used the zodiac (*mazzaroth*) to track their seasons and feasts. For example, the Jewish historian, Josephus, tells us that the Jewish year began when the sun was in "Aries," and the Passover on the fourteenth day coincided with the first full moon (Jos., Ant. 3:201).[26]

"The Matthean passage has been one of the most cherished events in history—cherished in part because that star heralded the birth of the Savior of mankind. Moreover, this passage mentions the star only four times, and it is definitely not astrological. On the other hand, the star undoubtedly was an astronomical phenomenon."[27] "Therefore, the event glorifies God and His Son and is the result of His work, whether that be a miracle or a natural occurring phenomenon."[28]

Archaeological Evidence

Today archaeologists are finding synagogues in northern Israel with zodiacs in mosaic floors. "In one Synagogue, found at Hammath Tiberias, there is a mosaic floor that depicts the traditional Torah shrine and Menorahs and a zodiac panel. In the center of this panel, the sun (god) Helios is shown riding in the chariot of the heavens above the sea, his arm raised in a gesture of might and blessing. He is surrounded by signs of the zodiac as identified in Hebrew."[29]

In another similar synagogue, found at Meroth, the evidence of the zodiac found in stones has perplexed some archaeologists. They suggest, "despite pagan associations, that the zodiac was perhaps adapted to the Hebrew calendar and seemed to have been a popular element of Jewish ichnography." Within this same article the question is asked, "What is the zodiac doing in a synagogue?"

"Meroth is not the only example. There are theories but no firm answer to the presence of the zodiac. Perhaps the zodiac was used to calculate time. Did magic coexist with Judaism at the time? Perhaps the zodiac described the divine order of the heavens as a symbol of God's deeds on earth."[30]

Interestingly, in this same synagogue at Meroth, a study room with a mosaic floor was excavated. Only partial remains have survived, but one surviving frame describes "the end of days" and depicts a large amphora of water. "On one side of the amphora is a wolf and on the other is a lamb, together with the inscription from Isaiah 65:25,"[31] which says, "*The wolf and the lamb shall feed together....*"

The combination of both the zodiac and an interest about end-time events in this one synagogue may provide us with a valuable clue as to what early fifth and sixth century Jews believed concerning the signs that may have come from the heavens. The zodiac may have something to do with the signs of the seasons or of the end-time warnings.

Jesus proclaimed that believers should learn the parable of the fig tree, and learn to discern from the signs of the "*times*" that it is near at the doors (Mt. 24:32-33). He also said in Luke 21:25-26 that the signs would be in the sun, moon, and stars, and on the earth distress of nations and waves roaring. He also said that men's hearts would be failing them for fear for looking after those things which are coming upon the earth; "*for the powers of heaven shall be shaken.*"

The Signs of the Second Coming

In accord with this, Jesus tells us that the Church will pass through an age of tribulation (Jn. 16:33), but that believers should be of good cheer because He has overcome the world. Jesus refers to this tribulation period in Matthew 24:5-14,29 as the "beginning of sorrows." At the end of the "beginning of sorrows" we should expect the appearance of the "sign" of the Son of man in the heavens (Mt. 24:30).

What sign is Jesus talking about? Could this be the sign that both Jew and Christian who lived in the Galilean area were looking for in the heavens, specifically in the zodiac? If this is true and God has prepared a sign in the heavens, are we going to be wise enough to recognize and respond to the message? Will we continue to ignore the declaration about the truth of God's Word—that the heavens do indeed declare the glory of God? Will we miss God's divine warning?

We are to be watching for the signs in the heavens that pertain to Jesus' return. Some early Church fathers recognized a need for the man of God to understand astronomy. Origen, writing to his former pupil Gregory in the third century, states, "I would wish that you should take with you...as much of Geometry and Astronomy as may be helpful for the interpretation of the Holy Scriptures."[32]

Therefore, Christians must steadfastly avoid any involvement with juridical astrology, while a knowledge of the science of astronomy will help us better understand God's Word—especially prophecy.

Combining the heavenly signs and the earthly signs gives a clearer witness and a better understanding of the question, "What time is it?" I believe that it is near—even at the doors. The signs seem to indicate that the time is close at hand, but what are the heavens declaring today about the Second Coming of Jesus Christ that many are unable to acknowledge?

We cannot expect to know unless we first rediscover the signs to be sought. What is the sign of the Son of man that will appear in the heavens (Mt. 24:29-30)?

The journey begins.

End Notes

1. Jay M. Pasachoff and Donald H. Menzel, *Stars and Planets, Peterson Field Guides*, (Boston, MA: Houghton Mifflin Company, 1992), p. 438.

2. Paul Davis, *The Mind of God*, (New York: Orion Publications, Simon & Schuster, 1992), p. 50.

3. Stewart Custer, *The Stars Speak, Astronomy and the Bible*, (Greenville, SC: Bob Jones University Press, 1977), p. 41.

4. James Bjornstad and Shildes Johnson, *Stars, Signs and Salvation in the Age of Aquarius*, (Minneapolis, MN: Bethany Fellowship, Inc., 1971), p. 18.

5. Ibid., p. 7.

6. Ibid., pp. 79-80.

7. Ibid., p 21.

8. Spiros Zodhiates, *Lexicon to the Old Testament*, (Chattanooga, TN: KJV AMG Inter. Inc., 1984), p. 1577. All notes used by permission.

9. Paul M. Steidl, *The Earth, the Stars, and the Bible*, (Phillipsburg, NJ: Presbyterian and Reformed Pub. Co., 1979), p. 188.

10. Yonathan Mizrachi, "Mystery Circles?" *Biblical Archaeology Review*, Vol. 18(4), (July/August 1992), p. 55.

11. John Edwin Wood, *Sun, Moon and Standing Stones*, (Oxford: Oxford University Press, Merrivale Books Limited, 1978), pp. 11-13.

12. Joseph A. Seiss, *The Gospel in the Stars or Primeval Astronomy*, (Philadelphia, PA: General Council Publication House, 1912), pp. 363-364.

13. Hugh A. Moran and David H. Kelley, *The Alphabet and the Ancient Calendar Signs*, (Palo Alto, CA: Bell's Book Store, 1969), pp. 13-14.

14. Ibid., pp. 62-65.

15. Ibid., pp.14-15.

16. Seiss, *The Gospel in the Stars or Primeval Astronomy*, p. 56.

17. Moran and Kelley, *The Alphabet and the Ancient Calendar Signs*, p. 18.

18. Ibid., p. 35.

19. Ibid., p. 37.

20. Seiss, *The Gospel in the Stars or Primeval Astronomy*, pp. 53-54.

21. Ibid., pp. 55-56.

22. Moran and Kelley, *The Alphabet and the Ancient Calendar Signs*, pp. 49-52.

23. Phillip E. Johnson, *Darwin on Trial*, (Washington, D.C.: Regnery Gateway, 1991), p. 134.

24. Merrill F. Unger, "Festivals, Ascertaining the New Moon," *Unger's Bible Dictionary* (Chicago, IL: Moody Press, 1985), p. 352.

25. Kenneth C. Fleming, *God's Voice in the Stars, Zodiac Signs and Bible Truth*, (Neptune, NJ: Loizeaux Brothers, 1981), p. 35.

26. *Illustrated Bible Dictionary*, Part I, "Calendar" (Intervarsity Press/Tyndale House Publishers, 1980), p. 223.

27. Bjornstad and Johnson, *Stars, Signs and Salvation in the Age of Aquarius*, p. 56.

28 Ibid., p. 61.

29 Denis E. Groh, "Jews and Christians in Late Roman Palestine, Towards a New Chronology," *Biblical Archaeologist*, (June 1988), pp. 80-93.

30. Zviilan Emmanuel Damati, "The Synagogue at Meroth," *Biblical Archaeology Review*, (March/April 1989), pp. 20-36.

31. Ibid.

32. Bjornstad and Johnson, *Stars, Signs and Salvation in the Age of Aquarius*, p. 81.

Chapter 2

Origins

The Origin of Symbols and Signs in Revelation

Revelation 12:1-4 may contain the astronomical signs or wonders that will announce the coming of God's wrath. Once I understood the symbolic and literal meanings of the information contained in this passage, the entire chronology of the Book of Revelation was revealed. God may be using alignments in His creation of the cosmos to indicate the time of the Second Coming of Jesus Christ, just as He did in the First Coming of Christ.

God's intended purpose for the creation of the cosmos was consummated by the placement and naming of the stars in the heavens. In Revelation 12:1-4, God has given us this unique alignment to announce or indicate the arrival of the days of final judgment.

Understanding the source of John's description (the constellations) makes it possible for us to rediscover one of the most significant truths in biblical studies, "the sign of the coming of the Son of man" (see Mt. 24:30), in the heavens. This sign may validate that the age of Christ's Second Coming is truly at hand and ready to be fulfilled. It may also indicate the beginning of seven years of ever-increasing tribulation on earth.

Jesus stands at the door of time waiting to return. World and prophetic history will enter into an appointed hour when God will rapture the

Church, redeem Israel, judge the world, defeat satan, and set up His everlasting Kingdom. The seventh and final world kingdom of great Babylon will awaken only to be destroyed by Christ. The destruction of this one-world kingdom was portrayed thousands of years ago by Daniel the prophet.

God gave King Nebuchadnezzar of Babylon a dream. The king saw in his dreams an image of a man with a head of gold, breast and arms of silver, belly and thighs of brass, and legs of iron. Its feet and ten toes were of mingled clay and iron. The ten toes of the image indicated the final phase of the world empires.

In the dream the king saw that the image was destroyed by a stone of divine origin. The stone hit the image upon its feet, totally destroying it. This part of the dream obviously disturbed the king. Daniel interpreted the dream for the king and told him that the image represented four major world empires that would continue in some form until the latter days, when God would destroy these worldly kingdoms and establish His everlasting Kingdom on earth. (See Daniel 2:31-45.)

Similarly, the crowned seven heads and ten horns of Revelation 12:3 also indicate the time when the seventh and final kingdom rises as a world dominating power. The ten horns of Revelation 12:3, 13:1, and Daniel 7:7 are the final phase of world government that will be destroyed by the Second Coming of Jesus Christ.

Predicting the exact day or the hour of the Lord's return is not possible, but the season will be recognized by those who *watch*. The blessing and the wrath of God will be experienced as certain signs are revealed.

The latter part of King Nebuchadnezzar's dream and the signs or alignments of Revelation 12:1-4 have not yet physically appeared. These final signs, coupled with world events, should leave little doubt to the wise witness.

Different Views of Creation

Scholars hold different views toward the Word of God and the world we live in. These views directly affect their interpretation of the Book of Revelation. Thus it is important for you to understand my view of God's Word and how it affects my interpretation of prophecy.

For example, there are liberal antagonists who proclaim that the universal flood account in Genesis was taken from the Gilgamesh Epic, which dates back to the second millennium B.C., before the writings of ancient Israel, and is therefore the source for the Genesis creation story. Some say, "The story undoubtedly had its origin in Mesopotamia where, unlike Palestine, river floods were, and are, a common occurrence."[1] This attack reduces the Bible to an evolutionary or mythological belief, that existed long before, and was then merely copied and altered by the Hebrews to suit their needs.

I decline to accept this as fact. This theory is a baseless lie. The Gilgamesh Epic is more likely unregenerate man's account of the global flood with distorted folklore that turns the truth into a lie. Satan's manipulation of the facts began in Genesis chapter 3 when he told Eve that she would not die if she ate the fruit from the tree of the knowledge of good and evil. (See Genesis 3:4.) Most people today still fail to see or acknowledge the long-term destructive effects that are born out of the short-term toleration of sinful desires and habits.

The same principle of deception is found in the mind of man concerning God's creation. For example, satan has used the theory of evolution to undermine the Genesis account of creation. By creating an alternative to God and the rejection of sin, many people succumb to the myth of evolution. Evolution has been promulgated as fact by some leading scientific writers. The affirmation of evolution as fact surprisingly exists in the face of overwhelming evidence to the contrary.[2] Evolution is a recent man-made myth, excludes the God of the Bible, and is the foundation for many destructive philosophies, including that of racism. The idea of race is totally foreign to the Bible. According to the Bible, God created all nations of men and we are all of one blood. Fallen man, though, does not see or understand God's purpose behind His creation.

Therefore, with man in mind, God created and named the stars and set them in their own place in the heavens for a chosen purpose. We know from Romans 1:18-20 that part of this purpose was to reveal the wrath of God to the natural man, so that he would be without excuse.

God's naming of the stars is a significant truth. We learn from the study of Scripture that when God gives a name or changes a name, it reveals something significant. For example, God changed Abram's name, "father of many," to Abraham, "father of many nations," and Jacob's name to Israel, "prince of God" (Gen. 17:5; 32:28). Consider also the names of Samuel, "name of God," or *Lo-ammi*, "not My people" (1 Sam. 1:20; Hos. 1:9). Similar examples persist throughout Scripture.

It is no wonder that God placed and named the stars so that they might also tell us something about Himself and the purpose of His creation and its relationship to His plan for redeeming man. Is it any marvel that the Psalmist, looking into the heavens and considering the message revealed in the names of the stars, would ask in Psalm 8:3-4:

> *When I consider Thy heavens, the work of Thy fingers, the moon and the stars, which Thou hast ordained; what is man, that Thou art mindful of him? and the son of man that Thou visitest* [will observe or attend to] *him?* (Psalm 8:3-4)

David was reminded of this by considering the message proclaimed by the sun, moon, and especially the stars in the heavens. This glorious message has been perverted by mythology, astrological mystics, and evolutionary thinking.

I would like to suggest that the curious reader carefully explore additional information concerning the names of the stars and the history of the constellations in books like *The Witness of the Stars* by E.W. Bullinger and *God's Voices in the Stars, Zodiac Signs and Bible Truth* by Kenneth C. Fleming. On the astronomical relevance of the cosmos and the Word of God, *The Stars Speak, Astronomy in the Bible* by Stewart Custer is recommended.

It is important to differentiate between astrology and astronomy. Jeremiah 10:2-13 is an example of God's condemnation of the misuse of creation, but Jeremiah is told not to be dismayed or amazed at the signs of the heavens as the heathen (*goim*) are, for their customs are vain, void of any truth. Jeremiah acknowledges, after receiving instructions from the Lord concerning heathen abuses, that God is to be feared, not the false gods of the heathen. The heathen feared and, therefore, worshiped the heavens—the very place that testified of the true God, the only God to be feared (Jer. 10:6-7).

Fear is limited to the worship of Jehovah God. Fear is reverence for the God who created the heavens. The awesome splendor of the vast universe and the order of our solar system testify that our God *is* and that He *is to be feared* because He transcends the knowledge of men and their experience of God's creation.

All this information and understanding must be taken into consideration as we progress in our study. This is especially true when studying prophecy because symbolism and literal references to the sun, moon, and stars can be confused. Hidden significance can mask the truth, leading to producing and promoting a lie. Scholars "must also enter into symbols, syntax, and literary structures of the book."[3] If the errors of astrology, mythology, and evolution are ever going to be exposed within our society, the relevance of the truth in scientific discoveries must be clearly related to the truth contained in God's Word.

The Cosmic Clock

We could view the universe as God's great prophetic and solar or cosmic clock. If we do, then it is about time that we learn how to read the "signs of the times" contained in this great clock; for I fear that the "*time is at hand*" and we are nearing the midnight hour of judgment (Mk. 1:15; Rev 1:3; 22:10).

It is a fact today that we depend upon the stars and the path of the sun through the zodiac to regulate time. Important religious holidays are still regulated by the signs in God's great cosmic clock. Currently, Easter and Pentecost are governed by the Hebrew lunar calendar. The date that we celebrate the resurrection of Christ is established by Passover, which the Jews celebrate on the first Sabbath after the vernal full moon. "The beginning of spring was the vernal equinox, about March 21; the next full moon might occur as much as a month later, and the next Sabbath a week after that. Consequently, the highest festival of Christianity oscillated in the sun calendar."[4]

Why did God instruct Israel to mark the feasts by watching and counting the phases of the moon? The phases of the moon are only 29.5305882 days long and not 30 days. Therefore, this would not allow for any yearly constancy in Israel's calendar.

"It is possible that the nations surrounding Israel were worshiping the stars and planets and God wanted to distinguish His people from the heathen neighbors and thus insulate them from pagan idolatry. '*The star of your god which you made to yourselves*' Amos 5:20-26. Even though Israel maintained a lunar calendar, it reconciled its calendar with the solar cycle of 365 days, 5 hours, and 49 minutes."[5]

Therefore, Israel had an early knowledge of the true length of a year. "The ancient Akkadians used the yearly appearance of the thin horizontal spring crescent moon and its close proximity to two 'twin stars,' Castor and Pollux, to mark the beginning of the year. They did this over 4,000 years ago. If the alignment failed to materialize until the third day of the month of Nisan, the ancient star gazers knew that the year was to be a full year or a year with 13 months. But because of the effects of 'precession' their calendars would still be off 1 day in 70 years."[6] (See Figure 7 on page 8 and Chapter 10 for more on this alignment.)

"In time it was noticed that the terrestrial seasons no longer bore their relationship to the traditional year. Eventually the shift was made to relating the event of spring and fall equinoxes to new signs of the zodiac. Thus, the constellation of the Ram (Aries) replaced the Bull (Taurus) as the leader. They also began recording the actual lengths of day and night to discover the official first day of spring. When 12 hours of day and night arrived they knew, as today, that spring had arrived."[7]

God is the supreme authority on time. He created the solar system and time itself must be adjusted according to God's timetable, purpose, and revelation—ultimately the end of this age. When God's Kingdom is established on the earth, it will be the year "1 C.R.," the first year of "Christ's Reign" over the kingdoms of the world. God will, at this time, set all things according to His righteousness, including our calendars, clocks, and theologies.

The cosmos declares the glory of God by its order and its history, and because of our ignorance, its fragmentary display of the gospel message in the names of the stars and its appointed signification as to the First and Second Coming of the Son of Man, Son of God.

"*And let them be for signs, and for seasons...*" (Gen. 1:14b). "*O Lord...who hast set Thy glory above the heavens...*" (see Ps. 8:1-6). "*The heavens declare the glory of God...*" (see Ps. 19:1-6). "*For we have seen His star in the east...*" (see Mt. 2:1-10). "*And then shall appear the sign of the Son of man in heaven...*" (Mt. 24:30). "*And there appeared a great wonder* [sign] *in heaven...*" (see Rev. 12:1-4).

What's the Point?

What time is it, relative to what God has planned for man? The question is not: Where are we in the solar system in relationship to the sun? But it is: Where are we in the process or passage of time in relation to what God has revealed in the Word of God, concerning the coming of His everlasting Kingdom? How close are we?

For example, we can read the Bible prophecies concerning the coming of the Messiah. Christians will read passages and realize that some of the prophecies have been fulfilled with the passage of time. "*And He shall set up an ensign* [banner to be noticed] *for the nations, and shall assemble the outcasts of Israel, and gather together the dispersed of Judah from the four corners of the earth*" (Is. 11:12). This passage was read by modern Israel when it was discovered on Masada by Jews who had returned. It is now set to be fulfilled (see also Ezek. 37).

Isaiah 53 was fulfilled with the crucifixion of Christ, but men today continue to reject even this clear revelation. Many other prophecies are still pending, but the real question is: How much longer? How distant are God's promises concerning His eternal Kingdom on earth? A Kingdom where death, hunger, pain, and suffering will end; a Kingdom that will command the lion and lamb to live together in harmony? How far are we from those blessed events? How close are we to the implementation?

Jesus inaugurated the first phase of the Kingdom of Heaven on earth by commissioning the Church, the body of born-again Christians. Christians are to continue gathering the constituency that will someday share the Kingdom with God on earth. It is my belief that the signs will soon be revealed to all the world.

This means that the "Day of the Lord" will finally be ushered in upon this world and everything that God has promised will be fulfilled.

> *Seek ye out of the book of the Lord, and read: no one of these shall fail, none shall want her mate: for My mouth it hath commanded, and His spirit it hath gathered them* (Isaiah 34:16).

The mate for what God's Word has prophesied is its fulfillment in time. As Jesus Himself is recorded to have said, "*The scriptures must be fulfilled*" (Mk. 14:49) and they shall be "*fulfilled in their season*" (Lk. 1:20). This word *season* is translated from the Greek word *kairos* and means "occasion, set or proper time."

But what is the appointed time of the "Day of the Lord"? God gave the prophet Habakkuk an answer to a question that he had concerning his watching for the Lord's judgment day. That answer gives us some interesting insights.

> *And the Lord answered me, and said, Write the vision, and make it plain upon tables, that he may run that readeth it. For the vision is yet for an appointed time* [fixed time, meeting place], *but at the end it shall speak, and not lie: though it tarry, wait for it; because it will surely come, it will not tarry* (Habakkuk 2:2-3).

The vision was to be written down because it was for a day in the future—a day when Habakkuk would not be around to tell it, but others would be able to read it and run to the Lord in faith. "*The just shall live by his faith*" (Hab. 2:4b). The Lord has appointed the time when His word of prophecy will be fulfilled. All prophecies of the Lord will meet their mate at the appointed hour. At the time of the end, the prophecies will speak and impart the truth.

In other words, what God's Word declares will happen *must happen*, and what God's Word predicts will appear *must appear* exactly as God's Word describes. If God's Word promises that there will be signs in the earth indicating the Lord's coming, then there will be signs as Jesus said (Mt. 24:6-8).

And if God's Word expresses that there will be signs in the heavens, indicating that the time is at hand, then there will be signs in the heavens that "*shall speak, and not lie*" (Hab. 2:3). "*Tell us, when shall these things be? and what shall be the sign of Thy coming, and of the end of the world?*" (Mt. 24:3)

As we can look to God's creation and tell the time or season, so we can look to God's creation and God's Word to determine where we are dispensationally regarding the implementation of the Kingdom of God, the gathering away of Christians by the Lord Jesus Christ, and the coming "again" of the Messiah to Israel.

If Christians understand what it is we are to be looking for (to happen or appear), then we will be warned. *"Many shall be purified, and made white, and tried; but the wicked shall do wickedly: and none of the wicked shall understand; but the wise shall understand."* (Dan. 12:10). *"But ye, brethren, are not in darkness, that that day should overtake you as a thief"* (1 Thess. 5:4).

Signs in World Events

Many writers in the area of prophecy have been looking for and cataloging the signs upon the earth, the distress of nations, earthquakes, famines, pestilence, wars, and rumors of wars (Mt. 24:6-7). In June's issue of "Zion's Fire," Marvin Rosenthal lists 137 significant signs of the Lord's Second Coming taking place in the world. As these signs continue to increase in scope and magnitude, they indicate the approaching "Day of the Lord," climaxing with the seven years of the Great Tribulation period. We can readily see the increasing tribulation pangs appearing like the labor pangs of a woman with child. These pangs indicate that the "Day of the Lord" is at hand.

A prophesied one world system is being set up right before our very eyes. For example, with the North Atlantic Free Trade Agreement (NAFTA) and the General Agreement on Tariff and Trade (GATT) now in place, the world has taken two giant steps closer to a global economy—and *we can expect other nations to follow suit.* Crucial events take place at such a rapid rate that as soon as they are recorded, a key event is predicted and weeks later it becomes a reality. NAFTA exploded in this fashion.

At the beginning of 1994, the media reported the desires of South American countries to be part of the revised NAFTA trade agreement with the United States. Later, the European community announced a major breakthrough in the GATT agreements, which are designed to set up a global economy that will be governed by a regional top secret tribunal. Ralph Nader and others are sounding the alarm against this type of autocratic governance because they see our national sovereignty and rights being eliminated.

A significant event occurred when the recent Russian elections produced a Russian fascist named Zhurvinowsky and his democratic party was victorious in the last election. Again, the hateful words of white supremacy and anti-Semitic rhetoric are being fanned by the choking winds of despair and helplessness.

If the New World Order disregards Russia and, as a result, the Russian people are relegated to poverty while other nations prosper, that catalyst could bring Russia out of the North and against Israel, fulfilling Ezekiel 38. After all, according to Zhurvinowsky, the Jews are largely responsible for the breakup and breakdown of the Russian Communist government. He is even threatening to use nuclear force, if necessary, to restore Russia to her glory. We have a close copy of Nazi Germany's philosophy with one impressive exception: Zhurvinowsky already has the "bomb."

These situations have more than a ring of biblical prophecy to them. It should sound sirens of alarm to those who are expecting the soon return of Jesus Christ, but only the wise will hear and understand. God's Word declares, "*A prudent man foreseeth the evil, and hideth himself: but the simple pass on, and are punished*" (Prov. 22:3).

As the fateful day approaches, famine will be partly responsible for the widespread pandemonium as it spreads through the world. When famine affects Russia, and I believe that it will, this could be the motivation for a fascist representative like Zhurvinowsky to initiate new acts of aggression across borders in a search for fertile food sources.

An invasion of Israel would take hold of the fruitful lands in the Middle East and thus take a spoil.

> *And thou shalt say, I will go up to the land of unwalled villages; I will go to them that are at rest that dwell safely, all of them dwelling without walls, and having neither bars nor gates* [have their defenses down], *to take a spoil, and to take a prey; to turn thine hand upon the desolate places that are now inhabited, and upon the people that are gathered out of nations* [describes the Israel of today], *which have gotten cattle and goods, that dwell in the midst of the land*, (Ezekiel 38:11-12).

The significant point about this passage is that I believe it will not be fulfilled until the *middle of the seven-year tribulation period* spoken of by Daniel and the Book of Revelation. If this is correct, we see the stage being set now!

For the fulfillment of this prophecy, Ezekiel predicts that a great army will come down out of the North, invading the land of Israel in the last days (Ezek. 38:1-8). Therefore, the only conclusion is that we are exceptionally close to the beginning of this seven years of world tribulation. Contemporary events in our world directly relate to the second, third, and fourth seal of Revelation 6 within the Church Age.

Similar events will intensify, as predicted, when the "Day of the Lord" approaches. The days ahead of us "will speak and not lie." Chaos will grow in the world as a result of growing economic, political, and social instability. The United States economy and social structure will collapse as a result of irresponsible government policies designed to please an ever-growing perverted and godless society.

The accomplishments and virtues of the gay community are presented as if to verify their innate goodness. The logic itself is perverted—they conclude that homosexuality is not a grievous sin because so many homosexuals accomplish and do so many good things. The Bible says, "*But they measuring themselves by themselves, and comparing themselves among themselves, are not wise*" (2 Cor. 10:12b), and "*All the ways of a man are clean in his own eyes; but the Lord weigheth the spirits*" (Prov. 16:2).

To the gay community and our country as a whole I seek only to impart some good advice: "Be not wise in thine own eyes: fear the Lord, and depart from evil" (Prov. 3:7) before it is too late. Everyone must compare themselves to the Word of God and the righteousness of Jesus Christ. If all were to do this, the conclusion would be that homosexuality is a sin that needs to be repented of and frustrated. Open homosexuality is an indictment against the perverseness, not the greatness, of our society. It is a sin that is produced by a godless society ripe for judgment.

The Seventieth Week of Daniel

For those who are not familiar with the prophesied seven years of tribulation, otherwise referred to as the "Seventieth Week of Daniel," let me explain. In Daniel 9:21-27 the prophet records the vision of seventy weeks. The weeks represent periods of seven years each. Therefore, 70 weeks equals 70 groups of 7, or 490 years.

Seventy weeks are determined upon thy people and upon thy holy city, to finish the transgression, and to make an end of sins, and to make reconciliation for iniquity, and to bring in everlasting righteousness, and to seal up the vision and prophecy, and to anoint the most Holy. Know therefore and understand, that from the going forth of the commandment to restore and to build Jerusalem unto the Messiah the Prince shall be seven weeks, and threescore and two weeks: the street shall be built again, and the wall, even in troublous times. And after threescore and two weeks shall Messiah be cut off, but not for himself: and the people of the prince that shall come shall destroy the city and the sanctuary; and the end thereof shall be with a flood, and unto the end of the war desolations are determined. And he shall confirm the covenant with many for one week: and in the midst of the week he shall cause the sacrifice and the oblation to cease, and for the overspreading of abominations he shall make it desolate, even until the consummation, and that determined shall be poured upon the desolate (Daniel 9:24-27).

The prophecy predicted that there would be 483 prophetic years (360 days for each year based on a lunar calendar) from the building of the wall until the coming of the Messiah. The wall was built by Nehemiah in approximately 445 B.C. From 445 B.C. to A.D. 30 is exactly 483 prophetic years. Daniel's prophecy indicates that the Messiah would be cut off after 483 years, or 69 weeks of 7's.

The Hebrew word for "cut off," *karath*, literally means "to cut" and was also used to indicate the cutting of a covenant (Dan. 9:26). In the making of a covenant, a sacrifice was used or cut to seal the agreement between two parties. Such a covenant was made or cut between Abraham and God: "*In the same day the Lord made* [cut] *a covenant with Abram...*" (Gen. 15:18). Jesus Christ sealed the New Covenant agreement between God and man with His own blood at Calvary's cross (Heb. 9:14-17).

Therefore, only 483 years of this 490 years of Daniel's prophecy have been fulfilled with the crucifixion, resurrection, and ascension of Christ. God has delayed the countdown of the last seven years. He has done this because Israel as a nation has rejected her Messiah. "*He came unto His own, and His own received Him not*" (Jn. 1:11). (See Romans 10 and 11 for more on this rejection of Christ.)

For almost 2,000 years God has been patiently calling all to repent of their sin and accept Jesus Christ as their Savior and Deliverer. But soon, the prophetic clock of Israel will begin ticking again. Then the final countdown of the last seven years of Daniel's prophecy will begin. In the middle of this seven-year period the newly constructed temple will be desecrated as prophesied in Daniel 9:27 and Matthew 24:15.

These final seven years are what we call the tribulation period or the seventieth week of Daniel, meaning the final group of seven years **(483 + 7 = 490 years).** The start of this final seven-year countdown will mark the end of the Church Age and the beginning of God's restoration and the salvation of Israel. But it will also mark the beginning of increased judgment, designed to convince an unrepentant world that it lacks acceptable righteousness and that it faces the imminent and total fiery judgment of God.

Christians Are Commanded to Watch!

Jesus tells Christians to watch for the signs of His Second Coming that precede the arrival of this final seven-year period. Christ will rapture His Church out of the world just as this final seven-year countdown begins—when He opens the sixth seal (Rev. 6:12-17). The Church will be in Heaven, delivered to the throne of God, while the world and Israel will be delivered to the time of Jacob's trouble (Jer. 30:7) or "The Great Tribulation." "*These are they which came out of great tribulation*" (Rev. 7:14).

The signs that Jesus tells us to watch for are famines, earthquakes, wars, rumors of wars, and pestilence. Some scholars and lay persons argue that the signs described in Matthew 24:6-8 are "nearly routine events"[8] and question the uniqueness and relevance of the signs. Although this is partly true, it must be concluded that it has never been more true and more relevant than it is today.

As a result of passing time, this question of Christ's return and the signs are more relevant because we are that much closer to the reality of God's Kingdom than any other generation. By concealing the exact time from man, God has held the hope of Christ's return open and imminent for every generation. But for the generation that will see the return of Christ there would be no need for God to continue to conceal, *as completely*, the appointed time; instead He would begin to reveal that the season is indeed at hand.

This is what is happening today. The Spirit of God is working in believers today to announce that the Lord's return is approaching fast. We should step back for a moment and ask the question: Why are so many people writing about the return of the Lord, and with such an ominous urgency? Billy Graham, commenting on his book entitled *Storm Warning*, says that it was written partially in response to the tremendous interest and the increased volume of questions that he has received regarding the end of the world. These questions were spawned as a result of the unrest, violence, fear, helplessness, and instability that is apparent everywhere on the earth. Books like *The Pre-Wrath Rapture of the Church* by Marvin Rosenthal and *1994* by Harold Camping, (with whom I strongly disagree because of his lack of consistent biblical hermeneutics), or *Armageddon, Oil and the Middle East Crisis* by John F. Walvoord, are books written by men who are theologically different, but who similarly believe the return of the Lord is fast approaching.

If we could put aside our theological differences for a moment, we would note that many men, though theologically different, are "born-again" saved individuals trying to respond to the leading of the Spirit, but who are limited by their theological bias. ***Apart from the bias, the message is the same—the Lord is coming back and it may be soon.*** This inescapable moment will be exciting, and we dare not ignore what the Spirit is saying to the Church. The message is to watch and warn!

To every generation that expects the return of Jesus Christ, God's Word repeatedly says, "Watch!" To the Church of Sardis (Rev. 3:1-6) Jesus says "watch" because He will come as a thief to those who are not watching. The Church of Sardis represents the root of the Reformation Church that began an era where the brethren increasingly watched for the Lord's return.

With each passing day the responsibility becomes more and more relevant because we are closer to God's appointed time. It is near the appointed time, a time appointed by God. God has determined when it will be and where the earth and moon will be in their orbits around the sun. He has foreordained the exact position of the stars, as well as set them for His purpose. It is well to remember that Jesus has said:

> *And there shall be signs in the sun, and in the moon, and in the stars; and upon the earth distress of nations, with perplexity; the sea and the waves roaring; men's hearts failing them for fear, and for looking after those things which are coming on the earth: for the powers of heaven shall be shaken* (Luke 21:25-26).

God ultimately knows what the spiritual status of mankind will be at that appointed time and God has already revealed some of the signs of the Second Coming of Christ. Within the revelation of His Word, God has told us to watch for signs that will be coming in the heavens, sun, stars, moon, and earth.

End Notes

1. Phillip K. Hitti, *The Near East in History: A 5000 Year Story*, (Princeton, NJ: D. Van Nostrand Company Inc., 1961), pp. 59-60.
2. Michael Denton, *Evolution: A Theory in Crisis*, (Bethesda, MD: Adler & Adler Publishers, Inc., 1985), pp. 305-306.
3. Leonard L. Thompson, *The Book of Revelation*, (New York: University Press, 1990), pp. 1-2.
4. Rudolf Thiel, *And There Was Light, The Discovery of the Universe*, (New York: Random House Publishing, Alfred A. Knopf, Inc., 1957), p. 53.
5. W.E. Maunder, *The Astronomy of the Bible*, (New York: Richard Coly & Sons, Lmtd., Bungay, Suffolk), p. 305.
6. Ibid., pp. 315-316.
7. Ibid.
8. Turner, "Structure and Sequence of Matthew 24:1-41," p. 7.

Chapter 3

Different Views

Time to Reflect

Many years ago, before I began my seminary training, I was a self-employed contractor. I worked with a general contractor, Dave Brown. Dave was a Christian and had another Christian man working for him. What I remember most about this other man was the watch that he wore. It was a very special watch because it had no working mechanical or electronic parts. In fact, it was nothing more than a flex-band with a crystal that revealed his hairy wrist underneath the crystal of the watch face.

I noticed the watch when I asked him for the time. He told me that he did not know because his watch was not a mechanical watch at all. "Instead," he explained, "it's a spiritual watch." He went on to explain, "Every time I look at my watch, I am reminded that I really do not know what time it is in relationship to the time of Jesus' return."

It is certainly true that no person can know, with absolute certainty, the day and the hour of our Lord's return, but we can determine, with some degree of certainty, when the age is nearing or when we are entering the season of time that will witness the Lord's return. Otherwise, why would Jesus have commanded believers to "watch" if there were not some intrinsic value for the one watching? This man's watch became a constant reminder that the Lord's return could happen at any time.

Theological and Eschatological Positions

The goal of my research has been truth. My goal has not been to prove a certain position, whether it be premillennial, postmillennial, amillennial, pretribulation, midtribulation, or posttribulation.

Those who are pretribulation and premillennial believe that Jesus Christ will rapture, or rescue, true believers just before or at the very onset of the seven years of tribulation, and that Jesus Christ will return with the raptured saints before the official implementation of the 1,000-year rule of Christ on earth.

"*And I beheld when He had opened the sixth seal...*" (see Rev. 6:12-17). "*These are they which came out of great tribulation...Therefore are they before the throne of God...*" (see Rev. 7:14-16). "*For God hath not appointed us to wrath...*" (1 Thess. 5:9). "*And her child was caught up unto God, and to His throne* [Body of Christ/Church with Christ, Christ is the man-child]" (Rev. 12:5b). "*And the armies which were in heaven followed Him upon white horses, clothed in fine linen, white and clean*" (Rev. 19:14).

Most pretribulation-premillennial theologians are dispensationalist, which means that they view the works of God recorded in the Bible as happening within different dispensations. The number of dispensations varies. Some believe in seven, while others believe there are as few as three or four. The seven dispensations are: innocence, conscience, government, promise, law, grace, and kingdom.

Each dispensation covered a period of man's history where God tested man in "respect of obedience to some *specific* revelation of the will of God."[1] Dispensationalist theology is based primarily on a contextual, historical, and literal interpretation of the Word of God—the same method that Jesus and the apostles used when they quoted or explained Scripture. Therefore, dispensationalists view the revelation of Scripture as being progressive. More of God's truth was understood as time progressed and more of God's revelation was received. The reception of the revelation has long ceased, but God is still illuminating believers to the truth of His Word through the ministry of the Holy Spirit.

Those who are posttribulation believe that Jesus will return after the seven years of the Great Tribulation on earth, while the midtribulationalist believes that Jesus will rescue the Church after three-and-a-half years of the tribulation.

Amillennialists do not believe in a literal 1,000-year reign of Christ. Most amillennialists are of the covenant theological background and view the Church as replacing or usurping Israel's place with God. Covenant theologians believe God will fulfill the promises that He gave to Abraham through the Church. Believers of this theology see no future restoration of Israel and, therefore, see little or no significance of Israel's return to Palestine. I find this position to be based on an allegorical interpretation of Scripture.

"Only dispensationalism does justice to the proper concept of progressive revelation. Covenant theology does include in its system different modes of administration of the covenant of grace, and although these modes would give an appearance of an idea of progressiveness in revelation, in practice there is extreme rigidity in covenant theology."[2] James Orr, a covenant theologian himself, confirms this:

> "It [covenant theology] fails to seize the true idea of development, and by an artificial system of topology, and allegorizing interpretation, sought to read back practically the whole of the New Testament into the Old. But its most obvious defect was that, in using the idea of the covenant as an exhaustive category, and attempting to force into it the whole material of theology, it created an artificial scheme which could only repel minds of simple and natural notions."[3]

My position before my study began was *pretribulation-premillennial* and that is what it remains after my study, but with some "major" modifications that were demanded by the results of my study. I admitted my biases in the very beginning so I could work to control them, move them, or adjust them as truth was revealed or established that challenged or exposed weakness in a certain position.

I have tried to be as objective as possible, but I realize that there is no such thing as total objectivity. My purpose is not to attack anybody else's position, but I do sound some warnings. I put forth the results of my study as a witness to the fact that I have taken the time to hold open the whole question of biblical prophecy in hope that we might be able to resolve some major discrepancies that have existed in some of the proof texts of the pretribulation, premillennial, and dispensational positions—all of which I still hold to, but again with "*major*" modifications.

The modifications have convinced me that this position is biblically prudent. As such, this study has led me to coin a new name—the "*born-again-pretribulation-premillennial*" position. This study has authenticated this theological and eschatological (study of end-time events) position as being the only one that is biblically prudent for a believer to hold. At first this conclusion may not appear warranted because of individual bias, but the certification will establish itself.

Other men have dared to put forth new ideas and challenges, and at the same time they have opened themselves up to attacks and years of word battles in journals and publications. Their ideas and challenges can help to expand our understanding of God's Word.

We can thank men like Rosenthal, even though some of us may disagree in a major way with many of his conclusions and positions. (Rosenthal is the author of the prewrath Rapture position. This position modifies the pretribulation and midtribulation position by arguing that the first half of the tribulation does not contain the wrath of God. Therefore the Church can and will go through at least half of the tribulation period, but will be raptured before the wrath of God is poured out.)

I do not agree with Rosenthal, but I thank him because my study was spurred on by a challenge that he issued to pretribulationalists, in his prewrath Rapture position of the Church, in which he asked for a one-text proof of a pretribulation rapture.[4] I will provide such a proof in this study, although a one-text proof is totally unnecessary for authentication.[5]

I encourage anyone who is bothered by any or all of the positions that currently exist today, or just this one, to put forth his own study, come to his own results, and finalize his own conclusions. Then live out to the fullest what you believe to be true.

The position that I put forth here has settled my heart and convinced me that the Book of Revelation not only belongs in the canon of Scripture, as some have wrongfully questioned, but is also a very fitting capstone to the Word of God.

The Book of Revelation is the key that unlocks and draws together all of God's truth from the beginning of Genesis through the Book of

Revelation itself. The Book of Revelation is seen as both complex and very well organized and very consistent with the whole body of Old and New Testament teachings. This is true of both prophetic and non-prophetic passages, which is exactly what the certifiable truth must correlate.

If we hold to a professed truth that argues against another Bible truth, then they must be reconciled or else confusion and conjecture will be the order of the day. The *"born-again-premillennial-pretribulation" position suggests some major chronological changes.*

The fact that I have come to the same conclusion, in spite of so many major changes, can best be explained with the following illustration.

While in school many of us may remember having math books that contained the answers in the back of the book. These answers were provided so we could check our final answers. The answers in the back of the book, however, did not give us the formulations or the running mathematics that resulted in the correct answer.

By knowing the answer, we knew what our figures must equal. If we checked our answer and it was wrong, we could go back and continue to adjust our calculations until we came up with the right answer.

If we simply went off to school with the right answer at the bottom of the page, our understanding and methodology for coming to that answer was flawed, incomplete, and hard to explain.

As the problem was put on the board, we may have learned that several of our steps, which led us to the answer, were wrong. But we continued to hunt for the difference between the answer in the back of the book and our first conclusion, and work out our formulations.

It was a case when two or more wrongs made a right, but not quite. This is because having the right answer does not make us right, or a mathematician. Knowing how to correctly add, subtract, divide, multiply, convert, reduce, and logically assemble the numbers in a proper order or sequence resulted in the correct answer and a passing grade for the class.

I believe that the *pretribulation-premillennial* position has most of the right answers, but many of those holding it cannot explain why or how they formulate all their conclusions.

Revelation tells us where we must end up. We know that the Church is not appointed to wrath; therefore, the Church cannot go through the tribulation period. As Dave Hunt says, "A post-tribulation 'Rapture' would be a classic non-event. [Because] there would be few believers if any believers in Christ to take to heaven. They would all have been killed, for such is the fate of those who refuse to take the mark of the beast (Antichrist) and worship his image."[6]

We have declared to know the answer because it is so obvious, but our explanation of the Book of Revelation has not always been based on good "formulation," or might we say, "good hard exegesis." It is for this very reason that the *pretribulation-premillennial* position has come under attack. The cracks in the formulation errors were obvious, and as a result this position has been rejected by some and held in suspect by others. But it must also be noted that the *pretribulation-premillennial* position best conforms primarily to a literal interpretation of the Scriptures.

If there is one thing that Harold Camping's book *1994* proves, it is the danger of symbolic interpretation and the dependency of the covenant and the amillennial positions on allegorical/symbolic interpretations. This is especially confusing when writing or attempting to explain prophetic Scriptures.

Some of the assumptions that have plagued the pretribulation positions are:

1. The first seal of Revelation 6:1-2 signifies the beginning of the seven years of Daniel's tribulation. It has been *assumed*, but not proven by anyone, that the first seal of Revelation 6:1-2 marks the beginning of the seven years of Daniel's tribulation.
2. The 24 elders must be representatives of the Church in Heaven.
3. The two witnesses have their ministry in the second half of the tribulation and not the first.

These are major assumptions that, when properly placed and proven, help to unlock the beautiful panoramic view that John gives to the Church of the last days.

Yet, these or other issues may never be totally settled until we are with the Lord. To say that we are no longer teachable would suggest that "we have arrived." To say that we have arrived is to affirm that we can no longer grow or mature. To say that we will never change does nothing but create a fortress mentality.

We must seek growth and understanding, and if change is warranted, God's Word will direct us toward the truth without making us victims of compromise. This is especially true when it means growth. Growth that is based upon the truth of God's Word should bring us into a closer relationship with the Lord Jesus Christ and make us more and more like Him.

After all, this is God's goal for us. This is what it means to become a son of God. Consequently, no man of God, while living in the flesh, can lay claim to a close proximity of this glorious goal of God—to be like Jesus Christ.

"*Not as though I had already attained, either were already perfect...*" (see Phil. 3:12-14). "*That we should be holy and without blame before Him in love*" (Eph. 1:4b). "*For they* [our fathers] *verily...chastened us after their own pleasure; but He* [God] *for our profit, that we might be partakers of His holiness*" (Heb. 12:10).

Let us lift our heads and hearts to God and say, "*Father, help us; help us to understand. Guide us with Thy Holy Spirit into all truth, that we may serve You better and with greater confidence and fidelity. Help us to understand what the Spirit is saying to the churches in these 'last days.'* "

The Problem With Theories

Theologians share similar problems, as do other fields of scientific inquiry. For example, the field of physics abounds with theories, counter theories, and new theories. Old theories are continually giving way to new ones. New theories can be good or bad, depending on one's bias. New theories often seem good in the beginning, but when faulty data reveals error, the theory should be reevaluated.

For example, scientists are being forced to reevaluate Darwin's concept of evolution and the origin of species in light of the new evidence pouring in that supports special creation. But the sinful intellect of modern man will not allow this switch to be easy.

Scientists and physicists usually learn from their mistakes and go on, but old theories sometimes die hard and slow deaths. This is also true in the area of theological studies.

Theology, like physics, is somewhat provisional in the sense that both put forth hypotheses. Quantum physics is based upon the known laws of the created universe. Theology, however, is based upon understanding the relationship between the eternal principles of God's Word and God's laws of nature.

Therefore, theology is just as complex, if not more so, as physics. The term *metaphysics* means "after physics." Therefore, questions that cannot be answered by physics are often relegated to metaphysics or theological studies. More and more scientists are trying to explain man's origins. But the questions remain: Is this a place where physicists belong? Can the questions of origin and who we are be answered by scientists?

The truth is, even the grandest of all explanation of origins, of how the universe and our world with all its complex life forms and interconnected systems of life support began, is at best a "good story" with huge gaps in known facts. What makes the story so convincing to most people today are the credentials of some of the "tale bearers" more than their actual understanding of the empirical data.

The stories of evolution, big bang, and quantum physics are too far afield for most people to investigate. But when the data is carefully considered, the "stories" abound with speculations and unproven hypotheses lacking hard facts. Even worse, many of the theories make no risky predictions that can be proven true or false, thus making it impossible for us to accept any of them.

Dr. Michael Denton, a renowned microbiologist, states, "There is little doubt that if this molecular evidence (DNA) had been available one century ago it would have been seized upon with devastating effect by the opponents of evolution theory...and the idea of organic evolution might never had been accepted."[7] Again he states that, "Despite the fact that no convincing explanation of how random evolutionary processes could have resulted in such an ordered pattern of diversity, the ideas of uniform rates of evolution is presented in the literature as if it were an empirical discovery. The hold of the evolutionary paradigm is so powerful that an idea which is more like a principal of medieval astrology than a serious twentieth-century scientific theory has become a reality for biologist...Yet in the face of this extraordinary discovery [in DNA research] the biological community seems content to offer explanations which are no more than apologetic tautologies."[8]

But theologians, while trusting in the leading of the Holy Spirit, have a great advantage over physicists and evolutionists. In a greater sense we have an additional advantage because we have the revelation of the God who claims to have been there when it all began—who was, who is, and who will be. This revelation is in the Word, history, and archaeology for us to draw upon.

The problem for us is finding the data and then correctly interpreting and assembling it. However, even after we assemble and interpret the data it is never really complete because time has a way of altering the data and at times producing new data. So we must do the best we can and avoid a fortress mentality, which will do nothing but run our studies aground.

God's Word Is Not Theory

On the other hand, the Bible makes literally thousands of predictions, many of which have been fulfilled. Some are being fulfilled today and we suspect that others will be fulfilled in the not too distant future. Just watch and see! God's Word must be fulfilled. Christians are often accused of practicing pseudoscience when they profess an unshakable understanding based on the creation account of Genesis.

Christians are often chided about believing in a flat earth because we believe and interpret the Bible as the literal revealed Word of God's truth. But Christians and the Bible do not teach that the world is flat;[9] scientists before Columbus did that. If scientists or misguided religious leaders before Columbus had read their Bibles, they would have known, like Isaiah and Job, that the earth was a circle and hung on nothing (Is. 40:22; Job 26:7).

Premature conclusions and unwarranted preclusions place destructive doubts in the minds of some people concerning the reliability of God's Word and His existence. Still, all the facts are not yet revealed. Scientists need to heed this solemn warning: ***Know your limits and know what and who it is you seek to replace or destroy before you destroy it, for it could lead to your own demise as well.***

Scientists, after all, are only men and sinners like everybody else. I love science and I believe that, in the end, science will be greatly elevated. This will occur when the facts that indicate a designed and ordered world are acknowledged openly by notable scientists and physicists, such as Paul Davis, Michael Denton, Stephen Hawking, and dare I say, Carl Sagan.

The facts of science and Scripture must be distinguished from theory. Science, on the other hand, is used to prove or disprove a theory, but is not the theory itself.

Therefore, if we are continually frustrated to prove or disprove a particular theory, whether it be creationism, evolution, or something in prophecy, it may be because we are not yet privy to all the facts. This would seem to indicate that God has limited man's understanding by creating a world that refuses to divulge its deepest secrets.

The deliberate concealment may be for the perpetuation of faith. In other words, God created a world with limited revelation that would require us to believe in Him by faith. He wants us to have faith in Him, evidenced by creation and by His Word. To combine the *facts of science* with the *Word of God* is most exciting and enlightening, but totally unnecessary for those who have come to God through Jesus Christ by faith alone. Faith in God must take place before God can enlighten our hearts and minds to the depth of truth contained in His Word.

> *Now faith is the substance of things hoped for, the evidence of things not seen* (Hebrews 11:1).

> *For by Him were all things created, that are in heaven, and that are in earth, visible and invisible...all things were created by Him, and for Him: and He is before all things, and by Him all things consist* (Colossians 1:16-17).

God will only reveal to man what is necessary for His Word and His will to be realized. For now, it seems that He does not want us to have a comprehensive understanding. This limitation frustrates the scientific "enlightened one's" thinking, and so be it. For example, the truth concerning organic evolution (the belief that life evolved from organic material) is that it is a kind of metaphysics because it propagates a theory of origins without "any" empirical data.

God has more important things to concern Himself with than man's thirst for knowledge. After all, according to Genesis 3:5-6, this is how we fell into "sin" in the first place.

> *For God doth know that in the day ye eat thereof, then your eyes shall be opened, and ye shall be as gods, knowing good and evil.*

And when the woman saw that the tree was good for food, and that it was pleasant to the eyes, and a tree to be desired to make one wise, she took of the fruit thereof, and did eat, and gave also unto her husband with her; and he did eat (Genesis 3:5-6).

If creationists want to conduct scientific experiments to prove the belief that we live in a created, designed, and purposeful world, then science should accommodate those who are willing to conduct such research. It is not healthy for science to so narrowly define the boundaries of what is acceptable science by deliberately precluding the intellect of the religiously devout.

This type of preclusion only draws science into a very dangerous type of narrow-mindedness and shortsightedness, which is always detrimental to the advancement of science. Science appears to set a double standard by accepting the stories of evolution as acceptable science. I have nothing against anyone who believes that evolution is true, but I have everything against someone who says that they "know" it is true. This is because I have taken the time to read the data, and the empirical evidence is just not there to make such an unwarranted conclusion.

On the other hand, for those of us who believe that God created our world, it is really not up to us to prove anything. We readily admit that we accept creation primarily on the basis of faith—first, faith in His revelation, the Bible; and second, by considering the evidence of the world around us...scientifically. How He did it is not as important as to why? Evolution is disturbing to Bible-believing Christians primarily for two reasons:

1. It claims something to be true that has not been proven to be true by good science.
2. It undermines the creation account of the Bible, which is not fully understood by anyone, without understanding fully the repercussions of such a fallacious claim upon the societies of the "real" world in which we live.

Crime, violence, rebellion, and disease can be the result of bad science as well as bad theology. This is especially true when science undermines the truth of good theology. We need to conduct our studies intelligently and honestly if truth is to be ours. This holds true in the study of science and in the study of prophecy. I will seek to combine the facts of astronomical science with the revelation of Scripture as we progress in our study of prophecy.

Now let us now consider, with our minds and hearts open, an outline of Revelation with the major tenets of what I have defined as the "*born-again-pretribulation-premillennial*" position.

End Notes

1. Charles C. Ryrie, *Dispensationalism Today*, (Chicago, IL: Moody Press, 1991), p. 22.

2. Ibid., p. 19.

3. James Orr, *The Progress of Dogma*, (Grand Rapids, IL: Eerdmans Publishing Co., 1952), p. 303.

4. Rosenthal, *The Pre-Wrath Rapture of the Church*, p. 280.

5. Karleen, *The Pre-Wrath Rapture of the Church, Is It Biblical?* p. 89.

6. Dave Hunt, *How Close Are We?* (Eugene, OR: Harvest House Publishers, 1993), p. 230. All notes used by permission.

7 Michael Denton, *Evolution: A Theory in Crisis*, Reprint, (Originally published Great Britain: Burnett Books, 1985; Maryland: Adler & Adler, Publishers Inc.), pp. 290-291.

8. Ibid., p. 306.

9. Bjornstad and Johnson, *Stars, Signs and Salvation in the Age of Aquarius*, p. 38.

Part II

The Book of Revelation

Chapter 4

It's Time to Understand Revelation 1–6

My Positional Statements

As we consider the Book of Revelation, I will present my position, explanation, and support of the following statements:

1. Seals one through five are open and may have been open for some time. The first seal was definitely opened by the Day of Pentecost because it involved the sending of the promised Holy Spirit to the Church. As for seals two through five, they have been progressively opened since Pentecost and will be acutely manifested in the last nine-month period that immediately precedes the start of the seven-year tribulation period. Seals two through four, when properly understood, will be recognized as the "beginning of sorrows."

2. Seal six includes the Rapture, which will occur with the realization that the "Day of the Lord" has come and will be followed by a pause of an indefinite period of time, which is used to seal the 144,000.

3. The "Day of the Lord" refers to the whole seven-year period, while the second half is specifically the high-water mark of God's wrath. Everything before the seventh trumpet will be warning judgments that

will serve as opportunities for repentance and salvation. The first four trumpets parallel the battle in the heavens of Revelation 12:7-12. Satan's kingdom, which will have taken over one-third of all creation, will be judged and darkened.

4. The seven churches have a dual meaning. They are seven literal churches, but the seven churches are also a representation of periods of history and events for the Church to pass through. The Church today is a result of those who have preceded us and specifically the history of the choices made by earlier Christians. A choice to be faithful, repent, overcome, stand firm, or not has had lasting consequences.

It will also be seen that the seven churches are divided into two groups of believers. Ephesus, the beginning or the Apostolic Gentile Church, was divided into two wings. One wing was made up of the faithful Smyrna, Sardis, and Philadelphia churches. The second wing included the unfaithful churches of Pergamos, Thyatira, and Laodicea. The cumulative message of the seven letters is ultimately written to the churches that will see the return of the Lord, which I absolutely believe to be the Church existing today.

5. The seals have a relationship to the seven churches and each seal parallels each respective church, but with cumulative and lasting effects throughout the Church Age and into the Great Tribulation.

6. The seventh seal commences with the beginning wrath of the "Day of the Lord," but the actual countdown of the seven-year period will begin earlier with the sixth seal. During this time the Church will be under increased persecution by the devil, but for a short time only.

7. At the end of the history of the Philadelphian Church, Christians will be raptured before the tribulation (which is coming upon the whole world) begins to unfold. The seven churches are representative of the whole Body of Christ on earth, as well as being the branches through which we can trace the evolving history of the Church through the ages. The letters to the churches need to be considered corporately and are revelations of the types of trials that the Body of Christ has and will continue to face through the ages—right up to the Rapture. These seven letters represent seven stages of purifying trials that will prepare the Bride for the Bridegroom.

8. The Laodicean churches are compossed of professing religious Christians who have not been born again. They are physically alive but spiritually dead, making them lukewarm and rejected by the Lord in the Rapture.

9. The two witnesses have their ministry in the first half of the tribulation period, are killed on Passover, and three-and-one-half days later are resurrected. This resurrection could happen on the morning of some future Easter Sunday.

10. The 144,000 are taken into the wilderness at the beginning of the first half of the tribulation period with the two witnesses, where they are literally fed, protected, and taught of God by His two witnesses.

11. The beast rules the second half of the tribulation, but his rule is cut short by the Lord's return. This is the eighth kingdom that replaces the short-lived seventh kingdom of the "New World Order."

12. The 24 elders are not representatives of the Church; they are the sons of God or ruling angels and have been before the throne of God since their creation.

13. Chapter 12 of Revelation is a key chapter of the book and is fundamental to understanding the Book of Revelation.

14. The woman of chapter 12 is Israel; the dragon is the devil. The man-child that will rule with a rod of iron is Christ, coming forth to rule all nations at the time of Israel's trouble. The child that is caught up to Heaven is the raptured Church with Christ before God's throne, poised to rule with Christ.

15. The wonders in the heavens—the woman, and the dragon of Revelation chapter 12—are the constellations Virgo and Hydra, indicating for us precisely that Israel's trouble must begin in the month of some future September or October. It is also a time of harvest and the moon at the feet of the woman is then the first new moon after the harvest full moon associated with the "Feast of Tabernacles."

16. The ten kings and the kings of the East represent the same nations. These nations are Muslim nations that rise up with the beast and destroy the woman, which had her roots in the history of Pergamos and confirmed her appointment with the judgment pronounced in the history

of Thyatira. The woman of Revelation chapter 17 represent the remnant of an unrepentant Laodicean Church that has bought into the mark of the beast. This is the remnant of a worldly unregenerate western Christianity that is destroyed by the dragon and the beast.

17. The history of the Bible needs to be seen from a perspective of three different ages (the Age of Sin, the Age of Righteousness, and the Age of Judgment).

18. Adam was the first son of God who fell from grace and died spiritually, plunging man into sin. All of mankind are sons of Adam, or sons of men in need of spiritual rebirth to once again become sons of God. Adam was a man who was the first, making him the first number "6" in the Age of Sin.

19. The Age of Righteousness began with Abraham and was fulfilled at the cross by Christ. Christ, being the second Adam in the second age is "66," but Christ was Son of Man, Son of God, being the first begotten from the dead and the one through whom all mankind must come to be born again.

20. The next man to come will be the son of perdition. He will also claim to be a Son of Man, the Son of God in the Age of Judgment (Jn. 14:30)—the age that we are now in and have been in since the cross. At the cross judgment was decreed, sin was defeated, and satan's head crushed. We now await the carrying out of God's sentence, which will occur at the end of this age when antichrist appears as a man or the third Adam. He is a fallen son of God and will come in the third age; therefore his number is "666." (These last three positional statements, 18-20, will not be covered in detail in this book, but will be handled in a future publication.)

These are the major tenets of my "*born-again-pretribulation-premillennial*" position and will be proven consistent with the whole counsel of God's inerrant Word and the unalterable witness of the cosmos and our solar system.

The cosmos is God's great prophetic time clock. Understanding this clock has helped me to tie the feasts of the Jews and the timing of the seal, trumpet, and vial judgments together. The chronology will be proven by a body of evidence that provides unequivocal proof for adjusting the current pretribulation chronology models.

So be warned! The study that we are about to embark upon will test the moorings of prophetic academia and will rumble throughout its hallways. Therefore let us not delay, for "the time of His Coming" is close at hand.

The Time Is at Hand

The word for Revelation, *apokalypsis*, means "to take off the cover or to unveil." If God has taken off the cover, why has there been so much confusion over the Book of Revelation? Part of the reason is it was written so long ago by a writer who was seeing things of the future that he literally did not have words to describe.

When John was shown a vision that revealed events of our day or beyond, he obviously found it perplexing because he was restricted to the terminology of his day. A tank, for instance, might be described as a scorpion with fire in its tail. Another reason for the confusion over Revelation is we have lost much of the everyday background and understanding of first century civilizations. First century astronomy is only one of the disciplines that we must come to understand if we are going to unlock the message of Revelation.

Understand, God is not locking away the message of Revelation from us, but our ignorance is, however, inordinately responsible. Therefore, the book will be filled with symbolic and forgotten language that can be, and no doubt has been, misunderstood.

In addition to future events, John was also describing events that were past, present, and relative to John's day. First, his descriptions must be considered and understood in the context of his day and then brought forward with their true meaning and relevance.

It is in this process of evaluation that the multitude of interpretations are produced. Add to all this the fact that John saw things in the heavens where the planets abide and the heavens where God dwells, and you have a formula for confusion and frustration.

But, a promise of blessing is given in the beginning of the Book of Revelation for those who would read, hear, and keep the prophecies that are written therein: "*Blessed is he…for the time is at hand*" (Rev 1:3).

This verse contains three active participles, which indicates that the Book of Revelation is not just a book to be read and set aside. The Book of Revelation is a book that one needs to actively read, actively hear, and actively guard.

The prophecies of the Book of Revelation are to be kept, held, and preserved or guarded with a definite purpose in mind. The purpose is to watch for the coming of the time when these things will be fulfilled. It is my belief that the appointed time is very near.

> *The Revelation of Jesus Christ, which God gave unto Him, to shew unto His servants things which must shortly come to pass; and He sent and signified it by His angel unto His servant John: who bare record of the word of God, and of the testimony of Jesus Christ, and of all things that he saw. Blessed is he that readeth, and they that hear the words of this prophecy, and keep those things which are written therein: for the time is at hand* (Revelation 1:1-2).

Revelation is an intensely spiritual book, written to those and for those who are spiritually minded. It is written to those who are "possessed" by the Spirit of God, with the Teacher of all wisdom dwelling in them.

> *Now we have received, not the spirit of the world, but the spirit which is of God; that we might know the things that are freely given to us of God. ... But the natural man receiveth not the things of the Spirit of God: for they are foolishness unto him: neither can he know them, because they are spiritually discerned* (1 Corinthians 2:12,14).

To understand Revelation, one is required to have knowledge of Old and New Testament writings as well as an appreciation for Jewish, Roman, Greek, and ancient Babylonian culture, history, and grammar. In addition, however, only those who endeavor to put on the mind of Christ can anticipate an understanding of this book. The Book of Revelation is for the spiritually maturing Christian, but the message needs to heard by all.

The book is specifically addressed to the churches (Rev. 2:7,11,17,29; 3:6,13,22). It is sent to seven churches that existed in Asia during the first century and, later, as the Body of Christ. We are told that believers are kings and priests by Jesus Christ Himself, who is the Prince of all the kings of the earth. We are to watch for the signs that will precede the Second Coming of Jesus Christ.

The coming in the clouds of Heaven represents the first part of the Second Coming—the Rapture . At that time, all those who are left behind will see Jesus, who was pierced for the sins of the world. They will wail (mourn or literally beat one's breast with grief). This will take place after the events of the sixth seal are unleashed (Rev. 6:12-17) and then the seven years of tribulation will proceed with the opening of the seventh seal.

> *JOHN to the seven churches which are in Asia: Grace be unto you, and peace, from Him which is, and which was, and which is to come; and from the seven Spirits which are before His throne; and from Jesus Christ, who is the faithful witness, and the first begotten of the dead, and the prince of the kings of the earth. Unto Him that loved us, and washed us from our sins in His own blood, And hath made us kings and priests unto God and His Father; to Him be glory and dominion for ever and ever. Amen. Behold, He cometh with clouds; and every eye shall see Him, and they also which pierced Him: and all kindreds* [tribes] *of the earth shall wail because of Him. Even so, Amen* (Revelation 1:4-7).

Who Will Escape?

Only those who have trusted in the blood of Jesus Christ alone to cleanse them from all their sin will be entitled to rule with Christ forever. They will also be the only ones to escape the tribulation that is coming upon the whole world. No amount of religious devotion or works will save anyone. Jesus must cleanse us from our sin, for we cannot cleanse ourselves.

Everyone needs a personal relationship with Jesus Christ that begins when we repent of our sins and turn to Jesus Christ in faith. We must ask

Him to forgive us and save us. Salvation from one's sins is a free gift that is given to those who prayerfully ask for it.

Those who are attempting to work their way to "Heaven" through systematic religious devotion will be denied because they are trusting in what they are doing rather than in what Jesus has done for them. "*Not by works of righteousness which we have done, but according to His mercy He saved us, by the washing of regeneration, and renewing of the Holy Ghost*" (Tit. 3:5).

Salvation is a work of the Holy Spirit of God and not religion. When we repent of our sins and give up trusting in what we are doing for God, which is really for ourselves, and instead trust in Christ, God then sends His Holy Spirit to dwell within the "*new-born*" believer. God then seals the new believer unto the day of redemption.

> *That we should be to the praise of His glory, who first trusted in Christ. In whom ye also trusted, after that ye heard the word of truth, the gospel of your salvation: in whom also after that ye believed, ye were sealed with that holy Spirit of promise, which is the earnest* [down payment that secures us for God] *of our inheritance until the redemption of the purchased possession, unto the praise of His glory* (Ephesians 1:12-14).

No one entering Heaven will be able to say that he did it. Those who enter into the Kingdom of Heaven will only be able to praise God because salvation is something that He does for people. There will be no boasting in Heaven; only praise for God and what He has done. "*That no flesh should glory in His presence*" (1 Cor. 1:29).

God has provided the gift of salvation through faith. Jesus' death on Calvary's cross satisfied the debt of sin to God. Jesus paid it all. Please! If you have not already done so, repent of your sin and dispense of any misplaced hope in a works-oriented salvation. Ask Jesus to forgive you, cleanse you, and save you today! Accept Jesus as Savior before it is too late.

Let us be confident of this one thing: none who truly repent and turn to Christ will be rejected. No matter how bad or ungodly one is, or has been, God wants all to be saved.

The Lord is not slack concerning His promise, as some men count slackness; but is longsuffering [patient] *to us-ward, not willing that any should perish, but that all should come to repentance* (2 Peter 3:9).

God has patiently waited for almost 2,000 years for men, women, and children to be saved, but time is running out. That which Jesus revealed to John and prophesied is near—even at the doors of time.

I am Alpha and Omega, the beginning and the ending, saith the Lord, which is, and which was, and which is to come, the Almighty (Revelation 1:8).

The Seven Churches Were the First

The seven churches of Asia were the first to receive the message contained in the Book of Revelation. No doubt they struggled with it, but all were called to respond to the message addressed to them—just as we are today. The seven churches, I believe, represent progressive properties of an age that would continue to develop throughout history.

As Christ's Church progressed through time, the Church would experience the purifying trials that the Book of Revelation forewarned. The seeds of the Gentile Church were planted in Asia. Today we can look to recorded history and see the fruit of the seeds that were sown. It is painfully obvious to us that what we now call Church history is, in fact, contained in the letters to the seven churches.

As early believers encountered the trials that God forewarned, then professing or practicing believers within the churches had to make personal choices. All those within the churches were called to repent, stand fast, be faithful, endure, be longsuffering, expose liars, promote good doctrine, weed out false doctrine, acknowledge His name, and defend His Word. This and more has worked to shape what we have come to know as Church history.

But the letters to the seven churches have revealed to Christ's Body, beforehand, what kind of trials lay ahead. The letters contain the key identifying characteristics of each Church period. The letters reveal what God saw within each church, both good and bad. Believers throughout the

Body of Christ are admonished to overcome these trials. The final outcome for each individual is not the same, but in fact, depends upon one's choices to overcome the trials of life and serve God.

It is recorded in the Gospels that Christ prayed that the Father would not take believers out of this world. Instead He asked the Father to equip them to serve Him in a world that would become increasingly hostile toward the truth of the gospel (Jn. 16:33; 17:11-26). This is exactly what the messages to the seven churches are—prescriptions or forewarnings of what could be expected as the Church, the Body of Christ, progressed through an age filled with sorrows and warnings.

The message to the seven churches is from Jesus Christ, the First and the Last. It is also a message to the first and last believers of the Church. The message of the seven letters and beyond is from the Alpha and Omega, and encompasses the beginning and the end of history.

The message to the seven churches was first delivered to the disciples of the Apostolic Church, Ephesus, and its faithful offspring Smyrna. Smyrna is the branch that bears today's faithful Church (see chart on page 90). Pergamos was also the offspring of the first Apostolic Church, but of the seed of those who had left their first love (Rev. 2:4). This branch ends with the budding, unfaithful Church of Laodicea experiencing greater tribulation in the first half of the tribulation period. In other words, the letters to the seven churches describe the Church from apostolic to apostasy.

> *Let no man deceive you by any means: for that day shall not come, except there come a falling away first, and that man of sin be revealed, the son of perdition* (2 Thessalonians 2:3).

The letters to the churches speak to the Church from its conception to its judgment. (Please note: the "Rapture" is a form of judgment when some are taken and some are left behind.) The "angel" of each church would speak to the churches throughout the days of the seven churches. The voice of the first angel was heard by the Gentile offspring of the Apostolic Church, represented in Revelation as the Church of Ephesus.

The work of the Spirit has continued throughout the days of the Church and it will continue until the days of the seventh angel and the seventh church. The message would span from the church that left its first love to the church that is "*wretched, and miserable, and poor, and blind, and naked,*" but does not know it (Rev. 3:17). It is going to take the Rapture and the nightmare of the first four warning trumpets of Revelation chapter 8, as well as the ministry of the two witnesses, to wake some professing Christians out of their sleep.

The Purging of the Church

The trumpet judgments are warnings of the inescapable wrath of God that is soon to follow in the second half of the tribulation. I believe this is why the last three trumpets have woes associated with them—they announce the absolute certainty of God's impending wrath. In other words, the woes in the final three trumpets make judgment so certain that those refusing to repent before the final trumpet sounds are as good as dead.

Many contemporary sorrows exist for Christians, and today's world is growing increasingly hostile toward biblical Christianity. However, the tribulation experienced throughout Church history is just the beginning of sorrows. These sorrows will continue to increase as the "Day of the Lord" draws near.

Church history began with a spiritually strong and vivacious Church in Jerusalem, which seeded Ephesus, but would see itself divided and weakened as the age progressed toward its completion (Rev. 3:2,8,18). In fact, the letter to the seven churches shows a twofold division. The faithful will see the "Day of the Lord" (beginnings with the seven-year tribulation) approaching and will, therefore, escape it. The unfaithful, yet professing to be of the Christian Church, will be taken by surprise and will end up going through the purifying trials during the first half of the tribulation and beyond if repentance is not realized.

Faith must be exercised—even unto death. The trials that God will allow to come into the world will have a twofold purpose. First, they purify professing believers by exposing their corruption or slackness. They need the new birth. Second, trials purge out or separate the idolater, the liar, the faithless, the fornicator, and such others, and reserve them for the day of judgment.

We must also try to consider these churches from the perspective of an eternal God rather than from our limited temporal perspective. God continually sees the works of every church that claims to be of the Body of Christ. He knows where they are and what their destiny will be. The Body has been warned and commanded to repent and to overcome. Christians need to heed what the Spirit has said and is saying to the churches that make up the Body of Christ. The eternal implication for each soul is a matter of individual choices.

The angel of the sixth church is speaking today and has continued to provide an open door of opportunity for today's missionary work. However, this door of opportunity will come to a dramatic close when the angel of the sixth church begins to sound the decrees of the sixth seal, which I believe includes the Rapture. In essence, the voice speaking to the seven churches in Revelation chapters 2 and 3 is the voice of the Spirit of God speaking through the seal judgments of Revelation 6.

The Rapture will be the first line of separation. At the Rapture, God will judge those who were faithful overcomers. First the dead in Christ, who overcame the trials of life and served and obeyed, shall rise. Then those born-again believers, which are alive and remain, will meet the Lord in the air. All true believers will be judged as overcomers and will receive the promise made to the Church of Philadelphia. They will be the ones rescued out of the hour of tribulation that is coming upon the whole world (1 Thess. 4:13-18; Rev 3:10). They will be Raptured out of the "Great Tribulation" as it begins to unfold (Rev. 7:14).

The coming of the "Day of the Lord" is clearly represented in Scripture as coming upon Israel as a woman in labor (Is. 13:1-11; Mt. 24:3-8; Rev. 12:1-4). When a child is born, the birth takes place at the height of the birth pangs. The child is begotten in much sorrow (Gen. 3:16). The child comes through much tribulation or sorrows, but does not experience the pangs of labor itself. The child experiences new life, while the mother endures the pangs of the delivery. This is Israel's relationship to the Church. As the Church is Raptured to God's throne, Israel will be experiencing great sorrows in the world (Mt. 24:29; Rev. 6:1-14; 12:1-4). This is the time of Jacob's trouble.

> *Ask ye now, and see whether a man doth travail with child? Wherefore do I see every man with his hands on his loins, as a woman in travail, and all faces are turned into paleness? Alas! for that day is great, so that none is like it: it is even the time of Jacob's trouble; but he shall be saved out of it. ...in the latter days ye shall consider it* (Jeremiah 30:6-7,24).

The Church will be delivered to heaven (Rev. 12:5b) and the woman (the faithful sealed remnant of Israel, which is 144,000 Jews from the 12 tribes of Israel in Revelation 7:1-14) will be led into the wilderness and nurtured back to spiritual health through the ministry of the two witnesses (Rev. 12:1-6,14).

The nation of Israel and the unregenerate remnant of the Church will be purged and chastised for their sins (Jer. 30:8-17; Rev. 3:18-19). This period will end with the destruction of the apostate "Christian" Church as it is destroyed by the beast and the ten kings allied with him (Rev. 17). The beast will also pursue the faithful remnant of the woman's seed, those "*which keep the commandments of God, and* ***have the testimony of Jesus Christ***" (Rev. 12:17b). These are those that were saved in the tribulation period and may consist of both Jew and Gentile just as the early Church did. In the process of pursuing this remaining seed of the woman, the harlot of "Christianity" is destroyed as well.

Those who are alive and are only professing, religious, worldly Christians will be rejected or spewed out of the Lord's mouth at the time of the Rapture. They will be treated as "afterbirth," or as the unfavored Esau. "*As it is written, Jacob have I loved , but Esau have I hated*" (Rom. 9:13; see also Mal. 1:2-3; Heb. 11:20).

The Raptured Church consists of the children of God—of the promised seed of Abraham. "*I will call them My people, which were not My people; and her beloved, which was not beloved*" (Rom. 9:25; Hos. 2:23). Those not beloved and born of God will go through the intense purging fire of the first half of the "Day of the Lord." They will have an opportunity to come to Christ, to be born again, but may have to pay with their lives if they make this decision (Rev. 20:4).

Those "professing Christians" left behind after the Rapture are of the Church of Laodicea that will see the warning trumpet judgments of God, but not the outpouring of the vials of God if they truly repent and are saved. The 144,000 sealed of Israel will be protected by God and will flee to the wilderness after the sixth seal because they will be convinced that the "Day of the Lord" has come (Rev. 7:16-17).

Consider the Promises

In order to understand the significance of the letters to the seven churches in Revelation, it will be necessary for us to consider the fact that the promises are made to the overcomers of all seven churches. These promises are for every believer and not just for the Asian churches (Rev. 2–3). These are promises to everyone who has spiritual ears to hear what the Spirit said to the churches.

The nature of the promises prevent us from precluding any believers. These promises embody such things as access to the tree of life, a crown of life, a new name, entrance into the new Jerusalem, the right to sit and rule with Christ over the nations, and so on. These promises are not just to the believers of the seven Asian churches, but to every "overcomer" throughout the Church Age, who overcome the trials of this life and remains faithful unto death or the Lord's coming.

"Overcomer" is best understood as a general designation applicable to all believers."[1] There is no doubt that we can clearly apply some of these eternal promises to the seven Asian churches. However, all the promises and warnings contained in the letters can be easily applied to the Church of today. The promise to rescue the faithful from the hour of Great Tribulation (Rev. 3:10), is clearly a promise to the Church that will witness the Rapture. The warning to remain faithful, unless the Lord "*come on thee as a thief*" in the night (Rev. 3:3; 16:15), is again a clear reference to Christ's coming at the Rapture.

So, while some of the promises and warnings apply to the seven early Asian churches, "all" the promises and warnings can be applied to what we now call the "extant Church." The Church found its way through history from the Apostolic "Mother" Church of Jerusalem and then to Ephesus, and culminating with the Church that contains assemblies of believers who have not denied the name of the Lord. They have kept His Word and are faithfully looking for the blessed hope of their salvation—the return of the Lord Jesus Christ.

Unfortunately, the Church also includes unfaithful assemblies that have long ago abandoned salvation in Christ alone and, even longer, the authority of God's Word. These churches have committed spiritual fornication and adultery. Today's ecumenical movement, through the National Council of Churches and the World Council of Churches, is a major offender of this great spiritual apostasy. Many of the professing Christians who are part of these movements are not even aware of the Lord's promised return that we identify as "the Rapture."

To an eternal God, there is absolutely no difference between those who have faithfully died trusting in Christ as their Savior and those who are found faithfully doing the Lord's will when He comes.

> *Who then is a faithful and wise servant, whom his lord hath made ruler over his household, to give them meat in due season? Blessed is that servant, whom his lord when he cometh shall find so doing* (Matthew 24:45-46).

The seven churches are the roots of the tree that we label as Christendom today. They exist in all their diversity as a picture of wheats and tares growing up collectively until the time of harvest. God will then send forth His angels, who will first bind the tares for burning and then gather the wheat into His barn (Mt. 13:36-40).

Many wrongly conclude that the parable of "the wheat and the tares" applies to the faithful and the lost world as a whole. I believe that this is too general. We must remember that the wheat and the tares are growing up together. The message of this parable is to a body of believers that contains both faithful and unfaithful Christians—which is exactly the condition of the Church today. The realization that they were left behind to endure the tribulation that is coming upon the world will cause the "religious" to weep and gnash their teeth when they could have escaped (Mt. 25:30).

The powerful message of Revelation to us today is that the Head of the Church, Christ, who stands in the midst of the candlesticks (the churches), sees and hears every work of His Body (Rev. 1:11–2:1). The Church is the "voice of many waters" that speaks for the testimony of Jesus Christ today. If any part of the Body of Christ refuses to hear what the

Spirit says, then that branch will be purged. "*For if God spared not the natural branches, take heed lest He also spare not thee*" (Rom. 11:21).

> *I John, who also am your brother, and companion in tribulation, and in the kingdom and patience of Jesus Christ, was in the isle that is called Patmos, for the word of God, and* ***for the testimony of Jesus Christ.*** *I was in the Spirit on the Lord's day, and heard behind me a great voice, as of a trumpet, saying, I am Alpha and Omega, the first and the last: and, What thou seest, write in a book, and send it* ***unto the seven churches*** *which are in Asia; unto Ephesus, and unto Smyrna, and unto Pergamos, and unto Thyatira, and unto Sardis, and unto Philadelphia, and unto Laodicea. And I turned to see the voice that spake with me. And being turned, I saw seven golden candlesticks;* ***and in the midst of the seven candlesticks one like unto the Son of man, clothed with a garment down to the foot, and girt about the paps with a golden girdle. His head and His hairs were white like wool, as white as snow; and His eyes were as a flame of fire; and His feet like unto fine brass, as if they burned in a furnace; and His voice as the sound of many waters.*** *And He had in his right hand seven stars: and out of His mouth went a sharp twoedged sword: and His countenance was as the sun shineth in His strength. And when I saw Him, I fell at His feet as dead. And He laid His right hand upon me, saying unto me, Fear not; I am the first and the last: I am He that liveth, and was dead; and, behold, I am alive for evermore, Amen; and have the keys of hell and of death. Write the things which thou hast seen, and the things which are, and the things which shall be hereafter; the mystery of the seven stars which thou sawest in My right hand, and the seven golden candlesticks. The seven stars are the angels of the seven churches:* ***and the seven candlesticks which thou sawest are the seven churches*** (Revelation 1:9-20).

Those who refuse to repent and return to the fundamental and loving truths of the faith will have their candlestick removed. They will literally cease to be part of the spiritual light and will be reserved for judgment (Rev. 2:5, 21-23). This does not mean, however, that they will cease to exist as an organized religious body. Those who refuse to repent will have to contend with the truth of God's Word speaking against their doctrines and their works (Rev. 2:16).

The children or descendents of those organized religions who continue to follow false doctrine, will be "killed with death" and be thrown into Great Tribulation (Rev 2:22-23). Those who give up, compromise the truth of God's Word, and give up on Christ's promises, will see His return "*as a thief*" coming in the night (Rev. 3:2-3).

Those who do not deny His name and continue to keep His Word will be separated from those who belong to satan. They will be "kept" from the tribulation that is coming upon the whole world (Rev. 3:8-11). Those who solely trust in their riches and works will be rejected and delivered into the chastening and trying tribulation of the trumpet judgments on the "Day of the Lord" (Rev. 3:18-20).[2]

The Historical Progression of the Seven Letters

Another significant aspect of the letters to the seven churches is the progressive nature of their motif. They progress from the days of the Apostolic Church, which hates the doctrine of the Nicolaitans, into a Church that will suffer physical persecution and imprisonment from the devil's ministers, and then grow into a Church great in its works but refusing to repent of its spiritual fornication. This Church is guilty of following a god that is not God, thus the claim of idolatry (Rev. 2:20). But within this Church, there is a separate group of believers who do not hold to its teachings—the doctrines of devils.

The motif then continues to progress to a spiritually weakened Church that suffers death, but has some that walk in white with the Lord. This indicates their faithfulness even unto death. These believers are also reminded to watch for the sudden coming of the Lord. Then the motif advances to a Church that has an open door of opportunity before them and a promise to escape the tribulation coming upon the whole world. Finally, the last Church is rejected and faces a closed door. It is this progressive nature of the letters that has led many scholars to parallel actual Church history with the letters to the seven churches—a parallel that is entirely legitimate.

The message contained in the letters to the seven churches becomes much more evident when we recognize these clear divisions. Consider the following chart to illustrate this fact.

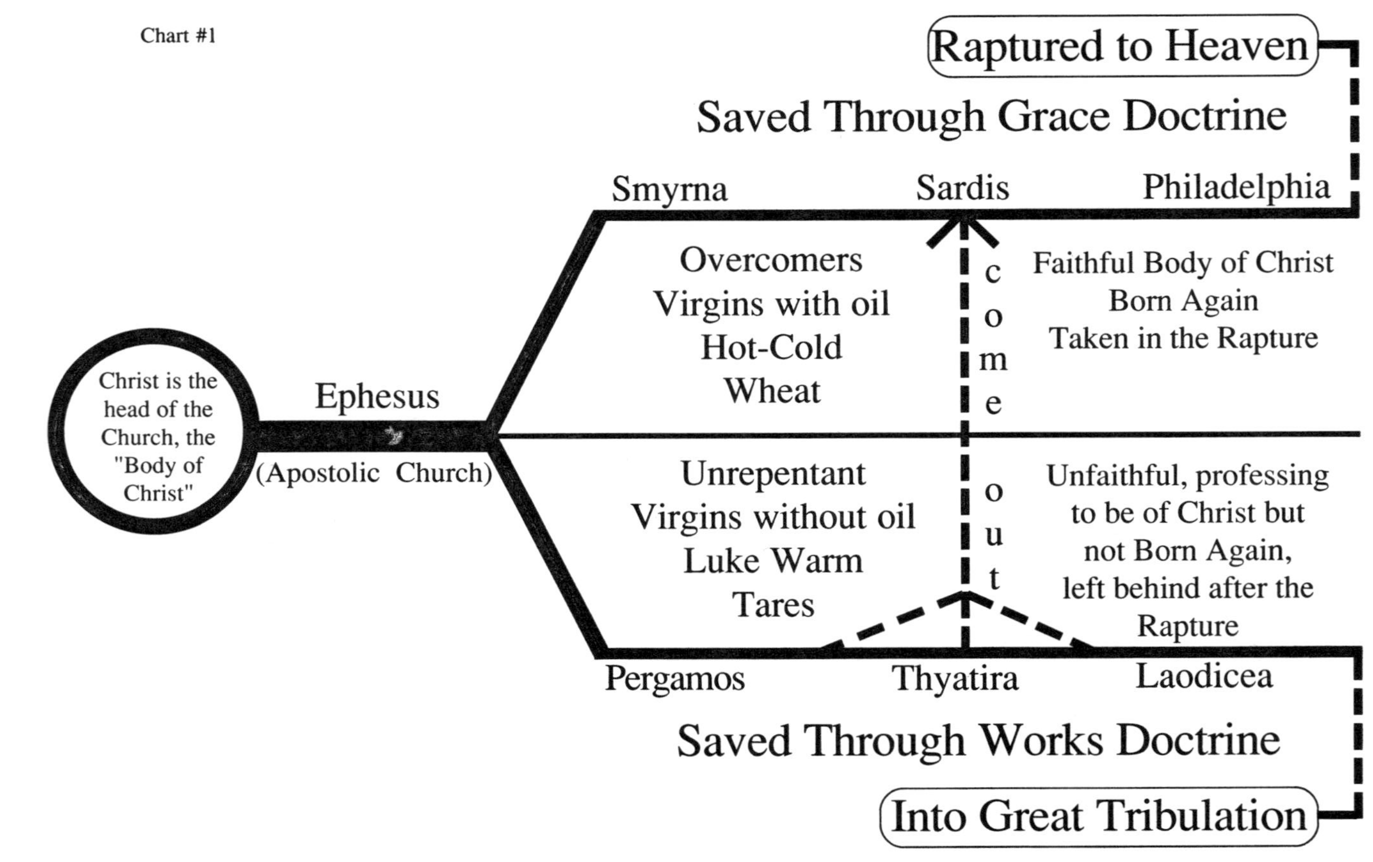
Chart #1
Raptured to Heaven
Saved Through Grace Doctrine
Smyrna
Sardis
Philadelphia
Overcomers
Virgins with oil
Hot-Cold
Wheat
c o m e
Faithful Body of Christ
Born Again
Taken in the Rapture
Christ is the head of the Church, the "Body of Christ"
Ephesus
(Apostolic Church)
Unrepentant
Virgins without oil
Luke Warm
Tares
o u t
Unfaithful, professing to be of Christ but not Born Again, left behind after the Rapture
Pergamos
Thyatira
Laodicea
Saved Through Works Doctrine
Into Great Tribulation

The seven churches equal or represent the whole Body of Christ throughout the dispensation of grace. Yet, as we can clearly see from the letters, the churches are not free from doctrinal error (Rev. 2:14,20). The letters not only serve to foretell the evolving patterns of the Church, but also provide an undisputed validation for the warnings contained in the letters. The warnings are addressed to the Body of Christ. They include calls for people to repent and commands for them to overcome obstacles and to boldly face challenges in the Church. The Church was to heed the warnings of judgment that would come, should the admonitions be left unheeded. Some of these judgments were already delivered by the horsemen of seals two, three, and four.

I have no doubt that some will continue to argue that each letter was addressed to a specific church with a unique message for that church alone. Therefore, it is demanded by those of this persuasion that the true interpretation must satisfy this assertion. However, the letters were to be part of an opened book that was to be sent to all the churches (Rev. 1:11).

The letters were addressed to the angels of each church—not the churches themselves. The angel of the seven churches are the stars that Jesus holds in His right hand, which represents the Holy Spirit, who in turn speaks to each church through the revelation of God's Word (Rev. 2:7,11,17,29; 3:6,13,22). In this same way, the Holy Spirit is still speaking to the Body of Christ through the Book of Revelation.

To verify this fact all one has to do is consider the introduction of the book, which contains the promise of a blessing to he who reads, hears, and keeps the words of the prophecies of the Book of Revelation. Case closed. My conclusion is that the Book of Revelation is a book written for the Church from the beginning of the Dispensation of Grace to the end of that same period.

The letter addressed to each individual angel of each church had something special and unique about it. The uniqueness of each church was used by God to address the whole Body of Christ—just as the nations of Babylon, Media-Persia, Greece, and Rome represented the major kingdoms of the world in the vision interpreted by Daniel. In the Book of Daniel these kingdoms also represent the system of a godless world government (Dan. 2:37-43).

Why select just these seven churches? Why not the church that was in Philippi, Thessalonica, or even Rome? Is there not a message for them as well? We believe that the whole argument that limits our understanding to a "past" or "local" relevance only works to blind us to the imminency of the true message to today's Church.

Could it be that these seven were chosen partly because of their geographical location and how they apparently form a geographical circle? Could the circle indicate a fullness of an age as the number seven itself indicates completeness? Geographically, it is most interesting that there is a break in the mountain range between the Church of Philadelphia and the Church of Laodicea. The first six churches follow the topography of the land and this break (or valley) before Laodicea may indicate a separation that takes place between the Philadelphian and the Laodicean churches.

I believe this separation could represent the separation judgment of the Rapture where the faithful will be taken and the unfaithful, lukewarm, professing only Christians will be left behind for the purifying, fiery trials of the first half of the "Seventieth Week of Daniel." Therefore, this view would place an emphasis on the location of the churches and their relationship to one another with their own unique problems.

The specific characteristics found in the letters to the seven were very real to the churches of Ephesus and Smyrna (things that are), but only prophetic warnings to the churches of Pergamos through Laodicea (things that will come to pass) (Rev. 1:19). These warnings were pointing out the seeds of doctrine and practice of these seven churches that would result in what we now see as a complex, confused, and divided Body of Christ.

This is why these seven churches correspond so readily to the historical development of the Church. "It is argued that the successive periods of Church history, as they have unfolded, are in themselves a substantiation of this viewpoint because of the high degree of correlation between them and the spiritual conditions outlined in the seven messages."[3] "Ephesus is manifestly a picture of the Church toward the end of apostolic time, whilst Laodicea pictures it as it shall be in the last time."[4]

The relevance of the letters to the churches is this: To the Church of John's day, the letters were partly specific and relative. The Church that existed first was addressed by the angel to the Church in Ephesus, while the latter six letters were prophetic warnings to the future churches, including the Church of today. In fact, only the last half of the sixth letter and the entire seventh are still to be fulfilled.

The open door, promised to the Church of Philadelphia, is currently being fulfilled through the greatest missionary outreach that the Church has ever known. But as the world steps closer to the great "Day of the Lord," this door of opportunity will be closed by God. Evangelism in Russia, other parts of Eastern Europe, and Asia could be the closing stages of this open door. When the Rapture occurs, this door will be slammed shut and the Church of Laodicea will find itself on the outside and facing the awesome reality of the first half of the tribulation period.

I want to clearly emphasize at this point that this Laodicean Church is not made up of saved, backslidden Christians, or others who believe they have lost their salvation. They are individuals who claimed they were Christians, but who were never truly baptized with the abiding presence of the Holy Spirit. This baptism only takes place at the moment one truly gives his life to Jesus Christ, repents of his sins, and asks Jesus to save him as only He can (Eph. 1:12-14; Rev. 3:15-20; Mt. 25:1-13).

Warning to the Churches

To further understand the message to the extant Church, let us consider, by comparison, the promises and warnings made to the seven churches within the context of Church history. The Church of Ephesus in Revelation represents the second generation of the Apostolic Church. "More than forty years had passed and the warmth of love that characterized the former generation of believers was not as discernible in its membership."[5] It is the first generation of Ephesus that the true Christian Church is firmly rooted. However, the unfaithful Church that is filled with doctrinal error also traces its roots back to the Apostolic Church.

In fact, every organized "Christian Church" authenticates its existence and establishes its authority by recognizing the Apostolic Church as its foundational body. But as the Church grew, so did the opportunities for corruption. With literally thousands of mystery religions that existed in the Roman empire at the time of Constantine's Edict of Milan in A.D. 313, corruption became epidemic.

This edict, which virtually made Christianity the state religion, produced a great influx of a new element into the Church. With this great influx of individuals from these "mystery religions," many of their rituals and rites were blended with Christian doctrine to accommodate the masses. In Third World countries, this practice continues to manifest itself in Roman Catholic missionary churches. The superstitions of local villagers were incorporated into Church traditions and rituals. But while corruption spread within the Church, there was always a body of believers that were enabled, through the abiding presence of the Holy Spirit, to overcome the corruption that flourished in the world around them. It is to this faithful body of believers that genuine Christianity owes its continuance.

> *Unto the angel of the church of Ephesus write; These things saith He that holdeth the seven stars in His right hand, who walketh in the midst of the seven golden candlesticks; I know thy works, and thy labour, and thy patience, and how thou canst not bear them which are evil: and thou hast tried them which say they are* ***apostles****, and are not, and hast found them liars: and hast borne, and hast patience, and for My name's sake hast labored, and hast not fainted. Nevertheless I have somewhat against thee, because* ***thou hast left thy first love****. Remember therefore from whence thou art fallen, and* ***repent****, and do the first works; or else I will come unto thee quickly, and* ***will remove thy candlestick out of his place, except thou repent****. But this thou hast, that thou hatest the deeds of the Nicolaitans, which I also hate. He that hath an ear, let him hear what the Spirit saith unto the* ***churches****; to him that* ***overcometh*** [*nikaw*] *will I give to eat of the tree of life, which is in the midst of the paradise of God* (Revelation 2:1-7).

Truth, and faithfulness to the truth, was preserved through the line of the Ephesus, Smyrna, Sardis, and Philadelphian churches, while corruption continued to spread within and through the spiritual fornication of the Pergamos, Thyatira, and Laodicean churches.

Historically, the Church of Smyrna is believed to be a church that John helped to establish. The great Church leader Polycarp, who was martyred at the age of 86 around A.D. 156–160, was said to have known the apostle John personally.[6]

"Out of the persecution of the early days of the Church of Smyrna exaggerated stories grew of persecution and fantastic miraculous happenings and superstitions. Some converts from paganism brought with them pre-Christian ideas so that, in the Church, the martyrs began to take on the role that the gods had earlier played in the old religion."[7] This perversion carried over to the Church of Pergamos and continues today.

The Church of Smyrna was not told to repent, but instead was admonished not to be fearful and to remain faithful unto death. The crown of life was their reward. The words of Polycarp at his death give evidence of such a faith. "The fire you threaten burns for a time and is soon extinguished: there is a fire you know nothing about—the fire of the judgment to come and eternal punishment, the fire reserved for the ungodly. But why do you hesitate? Do what you want."[8]

> *And unto the angel of the church in Smyrna write; These things saith the first and the last, which was dead, and is alive; I know thy works, and* ***tribulation, and poverty, (but thou art rich)*** *and I know the blasphemy of them which say they are Jews, and are not, but are the synagogue of Satan. Fear none of those things which thou shalt suffer: behold, the devil shall cast some of you into prison, that ye may be tried; and ye shall have tribulation ten days:* ***be thou faithful unto death****, and I will give thee a crown of life. He that hath an ear, let him hear what the Spirit saith unto the churches;* ***He that overcometh shall not be hurt of the second death*** (Revelation 2:8-11).

Pergamos was a church that began to decay. This church was committing spiritual fornication. It was combining the truth of the gospel with the lies of the mystery religions of that time. The perversions of partaking of food sacrificed to pagan idols was becoming a stumbling block to the Jews. They also had the doctrine of the Nicolaitanes, which is believed to be a doctrine that differentiated between the regular worshipers and church leaders. They created a laity and hierarchical church structure, which God hates. They were told to repent, and as we know from Scripture, this church did not repent (Rev. 2:21).

> *And to the angel of the church in Pergamos write; These things saith He which hath the sharp sword with two edges; I know thy works, and where thou dwellest, even where Satan's seat is: and thou holdest fast My name, and hast not denied My faith, even in those days wherein Antipas was My faithful martyr, who was slain among you, where* ***Satan dwelleth****. But I have a few things against thee, because thou hast there them that hold the doctrine of Balaam, who taught Balac* ***to cast a stumblingblock before the children of Israel, to eat things sacrificed unto idols, and to commit fornication****. So hast thou also them that* ***hold the doctrine of the Nicolaitanes, which thing I hate. Repent; or else I will come unto thee quickly****, and will fight against them with the sword of My mouth. He that hath an ear, let him hear what the Spirit saith unto the churches; To him that overcometh will I give to eat of the hidden manna, and will give him a white stone, and in the stone a new name written, which no man knoweth saving he that receiveth it* (Revelation 2:12-17).

After the Church of Pergamos came the Church of Thyatira, the forerunner of all ritualistic, mystic religions of today. This church with great wealth, works of charity, and faith received the sternest of all warnings. This church not only failed to root out spiritual fornication, but it also propagated spiritual adultery. The Church of Thyatira permitted (sufferest) the servants of God to succumb to the "*woman Jezebel, which calleth herself a prophetess*," and allowed her to teach and to seduce them into sacrificing to idols (Rev. 2:20).

Who is this "woman Jezebel"? Jezebel is that angel of light that has been appearing for years now. A warning goes out to the reader that what is about to be revealed may be shocking and offensive to some, especially if you are Catholic, but ***it is the truth.***

Once a Roman Catholic myself, I understand how difficult it may be for some to accept what is about to be said. A warning needs to be sounded for all those who think of themselves as "servants" of God. We are told that some professing to be servants of God will be seduced by this Jezebel. This prophetess appeared in A.D. 312 to Constantine after he prayed to the "Supreme God" for help.

The response was a sign, a cross in the noonday sky "above the sun," and with it the words, "Conquer by this." That night Christ appeared to him in a dream and commanded him to use the sign—presumably *CHI-RHO*, the initial letters of the name of Christ, as a safeguard in all engagements with his enemies.

> "This vision and Constantine's subsequent victory propelled the Church and state into a new age for which neither was prepared. Out of this new relationship between the Christian Church and a Christian emperor stemmed the history of Church-state relations in the later Roman Empire and throughout the Middle Ages."[9]

The prophetess Jezebel also appeared at Fatima in 1917 disguised as the "Virgin Mary" and again in 1961 to four Spanish children. If this was a vision of the Virgin Mary, she would have pointed to her Savior, Jesus Christ, as the only way of salvation, "*And my spirit hath rejoiced in God my Saviour*" (Lk. 1:47).

Jezebel has also appeared to Edgar Cacye and has given great and marvelous visions to all of her chosen about the end of the world, and has even given some of them the ability to predict future events. To Cacye, this woman Jezebel also gave powers to heal and see things in the future. None of the documented visions give the message of hope or redemption through Jesus Christ alone.

That single fact is how we know that these visions are not of God. They are contrary to the revelation of Scripture. This Jezebel has recently appeared in New Jersey and Delaware and has caused millions to stumble and fall into her snare. The messages, like astrological predictions, are very vague and without scriptural credibility. We are told to pray to Mary and that there is hope for the faithful. The devil likes it when Christians pray to Mary because Mary is powerless to hear or do anything with prayers to her.

Mary is just a woman of God who trusted in Jesus Christ to save her from her sins. "*For all have sinned, and come short of the glory of God*" (Rom. 3:23) and this includes Mary. Anyone who believes that Mary or any other saint can hear prayers is guilty of creating another god because only God is all-powerful, all-knowing, and all-present, and therefore able to hear and answer the prayers of the faithful.

Wake up! These visions are all part of a great deception. This deception is another clear sign that we are in the last days.

> *And with all deceivableness of unrighteousness in them that perish; because they received not the love of the truth, that they might be saved. And for this cause God shall send them strong delusion, that they should believe a lie* [Why?]: *that they all might be damned who believed not the truth, but had pleasure in unrighteousness* (2 Thessalonians 2:10-12).

Satan has preserved the kingdom of the fourth beast of Daniel, the Roman empire, by merging the remnants of it with the emerging Kingdom of God's Church. This is the spiritual fornication that the Lord first saw taking place in the Church of Pergamos. The seeds of this fornication were first planted by the second generation believers of the Church of Ephesus. They left their first love. "The love of first conversion had waxed cold, and given place to a lifeless and formal orthodoxy" (Alford).[10]

The Church of Pergamos was warned to repent, but it failed to do so. With Constantine the marriage between the mysteries and powers of Babel were securely enjoined to the teachings of Christianity. This is the Church of Thyatira (Rev. 2:18-23). The Lord calls this adultery and harlotry. This is why she is called the "MYSTERY, BABYLON THE GREAT, THE MOTHER OF HARLOTS AND ABOMINATIONS OF THE EARTH" (Rev. 17:5).

This "Mother" is the Roman Church that is working to gather the ritualistic and liberal denomination of Protestantism back under the title of Roman Catholic or the Roman Universal Church. Another way to put it is the "One World Church."

The Vatican has preserved the rule of the Roman empire and the mysteries of the Babylonian mystic religions. The Christian Church took over many pagan ideas and images. From sun-worship, for example, came the celebration of Christ's birth on the twenty-fifth of December, the birthday of the sun. (See "A Woman Rides the Beast" by Dave Hunt for the detailed history that warrants the preceeding conclusions.)

Those at the head of the New Age, Evolutionary, and Mother Earth movement would rather return to sun worship and the like. Francis Crick, the co-discoverer of DNA, raises this sentiment when he says, "Instead of

Christmas, I think our culture should celebrate Newton's birthday, which is also the twenty-fifth of December. If we're going to celebrate the winter solstice—which is what Christmas is—we might as well tie it to somebody modern rather than somebody.... Not everybody enjoys myths."[11]

The spirit of antichrist is alive and well, both inside and outside orthodox religion. Secret members of the "Club of Rome," "Illuminati," and "The Masonic Order" will someday reawaken the dominance of the Roman empire and religion over the world and call it the "New World Order." They will do this through the subversive activities of the Masonic Lodge. Many born-again Christians have become members of the Masonic Lodge and are unwittingly supporting and facilitating the rise of "One World Christian Religion."

Christians join these organization under the guise of pursuing harmless economic opportunities and downplay the sinister undercurrents of their advanced orders and rituals. They have taken the first step toward accepting the mark of the beast and are leading thousands of others to do likewise. "***Come out of her, My people!***" (Rev. 18:4)

Science, evolution, environmentalism, liberal Christianity, and geopolitical crisis management will be the subtle tools of satan to gather the world into his well-planned counterfeit kingdom of love, peace, and mutual toleration. When the prophecies of the sixth seal are carried out, the "Mother of all Crises" will compel the world to unite into a new world order. Any who supposes that it is just a coincidence that the Vatican and Israel have agreed to exchange ambassadors had better rethink the inferences of this timely agreement.

This agreement sets the stage for major prophecies to be fulfilled. "*...and causeth the earth and them which dwell therein to worship the first beast, whose deadly wound was healed...*" (see Rev. 13:12-18).

Those who refuse to attend to the Word of God will find themselves thrown into the worst tribulation that the world has ever known. Please! Turn to God and reject teachings that are opposed to Scripture. These visions are designed to defraud the individual who is sincerely searching for answers. Remember, satan is subtle, and the most proficient of deceivers. The world portrays demons as ugly, demonic, black beasts with horns and monstrous faces. But satan's Jezebel has been appearing to a select few as an angel of light.

For such are false apostles, deceitful workers, transforming themselves into the apostles of Christ. And no marvel; ***for Satan himself is transformed into an angel of light****. Therefore it is no great thing if his ministers also be transformed as the ministers of righteousness; whose end shall be according to their works* (2 Corintians 11:13-15).

We need to trust God's Word. Jesus is the Way, the Truth, and the Life and no man, woman, or child will be able to come to God and abide in Heaven without first coming to Jesus Christ (Jn. 14:6). Now is the time to get on both knees and ask Jesus to save you. Now is the time to run from these visions because they are of the woman Jezebel, that minister of satan sent to deceive the world into believing a lie. Accept the truth of God's Word now!

As we continue in our historic overview of the seven churches we note that God allowed the rider of the fourth seal to visit the Church of Thyatira in A.D. 1347 because people refused to repent of their sins of spiritual fornication and adultery. A warning was given from the Word of God (Rev. 2:16,21) and was ignored by the Church of Thyatira.

The truth of the Word of God was exchanged for the traditions of a superstitious (religious), corrupted, and a hierarchical leadership laboring, instead, to keep God's servants ignorant of the Word. As a result, many of the faithful have been made subservient and totally dependent on a priesthood officiating over their lives as "spiritual" mediators. This was partially overcome by the Reformation, but not until the Turks and the Black Death took their toll. "...the plague and the Turk. Both suddenly appeared on the scene about the middle of the fourteenth-century, and both were regarded by popular preachers as the scourge of God to punish the failings of Catholicism. Bubonic plague first struck Europe in 1347 in an epidemic known as Black Death, which in three years killed about one third of the inhabitants of the Catholic West...it remained endemic for centuries, causing many deaths from time to time...and during the fifteenth-century Europe could be described as a death-oriented society."[12] This judgment fulfilled God's promise to kill Thyatira's children with death as she refused to repent.

And unto the angel of the church in Thyatira write; These things saith the Son of God, who hath His eyes like unto a flame of fire, and His feet are like fine brass; ***I know thy works, and charity, and service, and faith,*** *and thy patience, and thy works; and the last to be more than the first.* ***Notwithstanding I have a few things against thee, because thou sufferest that woman Jezebel, which calleth herself a prophetess, to teach and to seduce My servants to commit fornication, and to eat things sacrificed unto idols.*** *And I gave her* ***space to repent of her fornication;*** *and she repented not. Behold, I will cast her into a bed, and them that commit adultery with her into great tribulation, except they repent of their deeds.* ***And I will kill her children with death; and all the churches shall know that I am He which searcheth the reins and hearts: and I will give unto every one of you according to your works.*** *But unto you I say, and unto the rest in Thyatira, as many as have not this doctrine, and which have not known the depths of Satan, as they speak; I will put upon you none other burden. But that which ye have already hold fast till I come.* ***And he that overcometh, and keepeth My works unto the end, to him will I give power over the nations:*** *and he shall rule them with a rod of iron; as the vessels of a potter shall they be broken to shivers: even as I received of My Father. And I will give him the morning star. He that hath an ear, let him hear what the Spirit saith unto the churches* (Revelation 2:18-29).

The Sardis Church occupies a special place in the growth of the Body of Christ. It represents those who came out of the corrupted Church and were persecuted throughout Church history (Rev. 2:24-27). These who came out of the Reformation period portray believers who, like Martin Luther, heard God calling His servants back to the Word of God. All this becomes more evident when one considers the promised judgments to the children of Thyatira and compares them to the judgment of the "Great Whore" (Rev. 2:21-23; 17:4-6,16-17). This is a body infiltrated and corrupted by the doctrines of devils, professing to be the faithful Church of Jesus Christ. They will be revealed as impostors. Come out of her!

Beware of false prophets, which come to you in sheep's clothing, *but inwardly they are ravening wolves. Ye shall know them* *by their fruits. Do men gather grapes of thorns, or figs of thistles? Even so every good tree bringeth forth good fruit; but a corrupt tree bringeth forth evil fruit. A good tree cannot bring forth evil fruit, neither can a corrupt tree bring forth good fruit. Every tree that bringeth not forth good fruit is hewn down, and cast into the fire.* ***Wherefore by their fruits ye shall know them*** (Matthew 7:15-20).

The usage of "whore" symbolizes unfaithfulness to Jesus by His Church as it does for Israel. "*...For their mother hath played the harlot...*" (see Hos. 2:1-13). The Church of Sardis is a spiritually weakened church. This church is to be watchful because its works are not perfect before God.

The Reformation Church struggled after its break from the Catholic Church. She labored to distance herself from the errors of tradition and neglect toward the Word of God. This struggle still continues in the ecumenical movement of today. This movement seeks to undermine the work of the independent, fundamental churches that are laboring to be faithful stewards according to God's Word. Economics and a doctrine of toleration, motivated by blind love, have caused many to compromise for the promises of growth and academic acceptability.

It is time to come out and return to the Word of God! It is time to overcome fears and doubt and simply trust in Jesus Christ and His Word. It is time to stand and defend the truth of God's Word, for it is the only way to be faithful.

And unto the angel of the church in Sardis write; These things saith He that hath the seven Spirits of God, and the seven stars; I know thy works, that thou hast a name that thou livest, and art dead. Be watchful, and strengthen the things which remain, that are ready to die: for I have not found thy works perfect before God. Remember therefore how thou hast received and heard, and hold fast, and repent. If therefore thou shalt not watch, I will come on thee as a thief, and thou shalt not know what hour I will come upon thee. Thou hast a few names even in Sardis which have not defiled their garments; and they shall walk with Me in white: for they are worthy. He that overcometh, the same shall be clothed in white raiment; and I will not blot out his name out of the book of life, but I will confess his name before My Father, and before His angels. He that hath an ear, let him hear what the Spirit saith unto the churches (Revelation 3:1-6).

The Faithful and the Unfaithful Churches

The letters to the churches, as well as Church history, divide the Body of Christ into two clear divisions. The Churches of Pergamos (3), Thyatira (4), and Laodicea (7) are tied together by the thread of judgment, while the Church of Ephesus (1), Smyrna (2), Sardis (5), and Philadelphia (6) are tied together with the thread of deliverance. Churches one, two, five, and six are faithful, while churches three, four, and seven are unfaithful. (See chart on page 90.)

And to the angel of the church in ***Philadelphia*** *write; These things saith He that is holy, He that is true, He that hath the key of David, He that openeth, and no man shutteth; and shutteth, and no man openeth; I know thy works: behold,* ***I have set before thee an open door****, and no man can shut it: for thou hast a little strength, and hast* ***kept My word, and hast not denied My name.*** *Behold, I will make them of the synagogue of Satan, which say they are Jews, and are not, but do lie; behold, I will make them to come and worship before thy feet, and to know that I have loved thee.* ***Because thou hast kept the word of My patience, I also will keep thee from the hour of temptation, which shall come upon all the world, to try them that dwell upon the earth.*** *Behold, I come quickly: hold that fast which thou hast, that no man take thy crown. Him that* ***overcometh*** *will I make a pillar in the temple of My God, and he shall* ***go no more out****: and I will write upon him the name of My God, and the name of the city of My God, which is new Jerusalem, which cometh down out of heaven from My God: and I will write upon him My new name. He that hath an ear, let him hear what the Spirit saith unto the churches* (Revelation 3:7-13).

And unto the angel of the church of the ***Laodiceans*** *write; These things saith the* ***Amen, the faithful and true witness, the beginning of the creation of God****; I know thy works, that thou art neither* ***cold nor hot: I would thou wert cold or hot****. So then because thou art lukewarm, and neither cold nor hot,* ***I will spue thee out of My mouth*** [rejected in the Rapture]. ***Because thou sayest, I am rich, and increased with goods, and have need of nothing; and knowest not that thou art wretched, and miserable, and poor, and blind, and naked*** [the rest of the chapter applies to those going through the tribulation and what they must do]: *I counsel thee to buy of Me* ***gold tried in the fire*** [the fire is the tribulation], *that thou mayest be rich; and white raiment, that thou mayest be clothed, and that the shame of thy nakedness do not appear; and anoint thine eyes with eyesalve, that thou mayest see. As many as I love, I rebuke and chasten: be zealous therefore, and repent. Behold, I stand at the door, and knock: if any man hear My voice, and open the door, I will come in to him, and will sup with him, and he with Me.* [Those trusting in Jesus after the door of the Rapture in Heaven is closed can only open the door in death. Jesus waits at that door for all those who will trust in Him at this time.] *To him that* ***overcometh*** *will I grant to sit with Me in my throne, even as I also overcame, and am set down with My Father in His throne. He that hath an ear, let him hear what the Spirit saith unto the churches* (Revelation 3:14-22).

First, compare the introductions of letters three, four, and seven.

Letter Three (Rev. 2:12): He that has a *sharp, twoedged sword* (*Judgment*).
Letter Four (Rev. 2:18): Son of God with *eyes of like a flame* and feet like fine brass or fire (*Judgment*).
Letter Seven (Rev. 3:14): The Amen, the faithful and true witness, the beginning of creation of God (*Judgment*).

Second, consider the description of Jesus Christ as He comes in judgment in chapter 19.

1. Faithful and true in righteousness, He *judges* and makes war (Rev. 19:11).
2. His eyes were a *flame of fire* (Rev. 19:12).
3. Out of His mouth *goes a sharp sword* (Rev. 19:15).

But now let us consider faithful churches one, two, five, and six.

Letter One (Rev. 2:1): The one holding the seven stars, walking in the midst of the seven candlesticks (*Holy Spirit*).
Letter Two (Rev. 2:8): The first and the last, which was dead and is alive (*Resurrection*).
Letter Five (Rev. 3:1): Has the seven Spirits of God and the seven stars (*Holy Spirit*).
Letter Six (Rev. 3:7): Holy, faithful, and true, has the key of David, one who opens and shuts (*Power to deliver*).

The letters to these four churches are from One "coming" with hope and assurance as opposed to One "coming" in judgment. Those remaining faithful will find themselves with the Lord dressed in robes of white (Rev. 7:9-17).

In the "end of the age" when harvest time comes, the Lord will send forth His angels to gather His Church. The wheat will be gathered out of the world and into the heavenly barn while the tares are left behind—earthbound for the fire (Mt. 13:40-43). All of this first harvesting of faithful souls will take place at the time of the Rapture.

Prior to the vial judgments being poured out, which takes place in the second half of seven years of tribulation, there will be a second harvesting. Souls trusting in Christ during the first half of the tribulation period (and partly into the second half) will be joined to the Church already in Heaven (Rev. 14:14-16).

Another aspect of these letters that we have already mentioned are the promises made to the overcomers in the churches. These are listed below:

1. Eat of the tree of life (Rev. 2:7).
2. Not be hurt of the second death (Rev. 2:11).
3. Eat of the hidden manna, a new name, a white stone (Rev. 2:17).
4. Power over nations, rule with a rod of iron, morning star (Rev. 2:26-28).

5. Clothed in white, not blot out his name, confess him before the Father and the angels (Rev. 3:5).
6. Make him a pillar in the temple of God, go out no more, bear the name of the city of God, New Jerusalem, and a new name (Rev. 3:12).
7. Granted the right to sit with Jesus in His throne as an overcomer (Rev. 3:21).

The above list incorporates promises that every true believer in Jesus Christ can rightfully expect to inherit, and not just the believers of a particular church. The promises are made to the Body of Christ as an incentive to overcome the spiritual barriers that the pilgrim might face.

But these promises speak loudest to the Church that experiences the Rapture. The Church to be raptured will also experience a heightening of the "beginning of sorrows." This final period of heightened sorrows could be a literal nine months of apparent global and cosmic disturbances that will warn "watchful" Christians of the Lord's imminent coming at the Rapture.

The tribulation will follow the Rapture, with a brief pause. This pause will facilitate the sealing of the 144,000 Jews (Rev. 7:1-8). The Rapture is the first phase of Christ's Second Coming. It is a phase that you cannot afford to miss out on.

Patterns in the Letters

In addition to what we have already pointed out, these two divisions in the churches are tied together by still another thread. The Church of Smyrna was told it would have tribulation ten days. The Church of Sardis was told to hold fast, repent, and watch lest Jesus come to them as a thief. The Philadelphia Church was promised that they would be kept from the hour of tribulation that was coming upon the whole world, which would try them that dwell on the earth (Rev. 2:10, 3:3,10).

If these letters were only meaningful to the churches of the first century, then why warn of His coming as a thief and why promise an escape from the Great Tribulation (Rev. 7:14)? This escape comes after the opening of the sixth seal, which introduces and includes the Rapture with the opening of the heavens.

> *And I beheld when He had opened the sixth seal, and, lo, there was a great earthquake; and the sun became black as sackcloth of hair, and the moon became as blood; and the stars of heaven fell unto the earth, even as a fig tree casteth her untimely figs, when she is shaken of a mighty wind.* ***And the heaven departed as a scroll when it is rolled together****; and every mountain and island were moved out of their places* (Revelation 6:12-14).

David Hunt makes a good point when he correctly compares the misunderstood First Coming of Christ to the confusion now surrounding the Second Coming of Christ. Just like the First Coming of Christ, His Second Coming is also divided into two events.

The first event, according to Hunt, is the "Rapture" and the second event is when Jesus returns with the saints that were taken up in the Rapture (Rev. 19:14). "...[what] the Old Testament prophets said of Christ's coming could not fit into one time frame and one event. Thus two comings of the Messiah were required, though the prophets didn't say so directly. There was no excuse for Christ's contemporaries not to realize what the Bible says. His return simply cannot fit into one time frame and one event." Hunt goes on to explain, "There must be two separate comings of Christ, both still future, which occur at two distinctly different periods of time. There is no other possible way to reconcile the otherwise contradictory statements in Scripture concerning Christ's return. According to Christ's own words, the conditions on earth at one coming will be the exact opposite of those at His other coming."[13] Today Christians are misinformed and unaware of the promised Rapture and how it initiates Daniel's Seventieth Week, which contains another separate coming of the Lord Jesus Christ.

It must also be noted that the seven letters are also related to the image of Christ, the One who is standing in the midst of the seven candlesticks and dressed in white to His feet (Rev. 1:13). The letters are linked in the introduction of each of the seven letters to the image by these descriptions: the One holding the seven stars and walking in the midst of seven candlesticks (Rev. 2:1); the First and the Last, or the Beginning and the End (Rev. 2:8); the One with the sharp two-edged sword (Rev. 2:12); the Son of God; the One with eyes of fire and feet like burning brass (Rev. 2:18);

the One who has the seven Spirits of God, even the seven stars (Rev. 3:1); the One that is holy and true and has the key of David (keys of hell and death) (Rev. 3:7); and finally, the Amen, the faithful and true witness, the beginning of creation (Rev. 3:14).

All these descriptions bind the image and the letters together into one beautiful picture of the Body of Christ with Christ as the Head. He is residing in the heavens, but speaking to the Church on earth through the ministry of the Holy Spirit—none other than the seven angels and the seven Spirits of God. This passage wonderfully illustrates the verbal inspiration of Scripture. This is why Jesus said this at the close of the book:

> *I Jesus have sent Mine angel* [singular] *to testify unto you these things in the churches* [plural]. *I am the root and the offspring of David, and the bright and morning star. And the Spirit and the bride* [while still in the world] *say, Come. And let him that heareth* [what the Spirit saith unto the churches] *say, Come. And let him that is athirst come. And whosoever will, let him take the water of life freely* (Revelation 22:16-17).

Jesus, interestingly enough, in this verse points to the fact that He is of the promised seed of David and that He is the bright and morning star. The bright and morning star is Venus. Venus alternates as a bright morning and evening star. Jesus' use of it reveals His deity because the Romans believed that the descendants of Eros, the goddess Venus, were gods. The passage combines the prophecies of David's eternal reign with first century Roman astrological beliefs. The seven churches in Asia Minor, a providence of Rome, would have known the significance of this symbolism.

But again, this imagery of Christ portrayed as the radiant Head of the Church is found in Revelation 10:1, "*...and His face was as it were the sun, and His feet as pillars of fire.*"

Turning our attention back to the vision of Revelation chapter 1, we note that the angels of the seven churches represent the seven Spirits of God, which is the Holy Spirit that Christ has sent into the world (Rev. 1:20; 2:1; 3:1; 4:5; 5:6). The white robe worn by Christ represents the faithful Body of Christ. The head of white wool is the purity of Jesus

Christ. The white robe from the shoulders to the feet symbolizes the faithful churches of Ephesus, Smyrna, Sardis, and Philadelphia. The eyes of flame, the feet of fine brass, and the two-edged sword that comes out of His mouth, depict that part of the Church that will be purified or separated for the fiery trials of the tribulation.

The breastplate of righteousness represents the righteousness of Christ that the true believer trusts in to preserve and protect his personal salvation and that enables him to stand in the day of judgment. "*Stand therefore, having your loins girt about with truth, and having on the breastplate of righteousness*" (Eph. 6:14).

The Seven Letters and the Seals

Another factor that supports the linkage of the warnings in the letters to the judgment of the seals is that, after Jesus ascended, He first took the scroll from His Father. He then opened the first seal (Rev. 6:1-2). Jesus' first priority was to send the Holy Spirit unto all believers. As He had promised, the Holy Spirit would make it possible for believers to "overcome the trials" that they would face throughout Church history (Jn. 14:16-26; 16:33).

Add to this the fact that Jesus also characterized Church history as the "beginning of sorrows" (Mt. 24:8). The first seal is, therefore, the sending of the Holy Spirit unto believers (Jn. 16:7; Acts 1:5,8; 2:1-4). Believers, in these letters, are consistently told to be overcomers because the Spirit or the angel of each church represents the Holy Spirit.

The Greek verb *nikaw* is translated in the King James Version "to overcome, to prevail and to conquer." Jesus overcame the world and prevailed to open the seven seals (Jn. 16:33; Rev. 5:5; 6:1). Jesus opened each seal as time progressed. The sixth seal may be opened soon, the phenomena associated with the sixth seal will bring the Church to the very brink of the tribulation period. The Spirit's message that comes through to every believer is "be one to overcome" and, with the message, the Holy Spirit gives each believer the power to overcome (Jn. 1:12-13,16-17; 16:7,13-15).

Persecutions and trials will increase just before the Rapture. Those persecutions and trials are followed by approaching signs of cosmic disturbances. In conjunction with the cosmic disturbances, the earth will witness increased volcanic activity and accompanying earthquakes. This activity will fill the upper atmosphere with volcanic dust and cause lunar eclipses to turn blood red "before" that great and notable "Day of the Lord." The Church Age ends with signs beginning to appear in the heavens (Joel 2:30-31; Acts 2:19-20). These signs in the heavens will continue to increase throughout the first half of the tribulation period. The first five trumpet judgments involve great events that either begin to take place in the heavens or fall from the heavens. (See Revelations 8:1–9:1.)

We can draw the inference that the letters to the seven churches are divinely written as a prophetic warning available throughout Church history and bearing a special warning for the Church that will experience the Rapture. Considering the composite message of the letters seems to indicate that before its Rapture, the Church will endure increased persecution at the hands of the devil (Rev. 2:10; 3:10).

The Church that will be rescued by the Rapture should be expected to better comprehend the letters because this Church has the advantage of history and progressive revelation as we approach the "Day of the Lord" (Dan. 12:3-4,9-10); "*...the wise shall understand.*"

We are approaching the opening up of the heavens, the Rapture of the Church. I believe it will be very soon and, therefore, I write with extreme urgency. Salvation in Christ is the *only* escape from what is coming. A saved "*born-again*" child of God will not go through the seven years of tribulation. Yet believers may go through some of the storms or sorrows that precede the Rapture. The Church has already progressed through the opening of seals one through five. Upon the opening of the sixth seal, the world will be devastated and Christians will be caught away to Heaven.

God has revealed these truths from His Word for the purpose of warning Christians in every Christian denomination. Christians are to watch and make sure of their calling (Mt. 25:1-13; 2 Pet. 1:10). Stop looking for miraculous signs and, instead, immerse yourself in God's Word. The day of judgment is fast approaching and those who prepare themselves will be watching and waiting for that final trumpet call. On that day all Spirit-filled believers in Christ will be called to "come up hither" (1 Thess. 4:13-17; 5:1-11; 1 Cor. 15:51-52). Praise God!

It Is Time to Make Sure You Are Saved

If there is any doubt concerning your salvation, now is the time to resolve this predicament. You need to accept the work of grace done by God for your sins on Calvary almost 2,000 years ago—now is the time. You must recognize yourself as a sinner, knowing in your heart and mind that you are doomed to an eternity in hell—not deserving the gift of salvation (Rom. 10:9-11).

The repentant sinner must realize that if God gave us what we deserved, we would all be destined for hell. But because of the grace and loving mercy of God, He sent His Son to die in our place, for our sin. Thus He provided a way for us to come to be saved—by trusting in His substitutionary death. Repent of sin and be saved by Him through His work of grace. "*For by grace are ye saved through faith; and that not of yourselves: it is the gift of God: not of works, lest any man should boast*" (Eph. 2:8-9). It is *not of religious piety.* In other words, there will be no one in Heaven who will be able to say, "I have done it." It is faith in what God has done for us that saves us, and not faith in what we have done for Him. Those who believe that their good or religious works will get them to Heaven are blind to the fact that faith *alone* in Christ is enough. "*My grace is sufficient for thee...*" (2 Cor. 12:9). If we do not ask God to save us, we will not be saved. So let go of everything that you thought earned a favorable judgment from God.

It requires humility and godly sorrow to be saved. God requires us to see ourselves as He does—hell-bound sinners whom He sent His Son to redeem. Let go—let God save you today. It is time! Let the Lord Jesus Christ become your righteousness (Jer. 23:6; 33:16).

Seals One Through Five Have Been Opened

The Rapture, then, is to be viewed as the harvesting of the first fruits (Rev. 14:4), the separating of the wheat from the tares, the taking of those who have oil in their lamps (Mt. 13:24-30; 25:1-13). Those left behind will be the ones who do not have oil in their earthly vessels (the Holy Spirit dwelling within), and have attempted, instead, to borrow from those that did.

The good servant (Mt. 25:14-30) will be rewarded at the Rapture, but the unprofitable servant (the one proclaiming to serve Christ, but in reality not knowing Him), will be thrown into outer darkness with those left behind after the Rapture (Mt. 25:30).

Jesus reminds us that the coming of the Son of man will be like the days of Noah (Lk. 17:24-37). People will be eating, drinking, and going about their daily routines; not giving even a second thought to the potential advent of the Lord's judgment. The same attitude persisted when the Lord judged Sodom. But, in the same day that Lot came out of Sodom, the Lord rained down fire and brimstone. The same circumstance will prevail when the Lord rescues believers from the world. Shortly after the Church departs this world, Christ's wrath will be revealed in the heavens and the world will know that the "Day of the Lord" has come upon them (Rev. 6:17).

The unbelieving world and empty vessels of Christianity will be left behind to endure the trials of the tribulation. The Lord will cause the earth to quake, the sun to be blackened, the moon to be turned to blood (*by a lunar eclipse*) and the stars of heaven (meteorites) will appear to fall to the earth (Rev. 6:12-17).

These events are components of the sixth seal, which immediately preludes the Rapture. The events of the sixth seal fulfill the prophecies concerning the moon turning to "blood red" before the coming of the "Day of the Lord" (Joel 2:31; Acts 2:19-20). Rosenthal is correct when he states that the sixth seal is the prelude to the Rapture.[14] However, he is wrong when he places the opening of the sixth seal (and thus the Rapture), within the second half of the tribulation period of the Day of the Lord. In fact, the sixth seal announces to the world that the "Day of the Lord's Wrath" has come.

The term "Day of the Lord" covers more than just the second half of the tribulation. There is evidence to suggest that the millennial age itself is included within the context of the "Day of the Lord."[15] The "Day of the Lord" comes as a thief in the night (1 Thess. 5:2). If the first six seals are limited to the first half of the tribulation, then expectation is realized and the surprise of the Rapture is denied. But by understanding that the seals are part of almost 2,000 years of Church history, a high degree of surprise can be maintained, except for those who are closely watching (1 Thess. 5:4).

Rosenthal makes the mistake of confusing the tribulation associated with the beginning of sorrows of the Church Age with the Great Tribulation of Jacob's trouble. He says, "Two points are of great significance. First, the sixth seal is opened after the Great Tribulation. And the Great Tribulation is cut short and ends before the end of the seventieth week."[16]

He inappropriately uses several verses (Mt. 24:29; Mk. 13:24; Lk. 21:23-25) to support the placement of the opening of the sixth seal. He argues that the phrases "*Immediately after the tribulation of those days*" in Matthew 24:29 and "*after that tribulation*" in Mark 13:24 is referring to the Great Tribulation. Rosenthal also uses Revelation 6:17 to propose that the coming of the great day of His wrath indicates the second half of the tribulation period, which is a false assertion.[17]

It is the beginning of the seven-year tribulation period. First Thessalonians 5:2 is enough to reject his conclusion. The "Day of the Lord" comes as a thief. If it comes within the tribulation period, there will be no surprise to those who are lost or saved. The sixth seal is opened prior to, not after, the start of the tribulation period. The sixth seal, like the final birth pangs before delivery, announces to the world that the "Day of the Lord," Daniel's seventieth week is come. With this seal the world is delivered into tribulation while the saved are delivered to God's throne (Rev. 7:9-17; 12:1-5).

Although Rosenthal's major tenet of a "pre-wrath Rapture" is incorrect, it is interesting that he notes that the first five seals are part of a purging of the Church. He limits the first five or six seals to three-and-one-half years, but the seals and their respective openings have been associated with the Church Age throughout the past 2,000-year process.

The horsemen of the Apocalypse are no different than the horsemen of Zechariah. "What do the horses symbolize? It is suggested that they represent the hosts of Heaven, the angels, but they are rather the symbols of the divine activity in the government of the earth."[18]

The horsemen of Zechariah were sent to work in behalf of Israel, but the horsemen of Revelation are sent in behalf of the Church. "When the prophet asks the angel for the significance of the horses and riders, the Angel of the Lord answers that they have been commissioned of the Lord to reconnoiter. God is actively interested in the conditions of earth, especially as they relate to His earthly people Israel."[19]

Chapters 1-6 of Revelation must be understood as events within the Church Age, then culminating with the Raptured Church at God's throne in Heaven (Rev. 7:9-17). It will be the Rapture of the Church that announces the end of this age. The tribulation period will proceed after a brief period of calm in order to seal the 144,000 Jewish servants of God. With the two witnesses, they will be God's messengers of salvation during the tribulation period.

As the sixth seal is opened, over a period of time, the world will experience greater and greater disturbances. How long a period is uncertain, but it is doubtful that it will be years. More than likely, the events of the sixth seal will cover a period of months. This period of months will immediately precede the coming of the "Day of the Lord" and conclude with the Rapture.

Seal one is the impregnation or the sending of the Holy Spirit into the world to indwell believers. Seals two to five are like the continuous sorrows that accompany childbearing. Seal six is the delivery of the child and is also the time of Israel's trouble. Therefore, as the birth pangs of a woman, when we see these things begin to happen, we look up—for our salvation draws close. This is why Jesus said that the wars, rumors of wars, famine, and earthquakes in diverse places are the "*beginning of sorrows*," but the end is not yet (Mt. 24:8). The sixth seal translates the Christians to be with the Lord and the remaining world into the "Day of the Lord's Wrath" (Rev. 6:17).

Seals two, three, and four are pangs felt and seen in the world while seal five depicts the pangs of the souls in the secret chambers of the "afterlife." The fifth seal exposes the desire and the restlessness of those who have died. They yearn to have their glorified bodies and their deaths avenged. We can gain some early second century Jewish insights to the fifth seal from the Apocrypha Book, II Esdras. In II Esdras 4:33-42, the prophet asks a question concerning the time of the end. The answer contains the illustration of a woman in birth pangs.

> *Then I answered as follows: How long then and when shall this come about? Why are our years few and evil? He replied to me thus: You cannot proceed faster than the Most High, for you want to proceed at your own pace while the one above [proceeds] for the many.* ***Have not the souls of the righteous in their storehouses inquired about these things, How long must we stay here? And when will the crop of our reward upon the threshing floor come?*** *Then Jermiel, the archangel, replied to them as follows: When the number of those like you is full; for he has weighed the age in the balance, and measured the times with a measure, and counted the times by number, and he will not*

disturb or rouse [them], ***until the fixed measure is attained*** (II Esdras 4:33-37, emphasis added).

Now compare that to what is recorded in Revelation 6:9-11.

And when He had opened the fifth seal, ***I saw under the altar the souls of them that were slain*** *for the word of God, and for the testimony which they held:* ***and they cried with a loud voice, saying, How long, O Lord, holy and true, dost Thou not judge and avenge our blood on them that dwell on the earth?*** *And white robes were given unto every one of them; and it was said unto them, that they should rest yet for a little season, until their fellow-servants also and their brethren, that should be killed as they were, should be fulfilled* (Revelation 6:9-11).

The parallels between these two passages are obvious. Both are talking about the departed souls crying out to God, "How long?" But as we continue to quote from II Esdras, we gain a valuable insight.

Then I answered as follows: O Lord, Lord, all of us are full of wickedness. Is not now perhaps on our account, on account of the sins of the inhabitants of the earth, the crop of the righteous held back? He replied to me thus: Go now and inquire of a pregnant woman if, when she has completed her nine months, her womb can hold back the foetus [fetus] *within it. I said, Certainly not, my Lord. He then said:* ***In the underworld, the storehouses of souls are comparable to the womb; for just as the woman about to bear [a child] strives to bring to an end the inevitable [anguish] of delivery, so also do these places strive to expel those things committed to them from the beginning. Then the things you want to see will be shown to you*** (II Esdras 4:38-43, emphasis added).[20]

As a comparison, II Esdras can assist in understanding that the souls under the altar can be rightly compared to a woman in birth pangs, waiting to be delivered (Rev. 6:9-11). When the brethren that should be killed, fill up that which the Lord has appointed, then Israel will enter into its time of trouble and the Church will have been raptured.

This, as we will see later, fits perfectly with the interpretation of Revelation 12:1-6. The birth of the child brings new life and relief to the child, but great anguish and pain to its mother. The faithful remnant of Israel is the mother of the Church, the child or offspring. This hints that the child, not the "man-child" of Revelation 12:5, is the Raptured Church.

The section that follows in II Esdras chapter 5 is that of the signs of the end. If our comparisons are correct, then this is the opening of the sixth seal being described.

> *But as to the signs: Look now, the days will come when those who inhabit the earth will be seized by great confusion, And the way of truth will be concealed, And the country of faith* [Israel] *will be barren. Injustice will be multiplied beyond that which you yourself now see* [A.D. 96-135.][21] *and become incomparably greater than anything you have ever heard about. Waste and trackless will be the nation you now see bearing rule* [Rome] *and men shall see it empty. If the Most High permits you to live, you will see [it] utterly confounded after the third [period].* [See Rev. 17-18.] *The sun will suddenly shine at night, and the moon in the daytime* [times will be changed]. *Blood will drip from the trees, stones will cry out, peoples will be in confusion, and the courses will be altered* [planets; consider also Rev. 8:7: "The first angel sounded, and there followed **hail and fire mingled with blood**, and they were cast upon the earth: and the third part of **trees was burnt up**, and all green grass was burnt up"]. *And one whom the inhabitants of the earth do not anticipate will reign, birds will migrate, the sea of Sodom* [Dead Sea] *will produce fish and one whom many do not know will cry out by night, but all will hear his voice. Chasms will appear in many places, And fire often be discharged [therefrom]; Wild beasts will leave their lairs, And women in their uncleanness will give birth to monsters.* [Effects of radiation on the developing fetus?] *Brackish waters will be found in sweet ones, And all friends will assault each other.* ["Survival of the fittest" mentality takes over.] *Reason will then be obscured, And insight confined to its chamber* [because the

Church is in heaven] *and sought in vain by many. Injustice and incontinence will be multiplied upon the earth* (II Esdras 5:1-10).[22]

This first century to early second century writing of II Esdras sheds some light on the unfolding of apocalyptic events at the time of the end. Although the Book of II Esdras is not recognized as authoritative Scripture today, it is, however, just as authoritative as anyone who currently writes concerning apocalyptic Scripture. The writer of II Esdras was a Jew who obviously was familiar with apocalyptic Scripture and symbolism. Other inconsistencies with Scripture account for this book being rejected as being authoritative Canon. It appears that the writer of II Esdras may also have been influenced by the writing of Revelation by John.

The traditional-historical approach (those who assert that Revelation is a book of past events) views Revelation from the perspective of background material in Greek or Oriental myths and Jewish tradition. "Most certainly the book draws upon these, especially the O.T., but it cannot be divested of its predictive element through suppositions of vagueness connected with its alleged apocalyptic language. It is a prophecy whose scope stretches forward to the return of Christ and beyond."[23]

However, what little we have extracted does agree with our conclusions of paralleling the seals with the beginning of sorrows in the Gospels. With or without II Esdras, our conclusion remains consistent with Scripture. In Chapter 6 we will conduct a much closer examination and comparison of Matthew 24 and Revelation 6.

The fifth seal is before the coming of the "Day of the Lord" and is part of the sorrows, while the sixth seal delivers the Church to God's throne. The unregenerate church, Israel, and the rest of the world are delivered to the "Seventieth Week of Daniel," the seven years of tribulation. "The casting of the unsaved remnant of the Church into end-time tribulation inevitably accompanies the deliverance of the saved remnant into Christ's presence. The two occur simultaneously, leaving the Church on earth without a single person whose profession of faith in Christ is genuine."[24]

A brief comparative look at the seals is very revealing. The first is sent out to overcome with a crown and a bow, riding a white horse. The second is riding a red horse and is sent to take peace from the earth and people are killing one another. The third is riding on a black horse and causes limited famine in the world. The fourth is a pale horse and it brings death by pestilence, the sword, and famine from the starving beast on the earth.

The nature of the first is clearly different from that of the second, third, and fourth. The latter three are clearly progressive and cumulative in nature, with the fourth incorporating the judgments of the second and the third. The second through the fourth seals are tribulations seen throughout history.

The fifth seal has nothing to do with the judgments on the earth except that it includes a request for God to avenge the deaths of the faithful witnesses of Christ. If the first four seals contain the beginning judgments of the "Day of the Lord," why are the faithfully departed not aware that God's judgment has begun? Instead they are given robes and told to wait.

Then we come to the sixth seal. The events of the sixth seal are clearly much more spectacular in nature and instantly affect the whole world. We have great earthquakes, and hail from heaven, the sun is darkened and the moon turns to blood, mountains move out of their place, and the heavens roll up like a scroll. The sixth seal is transitional and the whole face of the earth is shaken. With the events of the sixth seal fulfilled and the Church raptured to Heaven, it is now time to open the seventh seal.

The seventh seal simply opens the scroll and activates the trumpet judgments of the tribulation. The seventh angel then begins to speak to the seventh church and the world through the seven trumpet judgments. The opening of the seventh seal starts the tribulation; therefore, the sixth seal must include the Rapture. This is supported by the appearance of a multitude before the throne of God (Rev. 7:9-17).

The placement of this event between seals six and seven supports this conclusion. The sixth angel promised the sixth church that it would escape the tribulation that was coming upon the whole world, while the seventh angel told the seventh church that it was blind and naked. The seventh church was also counseled to buy of the Lord gold tried in fire. They were also reminded that the Lord rebukes and chastens those whom He loves (Rev. 3:19).

The fire is the first of four fiery trumpet judgments of the first half of the tribulation period (Rev. 8:6-12).

> ***And when He had opened the seventh seal,*** *there was silence in heaven about the space of half an hour. And I saw the seven angels which stood before God; and to them were given seven trumpets. And another angel came and stood at the altar, having a golden censer; and there was given unto him much incense, that he should offer it with the prayers of all saints upon the golden altar which was before the throne. And the smoke of the incense, which came with the prayers of the saints, ascended up before God out of the angel's hand.* ***And the angel took the censer, and filled it with fire of the altar, and cast it into the earth:*** *and there were voices, and thunderings, and lightnings, and an earthquake* [the beginning of judgment]. *And the seven angels which had the seven trumpets prepared themselves to sound. The first angel sounded, and there followed hail and* ***fire mingled with blood,*** *and they were cast upon the earth: and the third part of trees was* ***burnt up,*** *and all green grass was* ***burnt up.*** *And the second angel sounded, and as it were a great mountain* ***burning with fire*** *was cast into the sea: and the third part of the sea became blood; and the third part of the creatures which were in the sea, and had life, died; and the third part of the ships were destroyed. And the third angel sounded, and there fell a great star from heaven,* ***burning as it were a lamp,*** *and it fell upon the third part of the rivers, and upon the fountains of waters; and the name of the star is called Wormwood: and the third part of the waters became wormwood; and many men died of the waters, because they were made bitter. And the fourth angel sounded, and the third part of the sun was smitten, and the third part of the moon, and the third part of the stars; so as the third part of them* ***was darkened, and the day shone not for a third part of it, and the night likewise*** (Revelation 8:1-12).

The darkness that takes place after the fourth trumpet and may come at the end of the ministry of the two witnesses could have something to do with their deaths. Just as darkness spread across the land with our Lord's death, this darkness will accompany their deaths as well (Lk. 23:44). Another possibility is that it marks the end of the first half of the tribulation. The darkness announces increased doom and gloom. The darkening of one-third of the sun, moon, and stars could be calling attention to the imminent arrival of satan (Rev. 9:1-2,11).

Satan rules one-third of the host of Heaven and the darkening represents the darkening of his kingdom (Jude 6; Rev. 12:5).

The Beginning of the End

There are indications that the world does physically see some type of manifestation of the Lord after the opening of the sixth seal (Rev. 1:7; 6:16-17). The world becomes aware of the arrival of the "Day of the Lord's Wrath." This fact becomes apparent to the world because the sign of His coming has appeared in the heavens with the Rapture of the Church and the cosmic disturbances that accompany and follow it.

As a result of the judgment, the world is left in utter chaos. The events of the sixth seal will probably unfold gradually at first, but not as gradual as the events of seals two, three, and four have over the history of the Church. The events of the sixth seal will grow as birth pangs and will announce the coming of the "Day of the Lord" as the birth of a child (Mt. 24:8; Rev. 12:1-4).

We may begin to see some cosmic disturbance that affects other planets first and then the earth. The disturbance may start out with meteor impacts that cause earthquakes, in turn, may cause an increase in volcanic activity. Together these events will set in motion a series of devastating ecological effects that will work to warn the faithful that the "Day of the Lord" is indeed imminent. O.M. Mitchel, when considering the judgments of God, writes the following:

> "Is it credible that this earth is to be consumed by fire,—that the sun and moon are to be darkened,—that the stars of heaven are to fall,—that the skies are to be wrapped in flame, and be rolled up as a scroll,—are these oriental figures or dread realities, which at no distant day are to strike terror to the inhabitants of earth? I frankly confess I do not know how to answer these questions, and I do not believe that all the sciences and philosophy which

> now exist on earth, can fit an individual one particle for their comprehension or solution. There are those who find in the internal structure of the earth,—its volcanoes with their rivers of molten lava,—evidence that these sublime predictions are one day to be accomplished. I dare not thus point out to the All-wise the means to accomplish his purposes. I can only bow and reverently accept. And do you really believe that the day will ever come, when this great globe, with its rock-ribbed mountains, shall melt with fervent heat,—its oceans bellows flash into unmeasured volumes of fiery steam,—when flaming fire shall wrap the doomed planet and devour its very being, and blot it from its kindred family of worlds? I can only answer that I know of no special reason why earth should be eternal. Its destruction does not involve the well-being of the universe, and were it even blotted from existence it would but momentarily disturb the equilibrium of the great scheme of worlds, of which it forms an insignificant unit. But should God destroy its present form; should it indeed be baptized with fire; should it be purged and purified, God can bring it out of this terrific ordeal, not one atom of His matter lost, but all remodeled, restored, recreated, a new world filled with beauty, and joy, and perpetual happiness; where death—the wages of sin—shall never appear, and where neither tears, nor sobs, nor sorrows shall dim the beauty of its enchanting abodes."[25]

Possibly for a nine-month period, prior to the start of the "Day of the Lord," the world will experience a period of continuous and growing "natural" disasters. As a result of this increased activity, a fervor for prophetic writings and warnings can be expected. This fervor may produce a strong anti-Christian movement as the media focuses attention on the radical "Christian" factions that have fortified communes—such as the example in Waco, Texas.

Increased legislation and enforcement of religion may outlaw public gatherings that warn of the Lord's return. The outlawing of protesting against abortion clinics has already set the precedent for this.

The "Day of the Lord's Wrath" will come with the opening of the sixth seal, but God will order His angels not to hurt the earth until the servants of God are sealed (Rev. 7:3). There is a greater tribulation on the earth after the days of sorrows have been completed, but the great, stored-up wrath of God will be poured out "only" after God warns the world with the ministry of His two witnesses and the first four trumpet judgments, which are pronounced during the first half of the tribulation.

It must be noted that the seven trumpets are contained in the seventh seal and the seventh trumpet contains the seven vials. After the 144,000 Jews (12,000 from the 12 tribes of Israel) are sealed, the appointed time-out for the sealing will resume (Rev. 8:1).

The day is coming, and the opening of the sixth seal will cause great distress and destruction on the earth. It will be the beginning of the end. No more will it be said "*but the end is not yet*" (Mt. 24:6), for it will have come (Rev. 6:17). There will be nothing else to fulfill and this is why the four angels are told not to hurt the earth until the servants of God are sealed (Rev. 7:1-3).

Even with the opening of the seventh seal, the calm upon the earth will continue for a short space. It is clear that, even though the world will be aware that the day of God's wrath has come, there will be a temporary calm. It will be a morning when the birds will not celebrate the rising of sun and the arrival of a new day with their singing, for it will be a morning of "*thick darkness*" (Joel 2:2).

This morning will be darkened by a sunrise solar eclipse in Israel, which will affect the natural order of God's creation. After that, a building of the warning judgments will eventually lead to the unmixed pouring out of God's wrath on the earth in the second half of the seven-year tribulation (Rev. 14:10). (See Figure 2 on page 3.)

Perhaps the first indications of God's judgment will be observed by astronomers. "Perhaps as they set their telescopes for the rising of a particular star they will notice that it is seconds or even minutes late in its rising. This will indicate that the doom of the universe is near to the astronomer who, as a result, will stand aghast at such an event, for the powers of the heavens will be shaken."[26]

It must also be understood that until the final bowl or vial judgments are inaugurated, there will be time to repent and come to God (Rev. 9:20-21; 16:9,11). God will manifest Himself in judgment to those who scorned His Word and persecuted His people. Jesus Christ will reveal Himself to the world in progressive judgment (which is what the Book of Revelation portrays).

Every knee will bow and worship the Lord Jesus Christ. It is much better to bow to Him now as Savior rather than shamefully bow to Him later as the Righteous Judge (Is. 4:3-4). "*That at the name of Jesus every knee should bow, of things in heaven, and things in earth, and things under the earth; and that every tongue should confess that Jesus Christ is Lord, to the glory of God the Father*" (Phil. 2:10-11; see also Rev. 10:6).

The Church Will Have Tribulation

As we have said earlier, it is also clearly indicated by the seven letters to the churches that the Church will have tribulation to overcome throughout the days of the Church. Evidence of this Church Age tribulation can be found in Revelation 2:9-10, 22 and John 16:1-3. Matthew 24:15-22 clearly refers to the second half of the tribulation period, but in verse 25 Jesus refers them back to what He told them previously—"*I have told you before*"—about false prophets and messiahs (Mt. 24:11). Then in verse 26 Jesus begins to talk to the disciples about a time more relative to them. He tells them not to be deceived into following a false Christ, which is exactly what will happen to those who accept false Messiahs before and during the tribulation period. "*Wherefore if*" (*eav ouv*) someone tries to deceive you, believe it not.

The time between Christ's leaving and His return would be characterized as a time of false Christs and false Messiahs. Believers from the time of Christ unto today have had to deal with this problem. The faithful will be overcomers because greater is He that is in us than he that is in the world (1 Jn. 4:1-4).

Jews today are looking for the Messiah. The *Jerusalem Post*, dated January 29, 1994, ran a full-page ad that calls the world to receive Menachem M. Schneerson, a Jewish Rabbi, as the Messiah King.

Schneerson died in June of 1994 and the Lubavitcher movement was faced with the reality that they had placed their hopes in a false Messiah. Some of the faithful camped out at the grave site of Rabbi Schneerson, expecting him to be resurrected, but again their hopes were not realized. How sad it is to see so many thirsting for the truth, but refusing to accept

Jesus Christ as their true Messiah. They will, however, when He comes the second time and the signs of Christ's Second Coming are everywhere.

In the same paper edition was this headline: "**1994 is the deadline for peace with Syria-Rabin**." Why 1994? Does Rabin know something that we don't? If anybody doubts that the Jews are looking for and preparing for the Messiah, let them doubt no longer.

The conflict between the Church of Christ and the kingdoms of the world will continue right up to the sign of the coming of the Son of man. In the final days the devil will greatly increase persecution of the Church. The signs in the earth and the heavens will become more obvious for those who are watching. After the tribulation of these days and the days of false Messiahs and sorrows are fulfilled, the imminent signs of His coming will follow (Mt. 24:29). It must be noted that the tribulations the Church has suffered throughout its history have been at the hands of the devil, but his authority over believers is limited by the Lord (Jn. 16:1-4). Jesus, after all, prayed that God would not take us out of the world, but that we would be kept from evil.

This chronology of Church Age tribulation, which will be followed by the signs of His imminent coming, is further supported by Luke 21:12, where Jesus also tells of events that would characterize Church history (Lk. 21:10-11). He then clearly states that "*before*" all these things, the disciples would suffer persecution, but that they would be helped with the abiding presence of the Holy Spirit. "*For I will give you a mouth and wisdom which all your adversaries shall not be able to gainsay* [refute, *avtepo*] *nor resist*" (Lk. 21:15). This truth was realized in Acts 4:8-22 when Peter, being filled with the Holy Ghost, spoke out against the rulers of Israel and they could not say anything to refute (*avtepo*) them.

We must understand that the end-time events in the Gospels are not written chronologically. Just because events follow one another in the text does not mean that they necessarily follow in that order in chronological time. The connecting words and interconnecting markers of the Greek language must be considered very carefully. At the end of His teaching to the disciples, concerning the end of the world and His return, Jesus summarizes the signs of His coming.

In Luke 21:25 Jesus discusses the signs in the heavens, distress among nations, perplexity among nations, and sea waves roaring (all this can be set in motion by great earthquakes or meteors falling from the sky). Jesus is referring to the coming together of all the signs that point to the coming of the "Day of the Lord." These events will throw the world into a state of absolute panic and chaos. The panic and chaos will set the stage for the beast, antichrist himself, to rise to power.

The Lord will show signs in the heavens **before** that great and terrible "Day of the Lord" (Acts 2:19-20). (See Figure 2 on page 3.) There will be little doubt to the faithful that the Lord's return is imminent because the situation on the earth will progressively deteriorate. As the Rapture takes place, the world will finally begin to realize that the "Day of the Lord" has come (Rev. 6:16-17).

Astronomical evidence found in Scripture points to the fact that the blood red moon of Acts 2 and Joel 2 could be a lunar eclipse that helps to mark the season of the "Day of the Lord." For clarification, the "Day of the Lord" is referring to, at the least, the seven-year period of God's judgment as a whole, but the "Great Tribulation" is referring to a time in the second half of the seven years of the "Day of the Lord" when God pours out His final judgment on the world—specifically the bowl or vial judgments. Every event prior to the outpouring of the bowl judgments is a warning designed to call the world to repentance, which reveals the extreme, gracious mercy of God.

The signs that will appear in the heavens will gradually build until there is little doubt that the powers of the heavens have been shaken by the Lord of Hosts. Perhaps the meteor impacts that took place on July 16, 1994, are the beginning of the signs in the heavens. Jupiter was in the constellation Virgo at the time of these impacts and the eyes of the world were watching.

Some More Important Conclusions

We have clearly shown that the Church was told ahead of time that it would experience tribulation before the coming of the "Day of the Lord" (Jn. 16:33). This tribulation will become more pronounced as the Church approaches the inauguration of the "Day of the Lord." The Church, however, will be raptured out of the dawning days of the "Day of the Lord." This will be the "Great Day of Salvation" when the skies will open up and the Lord will gather His Bride unto Himself.

First they who are dead in Christ (cold and dead, but alive in Christ) and then we who are alive in Christ (hot and alive and living for Christ) will meet the Lord in the air (1 Thess. 4:13-18; 1 Cor. 15:51-53). Just as the fifth seal, which speaks to those faithful deceased saints waiting for the day when the Lord would raise their bodies and avenge their deaths upon an ungodly world (Rev. 6:10-11), precedes the sixth seal, which involves the Rapture of the Church, so the resurrection of the dead precedes the translation of the living faithful. "*...and the dead in Christ shall rise first: then we which are alive and remain...*" (1 Thess. 4:15-16).

Many souls are waiting in eternity, clothed in their white garments of righteousness. But those who are only professing Christians (lukewarm and alive, but not living for Christ) are those who grew up in the fields with the good wheat, as tares. They will be separated and left behind with the rest of the unbelieving world to be tried by fire, that their nakedness and poverty might be revealed by fire.

Those who are saved within the first half of the tribulation period are the Laodiceans that will overcome the beast and be added to the Lord during the tribulation period (Rev. 3:17-22).

The Rapture will shake the world and stir the unfaithful Christian Church out of its sleep. After the Rapture the Lord will seal 144,000 men of Israel, during an eerie calm, because God is now about to initiate the redemption of Israel. God will graft them back into the vine and once again focus His attention on the redemption of Israel, "the apple of His eye" (Rom. 11:23-24). Israel is the one whom He had forsaken, but with great mercies or compassion He will gather them (Is. 54:7).

Then, with the opening of the seventh seal, the "Day of the Lord" commences after a brief continuation of the calm. There will be another sign in the heavens that will mark the start of God's trumpet judgments. This sign will consist of a very timely and precisely located solar eclipse, which was prophesied in Isaiah 13:9-10: "*Behold, the day of the Lord cometh.... For the stars of heaven and the constellations thereof shall not give their light: the sun shall be darkened in his going forth* [at sunrise], *and the moon shall not cause her light to shine.*" Joel 2:1-2 speaks about a day of darkness. In Malachi it says, "*But unto you that fear My name shall the Sun of righteousness arise with healing in his wings* [this verse uses an ancient Assyrian description of a solar eclipse that appears as a winged eagle at the time of totality]" (Mal. 4:2a). "*And there appeared...a woman clothed with the sun, and the moon under her feet...*" (Rev. 12:1). (See Figures 3, 4, and 6 on pages 4, 5, and 7 respectively.)

Considering all these Scripture truths has helped me to better understand the meaning of Revelation 3:15 in the context of the Rapture. Cold and hot are acceptable, whereas lukewarm is not. "Lukewarm is a description of Church people who have professed Christ hypocritically, but do not have in their hearts the reality of what they pretend to be in their actions."[27]

"The Church [has] come under the dominance of pretending Christians."[28] Those who are dead and in Christ at the Rapture are characterized as being cold and those who are alive and in Christ at the time of the Rapture are characterized as being hot. But those who are alive and not in Christ are described as being only lukewarm. They are only half alive. They have physical life, born of woman, but have never been born again, born of God. They are "sons of men" but they are not "sons of God." They have had a physical birth but have not experienced a spiritual birth. They have never believed or accepted God's call to repent of their sin. They continued to trust in their own righteous deeds or religious practices for "their" salvation.

"Christians" in the Tribulation?

Those left behind after the Rapture are the Laodiceans (Rev. 3:14-22). These are the churches of the professing Christians who are rejected by the Lord and vomited out of His mouth because of the unreality of their profession. The Bride of Christ will be made ready (Rev. 19:7). But the marriage feast in Heaven will not take place until the last soul has been saved out of the Great Tribulation and added to the Church already in Heaven (Rev. 3:21; 13:10; 14:12-13; 20:4).

The only way a soul can pass through the door that has been closed after the Rapture, is through death. This is the door that Jesus is standing at and knocking after the Rapture. It is a door that only those on the outside can open by giving their life to Christ and dying at the hands of the beast as a result (Rev. 3:20-21; 20:4). In his Gospel John portrays Jesus as one standing at the door of death waiting for those who would follow Him into eternity (Jn. 10:7-12). Death is the wolf of John 10:12 that pursues us all our lives. When tribulation saints get to that door of death, the hired religious leader (hireling) will not be there. Jesus, however, who faithfully went before us and defeated death, waits at that door for those who faithfully trusted in Him (1 Cor. 15:54-58).

Dwight D. Pentecost writes concerning Laodicea: "This Church represents the final form of the professing Church, which is rejected by the Lord and vomited out of his mouth because of the unreality of its profession. If the Church goes into the seventieth week in its entirety and not just the professing portion of it, it would have to be concluded that this Laodicean Church is the picture of the true church. Several things are obvious then. The true Church could not go through the persecutions of the seventieth week and still remain lukewarm to her Lord. The early persecution of the tribulation would fan the sparks of truth that are already in the minds of professing Christians and turn their lukewarmness into a burning fire that results in their repentance or else it will consume their unrepentant heart all together. Such has always been the ministry of persecutions in the past."[29]

But the Laodicean Church is only that portion of the Church that was unfaithful, yet still retains a head knowledge of the Word of the Lord. Thus the warnings contained in Revelation "to those that have ears to hear what the Spirit is saying" (after Revelation 7) have a special significance for those professing Christians who find themselves within the tribulation period. Consider such passages as Revelation 13:9-10, 18; 14:12-13; 16:15 and consider reading them as one who is living in the days of Daniel's seventieth week. I guarantee the reader that the real significance of these passages will be seen for the first time.

> *If any man have an ear, let him hear. He that leadeth into captivity shall go into captivity: he that killeth with the sword must be killed with the sword. Here is the patience and the faith of the saints. ... Here is wisdom. Let him that hath understanding count the number of the beast: for it is the number of a man; and his number is Six hundred threescore and six* (Revelation 13:9-10,18).

> *Here is the patience of the saints: here are they that keep the commandments of God, and the faith of Jesus. And I heard a*

> *voice from heaven saying unto me, Write, Blessed are the dead which die in the Lord from henceforth: Yea, saith the Spirit, that they may rest from their labours; and their works do follow them* (Revelation 14:12-13).

> *Behold, I come as a thief. Blessed is he that watcheth, and keepeth his garments, lest he walk naked, and they see his shame* (Revelation 16:15).

If one believes that the Book of Revelation is interesting now, wait until the tribulation is upon the whole world. Then it will be the number one survival book in anyone's library.

Tribulation is part of our world today, but those who die in Christ are gathered to Him when they die. This will continue to be the case within the tribulation period. Those who die in Christ during the time of the "Day of the Lord" will be those who refuse to worship the beast. They will refuse to receive his mark.

This mark will identify those who wear it as a faithful worshiper of the beast. They will become a citizen of the "New World Order." "*And...causeth the earth and them which dwell therein to worship the...beast...*" (Rev. 13:12).

Those who have come to have faith in Jesus during the seven years of tribulation will be tested by being asked to worship the beast. They must refuse, but in doing so, they will be unable to buy or sell; they will be jobless, homeless, cast in prisons, and ultimately beheaded (Rev. 20:4).

The sheep and goats judgment will judge the peoples of the gathered nations after the tribulation for how they treated those who trusted in the Lord Jesus Christ during the tribulation (Mt. 25:31-46). What serves to support this understanding is the fact that the promises made to the overcomers of Laodicea are realized by those beheaded for refusing the mark of the beast in Revelation 20:4. "*To him that overcometh will I grant to sit with Me in My throne...*" (Rev. 3:21).

These passages indicate that they will find themselves sitting and ruling with Christ from God's throne. God will turn up the heat (increased judgment) in the second half of the "Day of the Lord," but He will still save those who have given over their lives to Christ. This will be possible, but it certainly will not be easy. If one will not give his life to Christ now, it will be that much more improbable then—but certainly not impossible. Not every believer who trusts in Christ during the tribulation period will be killed. Some will survive and those who risk their lives to help them will be rewarded as long as they avoid taking the mark of the beast. ***(Be careful how you treat God's faithful!)*** Within the tribulation of those days, God will reveal to all the world that He is and that His day of wrath has come.

In giving my final comment on the progressive history of the Church, it is clear that the Church has grown in numbers but dwindled in spiritual life. The Church will progress until it reaches a day that is characterized by a "*falling away*" or great apostasy (2 Thess. 2:3). The coming of the Lord will be preceded by a time of increasing apostasy from the center line of truth. "The verb (translated falling away in the KJV) from which the substantive is derived is (*aphistemi*), made up of the preposition (*apo*), 'from,' and (*histemi*), 'to place or stand.' In its strict sense, it means 'to place oneself away from or to stand away from someone.' It does not necessarily mean to remove oneself from someone or somewhere. This departing from someone does not necessarily imply wholehearted agreement or disagreement, but it is separating oneself for the purpose of not incurring the dangers of that association."[30]

This is exactly what is happening on a large scale today, even to those who once held to the fundamental truths of the faith. People are avoiding the labels of fundamentalism because association with fundamentalism means to be on the wrong side of modern scholarship, evangelical outreach, and relevant Bible teaching. Stephen Carter in his book *A Culture of Disbelief*, makes the point that religion is the counter weight of democracy. He cites Soren Kiekegoard and points out that when religion becomes part of the state, it then ceases to be Christianity.[31]

Carter confesses to be a committed Christian, yet he does not regard the Bible as an inerrant authority. He says, "...as a committed Christian, I also do not share the particular vision of biblical inerrancy."[32] Mr. Carter says that Christians should stand for what they believe to be true and right—even if it means suffering for it. The concept is right, but it often places him on the opposite side of many major evangelical issues. I believe this is because he does not accept the Word of God as an inerrant authority. The distance is growing between Christians who accept God's Word as inerrant (without error) and those who do not.

End Notes

1. Thomas, *Revelation 1–7: An Exegetical Commentary*, p. 152.
2. Ibid., pp. 145-146.
3. Ibid., p. 509.
4. John Peter Lange, *The Revelation of John, Lange's Commentary*, E.R. Craven, ed. (Grand Rapids, MI: Zondervan, 1968), p. 139, as cited by Thomas, *Revelation 1–7: An Exegetical Commentary*, p. 509.
5. Ibid., p. 141.
6. Tim Dowley, John H.Y. Briggs, Dr. Robert D. Linder, and David Wright, eds., *The History of Christianity*, (Grand Rapids, MI: Eerdmans Publishing Co., 1977), pp. 72, 80-81.
7. Ibid., p. 83.
8. Ibid., p. 81.
9. Ibid., p. 130.
10. Thomas, *Revelation 1–7: An Exegetical Commentary*, p. 140.
11. Daniel Voll, "Soul Searching With Francis Crick," *Omni*, (Feb. 1994), p. 52.
12. Dowley, Briggs, Linder, Wright, *The History of Christianity*, pp. 346-347.
13. Hunt, *How Close Are We?* p. 107.
14. Rosenthal, *The Pre-Wrath Rapture of the Church*, p. 153.
15. Dwight J. Pentecost, *Things to Come*, (Grand Rapids, MI: Zondervan, 1980), p. 231.
16. Rosenthal, *The Pre-Wrath Rapture of the Church*, p. 152.
17. Ibid., pp. 172-173.
18. Charles L. Feinberg, *The Minor Prophets*, (Chicago, IL: Moody Press, 1977), p. 275.
19. Ibid., p. 276.
20. Jacob M. Myers, *I & II Esdras*, (Garden City, NY: Doubleday & Co. Inc., 1974), pp. 165-166.

21. Ibid. See page 129 for more details. Though the vision of II Esdras may have undergone revision, it appears fairly clear that it received its main thrust from the events in the Vespasian-Domitianic period (A.D. 69–96).

22. Ibid., pp. 166-167.

23. Thomas, *Revelation 1–7: An Exegetical Commentary*, p. 30.

24. Ibid., p. 146.

25. O.M. Mitchel, *Astronomy of the Bible*, (New York: Blakeman & Mason, 1863), pp. 278-280.

26. Ibid., pp. 276-277.

27. Albert Barnes, *The Book of Revelation*, (New York: Harper, 1851), p. 1570; and John F. Walvoord, *The Revelation of Jesus Christ*, (Chicago, IL: Moody, 1966), p. 92, as cited by Thomas, *Revelation 1–7: An Exegetical Commentary*, p. 308.

28. Ibid.

29. Pentecost, *Things to Come*, pp. 212-214.

30. Spiros Zodiates, *The Hebrew Greek Key Study Bible*, (Chattanooga, TN: AMG Publishers, 1985), p. 1468, notes on 2 Thess. 2:3.

31. Stephen Carter, *The Culture of Disbelief*, (New York: Basic Books Publishers, Div. of Harper Collins Pub. Inc., 1993), p. 81.

32. Ibid., p. 161.

Chapter 5

The Vision of Revelation 1:9-20

A Different Understanding

It has often been cited from men of various eschatological positions that it is impossible to understand the Book of Revelation without first understanding the Book of Daniel. Yet this is exactly what many are doing.

Of all the books of the Old Testament that John alludes to, Daniel is the most frequent.[1] Daniel interprets the vision of King Nebuchadnezzar's dream (Dan. 2:31-45) as a man's image, which consisted of a head of gold, breast and arms of silver, belly and thighs of brass, legs of iron, and feet of iron and clay. We know that the metals and body parts represent kingdoms of the earth that grow in military strength and numbers, but are inferior in moral purity from the previous kingdom (Dan. 2:39-45).

This image of a man was God's way of laying out the prophetic history of the kingdoms of the world. Within the reign of the last kingdom, when ten kings are ruling, God will begin to set up an everlasting Kingdom that will never be destroyed and will stand forever (Dan. 2:44). In other words, the last phase of the worldly kingdoms will overlap the beginning phase of God's Kingdom. In the end, the worldly kingdoms will be destroyed when Christ returns to rule and reign on earth (Dan. 2:45).

The image in the Book of Daniel is that of a man who neither hears, speaks, or sees. Daniel, as the man of God, must interpret the dream for Nebuchadnezzar. Later Nebuchadnezzar ordered that the image of his vision be constructed and commanded all to worship the image that represented the kingdoms of the world. This image contained all the characteristics of the kingdoms of the world and they committed idolatry by worshiping the created more than the Creator.

Taking this skeletal understanding over to the Book of Revelation and applying it to the vision of Revelation 1:9-20, we can see that God has done something similar to reveal the characteristics and prophetic history of the "Kingdom of God" on earth. This Kingdom of Heaven was inaugurated at Pentecost and will continue forever, for the gates of hell will not prevail against it; it is an everlasting Kingdom (Mt. 16:18; Dan. 2:44).

Robert L. Thomas addresses this comparison when he speaks concerning the content of Revelation. "The data to be shown the churches, that is, the content of the revelation, are described by the highly significant words (*ha dei genesthai*, 'things that must happen') (1:1). They depict a theme of longstanding interest that has its roots in the O.T. These 'things must happen' first come into view in Daniel's description and interpretation of Nebuchadnezzar's dream about the great statue (Dan. 2:28 [LXX]; cf. also 2:29,45). The statue stands for four kingdoms and a stone cut without hands out of a mountain that destroys the statue, stands for an everlasting kingdom that will supersede the other four. The prophet, using the king's dream as a vehicle, clearly predicts the eventual establishment of God's kingdom on earth."[2]

Unlike the lifeless image of Nebuchadnezzar's dream, the "living" body of Jesus Christ is the image that God has given as a predetermined picture of what the Church should be. The vision that John saw in Revelation 1:9-20 is of paramount significance. The vision that John saw was of the glorified and ascended Christ.[3] The vision also represents the Body of Christ as the Kingdom of God.

> *Till we all come in the unity of the faith, and of the knowledge of the Son of God,* ***unto a perfect man****, unto the measure of the stature of the fulness of Christ: that we henceforth be no more children, tossed to and fro, and carried about with every wind of doctrine, by the sleight of men, and cunning craftiness, whereby they lie in wait to deceive; but speaking the truth in love, may grow up into Him in all things,* ***which is the head****, even Christ: from whom the whole body fitly joined together and compacted by that* ***which every joint supplieth, according to the effectual working in the measure of every part****, maketh increase of the body unto the edifying of itself in love* (Ephesians 4:13-16).

God first predetermined that we, the Body of Christ, should be holy (Eph. 1:4; Heb. 12:10). In comparison to the decaying image of Nebuchadnezzar (from gold to iron and clay), the image of Christ in Revelation chapter 1 is absolutely pure from head to foot. Christ is wearing a "pure gold" breastplate of righteousness. His head of hair is "pure white" and His feet blaze in the refining fire of His righteous judgment.

Thus, Jesus has provided us with a literary picture of His Church, the "Body of Christ" and the Kingdom of God, which is at hand. The fiery eyes of discernment and wisdom lay all the works of the Church naked. With the sword of His mouth, the Word of God, He directs the Spirit of God to continually speak to the churches, that they might be purified.

Those who repent will avoid the final fiery judgment. They will be the believers who overcome the trials of life through the blood of the Lamb and the word of their testimony (Rev. 12:11). These trials come because of the incompatibility of the kingdoms of the world and the Kingdom of God on earth—kingdom against kingdom (Mt. 24:7).

The vision of Christ is one of "penetrating intelligence" and "His movement among the churches [is] to enforce standards of moral purity."[4] The vision that John sees portrays One standing in the midst of seven golden lampstands and holding seven stars in His right hand. As previously stated, this is a picture of Christ, the Head of the Church, sending the seven Spirits of God into the world to help believers and assist them in overcoming the trials of this world.

John begins to receive understanding of the vision because the vision is that of Christ Himself who is speaking directly to him (Rev. 1:20). The seven stars are seven angels and each messenger is dispatched with a specific announcement designed to admonish and/or encourage the Church. These seven messengers are none other than the seven Spirits of God.

The letters were sent to all the "churches," not just a specific church assembly. Individuals of every church are admonished to hear what the Spirit is saying. The invitation at the end of each letter "to hear" portrays the vision of the Son of Man speaking through the *Spirit*, rather than in oral words spoken directly to the prophet.[5]

The Letters and the Vision

The letters continue the interpretation of the mystery of the vision of Christ that John saw. Each church is connected to the overall vision of Christ by the introductory names of the One addressing the Church. The churches are to the vision of Christ what the kingdoms of Babylon, Media, Persia, and Greece were to the vision of Daniel 2. Just as the head in Daniel's vision is Nebuchadnezzar, so the seven golden lampstands represent the physical nature of the seven churches of Asia, signifying the roots of the Gentile Church.

The spiritual life of each church is sustained by the right hand of power through Christ. The spiritual body of believers is represented by the burning candles established upon the lampstands. The lampstands represent the physical church, which can be removed (Rev. 2:5). The white robe, in the vision of Christ, depicts the greater or universal Body of Christ protected by the golden breastplate of the righteousness of Christ.

The introductory names of Christ given to the seven churches are the chronological time indicators, which have only become germane through our study. Each letter to the seven churches opens with a significant introduction. "*Unto the angel of the church of Ephesus* [or Smyrna or Pergamos] *write; These things saith He that holdeth the seven stars* [or the first and the last or He who has the sharp twoedged sword]" (Rev. 2:1).

The most convincing evidence of this relevancy is the church of Laodicea who is addressed by the "*Amen*" (Rev. 3:14) meaning "so it is" (when "amen" is usually found at the end of an oracle). This is followed by the phrase "*the faithful and true witness, the beginning of the creation of God*" (because the Word of God is something that is sure to be fulfilled).

Therefore, the vision of Christ (Rev. 1:9-20) is the great mystery of the Body of Christ and is explained in the letters to the seven churches in Revelation chapters 2 and 3. The Church of Laodicea represents the end of the history for professing churches. They will be rebuked and purged by fire (as represented in the vision seen by John) with the feet of Christ glowing white hot in the refiner's fire.

The feet represent the end of the age and judgment, just as it does in Daniel. Church history will end with the righteous judgment of Christ. Judgment will commence with the Rapture, then come the trumpet judgments, and finally just before His return He will purge the world by pouring out His wrath on those who have refused to repent and chose to worship the image of the beast. The world system of corrupt morals, global economics, and apostate religion will be replaced with the theocratic Kingdom of God on earth—Hallelujah!

Throughout Church history, Christ has been revealing the works of those who say they are Christians. In every letter to the churches Christ acknowledges the works of each church and pronounces His approval and/or disapproval. An admonition is given to believers, for example, to repent, to stand fast, or to remain faithful. To those who overcome there is a reward. However, for those whose works are tested and found wanting, they will suffer loss, but will be saved (if they are truly sons of God) because God rebukes those whom He loves (1 Cor. 3:9-18; Heb. 12:7-10; Rev. 3:19).

The letters to the seven churches must be viewed as the Lord's warning to the whole Body of Christ. Throughout Church history the Spirit has spoken. God has never clearly revealed when Jesus would come again, but to the Church that remains to see His coming, clearer signs of Christ's impending return will be given.

The work of the Spirit within the Body is also revealed as a work to purge, protect, purify, and direct the Body of Christ to its ultimate destiny. The destiny for the Bride of Christ is to make herself ready for the marriage feast in Heaven (Rev. 19:1-10).

With the "command to hear" at the end of each letter to the churches comes a broadened focus. It certainly includes a call to the churches of

Ephesus and Laodicea,[6] but the call is wider and extends to all the churches throughout history. (See Figure 1 on page 2.)

The purging of the Church of Laodicea will come at the hands of the two witnesses in the first half of the tribulation period that is coming upon the whole world. The first four trumpets are fiery judgments of purging brought upon an unrepentant world and the kingdoms of satan.

While the trumpet judgments are being carried out on earth, a battle will be raging in the heavens between satan and his angels and Michael and the faithful host of Heaven (Rev. 12:7-12). The only ones who will be divinely protected against these judgments are the 144,000 of Israel, who are sealed with the seal of God and have fled to the wilderness with the two witnesses. Figure 1 shows how the seals are associated with the history pertaining to the Body of Christ within the dispensation of grace.

We will briefly look at chapters 4 and 5, then consider the corollary points of the seven seals and the seven churches to these chapters.

Insights From Revelation Chapters 4 and 5

In chapter 4, John sees a door opened in Heaven and again hears a voice as a trumpet (Rev. 1:10), which calls him to come up into the heavens for the purpose of showing him things that are inevitably [*dei*] after this [*meta tauta*]. John, in the Spirit, is taken through this opened door where he sees the throne of God.

John's description leaves little doubt that he is looking into the very throne room of God, which he describes in all its grandeur. His description closely parallels the vision of Isaiah 6:1-4 on every major point. However, in addition to Isaiah's description of the four seraphims, each having six wings and continually praising God as being holy, holy, holy, John also describes seven burning lamps that are before the throne of God, which are the seven Spirits of God.

John also sees 24 seats before God's throne with 24 elders, clothed in white raiment and having crowns of gold (Rev. 4:4). John records the worship of these 24 elders in Heaven as they cast their crowns before the throne of God. They acknowledge God's worthiness to receive glory, honor, and power because He has created all things, for it was His will that they are and were created (Rev. 5:12).

The focus of chapter 4 is the beginning, the Alpha of God. The God of the universe who created all things is the One who holds creation together. The words of all wisdom are formulated by combining the individual symbols of the alphabet. These symbols and their meaning had their origin with God who placed them in the cosmos in the form of constellations for man to learn and copy. The 4 beasts and the 24 elders are part of this eternal, divine order that God has created to serve Him, and are recorded in the four winds of the cosmos.

The constellations were originally designed so the sun, at the time of the summer solstice, was in the middle of *Leo*, the Lion; at the time of the spring equinox in the middle of *Taurus*, the Bull; and at the time of the winter solstice, in the middle of *Aquarius*, the Man. The fourth point, which held the sun at the autumnal equinox, was a flying eagle, *Aquila*,[7] representing the wounded heel, at the tail of the serpents in the constellation *Scorpio*. (See Figure 4 on page 5.)

Therefore, as in the vision of Revelation 4:7, in the constellation figures (the Lion, the Ox, the Man, and the wounded Eagle of Scorpio) we have a representation of the orders of the heavenly angels and the gospel story.

The 24 elders are figured in the remaining 24 constellations of the lunar zodiac that together make up the 28 constellations, of which the moon traverses every month from new to full moon during the course of a lunar year.[8]

"The 28 steps are called the *Mansions of the Moon*."[9] This gives evidence then, that before the written revelation of God's Word, God wrote the witness of His divine order in the constellations of the stars. This witness has been lost to the perversions of mythology and astrology.

The overall significance of this vision symbolically depicts the One sitting on the throne in the center of the universe as the One who created and regulates the cosmos. Therefore the constellations of the primeval days of creation represent the angels of God, through which God regulates the universe. There is nothing in the patterns themselves to indicate the meaning attached to them; the meanings were revealed first and were then associated with groups of stars.

"Like symbolic road signs, the meaning is first revealed and then the symbol."[10] As writing became the standard medium of communication, the original message of the constellations was lost to astrology and mythology. The stars of the constellation tell the redemption story, while the names of the constellations represent the orders of the universe that are charged with the oversight of God's revealed will. This is why angels are often referred to as "*stars*" (Rev. 8:10-11; 9:1; 12:4). It is a leftover from the primeval witness of the stars.

Christ, whose face is as the sun (Rev. 10:1), holds the seven stars or seven angels of the Church in His right hand (Rev. 1:16,20; 2:1; 3:1). Man is "without excuse"; creation and its order declare the glory of God (Rom. 1:20).

The sum of what I am saying here is that when God created the universe, He created it in such a way that it would declare His existence and glory. If you want evidence that God exists, go out on a clear dark night and look into the heavens. The order and design of the constellations declare His very power and Godhead (Rom. 1:20).

John, who understood the language of the stars and planets, incorporated its confirming message into The Revelation. Therefore, the crowns of the elders probably represent positions of authority held by those angels who rule over some part of God's created universe. The gold crowns are specifically victor's crowns [*stephanos*], however, and indicate that those wearing them have won some type of victory with the God of Heaven.

The general view that the 24 elders are a representative group of the Church or Israel as it is linked to the 24 orders of priests found in the Old Testament, is an insufficient conclusion. The case for believing that the 24 elders are representative of the Raptured Church in Heaven is built on the premise that the first seal is the beginning event of the tribulation period (Rev. 6:1).

Therefore, if this passage is regarded as chronological, then it would seem to eliminate the possibility that the 24 elders are angels. At this point, they have already been judged and rewarded with their crowns. The conclusion is then made that these 24 elders represent the rewarded Church in Heaven.

The same conclusion is given as an argument for refuting the idea that these 24 elders are representatives of Israel. In addition to this, the white robes and crowns are paralleled to the white robes and crowns promised to the Church for rewards of endurance (Rev. 3:5; 2:10).

Pretribulation expositors have used this argument and the absence of the Church after chapter 3 as proof that they are raptured prior to the beginning of the "Day of the Lord." However, the angels of Heaven are also fighting a spiritual battle on behalf of believers. Examples of this are clearly found in Scripture with angels warring against princes who belong to the legions of satan (Dan. 10:13,20; 12:1; Jude 9; Rev. 12:7-10).

The crowns that the elders possess could be their reward for the victories won while fighting heavenly battles. Recent New Testament scholarship has tended to abandon the traditional interpretation in favor of identification of these elders as angels.

N.B. Stonehouse concludes his support by saying that "these elders are angels [by sighting that the] late expositors, do not appear to do justice to the implications of the current critical text, which records a song celebrating the redemption of a diverse multitude, *but which evidently ascribes the song to beings who are distinguished from the redeemed.*"[11] Probably most New Testament scholars today interpret the elders as angels.[12] The 24 elders are angels.

Indeed, the interpretation of the Greek text of Revelation 5:10 from the third edition from the United Bible Society should be translated, "And he made **them** [*autous*] to our God kings and priests **and they will reign** [*basileusousiv*] upon the earth."

The song that the 24 elders are singing is about someone other than themselves. The song is about what the Lord Jesus Christ did for the holy ones, the saints whom He redeemed, and whose prayers they were offering up to the Lord. This does associate them with the Church, but it does not prove that these 24 elders represent the Church, especially the Raptured Church. Such a position is, at best, an assertion, and we must be careful not to build upon such a shaky foundation as this. Therefore, the conclusion that the 24 elders are representatives of the Raptured Church must be set aside as a key proof of a pretribulation Rapture.

Since this section of Revelation is focused on the sovereignty of God over His creation, we might do well to conclude that these 24 elders have been before the throne of God since creation.

The sons of God are found presenting themselves before the Lord (Job 1:6; 2:1). Who are these sons of God? Could they be the same 24 elders that we see in Revelation 4 and 5? Among them, but not necessarily numbered with them, was satan accusing Job?

It makes much more sense to look at the 24 elders as commanding angels of the Lord. Maybe these 24 elders are the dedicated harpers of God that play His songs (Rev. 5:8; 14:2).

The bottom line, however, is that it is totally unnecessary to prove and propagate that these 24 elders are the representatives of the Raptured Church to maintain a strong pretribulation position. In fact, by giving up this shaky position, we can open up the true chronology of the events recorded in the Book of Revelation.

Chapter 5 of Revelation focuses on the redeeming work of the Lamb. It displays His work of redemption that qualifies Him to open the seals and in turn open the book (Rev. 5:5). The fact that John cries and laments over the failure to find a man worthy of opening the book must mean that his hopes of redemption and reward must somehow be connected to the opening of the seals and/or the reading of the scroll.

John then describes the Lamb in the midst of the throne of God. The Lamb appears as One who was slain, having seven horns and seven eyes, which are the seven Spirits of God (Rev. 5:6). The number seven here indicates the fullness of the Spirit of God that the Lamb possesses upon His arrival at the throne of God, which takes place when Jesus ascends to Heaven after His resurrection.

Jesus received the Spirit of God without measure (Jn. 3:31-34) and He was sealed by the Father (Jn. 6:27). "*For in Him dwelleth all the fulness of the Godhead* [deity] *bodily*" (Col. 2:9). If Jesus Christ (both one hundred percent man and one hundred percent God) did not return to His Father's throne with His sinlessness and His deity, He would not have been qualified to receive the book from His Father to open the seals. Thus, He could not have sent the Comforter (Holy Spirit), the One who empowers the believers to overcome the world.

This is exactly what the devil tried to prevent many times by tempting the Lord Jesus Christ in His earthly ministry, but of course failed. John is shown a twofold heavenly vision in chapters 4 and 5, spanning from creation to the days of final judgment. Chapter 4 is of the Lord God Almighty, Creator of everything that exists. He is sitting on His throne with voices, thunderings, and lightnings proceeding forth and with the seven Spirits before the throne—burning as seven lamps. In chapter 5, John observes the slain Lamb coming forward and receiving the scroll from the Father who sits on the throne.

Finally, both the Son and the Father are united again in the heavens at His throne (Rev. 5:13). Once again, Christ has the glory, honor, and power that He had always enjoyed with the Father before the beginning of what is understood as *temporal time, space, and matter.*

It was this position that He left behind when He left the glories of Heaven to redeem man to God (Jn. 17:5). Therefore, John was witnessing the throne of God without the Son of God present and then he witnessed the return of the Son of God after His victory on Calvary.

The events in Revelation 4 and 5 are not necessarily chronological to the previous chapters in anything other than that the vision was simply what John saw or was shown next. The things that John saw in chapters 4 and 5 would prepare him and us to understand what is revealed next in the visions that immediately followed—the opening of the seals and the trumpet judgments.

These things follow the events that he had already seen (Rev. 4:1) and further explain some of the previous visions as well. Chapters 4 and 5 of Revelation help us to appreciate the long redemptive history, patience, sacrifice, and sovereignty of our great God and Savior, the Lord Jesus Christ (Tit. 2:13).

These two chapters also help us to understand the significance of Chapter 6 and how the opening of the seals relate to the Church, the Body of Christ, who were left in the world to continue the work of the gospel. At the same time, God uses the "time" to purify and sanctify them who are truly born-again sons of God through faith in Jesus Christ.

End Notes

1. Thomas, *Revelation 1–7: An Exegetical Commentary*, p. 41.
2. Ibid., p. 53.
3. Ibid., p. 105.
4. Ibid., p. 105.
5. Ibid., p. 151. (See also F.J.A. Hort, *The Apocalypse of St. John*, [Macmillian, 1908]; and Isbon T. Beckwith, *The Apocalypse of John*, [London: Macmillian, 1919].)

6. Ibid.
7. Maunder, *The Astronomy of the Bible*, p. 167.
8. Ibid., p. 255.
9. Seiss, *The Gospel in the Stars or Primeval Astronomy*, p. 364.
10. Fleming, *God's Voice in the Stars*, p. 15.
11. N.B. Stonehouse, "Paul Before the Areopagus," *Westminster Press Theological Journal*, Vol. 20 (Nov. 1957), pp. 112-114.
12. John F. Walvoord, *The Revelation of Jesus Christ*, (Chicago, IL: Moody Press, 1993), p. 118.

Chapter 6

The Seals

The Opening of the First Seal

The opening of the first seal is the next recorded event following the ascension of Christ to His Father's throne. This chronology supports the fact that the opening of the first seal is the sending of the Holy Spirit into the world (the seven Spirits of God to do His will in the Church and in the world).

In the Church, the Spirit would seal, teach, comfort, and guide in all truth as well as teach about the trials, judgments, and rewards to come.

> *And I will pray the Father, and He shall give you another Comforter, that He may abide with you for ever; even the Spirit of truth...I will not leave you comfortless: I will come to you. ... But* ***the Comforter, which is the Holy Ghost, whom the Father will send in My name, He shall teach you all things...*** (John 14:16-18,26).

Jesus, in His concern for those about to seduce the Church away from truth, reminds the disciples that all believers will receive the anointing of the Holy Spirit. The abiding Holy Spirit "*teacheth* [us] *of all things*" (1 Jn. 2:27) and will help the believer overcome the lies of the world and remain in Christ with confidence and without shame unto His appearing (1 Jn. 2:27-28).

In the world the Spirit will work through believers to convince or convict the world of its sin, righteousness, and judgment (Jn. 16:6-11). He convicts of sin, because they believe not in Jesus Christ; and of righteousness because the world rejected and crucified Him. Yet, He ascended to His Father victoriously. Finally, the Spirit convicts of judgment because the prince of this world is judged (Jn. 16:9-11).

The world is not convinced that a judgment is coming. As such, part of the ministry of the Spirit of God is to overcome the world's resistance to truth. God does not receive any pleasure out of the death of the wicked. God desires that "all should come to repentance" (2 Pet. 3:9). God has given the world abundant opportunities to hear the gospel and be saved before the sentence of wrath is carried out.

It was expedient for Christ to go to the Father to receive the scroll and to open the first seal, thereby sending the Holy Spirit into the world to begin the final phase of God's redemptive program, the Age of the Church, the beginning of the Kingdom of God. "The declaration of Revelation 5:7 consummates the revelation of His person and authority. He takes the book out of the right hand of the One (God the Father) sitting on the throne."[1]

The most conclusive proof that the first seal of Revelation 6:1-2 is the sending of the Holy Spirit and the beginning of the Church, can be found in the twofold prophecies of Joel 2:28-32 and their partial fulfillment in Acts 2:16-21. Both of these passages reveal the beginning and concluding "days of the Church" on earth. The end of the "days of the Church" will be marked by increased volcanic activity, earthquakes, a darkening of the sun, and a blood-red full moon in eclipse, "*...before that great and notable day of the Lord come*" (Acts 2:20). The first and sixth seals, Revelation 6:1-2,12-17 mark the beginning and end of the Dispensation of Grace.

For example, consider Acts 2:16-21:

> *But this is that which was spoken by the prophet Joel; and it shall come to pass in the last days, saith God, **I will pour out of My Spirit upon all flesh: and your sons and your daughters shall prophesy, and your young men shall see visions, and your old men shall dream dreams: and on My servants and on My***

> ***handmaidens I will pour out in those days*** [Church days] *of My Spirit; and they shall prophesy: and I will shew* ***wonders in heaven above, and signs in the earth beneath*** [beginning of sorrows]*; blood, and fire, and vapour of smoke:* ***the sun shall be turned into darkness, and the moon into blood*** [pangs of birth], ***before that great and notable day of the Lord come****: and it shall come to pass, that whosoever shall call on the name of the Lord shall be saved* [raptured] (Acts 2:16-21).

The events in Acts mark the beginning and the end of the Church Dispensation. The Church began on the Day of Pentecost with the sending of the Holy Spirit.

> *And when the day of Pentecost was fully come* [when the first seal was opened]...*And suddenly there came a sound from heaven* [noise of thunder when the first seal was opened] *as of a* ***rushing mighty wind*** [the arrival of the Holy Spirit sent from Heaven], *and it filled all the house where they were sitting* (Acts 2:1-2).

But Acts 2 also gives information that has not been totally fulfilled. Verse 19 parallels the "beginning of sorrows" recorded in the Gospels. "*And I will shew wonders in heaven above, and signs in the earth beneath...*" (Acts 2:19; see also Mt. 24:6-8; Mk. 13:7-8; Lk. 21:9-11).

Acts 2:20 parallels the sixth seal of Revelation 6:12-14. Therefore, Acts 2:16-21 conclusively supports the belief that the opening of the first seal was the sending of the Holy Spirit, and that the sixth seal marks the pretribulation Rapture of the Church and the beginning of the "Day of the Lord."

Why include these signs of a darkened sun and a blood-red moon with a prophecy that indicates the beginning of the Church? They mark the end of the Church Dispensation!

> *And I saw when the Lamb opened one of the seals, and I heard,* ***as it were the noise of thunder****, one of the four beasts saying, Come and see. And I saw, and behold a white horse: and He that sat on him had a bow; and a crown was given unto Him: and He*

> *went forth conquering, and to conquer. ... And I beheld when He had opened the sixth seal, and, lo, there was a great earthquake; and the sun became black as sackcloth of hair, and the moon became as blood; and the stars of heaven fell unto the earth, even as a fig tree casteth her untimely figs, when she is shaken of a* ***mighty wind*** [this is the departing of the Holy Spirit with the Church, or the Rapture]. *And the heaven departed as a scroll when it is rolled together; and every mountain and island were moved out of their places* (Revelation 6:1-2,12-14).

The seals represent the tribulation that will be in the world because it rejects the ministry of the Holy Spirit. "*And the way of peace have they not known*" (Rom. 3:17). The seals are the sword of division, the gospel message that will cause unrest between kingdoms.

> *Think not that I am come to send peace on earth: I came not to send peace,* ***but a sword.*** *For I am come to set a man at variance against his father, and the daughter against her mother, and the daughter in law against her mother in law. A man's foes shall be they of his own household. He that loveth father or mother more than Me is not worthy of Me: and he that loveth son or daughter more than Me is not worthy of Me. And he that taketh not his cross, and followeth after Me, is not worthy of Me. He that findeth his life shall lose it: and he that loseth his life for My sake shall find it* (Matthew 10:34-39).

Seals one through six cover the days of the Church on earth. The Church of Ephesus, the first church in Revelation, to the Church of Philadelphia, the sixth church, parallel this same period.

The seventh seal introduces the world and the seventh church of the unsaved Loadiceans to seven years of tribulation after the Rapture

Old Beliefs Die Hard

For too long now, it has been assumed that the opening of the first seal has intimated that this was the beginning of the "Day of the Lord" and the start of Daniel's Seventieth Week. This assumption has caused much confusion as to the order and sequence of the seals, trumpets, and vials of the Book of Revelation.

There are at least 16 views regarding the chronology of the seals, trumpets, and vial judgments. For example, David Hunt, who for the most part does an excellent job in supporting the pretribulation position of the Rapture, says, "To place the Rapture at the end of Revelation 6 just prior to the opening of the seventh seal by Christ is an '*impossible timing.*' " Hunt goes on to recount how the seal judgments take peace from the world and cause famine and war. But he makes the unfortunate mistake of not stopping there because that is all that the text says. Instead he adds, "and unprecedented upheavals of nature."[2] (Emphasis added.)

The exaggeration by Hunt is to help validate the assumption that seals two, three, four, and five cause unprecedented upheavals. If this were the case, it would then support the position that the tribulation period begins with the opening of the first seal, but it is inconsistent with the greater body of truth. It is interesting that David Hunt forgets to mention the first seal. Why? There is no judgment or woe associated with the first seal.

This distinction should not be overlooked but expounded upon. It is also important to point out that it is not until the *sixth* seal is opened that "unprecedented upheavals" take place in "nature." This is the seal that I believe contains the Rapture. The judgments contained in seals two, three, and four are nothing new, but are contemporary events of every age.

The world has never known peace or the way of peace (Rom. 3:17). Jesus said that He came not to send peace on the earth but a "*sword*" of division (Mt. 10:34-36). But at the same time Jesus says to believers, "*Peace I leave with you, My peace I give unto you...*" (Jn. 14:27).

Famines, wars, and pestilence continue to be a part of our history, but they are growing in scope and magnitude with each passing century. According to the Carter foundation, there are over 133 wars in the world. Undoubtedly, these conditions will worsen as we get closer to the "Day of the Lord" and the Rapture. Some writers are partaking in some deliberate exaggeration for the effect of proving an assertion. However, the effect is blinding many from the real truth of the seals.

"I once was blind, but now I see." By stepping back, taking a fresh look at prophecy, and admitting that there were some very broad assumptions being made by pretribulationists, it became clear to me that substantial proof texts for a pretribulation Rapture were being overlooked. As a result, I determined to compare Scripture with Scripture and let God's Word interpret itself, seeking only the truth.

The God of the Bible is not the author of confusion; "people" are. There has been too much confusion and reliance on subconscious protection schemes designed to prove or protect a certain position. Hunt is right to refute the prewrath position of Marvin Rosenthal, but he does it for the wrong reasons. Rosenthal, Hunt, Walvoord, and many others have assumed that seal "one" begins the seven-year count down, but it does not! (Please do not mistake my focus on Dave Hunt as a personal attack. I do not want to wound anyone. I respect and recommend Dave Hunt's books and only use this example to show how easy it is for very good men to assume something to be true in prophecy and have it affect one's understanding of end-time chronology.)

The judgments contained in seals two, three, and four parallel what Jesus called "*the beginning of sorrows*" (Mt. 24:8). (See Figure 1 on page 2.) Nation against nation and kingdom against kingdom is equivalent to the sword of seal two or the taking away of peace.

Famines clearly equate with the third seal. Seal four, which is primarily death, equates with the pestilence of Matthew 24:7. The earthquake parallel of Matthew 24:7 is found within the sixth seal. Jesus called these "the beginning of birth pangs."

The preferable placement of the sixth seal, then, is at the end of the birth pangs. So the events of the sixth seal are best understood as preliminary to what Jesus places immediately after the "beginning of sorrows" and before the opening of the seventh seal and the progression of God's wrath.

Israel's entrance into her time of trouble will be preceded by birth pangs (Rev. 12; Is. 13:7-9; 66:8). The seals are the birth pangs and the history of Israel's travail during the history of the Church. The pangs of sorrow began when Christ was crucified and rejected by His own and as the Church was conceived.

For those who doubt the validity of this, consider the fourth seal. The fourth seal addresses death while Matthew 24:7 calls it pestilence. By comparing Scripture with Scripture, it can be easily understood that these seals are relative to the history of the Church Age. Matthew 24 correlates the seals and the letters to the seven churches.

Understanding Matthew 24:1-31

The interpretation of Matthew chapter 24 is critical to any study of prophetic Scripture. The similarity between Matthew 24:6-8 and Revelation chapter 6 has been recognized by some leading scholars to be potentially very significant. This is especially true of the current studies now being conducted by dispensational scholars.[3]

Therefore, it will be necessary to demonstrate how the chronology of the seals, the Rapture, the sealing of the 144,000 (which are 12,000 Jews from each of the 12 tribes of Israel that will be sealed by God and thus divinely protected throughout the tribulation period), and the start of the tribulation period reconciles with Matthew 24.

Matthew 24 begins with Jesus departing the temple area and resting with His disciples on the Mount of Olives. Jesus instructs the disciples concerning the destruction of the temple, "*See ye not all these things? verily I say unto you, There shall not be left here one stone upon another, that shall not be thrown down*" (Mt. 24:2).

This generates three questions among the disciples: (1) When shall these things be? (2) What will be the sign of Thy coming? (3) When will the end of the world come? (Mt. 24:3) These three questions are answered in the text that follows.

The first question concerns the destruction of the temple. Verses 4 and 5 instruct the disciples to be careful of deception by false Christs. This clearly describes the atmosphere surrounding Jerusalem at the time of the temple's destruction in A.D. 70 by the Roman General Titus. "Numerous false prophets deluded the people at this time. They were hired by the tyrants to urge the people to wait for help from God, to keep them from deserting."[4]

In verse 6 Jesus continues to instruct the disciples about the news of war and all the rumors that will encompass these wars. The rumors, no doubt, will involve those who will be declaring the end of the world and the coming of the Messiah. Jesus clearly tells them that these things must come to pass, but the end is not yet. The end that Jesus is referring to is the end of the world and that answers questions one and three.

Jesus assures the disciples that although they will experience internal and external troubles in Jerusalem, these things are not the end of all things, nor the sign of His coming to power.

A Brief History of Israel

With the destruction of the temple in A.D. 70, the nation of Israel and the world passed into the age of the sixth worldly kingdom (Rev. 17:10). This kingdom is a kingdom within the Church Age. The Church was officially conceived on the Day of Pentecost, but when the nation rejected Jesus as their Messiah, Jerusalem was judged. God had sent forth His Spirit into the world to indwell believers and help them overcome sin, self-righteousness, and disbelief.

Because Israel first rejected Jesus Christ as her King Messiah, God allowed the horsemen that He had commissioned to this age, to destroy Israel as His Word foretold. "*For a small moment have I forsaken thee: but with great mercies will I gather thee*" (see Is. 54:6-8; Rom. 10:21; 11:11).

> *For the wrath [orge, anger] of God is revealed from heaven against all ungodliness and unrighteousness of men, who hold the truth in unrighteousness; because that which may be known of God is manifest in them: for God hath shewed it unto them* (Romans 1:18-19).

Israel had received the Word of God through the prophets, yet she knew not the time of her visitation.

> *And when He was come near, He beheld the city, and wept over it, saying, If thou hadst known, even thou, at least in this thy day, the things which belong unto thy peace! but now they are hid from thine eyes* [Rom. 1:21-22]. *For the days shall come upon thee, that thine enemies shall cast a trench about thee, and compass thee round, and keep thee in on every side* [Titus in A.D. 70], *and shall lay thee even with the ground, and thy children within thee; and they shall not leave in thee one stone upon another; because thou knewest not the time of thy visitation* (Luke 19:41-44).

This is why Jesus said, "*For nation shall rise against nation, and kingdom against kingdom: and there shall be famines, and pestilences, and earthquakes, in divers places*" (Mt. 24:7). This passage clearly parallels seals two, three, and four of Revelation chapter 6.

Israel first lost her internal peace with many factions positioning for power. Fighting broke out in May of A.D. 66 in Caesarea between Jews and Greeks over a land dispute and the mock sacrifice of a bird by a zealous Greek. The mistreatment of the Jews by Florus, Governor of Sebaste, infuriated Jerusalem. Florus later marched on Jerusalem with the intent to drive the Jews to revolt, that he might "pillage the city."[5]

Rebellion grew throughout Israel and the nation split over King Agrippa's insistence that the people obey Florus until Caesar sent a successor. The palace in Jerusalem was attacked by a revolutionary party that refused to listen to follow the leadership of the corrupted temple priest.[6] Skirmishes broke out all over Israel and the sounds and rumors of war were everywhere. Josephus and his men attacked Sepphoris in the spring of A.D. 66.

This attack infuriated the Roman Emporer Nero. He sent his troops into Galilee and killed anyone "capable of bearing arms."[7] Joppa, Gamala, and almost all of Galilee fell under the bloody sword of the relentless Roman army. Rome itself was rocked by insurrection and internal fighting. During all of this, Christianity continued to spread throughout the Roman empire.

Bands of robbers roamed the country side, stealing and killing. Indeed, the province of Judea was torn by civil dissension as parties for peace and war fought for supremacy in every city. "They eventually ruined the city, consuming those supplies that might have been sufficient for the combatants, and bringing on the people the miseries of sedition and famine."[8]

Simion (son of Giora) was proclaimed as the "savior and guardian" of the city in the spring of A.D. 69. This Simion was just another tyrant, even worse than the tyrant John that ruled before him. "In Rome...the Emperor Galba had been murdered and Otho succeeded, but Vitellius was chosen emperor by legions of Germany."[9] Eventually, Vespasian was acclaimed as emperor. With civil unrest settling down in Rome, Vespasian sent his son Titus in December of A.D. 69 "to crush [the city of] Jerusalem."[10]

The city was so divided that three warring camps "burned each others food supply" while the city was soon to be besieged by Roman soldiers. Eventually Jerusalem would be destroyed by a "self-imposed famine."[11] "Titus camped with his army about four miles from Jerusalem near Gibeah. Taking 600 horsemen with him, he rode forward to reconnoiter the city's strength and ascertain the mood of the Jews, for he had learned, as indeed was the fact, that the people wanted peace but were dominated by rebels."[12]

When Titus later besieged the city and the siege raged on, famine raged through Jerusalem as well. Rebels took all the food they could find from homes, "while the poor starved to death by the thousands."[13] "*A measure of wheat now sold for a talent*," and when it was no longer possible to gather herbs after the city was walled in, some "searched the sewers for offal or ate cow dung."[14] (Emphasis added.)

This brief account of Israel's history from A.D. 66 to 70 clearly demonstrates that Israel suffered from a threefold judgment:

1. Peace was taken from the land and fighting broke out (seal two: Rev. 6:3-4). "Little disagreement exists over the general nature of the second seal. It brings war, internal strife, and international and civil strife to the world (Swete; Charles; Beckwith; Walvoord)."[15]
2. Famine was in the land; three measures of wheat sold for a penny—but the church prospered, "*hurt not the oil and the wine*" (seal three: Rev. 6:5-6).
3. The Roman siege of Jerusalem caused the divided factions to kill each other, famine to increase, and death by the sword to multiply (the judgment of seal four: Rev. 6:7-8).

The seals are the agents of God's divine power and carry out His will in the world. The seals relate to the commissioning of the seven Spirits of God and the divine work that is to be carried out during the Church Age.

Seals two, three, and four have been opened and the riders of the horses of the Apocalypse have been commissioned to purge out unbelief and unrighteousness. These horsemen began their mission with Israel and continue today to purge out sin and judge unrighteousness in the world. They collectively warn of the ultimate judgment that will follow this Age of Grace.

Judgment will be especially true for those nations that have heard the truth of the gospel and continue to reject it. The Christian Church and the gospel first spread through parts of the Middle East and Africa, yet most of these nations today are not Christian. This is why most of them are only Third World countries today and suffering poverty, internal unrest, famine, wars, and pestilences—they and their fathers have rejected the truth of the gospel.

God does not bless disobedience. Somalia and Rwanda will never prosper and overcome its famine and unrest until the gospel of truth is accepted. Even if the United Nations pours 50 billion dollars in aid into Somalia, it will not result in any lasting change.

America has been historically blessed because it was founded on the truth of the Christian gospel. America has also been a haven for the gospel and a bastion of support for Israel, but all of this is beginning to change.

> *Boast not against the branches. But if thou boast, thou bearest not the root, but the root thee. Thou wilt say then, The branches were broken off, that I might be grafted in. Well; because of unbelief they were broken off...Be not highminded, but fear: for if God spared not the natural branches* [Israel is the natural branch], *take heed lest He also spare not thee* (Romans 11:18-21).

The same atmosphere that existed in Israel prior to the fall of A.D. 70 is once again making headlines in the world. Deep divisions exist between those who want peace at any price and those who want to cleanse the land of every non-Jew. The United States, the only superpower left, like Rome in A.D. 66, is decaying from within and is on the verge of moral, civil, and economic collapse.

When the U.S. collapses (and it will collapse by design), this will stimulate Arab nations to attack Israel. The Lord is setting the stage for the seven years of Daniel's tribulation and the signing of a seven-year peace treaty between Israel and its Arab neighbors. Economic, political, and social orders and conditions are in chaos in the world, but these conditions will get much worse, and very soon.

In verses 4 through 8 of Matthew 24 Jesus disclosed to the disciples the characteristics of the Church Age from Pentecost to the present. Nations are still rising up against nations and the kingdom of darkness is still rising up against the kingdom of light—the Kingdom of Heaven. Jesus described these judgments as the beginning of birth pangs. The questions from the disciples to Jesus were centered around their concern for the coming of the Kingdom of God. The disciples at this juncture did not understand that Jesus was first going to die, be resurrected, and ascend to Heaven. They were not expecting Him to leave and then return. They were asking Him about the Kingdom. Just before Jesus ascended to Heaven the disciples asked Him again, "*Lord, wilt Thou at this time restore again the kingdom to Israel*?" Jesus' response reveals that *it was not for them "to know the times or the seasons, which the Father hath put in His own power"* (Acts 1:6-7).

The Lord had revealed many wonders to the disciples, but revealing the times in general (*chronos*) or the seasons (*kairos*), specific times of the Kingdom, was not going to be one of them. Had Jesus done so, He would have destroyed the hope of His imminent return. However, Jesus did promise to send them the Holy Spirit (the opening of the first seal), who would enable them to go unto the uttermost parts of the world as His witnesses (Acts 1:7-8).

The opening of the first seal sent the Holy Spirit to believers and empowered them to overcome the trials and problems of the world (Rev. 6:1-2). It was not for them to know, but when that season and that time does come, believers will know because they are "*not in darkness*" (1 Thess. 5:1-9).

We know that we will be rescued because God has not appointed us to wrath (*orge*). "The Rapture *will not* come as a thief in the night to true believers"[16] because believers are not of the night. We are children of light. The coming of the Lord as a thief in the night is for those who are in unbelief and, therefore, darkness concerning the Second Coming of Christ.

In Matthew 24:9-14, Jesus speaks to what will befall believers from the beginning of Pentecost to the day of the Rapture. What Jesus describes in verses 9 through 14 of Matthew chapter 24 fits perfectly with the characteristics of the letters to the seven churches.

The comparisons on the following pages show significant parallels to warrant the conclusion that these six verses in Matthew 24:9-14 are, in fact, referring to the Church Age.

Compare verse 9 with the Church of Ephesus, which represents the late Apostolic Church. Note the significant agreement. "*Then* [or now] *shall they deliver you up to be afflicted, and shall kill you: and ye shall be hated of all nations for My name's sake* (Mt. 24:9). "*And* [thou] *hast borne, and hast* ***patience,*** *and for* ***My name's sake*** *hast laboured, and hast not fainted* " (Rev. 2:3).

> "They had so persevered (*dia to onoma mou*), '*because of My name.*'...The name of Christ [is the] gospel revelation through which He makes Himself known...The identical phrase occurs in Matthew 10:22 and 24:9 in context where Christ's persecuted followers were engaged in spreading the gospel. Before leaving earth Jesus had predicted the very thing that Ephesian Christendom was now experiencing."[17]

The parallel passage in Luke 21:12-19 contains more detail on the first two verses of this section of Matthew. Luke 21:12, 17 indicates the tribulations that believers will endure is for "*My name's sake,*" but Luke 21:19 ends with, "*In your patience possess ye your souls.*" The Apostolic Church has dramatically fulfilled the prophecy of Matthew 24:9 and Luke 21:12-19. The Apostolic Church is identified with and as the Church of Ephesus in Revelation 2:1-11 and was persecuted and delivered up to synagogue leaders, cast into prisons, and brought before kings and rulers for "*My name's sake.*"

They were given wisdom beyond their ability to speak and their adversaries were not able to "*gainsay*" or "*speak against it*" (see Lk. 21:15, Acts 4:14). They were betrayed by parents, brothers, relatives, and friends. Some were even put to death (Lk. 21:12-17). All of this was literally fulfilled in the lives of the first Church fathers (Acts 4:1-21; 5:17-23; 7:54-61; 25:1-27).

The churches of Revelation chapters 2 and 3 represent Church history. These Church ages or periods overlap and intertwine just as the root system of any well-aged organic plant.

Next, if we compare Matthew 24:14, "*And this gospel of the kingdom shall be preached in all the world...*" to the promises made to the Church of Philadelphia, we note the open door promise. This open door is believed by some to be a final door of opportunity for missionaries to preach the gospel to every nation.[18] I concur with this conclusion. This door is open today, but we are beginning to hear sounds and see signs of it closing.

The comparisons of Matthew 24, Mark 13, and Luke 21 are significant for their difference as well as for their agreements. It is clear that the desolation of Luke 21:20 is different from the "Abomination of Desolations" spoken of by Daniel and recorded in Matthew and Mark. Luke speaks of a "*wrath upon this people*," not the world (Lk. 21:23). He also records the prophecy of the captivity of Jerusalem "*into all nations*" that will continue "*until the times of the Gentiles be fulfilled*" (Lk. 21:24).

The difference in the passage that follows, however, is most significant because it only says that there will be signs in the heavens, while the parallel passages in Matthew 24:29 and Mark 13:24 say respectively, "*Immediately after the tribulation of those days shall the sun be darkened...*" and "*But in those days, after that tribulation, the sun shall be darkened....*"

Jesus did not reference the prophecy of the darkening of the sun to the destruction of Jerusalem in Luke because He knew that a very long Church Age was to follow, which would be filled with relative tribulation for active believers (Jn. 16:33) and be finalized with the fulfillment of the prophecies labeled as the "beginning of sorrows." (See Figure 2 on page 3.)

The "beginning of sorrows" ends just before and with the beginning of the "Day of the Lord" and Daniel's Seventieth Week. Daniel's "Week" is a focus on Israel's redemption and ***only with the true Church already gone—raptured***—can this be possible. Luke, while giving the same list of these sorrows, adds that there will be fearful sights and great signs appearing in the heaven.

But Luke fails to label his listing as the "beginning of sorrows" like Matthew and Mark did. Why? The answer is because the addition of sights in the heavens takes us beyond the "beginning of sorrows" and into the beginning of the "Day of the Lord."

> *Behold, the day of the Lord cometh, cruel both with wrath and fierce anger, to lay the land desolate: and He shall destroy the sinners thereof out of it. For the stars of heaven and the constellations thereof shall not give their light: the sun shall be darkened in His going forth, and the moon shall not cause her light to shine* (Isaiah 13:9-10).

Those not recognizing these truths will confuse their conclusions. There are diverse tribulations referred to in the Bible and they must be distinguished from one another using all the tools of exegesis. Luke 21:20-24 is making a clear reference to the tribulations of the Church, the destruction of Jerusalem in A.D. 70, and the coming of the "Day of the Lord" with "signs in the heavens."

Matthew and Mark make reference to the Church and its 2,000 years of varied tribulation, while looking for Christ's return; to the second half of the great tribulation, involving Judea and the world; and to the signs of the coming of the "Day of the Lord."

The beginning of the first three-and-one-half years of Daniel's Seventieth Week is referenced in these Gospel accounts with the appearance of signs in the heavens. The first half of Daniel's "Week" is a transitional period in which God begins to use the witness of the two witnesses of Revelation 11 to convince Israel and the world of their sin, lack of righteousness, and of the judgment that is scheduled for the world.

With the Church raptured to Heaven, God's witness in the world is removed. But the two witnesses, with the 144,000, will take over this responsibility.

The Laodicean Church represents that part of the Christian Body that "*is not saved*" and will be left behind to go through the first half of the tribulation to try its works and righteous deeds. The fires of the first four trumpet judgments will reveal their nakedness (Rev. 3:18) and their need to trust in Jesus as their personal Lord and Savior before satan is cast out of Heaven and confined to earth for the final judgments of God (Rev. 9:1; Rev. 12:9).

Trusting in Christ at that time will be at great personal risk and expense. Therefore, it is better to come to one's knees now and escape the revealed and revealing judgments of God. "*For whosoever shall call upon the name of the Lord shall be saved*" (Rom. 10:13).

With these comparisons, it is possible to conclude that Matthew 24:9-14, is clearly referring to a time within Church history. This history will conclude with the Rapture, which is not indicated in the text until Matthew 24:27: "*For as the lightning cometh...so shall also the coming of the Son of man be.*"

> *In a moment, in the twinkling of an eye, at the last trump: for the trumpet shall sound, and the dead shall be raised incorruptible, and we shall be changed* (1 Corinthians 15:52).

These truths have been hidden until the season of the Lord's return. The time of Jesus' return is near! As a believer I see the signs all around us and I expect the Lord's return to be in my lifetime.

Let's compare these passages to the seven churches.

> Matthew 24:9
> *Then shall they deliver you up to be afflicted, and shall kill you:* ***and ye shall be hated of all nations for My name's sake.***

Luke 21:12-15 expands on this thought. This is the beginning of the Church and starts off as almost completely Jewish. Soon it transforms into a Jewish and Gentile Church with the work of Paul.

> Church of Ephesus
> *I know thy works, and thy labour, and thy patience, and how thou canst not bear them which are evil: and thou hast tried them which say they are apostles, and are not, and hast found them*

liars: and hast borne, and hast patience, and ***for My name's sake*** *hast laboured, and hast not fainted* (Revelation 2:2-3).

Matthew 24:10
And then shall ***many be offended, and shall betray one another, and shall hate one another.***

Luke 21:16-19 expands on the problems that the Smyrna Church would face. These first two churches are transitional from Jew to Gentile Church.

Church of Smyrna
I know thy works, and ***tribulation****, and poverty, (but thou art rich) and* ***I know the blasphemy of them which say they are Jews, and are not****, but are the synagogue of Satan. Fear none of those things which thou shalt suffer: behold, the devil shall* ***cast some of you into prison, that ye may be tried; and ye shall have tribulation*** *ten days: be thou faithful unto death, and I will give thee a crown of life* (Revelation 2:9-10).

Matthew 24:11
And many ***false prophets*** *shall rise, and shall* ***deceive*** *many.*

Church of Pergamos
*I know thy works, and where thou dwellest, even where Satan's seat is: and thou holdest fast My name, and has not denied My faith...****But I have a few things against thee, because thou hast there them that hold the doctrine of Balaam, who taught Balac to cast a stumblingblock****...* (Revelation 2:13-14).

Matthew 24:12
And because ***iniquity shall abound****, the love of many shall wax cold.*

Church of Thyatira
*I know thy works...****I have a few things against thee...that woman Jezebel, which calleth herself a prophetess, to teach and to seduce My servants to commit fornication...and she***

repented not. *... And I will kill her children with death...* (Revelation 2:19-23).

Matthew 24:13
*But **he that shall endure unto the end,** the same shall be saved.*

Church of Sardis
*Remember therefore how thou hast received and heard, and **hold fast and repent**...I will come on thee as a thief...they shall walk with Me in white...* (Revelation 3:3-4).

Matthew 24:14
And this gospel of the kingdom shall be preached in all the world *for a witness unto all nations; and then shall the end come.*

Church of Philadelphia
...I have set before thee an open door, and no man can shut it... *thou...hast kept My word, and host not denied My name. ... I also will keep thee from the hour of temptation, which shall come upon all the world, to try them that dwell upon the earth* (Revelation 3:8,10).

Nothing is said in this section in Matthew about the first half of the tribulation. The text instead jumps directly to a clear reference of the middle of the tribulation in verse 15. (See Daniel 9:26-27.) This is because God will continue to witness in the first half of the tribulation through the ministries of the two witnesses, the fiery trial of the first four trumpet judgments, and the 144,000 sealed servants of God. [They will be like 144,000 evangelists.] ***Then the end will come.***

The first four trumpet judgments are fiery judgments that parallel the power of the two witnesses. Fire proceeding out of their mouths indicates that they command or direct this fire ***from Heaven*** with the words of their mouth. They have the power to turn waters into blood and to smite the earth with plagues (Rev. 11:5-6). The overriding characteristic of the first four trumpet judgments are "***signs from the heavens***."

Revelation 8:7-10
The first angel sounded, and there followed hail and fire *mingled with blood, and they were cast upon the earth: and the third*

part of trees was burnt up, and all green grass was burnt up. ***And the second angel sounded, and as it were a great mountain burning with fire*** *was cast into the sea: and the third part of the sea became blood; and the third part of the creatures which were in the sea, and had life, died; and the third part of the ships were destroyed. And the third angel sounded, and there* ***fell a great star from heaven, burning as it were a lamp****, and it fell upon the third part of the rivers, and upon the fountains of waters.*

Church of Laodicea
Because thou sayest, I am rich, and increased with goods, and have need of nothing; and knowest not that thou art wretched, and miserable, and poor, and blind, and naked: ***I counsel thee to buy of Me gold tried in fire,*** *that thou mayest be rich; and white raiment, that thou mayest be clothed...As many as I love, I rebuke and chasten: be zealous therefore, and repent. ... To him that overcometh will* ***I grant to sit with Me in My throne, even as I also overcame...*** (Revelation 3:17-21).

How did Jesus overcome the world? He did it through His death and those who are of the Laodicean Church will have to do the same during the first half of the tribulation. Salvation will be possible up until the vials are poured out.

Revelation 20:4
And I saw thrones, and they sat upon them, and judgment was given unto them: *and I saw the souls of them that were beheaded for the witness of Jesus, and for the word of God, and which had not worshipped the beast, neither his image, neither had received his mark upon their foreheads, or in their hands; and* ***they lived and reigned with Christ a thousand years.***

Understanding Matthew 24:15-28

David L. Turner states, "This section of Matthew 24 is commonly held by dispensationalists to [be tied] directly to a futurist view of the abomination of desolation in Daniel 9:27; 11:31; 12:11 ...Daniel 9:27 '...in the midst of the week...' in particular looms large as a precise indicator of time of the fulfillment of Matt. 24:15, the middle of the seven year eschatological tribulation period...Thus Matthew 24:15-28 is locked tightly into the second half of Daniel's seventieth week, with little or no reference to the destruction of the temple in A.D. 70."[19]

I agree with most of this, but I believe that only verses 15 through 24 relate to the second half of Daniel's seven years of tribulation. Verses 23 through 24 concern the false works of the second beast of Revelation 13:11-18, who will try to deceive the world and the 144,000 elect Jews or Israel of God.

Verses 25 through 28 now address the question of His coming and the false Christ. "*Behold, I have told you before*" [*idou proeirhka umin*]. The perfect verb here clearly indicates that Jesus is now telling the disciples of something that He has already told them. Jesus refers His disciples and every reader back to the subject of false Christs who will manifest themselves throughout the Church Age tribulations.

He rehearses what some will say, "*Wherefore if they shall say unto to you, Behold, He is in the desert; go not forth: behold He is in the secret chambers; believe it not*" (Mt. 24:26). Christ then tells them that His coming will be as lightning out of the East. He will come in the twinkling of an eye and there will not be time to tell anyone to come or go; therefore, all such claims will be false (1 Cor. 15:51-52).

Matthew 24, verses 27 and 28, are referring to the Rapture of the Church at the end of the Church Age, the end of the beginning of sorrows, after the tribulation of those days. The sixth seal will be opened and the Church will be delivered to the throne of God and the world will be delivered into tribulation. Christ will be at His Father's throne and the Bride of Christ will be gathered there with Him (Jn. 14:3; Rev. 7:9-17; 14:2-5; 12:5).

Verses 29 through 31 will take the Church into the beginning moments of the first half of the tribulation. Immediately after the tribulation of the Church Age, the beginning of sorrows, climaxing with great pangs of trouble, will cause the earth to reel, the sun to be darkened, the moon to not give her light, the stars to fall from heaven, and the powers of heaven to be shaken.

All this corresponds perfectly with the sixth seal. Luke 21:25 adds the description of mourning nations and the effects of an earthquake to this text: "*upon the earth distress of nations, with perplexity; the sea and the waves roaring.*" The sixth seal, therefore, may bring about the Rapture of the Church as it represents the intensified pangs or contractions just before and with the birth of the age of tribulation.

The seventh kingdom, the New World Order, and the Seventieth Week of Daniel will all commence with the climatic chaos of the sixth seal. Israel and the world will have entered the time of Jacob's trouble, but the Church will have been Raptured to Heaven.

> *And I beheld when he had opened the sixth seal, and, lo, **there was a great earthquake**; and the **sun became black as sackcloth of hair, and the moon became as blood; and the stars of heaven fell unto the earth**, even as a fig tree casteth her untimely figs, when she is shaken of a mighty wind. And the **heaven departed as a scroll when it is rolled together; and every mountain and island were moved out of their places*** (Revelation 6:12-14).

The earthquake of the sixth seal may indicate the resurrection of the dead, while the rolling back of the heavens indicates the Rapture of the living saints. "*the dead in Christ shall rise first: then we which are alive and remain shall be caught up together* [raptured] *with them...*" (1 Thess. 4:16-17).

There was an earthquake associated with the resurrection of Christ (Mt. 27:53-54, 28:2). The earthquakes in divers places, listed last, could indicate the resurrection of many different souls all over the earth (Mt. 24:7). With the power of the heavens shaken, the world will know that the "Day of the Lord's Wrath" has come and the nations of the earth will mourn when the "sign of the Son of man" appears in the heavens (Mt. 24:30).

They will seek to hide from the face of the wrath of the Lamb, revealed in the heavens with the opening of the sixth seal (Rev. 6:15-17). There will be a pause after the chaos of the sixth seal and the 144,000 elect of God will be gathered from the four corners of the earth—these 144,000 are all Jews—12,000 from 12 different tribes of Israel (Rev 7:1-8). These elect are Jews and the chosen people of God.

At the same time, God will gather those who are His from the ends of Heaven and then the cosmic battle will begin to cast satan and his angels out of Heaven (Rev. 12:6-10).

"*And there was war in heaven: Michael and his angels* [gathered for the battle] *fought against the dragon...*" (Rev. 12:7). The Church, the offspring of the faithful Jewish remnant, will be the focus of the battle. Satan will try to intercept the Raptured Church, but God will send Michael and His angels to stand for the children of the faithful remnant of Israel at that time (Dan. 12:1).

Michael and his angels battle satan and his followers (Rev. 12:7-10). Satan also accuses the brethren before the throne of God day and night (all the time) until he is cast out of Heaven. Satan and his angels, while fighting to remain in the presence of Heaven, have their attention averted away from the earth.

Satan will be cast out of Heaven at the middle of the tribulation period (Ezek. 32:7; Rev. 12:9-10). With the Church in Heaven, no place is found for satan and His angels anymore there (Rev. 12:8).

This heavenly battle might also help to explain why men's hearts might be failing them, "*...for fear, and for looking after those things which are coming upon the earth: **for the powers of heaven shall be shaken***" (Lk. 21:26). The battle taking place in the heavens may last for three-and-one-half years and as such would help to explain why the first half of the tribulation period is relatively peaceful between the nations on earth—as compared to the second half when the wrath of God is poured out and satan is revealed (Rev. 12:6-10).

It is satan's ouster from Heaven that marks the beginning of the Great Tribulation on the earth. The first woe of the fifth trumpet (Rev. 9:1-12) and the woe of Revelation 12:12 correspond to the same event. These two correlate in the first of three devastating woes in the Book of Revelation.

The text of Ezekiel 32 clearly supports this chronology. The first four trumpet judgments darken satan's kingdom. One-third of the trees, grass, rivers, and seas are burnt or turned to blood (Rev. 8:1-11; Ezek. 32:5-6). In the fourth trumpet one-third of the sun, moon, and stars and the day and night are darkened (Rev. 8:12).

> *And when I shall put thee out, I will cover the heaven, and make the stars thereof dark; I will cover the sun with a cloud, and the moon shall not give her light* (Ezekiel 32:7).

The fifth trumpet is then alluded to in the last section (Rev. 9:1-11; Ezek. 32:17-32). An interesting point that I only want to mention at this time is that the text also indicates that "*The sword of the king of Babylon will come upon thee*" (Ezek. 32:11). This last usage of Babylon in Ezekiel's text then supports the theory that Gog and Magog are code words for the King of Babylon. This is because the placement or the timing matches up Revelation 8:13; 9:1; 12:15; and Ezekiel 38–39 as part of the fifth trumpet judgment. (See Chapter 9 of this book, Isaiah 13–14, and Revelation 12.)

The sequence of the judgments of Revelation follow the same overall pattern of the Book of Ezekiel. Lamentations (beginning of sorrows), mourning (soundings, trumpets), followed by woe (woe, woe, woe) (Ezek. 2:10). Ezekiel, a watchman, warned Israel before the destruction came. Who is standing today as a watchman for signs of God's judgment?

If we see these signs, why aren't we sounding the warning? This we must do, lest the blood of the wicked be on our hands (Ezek. 3:18; 33:6). These two passages of Ezekiel function as grammatical brackets around the two great judgments of God. The first time Jerusalem fell to Babylon, and the second time will be in the end of days. Just as sure as it came the first time, so too will it come the second time (Ezek. 33:21-33)

The rest of Matthew 24:32-44 and 25:1-30 are parables intended to teach a heavenly truth, using earthly illustrations about all the various groups that are affected or included in the previous verses. Instructions are given on how to determine the signs of the times and we are admonished to watch for these signs.

The sequence of the parables that follow is most interesting: (a) There is a parable that addresses the faithful and the unfaithful servants of the physical body of Christ; (b) the parable of the ten virgins differentiates between those taken in the Rapture and those left behind; (c) next, we see the parable that concerns the judgment of rewards after the Rapture of the servants of God; and (d) this is followed by the return of the Lord in all His glory and the sheep and goats judgment of the nations.

As shown, the Gospels are in complete agreement with this understanding of the sixth seal, which incorporates the Rapture and the introductory moments of the tribulation period. This is the truth and God's Word confirms it. The seals are not part of the seven years of tribulation.

They precede the tribulation period, just as the discomforts and pangs of pregnancy accompany childbearing for nine months.

The progression of the parables that follow Matthew 24:1-31 is significant in chronology because they perfectly complement the order of events teaching a pretibulational Rapture.

The parables track from the beginning of the Church Age to the start of the Millennium:

1. The parable of the fig tree (Mt. 24:32-33). Learn how to determine the signs of the times—when the season of the end will come.

2. Learn and understand that this age will not pass away until all of Jesus' words are fulfilled. Everything that He said will come to pass (Mt. 24:34-35).

3. The lesson of Noah (Mt. 24:36-44). All need to learn from the first time when the Lord destroyed the world.

People did not believe that the end would come. They watched Noah build the ark and ignored the signs of judgment. They should have learned that, as the ark was nearing completion, the floods would not be far behind. Even as the animals were being gathered, the world continued to eat, drink, and marry *until the flood came and took them away.* Then they understood, but it was too late. The ark left its mooring, but Noah and his family were saved out of the flood. Those taken away by the flood were destroyed.

4. The lesson of Noah is applied and clarified (Mt. 24:40-41). When the Lord comes He will be selective; He will leave one and take the other. The illustration applies to both men and women. The ones left are saved. They will be left standing before the Lord, while the rest of the world will reel from the devastating effects of the sixth seal. The same flood that destroyed the world delivered or lifted Noah and his family to safety. This is also the nature of the sixth seal.

5. We will not know the exact hour (Mt. 24:42). The ultimate admonition is for all to diligently watch because we do not know the "*hour*" of the Lord's return. This is the first part of the Second Coming of the Lord at the Rapture.

6. This coming is as a thief in the night (Mt. 24:43). Because of the nature of His coming, it will require constant watching to avoid being surprised.

7. Just when the return of Christ is thought to be improbable, He will come (Mt. 24:44). The Son of man will come in such an hour that people will think it impossible. At such a time, believers should expect His return. This passage describes the attitude of our modern sophisticated world of today. Some wrongly conclude that the promise of the Rapture is too spectacular to really be believed as true. But in the very beginning of this teaching section, Jesus assures the faithful that all these things will be fulfilled before this generation or age passes away (2 Pet. 3:3-4).

8. Serve while you can (Mt. 24:45-51). During the Church Age we need to be faithfully serving the Lord. Those who faithfully serve the Lord will be looking for His return. The unfaithful servant will have no desire for the Lord to return and will ultimately be left behind with the hypocrites.

9. The parable of the ten virgins (Mt. 25:1-13) clearly teaches the pretibulation Rapture. Nothing is said about suffering prior to this—only serving. The five virgins, *with oil in their lamps*, do not slumber in ignorance while the Lord delays His coming. Those who are of the Kingdom of Heaven will be wise and serve the Lord while they can. The foolish virgins, *without oil in their lamps*, are those who profess to be Christian without being born again.

Carnal "Christians" who think they can lay claim to salvation without demonstrating any of the fruit of the Spirit are self-deceived. They are empty vessels. These five virgins will run to their houses of worship when the birth pangs of the sixth seal begin to develop. Faithful virgins are the opposite of fornicators and adulterers. They faithfully wait for the Lord while living for Him. True believers do not mix the truth of the Word of God with the religions that descended from Babylon—this is spiritual fornication.

The slumbering virgins think that they can somehow escape by running to those who make merchandise of salvation (e.g., the selling of indulgences). The Rapture will come and they will be left behind. The door will be closed and the Lord will reject them because He never knew them. These are the Laodiceans who will go into the tribulation and are told by the Lord to *buy of Him gold tried in fire* (Rev. 3:18). The faithful virgins stand with the Lord at the marriage feast.

10. The Bemas Seat Judgment (Mt. 25:14-30) are rewards for what one has done with his salvation and will be determined in Heaven, while the world enters into the first half of the tribulation. Those who have used or invested their talents wisely will be rewarded with the words, "*Well done, thou good and faithful servant*" (Mt. 25:21).

They will receive additional responsibilities because they proved themselves faithful over a few things. They will also be invited into the joy of the Lord. The unfaithful, wicked servant will make excuses for his inaction. He will claim that he feared the Lord because he knew He was a hard master and required fruit of what he had been given.

There is a special warning here to those Christians who claim to have very little to give to the Lord. The warning is: Invest what talent you have (no matter how insignificant) or risk suffering loss. "*...Whosoever shall lose his life for My sake and the gospel's, the same shall save it*" (Mk. 8:35).

The bottom line is that those who hide their salvation by investing their time and substance into the things of the world, will suffer loss in Heaven. Christians who are irresponsible while on earth will not be given any responsibilities in Heaven. They will not know what is happening. They will not understand why things are happening. They will be left out and in the dark concerning the things of Heaven. They will lament to each other; still they will be saved (Mt. 25:30; 1 Cor. 3:15). They will be vessels of dishonor (2 Tim 2:19-21). They are vessels on display in the Kingdom of Heaven.

11. The Second Coming of Christ (Mt. 25:31-46). Verse 31 clearly illustrates the time when Christ returns to rule the earth (Rev. 19:11-21), after the marriage feast (Rev. 19:1-10). This is the sheep and goats judgment of the nations, which is different from the Great White Throne Judgment that follows the millennial reign of Christ.

Because of the context of this parable and the time of the judgment (right after the tribulation), it appears that the people of the gathered nations will be judged for the way they responded to the persecution of those who become Christians during the tribulation. With the Lord living and ruling in Jerusalem, it appears that some will be judged faithful on the merits of their works, but this is not true. Their works show that they did it for the Lord in whom they trusted—"*ye have done it unto Me*" (Mt. 25:40).

Those who exercised compassion and service toward the brethren of Christ will be rewarded, while those who failed to exercise mercy will go into everlasting punishment. Satan will be released to test the nations after the thousand-year reign of Christ. The remnants of Gog and Magog (Babylon and the king of Babylon) will be destroyed along with satan and his followers. After this all the dead will be resurrected and be gathered before the Lord and will be judged according to their works at the Great White Throne Judgment.

Chapters 24 and 25 of Matthew harmonize the chronology of a pre-tribulation Rapture. Christ warned and prophesied concerning the destruction of Jerusalem. Jerusalem was destroyed because of its unbelief. He warned the disciples and their followers about false Messiahs and the tribulations that would follow. First, there would be a time of sorrows but the end was not yet. The Church would endure trials and tribulation as the Kingdom of God struggled against the kingdoms of the world ruled by satan. The servants of God were clearly told that Christ's coming would be as lightning out of the East and as a thief in the night. We were given assurances that everything that Christ said would be fulfilled. Christ gave illustrations from the Old Testament and used parables that pointedly teach all to *watch*!

We are to watch for the signs of His coming while serving Him and investing our time and talents into the Kingdom of God (Mt. 6:33). We are to be filled with the fruit of the Spirit and be bearing fruit in our lives because it is what the Lord requires of all good and faithful servants. Finally, we were given a glimpse of what it will be like in Heaven after the Rapture (Rev. 7:9-17).

The servants of the Lord Jesus Christ will be judged for their faithful service and rewarded appropriately. The last parable portrays Christ returning in glory at the end of the tribulation and conducting the judgment of the nations prior to the start of the Millennium. The progression of the parables complements our chronology of the seals.

There is no need to twist or bend the meaning. We do not have to search for hidden meaning. Understanding the truth of the chronology of the seals has unlocked all of prophetic Scripture—all because we recognize that the sixth seal includes the Rapture and delivers the world to the tribulation and because the "time" of its fulfillment is at hand.

It is time to accept the truth of the seals and acknowledge that they relate to what history records from A.D. 30 to the present. The six seals are part of the sixth kingdom, but the seventh seal begins the seventh and final kingdom of Revelation 17:10, which is also the beginning of Daniel's Seventieth Week.

Matthew 24 and 25 support a pretribulation eschatology as long as one's chronology of the seals is equated to Church history and not placed within the first half of the tribulation period. If Marvin Rosenthal would make this adjustment to his chronology (moving the beginning of sorrows outside of the first half of Daniel's Seventieth Week) he would have to immediately return to a pretribulation position and abandon his prewrath Rapture position.[20]

The sixth seal—the number of man—I believe is where the Rapture of the Church and the coming of the Lord to "snatch away" His Bride to Himself and deliver the world into the tribulation takes place. Just as the Noachian flood took unbelievers away and left Noah, his family and all the animals high and dry in the ark, so the sixth seal will have this same dual objective for the Raptured Church and the world lost in darkness.

Understanding More About the Fifth Seal

The unique nature of the fifth seal needs consideration. Is the fifth seal a judgment?

No! Instead, it is a *call for judgment.* In fact, it is a call for God to avenge the deaths of those who were slain for the Word of God. If pretribulationalists believe that the first seal is the beginning of the tribulation and that Church is raptured before the start of the tribulation, who are those killed for the Word of God during the tribulation (Rev. 6:9-11)?

Remember, during the first half of the tribulation Israel is to be at peace, according to Daniel 9:27. The seven-year peace covenant will occur at the beginning of the seven-year period and usher in the seventh king (Rev. 17:10).

If seals two, three, and four are the wrath of God being poured out upon the world, why do the souls under the altar cry out for the Lord to judge and avenge their blood on those who dwell on the earth? If the first seal begins God's judgment, why do they ask "*How long, O Lord?*" and why does the Lord tell them to wait?

They cry out because these souls are the ones who have died throughout Church history. They died aware of the promises and they are waiting for the judgment, resurrection, and the Rapture. It must be noted that "John only saw the souls, because their bodies *had not yet been resurrected*"[21] (emphasis added). If seal one is the beginning of the tribulation and the pretribulation position is correct, then the resurrection would have already taken place.

But seal one is *not* the beginning of the tribulation; therefore, the Rapture must take place after the fifth seal. In every dispensation of time God has sent the Comforter to comfort and clothe the departed souls of believers. This is what the fifth seal represents.[22]

The story of Lazarus and the rich man teaches this truth (Lk. 16:19-31). The dead in Christ will rise first (1 Thess. 4:16). These seals (the beginning of sorrows) contain the persecutions that deliver the world to the start of the tribulation period. They have little to do with the wrath of God within the tribulation, but they have everything to do with the tribulation throughout Church history, from Pentecost to the Rapture.

Any understanding[23] of the seals must explain seals one and five. Insisting that they are part of the tribulation judgments does not fit the bill. These first four seals are the eyes of the Lord that have gone forth into the dispensation of the Church to fulfill the will and the Word of God. This is not the first dispensation that we see these horsemen operative, for we see them during Zerubbabel's day in Zechariah 6. When Zechariah saw the four chariots with the red, white, black, grizzled, and bay horses, he said to the angel, "*What are these, my lord?*" The response was, "*These are the four spirits of the heavens, which go forth from standing before the Lord of all the earth*" (Zech. 6:4-5).

These four spirits are the same as the first four seals of Revelation chapter 6. But in Revelation we have seven seals. Where are the other three seals in Zechariah? The answer is in chapter 4. There Zechariah sees a vision of a menorah (a lampstand with seven lamps). To each side of the lampstand are standing two olive trees, which are the two witnesses of God. The lampstand with the seven lamps and seven pipes represent the seven Spirits of God sent on Israel's behalf. Note how both the horsemen of Zechariah chapter 6 and the seven lamps are described as those "*which go*" or those "*which run to and fro through the whole earth*" (Zech. 6:5; 4:10).

In Revelation chapters 1 and 6 we find parallels to the description of the seven golden lampstands (Rev. 1:12,20). The seven stars in the right hand of Jesus are the seven angels sent to the seven churches, which the seven lampstands represent.

At the beginning of the tribulation Jesus will hold a rod of iron in His hand. He will no longer restrict revealing Himself through the convicting ministry of the Holy Spirit. At the beginning of the tribulation, Christ will begin to reveal Himself in manifold judgments (Rev. 12:5,19:15).

We know from Revelation 3:1 that these seven stars are also the seven Spirits of God. As we consider the seven letters to the seven churches, we learn that it is the Spirit of God speaking.[24] Then we discover seven lamps burning before the throne of God which "*are the seven Spirits of God*" (Rev. 4:5). Finally, here is the last reference to the seven Spirits of God:

> *And I beheld, and, lo, in the midst of the throne and of the four beasts, and in the midst of the elders, stood a Lamb as it had been slain, having seven horns and seven eyes, which are the seven Spirits of God sent forth into all the earth* (Revelation 5:6).

This last reference to the seven Spirits of God comes at a time when Jesus receives the book with the seals "still" in place. The removal of the seals is the next action. With a thundering voice, the Lamb (the Lion of Judah) dispatches the Spirits one by one to the earth to oversee His Church and His Kingdom. Each seal is opened and sent—fulfilling God's will.

Initially, at Pentecost, Christ sent the Comforter as He had promised. The Comforter was sent to indwell the believer and empower him to overcome satan and the tribulations of the world. Jesus sent the Spirit into the world to establish believers as kings and priests—initiating the first phase of the kingdom of God on earth. "*Not by might, nor by power, but by My spirit, saith the Lord of hosts*" (Zech. 4:6).

The first seal represents the sending of the Holy Spirit with a bow in one hand, indicating that He is not sending the Spirit into the world with military might and power. "The bow traditionally has been associated with one who is a warrior. Frequently it is a symbol for victory (cf. Zech. 9:13-14) (Lenski; Ladd)."[25]

By His work on Calvary and by His Spirit and Word He overcame and continues to overcome the world (Jn. 16:33). At the end of the tribulation Jesus will come in might and power to destroy the evil in the world (Rev. 19:11-21). Suggesting that the bow in the hand of the rider of the white horse is the spirit of antichrist sent to conquer the world by peace, dismisses a storehouse of scriptural evidence to the contrary.[26]

God sent His Spirit during Zerubbabel's day to be sure that His will was done in the world—particularly that which concerned the completion of the temple. If Zerubbabel needed to have a mountain flattened, God would do it (Zech. 4:7). And if God needs the Dome of the Rock removed so that the "third temple" can be rebuilt, He will do that as well.

The Bible clearly indicates the need for the third temple to be built (Ezek. 40–47; Dan. 9:27; Mt. 24:15; 2 Thess. 2:4; Rev. 11:1).

In an interview with Michael Greenspan of "Jerusalem Online" July 17, 1994, Rabbi Chaim Richman, head of the Temple Institute, stated that "his organization is trying to raise the awareness of both Jew and Gentile of the central role that the temple plays in the reconciliation of man to God. Already the Institute has manufactured the sacred temple objects and they exist once again for the first time on the face the earth in nearly 2,000 years." Greenspan commented that "the rebuilding of the temple would be the closing event of a 2,000 year historical circle." He also asked, "If Israel rebuilds the temple, will the Messiah come?"

The answer, I believe, is yes! If the world really wants to know the answer, simply let Israel rebuild its temple and wait seven years and they will see Jesus returning with the armies of Heaven.

The only differences between the riders of Zechariah and Revelation are the economies and the existing earthly kingdoms of each. The Old Testament economy records Israel as the focus and instrument of God's work. The New Testament economy clearly demonstrates God working through the Church.

Comparing the order of the horses of Revelation chapter 6 with Zechariah 6, the white horse is probably listed third in Zechariah and first in Revelation because in the Age of Grace the Holy Spirit needed to first indwell believers. God is working through the Spirit-filled Church today. Likewise, the Spirit of God was also sent to the earth to fulfill all the events necessary in the kingdom of Zechariah's time—the Kingdom of the Medes and the Persians.

Solomon's kingdom was the first glorious kingdom of Israel and it followed the fall of the first great kingdoms of the world. It was during this kingdom that Israel appeared to rule the world. The temple was built and God dwelt in the "Holy of Holies." Israel's glorious kingdom decayed very slowly and was totally destroyed in 586 B.C. by the next world empire—Babylon. Babylon was succeeded by the Medes and the Persians, which was the third world empire. This third world empire was the ruling kingdom during the time that the temple was rebuilt.

After studying 16 known chronological views of the seal, trumpet, and vial judgments, all conclude that the final seven years of Israel's trouble begins with the opening of the first seal. But this conclusion ignores the nearly 2,000 years of Church and world history that has elapsed since Calvary.

No one can reasonably conclude that the recent explosion of knowledge in the last century is an accident. The reality of Israel being a nation now and discussing a peace treaty, while actively making preparations to rebuild the third temple, is a contemporary example of God working behind the scenes to fulfill the Word of God.

Presently, the Spirit of God and the following three horsemen are at work in the world, affecting history for the glory of God. The world was shocked by the collapse of communism, the breakup of Russia, and the open door of opportunity for evangelism. Why is this happening now? Many Christians were disappointed with Clinton's rise to power because of his open support for gays in the military and in his administration as well as his pro-abortion and social government setbacks. Why now?

Recently, others were startled when Zhurvinowsky and his party received the majority of votes in Russia. Why now? Why is the United States and the world now experiencing more and more devastating natural disasters? Because it is "time"! It is time for the world to give account. Man is also getting too close to the secrets of life itself. Such power in the hands of fallen, sinful man would be very dangerous.

When the recent "Super Collider" project in Texas was cancelled by Congress, scientists justified the costs because they claimed the project had the power to reveal the powers of creation itself. Such power they contended, would more than offset the cost of a measly 11 to 14 billion dollars.

Jesus has sent the first four riders of the Apocalypse into the world. When Jesus opens the sixth seal, the world will experience many "natural" upheavals. These upheavals will cause many to fear as they contemplate the consequences of what has come upon the earth. The sixth seal includes the Rapture of the Church and introduces the world to the beginning of seven years of ever increasing tribulation and judgment—for the "Day of the Lord" will have come (Rev. 6:17).

In the letters to the churches, specific information is found regarding God's plan and purpose for His Son's Bride, the Body of Christ. As we consider the seals, should we, like so many others, assume also the opening of the book?[27] In agreeing with Ladd, a posttribulation commentator, the breaking of the seals are not stages in the opening of the book, but only *preliminary* to the actual opening of the scroll.

That which is *preliminary* to the opening of the scroll is the completion of God's program for the Church. This is revealed in the letters to the seven churches and certified as being fulfilled in and with the opening of the seals. As time passes, God removes one seal after another according to His perfect plan. As seals are removed, understanding will come to the Church that the season of the "Day of the Lord" is approaching.

This will continue until the opening and fulfillment of the events associated with the sixth seal. The result will be the Rapture of the Church, leaving the world precariously set for the opening of the seventh seal and the reading of the scroll. As the Lord told Daniel, these things are sealed up until the time of the end (Dan. 12:9).

The events of Daniel's final seven years will be written into the pages of world history when the seventh seal is removed and the sixth seal is fulfilled. This new chapter of world history will carry the title, "*God Is*!" or "*The Day That Jesus Came Back.*"

One final consideration—Hunt and others also argue that the "second seal [takes] peace from the earth." This insinuates that the peace taken away was instituted by the prince that was prophesied by Daniel 9:26 *and the first seal.*[28]

According to Daniel 9:27, this peace covenant is not broken until the middle of the tribulation. Therefore, the second seal would have to come just after or at the middle of the tribulation, leaving only the first seal within the first half. Now this is what I call "impossible timing." Instead, a more legitimate scenario may develop.

Presently Israel is attempting to negotiate peace with its Arab neighbors. Why? They want peace. Why do they want it? It was taken from them. The Bosnians and the Serbians and the world are struggling to come to a peaceful settlement. Why? They do not have peace. Suppose the peace talks between Israel and the Arabs break down a really bad regional war breaks out in Israel.

Rabbin himself was quoted as saying that 1994 was the year that peace must be formulated. Later he berated an Israel Defense Force, IDF general for predicting that Israel would be at war in 1995. For our purposes here, let us assume that this potential war is so bad that Israel or the Arabs resort to nonconventional weapons.

As a result, the death toll and devastation becomes great.The New World Order steps in and negotiates and implements a seven-year peace plan. Maybe Israel will become desperate enough to warn Syria and others that unless peace is agreed to, they will use nuclear weapons to insure their enemies' defeat. This would present antichrist, who would be part of this newly formed or forming "World Order," with an ideal opportunity to catapult himself to center stage.

By instituting his peace agreement, peace would come not only to the Middle East but to the whole world. Before the peace treaty is implemented, though, the world is rocked by the major upheavals of the sixth seal. The ensuing chaos forces the world to consolidate for security reasons. The world leaders negotiate and implement a New World Order. As part of this "New Order," a peace treaty between Israel and its Arab neighbors is legislated.

One condition of this treaty would allow Israel to rebuild the temple, becoming the symbol and center of global peace. It could happen that the Lord will coordinate the opening of the sixth seal with the initial implementation of the peace accord and the dedication of the new temple in Israel. As a result, great natural disasters and cosmic events begin to happen, causing great fear in the hearts and minds of men and women (such as the panic that the aftershocks cause earthquake victims in California to experience).

Christians will continue to warn the world of the imminent danger and the coming of the Lord and the Rapture. The world will not take them seriously and continue about their business—marrying, partying, and such. The Rapture could take place as these natural disasters develop. The world community will be deceived into believing that the unexplained absence of many individuals is simply the result of the worldwide chaos and destruction.

The events of the sixth seal cannot effectively warn people of the Rapture because it includes the Rapture. "*As it was in the days of Noah... and they knew nothing about what would happen until the flood came and took them all away...*" (Mt. 24:37,39 NIV). The floodwaters took both Noah and the world away.

The Rapture will take the world by storm and provide its own cover and concealment with the sequential upheavals within the sixth seal. These events will disrupt most of the world, if not all of it. After the Rapture and the chaos of the sixth seal, the world may move its world headquarters for peace to Jerusalem (Hebrew, *shalom*), the city of peace. New York and the United Nations may be destroyed as a result of worldwide cataclysm.

The Rapture will take place either before or after the treaty is ratified. Either way, as a result of the Rapture, which will catch away untold millions of Christians, and the cosmic events, the world will know that the "Day of the Lord" has come.

However, the devil will use a strong delusion to deceive those who remain. At this time, the two witnesses of God will appear on the scene and begin to announce the judgment of God. The Lord will probably let the world know that He has taken believers to Himself or He may supernaturally declare to the world that His Day has come. In some manner, the world will know that the destruction has marked the beginning of the wrath of God.

The Bible indicates that men both great and small will seek to hide themselves from the face of Him that sits on the throne, and from the wrath of the Lamb. "*For the great day of His wrath is come*" (see Rev. 6:16-17).

It will have come because all that needed to be fulfilled according to God's Word has been fulfilled. It is now time to open the seventh seal and commence with the trumpet judgments of the first half of the "Day of the Lord." This scenario, should it happen, fulfills all the requirements of Scripture.

What Exactly Is a Seal?

A seal is not just a blank ball of wax or clay. A seal usually contains the name of the one who placed the seal and, without his authority, it cannot be broken. The names given in the introduction to each of the seven letters to the churches may be an indication of a seal being removed. Consider the introduction to the Church of Ephesus: "*...write; These things saith he that holdeth the seven stars in His right hand, who walketh in the midst of the seven golden candlesticks* [churches]" (Rev. 2:1). Now if the seven stars represent the Holy Spirit, and I believe that they do, then this would support our understanding that the opening of the first seal involved the sending of the Holy Spirit to the Apostolic Church at Pentecost.

Ephesus was the church that left its "first love." A seal usually contains the name of the witness who is authorizing or certifying the contents of that which is sealed, and in this case the contents of the scroll. If the seals are to be all opened at the same time, why have seven of them? The fact that there are seven seals indicates that there is more than one witness—as is the case of the Roman seal (*katasphragizo*) (Rev. 5:1).

"This book reminds us of Roman law with the seal of the tester and six witnesses. The sealed book is a double document. Only the Lamb can undo this seal. One seal is broken after the other (Rev. 6:1-17). [As a result]...eschatological events move forward with the breaking of the seals."[29] The seals are linked to the fulfillment of the prophecies that the Church would pass through world history.

As the Body of Christ progressed through the ages, Christ sanctioned the opening of each seal and sent forth His messengers into the world. He will continue this process until the Church is made ready and He authorizes the opening of the sixth seal.

Who Is the Rider of the First Horse/Seal?

Concerning the identification of the first seal with the ministry of the Holy Spirit, the evidence is extremely convincing. Some scholars insist that the first horseman, if consistent with the other three, must also be of an evil nature. "Since the other three are evil powers of destruction and death by which God executes judgment, the white horse must be similar in kind."[30]

This conclusion is a mistake. In fact, the events of the Church Age do not differ from what God decreed for Jerusalem prior to the Babylonian captivity. God continually called Israel and Judah to repentance long before judgment came, but Israel and Judah refused to repent. Consequently, God took peace out of the land, brought famine, then pestilence, and finally allowed death and destruction by the sword at the hand of Babylon (Ezek. 6:11; Jer. 14:12; 21:7). At the same time, God removed the good figs to Babylon and preserved them in captivity (Jer. 24:3-7).

Therefore, while the Lord was executing judgment upon Judah, He was also working to preserve and restore the faithful remnant of Israel. From this we can see the dynamics of the seal judgments within the Church Age as they work to implement the promises and warnings contained in the letters to the seven churches. This age, the beginning of sorrows, started with the sending of the Holy Spirit into the world (Acts 2:1-4).

One of the main difficulties with not understanding the first seal as being closely associated with the ministry of the Holy Spirit, is the failure of modern scholars to adequately explain the white garb worn by the rider on the white horse. Other interpreters have pointed out the obvious similarity between this white horse and the rider and vision of the conquering Christ (Rev. 19:1-11).

> "There Christ rides a white horse and wears many diadems on His head....The color white may be taken, however, as a clue to the identity of the first horseman, for in The Revelation, ***white is always a symbol of Christ***, or of something associated with Christ, or of spiritual victory. Thus, the exalted Christ has white hair as wool (Rev. 1:14); the faithful will receive a white stone with a new name written on it (Rev. 2:17); they are to wear white

> garments (Rev. 3:4,5,18); the 24 elders are clad in white (Rev. 4:4); the martyrs are given white robes (Rev. 6:11) as is the great numberless throng (Rev. 7:9,13); the son of man is seen on a white cloud (Rev. 14:14); in the final judgment, God is seen seated on a white throne (Rev. 20:11). *In view of this extensive evidence, we may look for some interpretation of the white horse that connects it with something associated with Christ and spiritual life.* This is further supported by the fact that, unlike the second to the fourth seals, the first has no woe connected with it.[31] (Emphasis added.)

The first seal personifies a rider going forth conquering and to conquer. The double form of the verb here is (*nikon* and *nikese* from *nikaw*), which the King James Version translates "overcome" throughout Revelation chapters 2 and 3. When this is considered in relationship with the use of this same verb to what the Spirit says to the seven churches (Rev. 2:7,17,26; 3:5,12,21), to be overcomers and inherit the promises of God, it becomes more plausible to consider the first seal as the sending of the Holy Spirit into the world.

It is also used of Christ to describe Himself as One who has prevailed or overcame to be worthy to open the seals and the book (Rev. 5:5). The verb *nikao* is also used in Revelation 11:7 in reference to the beast overcoming the two witnesses of God. This event must takes place at the middle of the tribulation period because of Daniel 9:27, which clearly states that a peace covenant is broken in the "*midst of*" the final week.

This final week represents the seven years of the tribulation period. Some might argue that Revelation 11:7 is supportive evidence for identifying the rider of the first seal as the beast or antichrist, but it is a weak assertion.

The overcoming of the two witnesses is not by peace and it is not at the beginning of the tribulation period. Those who take such a position isolate the first seal from the six seals that follow. If the first seal represents the antichrist coming, disguised as the harbinger of peace for three-and-one-half years, then the events of the remaining seals, as well as the first four trumpet judgments, must be explained within this context of "the peace covenant" in Daniel 9:27.

During the Age of Grace the spiritual pilgrim will either be an overcomer or one who is overcome by the devil and his devices in the world in which we live. We are in the dispensation of "grace." God has withheld judgment until the appointed day and has not sent His Spirit into the world to destroy but to *convince the world of its sin, its lack of righteousness and of the judgment* that is coming (Jn. 16:8-11).

He has sent the Spirit to work in the world through the preaching and teaching of the Word of God; thus the imagery of a rider with only a crown and a bow. The sixth seal and the first seal both contain imagery taken from the pages of ancient astronomy.

> *And I beheld when He had opened the sixth seal, and, lo, there was a great earthquake; and the sun became black as sackcloth of hair, and the moon became as blood* (Revelation 6:12).

The imagery of the rider of the first seal riding across the sky with a bow finds root in Assyrian astronomical writings and is found referencing a winged angel that is associated with solar and lunar eclipses and symbolizing divine protection. "The Assyrian 'Ring with Rings' is found on monuments and is always shown floating over the head of the king, and is designed to indicate the presence and protection of the Deity."[32] (See Figure 5 on page 6.)

Thus, John's rider with a bow was used to signify the divine protection of the Holy Spirit being sent into the world to overcome the world and provide divine protection for believers. This was initiated with the opening of the first seal (Rev. 6:1-2). (See Figure 5 on page 6.)

God has also allowed this age to be one that will experience famine, earthquakes, pestilence, and war as a result of disobedience to His Word. This is the purpose of seals two, three, and four. These are the causes of many sorrows, especially in today's God-forsaking societies.

"The former form of nikao, nikon found in Rev. 6:2 ('conquering'), portrays the rider's career as one marked by a long series of victories. The latter form, nikese ('that He might conquer'), points to an ultimate victory."[33]

Walvoord, Thomas, and others object to associating the first rider with the Christ because they mistakenly suggest that the victory of the first rider is to be temporal. This is in spite of the cumulative aspect of the verbs ("conquering and to conquer"). But even if they were right about the temporal nature of the victory,[34] the Holy Spirit will continue to hold down the mystery of iniquity until He has been taken out of the way (2 Thess. 2:7). Their argument, therefore, is spurious.

The Laodiceans are counseled to overcome the world even as Christ had overcome the world through His death and resurrection. In the first half of the tribulation the Laodiceans will be required to do the same (Rev. 3:21). Christ told His disciples that in the world they would have tribulation, but that they were not to fear because He had overcome [*nikao*] the world (Jn. 16:33).

It is through the ministry of the Holy Spirit that believers can overcome the trials of this life. It is also through the ministry of the Holy Spirit that God will purge His Church of the idolater, fornicator, and liar. The Spirit calls professing Christians to repentance.

To those who repent, overcome, and receive the Spirit of God (are born again), the promises of God are reserved for them. Those who refuse to repent are reserved for judgment, now and later, via the implementation of the second, third, and fourth seals. These seals are effected in the world when Jesus sees, through the eyes of the Holy Spirit, the conditions in the world deteriorating and threatening the spiritual life of His Body of believers as they attempt to work the will of God and fulfill His Word.

The Oil & Wine of the Third Seal

Proof that the seal judgments are part of Church history is also clearly demonstrated in the opening of the third seal. This seal brings a famine, but the oil and wine are not to be hurt (Rev. 6:5-6). The hurt of a famine is not just to the crops, but to those who depend on the crops. The reference to oil and wine then could be a symbolic reference to those who are the first fruits of the Holy Spirit.

Therefore, the command not to hurt the oil and the wine could be understood as these judgments are not meant for believers, but for unbelievers. This is part of the ministry of the Holy Spirit. "*And when He is come, He will reprove the world of sin, and of righteousness, and of judgment*" (Jn. 16:8).

This is exactly what seals two, three, and four accomplish. This command to not hurt the oil and the wine is similar to the command not to hurt them who have the seal of God. The grass, trees, and green things are also not to be hurt. Only those who have not the seal of God are under divine judgment (Rev. 9:4).

"The prohibition ('do not hurt'), addressed presumably to the third rider, is phrased so as to forbid even the beginning of damage to the wine."[35] Some suggest that because wine and oil are the commodities of the wealthy, then this means the privileged life style of the rich will remain intact.[36]

It is hard to imagine a famine from the hand of God, selectively set against only the poor. On the other hand, if the riders are dispatched by the Lord to fulfill His will in the world, then it would be better to conclude that the oil and the wine make reference to those "filled" with the Spirit of God. Therefore, those with the seal of God are protected from the famines.

This protection can be evidenced in Acts 11:28.

> *And there stood up one of them named Agabus, and signified by the spirit that there should be great dearth* [*limos*, "scarcity or famine"], *throughout all the world: which came to pass in the days of Claudius Caesar* (Acts 11:28).

The Spirit warned believers ahead of time so that the coming famine would not even begin to hurt the brethren. Believers are anointed with the Holy Spirit (1 Jn. 2:27) and sealed with the Holy Spirit of promise (Eph. 1:13-14).

The sending of the Holy Spirit is the rider of the first seal. The riders of the second, third, and fourth horses are directed by the one wearing a "victor's" crown and riding the "white" horse of the first seal.

> *Ye are of God, little children, and have overcome* [*nenikekate*, perfect verb form "victorious over"] *them: because greater is He that is in you, than he* [the spirit of antichrist] *that is in the world* (1 John 4:4).

It was expedient for Christ to go away to send the Holy Spirit, the Comforter, to believers (Jn. 16:7). Before God sent the riders of judgment into the world, He first sent the Holy Spirit into the world to seal, protect, and purchase for God those who first trusted in Christ. This is similar to the sealing of the 144,000 of Israel, which are sealed prior to the start of the trumpet judgments (Rev. 7:1-3).

Consider the miracle at the marriage feast of Cana (Jn. 2) that teaches that the day of the "New Wine" has come. The "worse wine, with which ordinarily in the beginning is made typifies also Mosaic Judaism, which was destined to give place to the better wine of the (liberating) gospel....His death which substitutes for the previous imperfect purifications the true purification through the blood of Christ, in consequence of which is given the joyous wine of the Holy Spirit."[37]

The New Testament agreement has come and this has fulfilled God's covenant promise to send His Holy Spirit—a new wine to dwell in men's hearts (Ezek. 36:25-29; Mt. 9:17).

The Holy Spirit is also clearly associated with the use of oil in the Old Testament. Having the oil indicates the presence or effectual working of the Holy Spirit in one's life.

> *Then Samuel took the horn of oil, and anointed him in the midst of his brethren: and the Spirit of the Lord came upon David...* (1 Samuel 16:13).

Matthew chapter 25 is the parable of the ten virgins. Five of the virgins had oil in their lamps and five did not. The Church is the first fruits after Christ (1 Cor. 15:23). Believers have the firstfruits of the Spirit (Rom. 8:23) and they are the firstfruits of God and the Lamb (Rev. 14:4). Therefore, the first five seals are part of this Dispensation of Grace.

Another clue to the meaning of the seals can be found outside Revelation. As we said earlier, some commentators have pointed out that there is a similarity between the structure of the seven seals and the Olivet Discourse found in Mark chapter 13 and Matthew chapter 24.

Mark 13:5-13 describes the beginning of sufferings or better, the "beginning of woes." The Kingdom of God will not be established immediately. This also explains the appropriateness of the imagery of the first seal, a crowned rider with just a bow. But the future generations of the Church Age will be visited by periods of wars and rumors of wars, conflict, earthquakes, and persecutions even to the point of death.

Matthew adds that there will also be famines (Mt. 24:7).[38] These preliminary periods of trouble will be followed by a time of great tribulation such as the world has never seen before. After this, the Kingdom of God will be realized with the coming of Christ, who will exchange the arrowless bow for a rod of iron, which will smash to pieces the kingdoms of this world. Then He will begin to rule and reign on earth. But even during this time of great trouble, the gospel must be preached as a witnesses to all nations before the end can come (Mk. 13:10).

The rider of the first horse with a bow and no arrows is the Holy Spirit going forth into all the world, working through believers to bring souls to Jesus Christ. But for those who reject God's first messenger, three others wait to do His bidding. Once these seals are opened and active, they continue to grow in scope and magnitude right up to and maybe throughout the Seventieth Week of Daniel.

The seventh seal is the beginning of Jacob's trouble, while the fifth relates to the promise for those who died in Christ. The sixth seal relates to the promises made to those who will be resurrected or alive and in Christ as the Rapture dawns. These promises were received by the Church of Sardis (Rev. 3:5) and the Church of Philadelphia (Rev. 3:10).

Summary of the First Six Chapters in Revelation

To summarize, then, everything from chapters 1 through 6 of Revelation concerns events that will be fulfilled within the Church Age—up to and including the Rapture of the Church. I have labeled this period as the "beginning of sorrows." The opening of the sixth seal includes God's rapturing of the Church. As a result of the Rapture and the upheaval that comes with it, the world knows that the "Day of the Lord's Wrath" has come. The "professing only" unregenerate Christians are left stranded and are reserved for the refining fire of the first half of the tribulation—these are the rich, but blind, Laodiceans.

Before events can continue to unfold in chapter 8, the 144,000 need to be sealed (12,000 from each of the 12 tribes of Israel). It is at this point that this elected remnant of Israel will go into the wilderness with the two witnesses sent by God. The Raptured Church will be taken out of the world in the very midst of the beginning of the "Day of the Lord's Wrath."

John recorded seeing the Church before the throne of God after the opening of the sixth seal. We want to emphasize that the Church is specifically found at the throne of God singing praise, thanks, and power to the Lamb and God. They are the ones who overcame by the blood of the Lamb and the word of their testimony (Rev. 7:9-17; 12:11).

End Notes

1. Walvoord, *The Revelation of Jesus Christ*, p. 115.
2. Hunt, *How Close Are We?* p. 238.
3. Turner, "The Structure and Sequence of Matthew 24:1-41, p. 27.
4. Paul L. Maier, trans. & ed., *Josephus: The Essential Writings*, (Grand Rapids, MI: Kregel Publications, 1993), pp. 361-362.
5. Ibid., pp. 281-283.
6. Ibid., p. 285.
7. Ibid., p. 295.
8. Ibid., p. 315.
9. Ibid., p. 326.
10. Ibid., p. 328.
11. Ibid., p. 330.
12. Ibid., p. 331.
13. Ibid., p. 347.
14. Ibid., p. 351.
15. Thomas, *Revelation 1–7: An Exegetical Commentary*, p. 425.
16. Marvin J. Rosenthal, "The Day of the Lord," *Zion's Fire*, Vol. 5, No. 3, (May/June), p. 5.
17. Thomas, *Revelation 1–7: An Exegetical Commentary*, p. 245.
18. William Barclay, *Letters to the Seven Churches*, (Philadelphia, PA: Westminster Press, 1978), p. 101.
19. Turner, "The Structure and Sequence of Matthew 24:1-41," p. 10.
20. Rosenthal, "The Day of the Lord," p. 6.
21. Thomas, *Revelation 1–7: An Exegetical Commentary*, p. 443.
22. Ibid. See pp. 440-447 for more discussion on the identity of the souls of the fifth seal.

23. Ibid. See pp. 413-424 for Thomas' discussion on eight different positions of the first seal. None clearly intimates that the rider of the first seal is the sending of the Holy Spirit to indwell the believers.

24. R.C.H. Lenski, *The Interpretation of St. John's Revelation* (Philadelphia, PA: Clarence Larkin, 1919); and George Ladd, *A Commentary on the Revelation of John*, (Grand Rapids, MI: Eerdmans Publishing Co., 1972), as cited by Thomas, *Revelation 1–7: An Exegetical Commentary*, p. 151.

25. Ibid., p. 422.

26. Walvoord, *The Revelation of Jesus Christ,* p. 127.

27. George Ladd, *The Book of Revelation,* (Grand Rapids, MI: Eerdmans Publishing Co., 1971), p. 95.

28. Hunt, *How Close Are We?*, p. 238. Used by permission.

29. Gerhand Kittle and Gerhard Friedrich, eds, *Theological Dictionary of the New Testament,* 10 Vols., (Grand Rapids, MI: Eerdmans Publishing Co., 1974), D.,2.,b., p. 1129.

30. Ladd, p. 97.

31. Ibid., pp. 97-98.

32. Maunder, *The Astronomy of the Bible*, p. 126.

33. Thomas, *Revelation 1–7,* p. 424. See also: Isborn T. Beckwith, *The Apocalypse of John,* p. 519; J.A. Seiss, *The Apocalypse,* p. 315; Archibald Robertson, *Word Pictures in the New Testament,* 6 Vols., 6:340; R.C.H. Lenski, *The Interpretation of St. John's Revelation,* p. 223. *Nikese* is an aorist subjunctive. The cumulative aspect of the conquest is what is emphasized in this use of the tense.

34. Thomas, *Revelation 1–7: An Exegetical Commentary*, p. 424.

35. Ibid., p. 434. The aorist is ingressive: "do not begin to hurt"; J.H. Moulton and G. Milligan, *The Vocabulary of the Greek Testament,* (Grand Rapids, MI: Eerdmans Publishing Co., 1974), 1:124-125.

36. Ibid., p. 434.

37. Frederick Louis Godet, *Commentary on the Gospel of John,* Vol. 1., (Grand Rapids, MI: Zondervan Publishing Co, 1893), p. 354.

38. Richard Bauckham, *The Climax of Prophecy*, (England: T&T Clark, 1989), pp. 97-98.

Chapter 7

The Pretribulation Rapture Confirmed

We Have Separation

Revelation chapter 7 begins with four angels holding the four winds of the earth so the four winds do not blow. This serves as a kind of calm in the midst of a storm. The Church has just been raptured and separated unto the Lord. With the events of the sixth seal, the Lord has revealed His "Day of Wrath" to the world. The word *day*, in this context, (*hmera*) means "the period of time that dawns or reveals the coming of the Day of Wrath" (Rev. 6:17).

The Rapture and the cosmic events related to the sixth seal are the dawning of the Seventieth Week of Daniel. By this, the world comes to the realization that it has come to the appointed time when God's wrath is revealed from Heaven. But with the dawn comes the morning sunrise, and with this sunrise, an eerie silence. (See Figure 2 on page 3.)

This silence will cause men to ponder and consider in their hearts and minds what is about to happen. This pause and silence may come after months of increasing world cataclysmic events and may share an affinity with the silence of the seventh seal, which lasts but a short space of time (Rev. 8:1).

The angel who speaks to the four angels, "*to whom it was given to hurt the earth and sea*" (Rev. 7:2), may be the same angel before the altar of God with the golden censer in his hand (Rev. 8:3-5). The first four trumpet judgments do not commence until this angel returns from the earth after sealing the 144,000, and casts a censer filled with fire from the altar to the earth.

The pause in Revelation 8:1 is for the sealing of the 144,000 Jews in the land of Israel. They will be sealed for divine protection against the trumpet judgments, "*hurt not the earth…till we have sealed the servants of our God in their foreheads*" (Rev. 7:3; see also 9:4).

The sealing of the 144,000 clearly takes place at the beginning of the tribulation period. It is at this time that the two witnesses must come to the 144,000 and begin their three-and-one-half year ministry (Rev. 11:2-3). Therefore, just as Jesus spent three-plus years teaching His disciples before His resurrection, so too will His two witnesses teach the 144,000 before their death and resurrection (Rev. 11:9-13).

These two witnesses will be filled with the Holy Spirit (Zech. 4:2-14) and will pour forth the teachings of God to the 144,000, the elect of God. They will cause the inhabitants of the earth to fear God and effectually work to bring some to repentance before the final judgments, contained in the vial judgments, are realized (Rev. 15:1–16:17). They will utilize the first four trumpet judgments to bring the world to repentance, just as God used the first four seals during the Church Age.

This is why we recognize similarities between the powers of the two witnesses and the descriptions of the first four trumpet judgments (Rev. 8:2-12; 11:5-6). Similarities exist because they are parallel judgment events. These similarities require us to place the ministry of the two witnesses into the first half of the Seventieth Week of Daniel.

Once the tribulation is inaugurated, and after the 144,000 Jews are sealed, John calls our attention to a scene in Heaven. There he sees a great multitude, which no man can number, gathered before the throne and before the Lamb. These are the many waters that belong to the Lamb, the voice of the Lamb in the world during the days of the Church on earth.

"*And His voice* [Christ] *as the sound of many waters*" (Rev. 1:15b). "*And I heard a voice from heaven, as the voice of many waters…*" (Rev.

14:2). *"And I heard as it were the voice of a great multitude, and as the voice of many waters ..."* (Rev. 19:6).

See Revelation 17 verses 1 and 15 for the definition of "many waters." It is a mixed multitude of people. These are the ones who will come out of the great tribulation as the appointed hour dawns upon the earth (Rev. 7:14).

The true Church will find itself being raptured out of the dawning days of the "Day of the Lord." They will be clothed in white robes crying with a loud voice, "Salvation to God," and worshiping Him and the Lamb with the all the angels, and the 24 elders and the 4 living ones, *"Saying, Amen: Blessing, and glory, and wisdom, and thanksgiving, and honour, and power, and might, unto our God forever and ever. Amen"* (see Rev. 7:10-12).

What a glorious scene it will be at the throne in Heaven when Jesus Christ sounds the trumpet and gathers His Bride unto Himself as the Church is caught up to meet Him in the air.

> *For the Lord Himself shall descend from heaven with a shout, with the voice of the archangel, and with the trump of God: and the dead in Christ shall rise first: then we which are alive and remain shall be caught up* [*harpazo*, raptured] *together with them in the clouds to meet the Lord in the air: and so shall we ever be with the Lord"* (1 Thessalonians 4:16-17).

The faithful will be serving Him night and day in His temple and the Lamb will feed them, heal them, wipe away their tears, take away their sorrows, and provide for them fountains of living waters. These are waters of eternal life, waters that will satisfy the soul and make it possible for us to live forever and ever with the Lord.

This is the first and clearest evidence of a raptured multitude in the Book of Revelation. The use of *he soteria* in Revelation 7:10, in this context, "suggest the connotation of 'victory.' John never uses *sozo* ('I save') to denote salvation from sin as other New Testament writers do (Caird). It is questionable as to whether he uses the noun *soteria* in this sense too."[1]

Therefore, John's use of the noun here may be used to indicate the victory (*nikos*) won through Jesus Christ at the time of the Rapture; *"But thanks be to God, which giveth us the victory through our Lord Jesus Christ*" (1 Cor. 15:57).

Attempts to identify the Church in Heaven prior to this passage in the Book of Revelation are based on speculation. Such claims are fraught with problems lacking hard exegetical evidence. One consistent identifying key of the Church in the Book of Revelation is the fact that the Church is promised to be gathered to the throne of God and is found at or before the throne of God (Rev. 3:21; 7:9,10,15; 12:5b with Christ; 14:3,5; 19:5-8; Jn. 14:3; 1 Thess. 4:17).

Why is this multitude found with palm branches in their hands and why are they singing thanksgiving and salvation? These are clues for us as to "when" the Rapture will take place—clues to "what season," not "what day."

> "The Feast of Tabernacles, which is reflected in this scene. *Skenosei*, 'be (be a) tabernacle,' [is translated 'dwell' in Revelation 7:15. This] was a feast of rest (Deut. 16:13-15).... The cry 'salvation' in Revelation 7:10 recalls the 'Hosanna,' or 'save now,' uttered during the feast (Lee)."[2]

The white robes that the multitude wear indicate a victory that they won through Jesus Christ. "The palms carried in their hands, *kai phoinikes en tais chersin auton*, 'and palm branches were in their hands,' confirm the victory symbolism. [The use of palms were] prominent at the Feast of Tabernacles."[3]

Palm branches were also part of the triumphal entry of Jesus Christ into Jerusalem (Mt. 21:8; Mk. 11:8-9; Lk. 19:38; Jn. 12:13). The fact that this entry is recorded in the four Gospels gives indication to its significance. Jesus rode into Jerusalem on a "young ass," not to conquer world powers, but to conquer sin and death and to win salvation for those who believed and trusted in Him.

At His Second Coming He will ride a great white horse, carrying a rod of iron, and He will yield all the power and authority of the One who rightfully sits at the right hand of God. The chiastic structure or inverted parallelism of Psalm 118, the last Psalm of the Hillel (hallelujah) that was recited during the Feast of Tabernacles, alludes to *two comings and triumphs of the Messiah.*

> *The Lord is my strength and song, and is become my* [1] *salvation. The voice of rejoicing and salvation is in the tabernacles of the righteous: the right hand of the Lord doeth valiantly.* ***The right hand of the Lord is exalted:*** *the right hand of the Lord doeth valiantly. I shall not* [2] *die, but live, and declare the works of the Lord*" (Psalm 118:14-17).

The right hand is recorded as doing valiantly *twice.* The Hebrew word for valiantly, *chayil,* meaning primarily "strength, army, and power," is a military term. The central theme of Psalm 118 is the exaltation of the right hand of the Lord, which is Jesus Christ.

"*Who is he that condemneth? It is Christ that died, yea rather, that is risen, who is even at the right hand of God, who also maketh intercession for us*" (Rom. 8:34). Jesus is the right hand of the power of God. The Jews knew that He who sat to the right side of God claimed to be an equal with God.

> "*Bathsheba therefore went unto king Solomon...and* [Solomon] *bowed himself unto her, and sat down on his throne, and caused a seat to be set for the king's mother; and she sat on his right hand* (1 Kings 2:19).

"A person of high rank who puts anyone on his right hand gives him [or her] equal honor with himself and recognizes [them] as of equal dignity"[4] (Mt. 26:64-65; Acts 2:25-37; 5:29-33; 7:56-57; Heb. 1:1-3; 12:2).

"The right hand or the right side is preferred (Acts 3:7), hence God is said to be at the right hand of the person whom He helps as the enemy is to the right of him whom he seeks to overcome and the accuser to the right of the accused. By the right hand the whole man is claimed."[5]

Therefore, the celebration taking place in Revelation 7:9-17 draws strong parallels to the celebration of the Feast of Tabernacles and especially to the final day of celebration—the great day of salvation: "Hassana Rabba. "This multitude has now entered into a heavenly rest, another symbolic feature of the tabernacles celebration."[6]

Because the Feast of Tabernacles also commemorates Israel's dwelling in tents (tabernacles) during their exodus from Egypt, this would also suggest that it is the time when the 144,000, the faithful remnant of Israel, will go into the wilderness. God will not only shelter or tabernacle believers in Heaven (Rev. 7:15), but He also will shelter, feed, and protect the 144,000 elect of God in the wilderness, at the *beginning* of the tribulation (Rev. 7:3, 9:4, 12:6,14, 14:1).

Thomas, Beckwith, and Walvoord might cite that the main problem with this view is that it cannot account for the placement of the vision as early as chapter 7, nor account for the heavenly scene.[7] Once again, by understanding that the sixth seal is the Rapture at the beginning of the tribulation, we are not faced with the problem of reconciling this with the vision's early placement and can account for the *heavenly scene as the celebration of the "pretribulation Raptured Church" in Heaven.*

October and the Feast of Tabernacles

As stated previously, these parallels to the Feast of Tabernacles in Revelation chapter 7 offer us a clue as to the season of the Rapture and/or the start of the tribulation. (See Figure 2 on page 3.) The Feast of Tabernacles was celebrated in the month of Tishri on the fifteenth through twenty-first day (October).[8]

Remember that the seasons, along with the Jewish feasts, are determined by the lunar cycles of new and full moons in conjunction with the earth's orbit around the sun. The Feast of Tabernacles begins with the full moon, which arrives about 14 and half days after the new moon, Tishri 1 to Tishri 15. Lunar eclipses can only take place during the full moon phase.

(See Chapters 10 and 11 for astronomical data that shows how the lunar and solar eclipses are related to the coming of the "Day of the Lord." *When considered corporately, the Scriptures [Is. 13:10; Joel 2:31; Acts 2:19-20; Rev. 12:1-4], clearly point to the month of Tishri in late September and early October.*)

Revelation Chapter 8

Chapter 8 continues after the parenthetical thoughts of chapter 7. With the sealing of the 144,000 and with the Church securely in Heaven, God will begin to convince the world of its sin, lack of righteousness, and the impending total judgment. He will use the ministry of the 144,000 Jews, led by the two witnesses, to accomplish this.

The negative fruit of their ministry will produce a growing resentment as people blame them for the plagues that are evidenced against the world. The 144,000 will separate themselves from those who remain in Jerusalem, who agreed to live under the compromising terms of the seven-year covenant made with the beast. The 144,000 will be like the Orthodox Jews in Israel today who vehemently object to land compromises with the PLO or others.

The 144,000 will separate themselves from national Israel, who agrees to the "New World Order" peace agreement. At this point, however, the world will not be able to discern that the beast is empowered by satan, the dragon. Satan will gradually manipulate and deceive the world into accepting him as the long-awaited Messiah. Many will grow to resent the ministry of the two witnesses who are telling the world to fear God and worship Him who sits on the throne in Heaven.

The world will be divided over who and what to believe. Should the world believe the two witnesses who are raining fire down upon wickedness and rebellion, or should they believe this great world leader who comes in the name of peace and prosperity for all, while performing wondrously deceptive miracles of his own?

> *And he doeth great wonders, so that he maketh fire come down from heaven on the earth in the sight of men, and deceiveth them that dwell on the earth by the means of those miracles...*" (Revelation 13:13-14).

Paul's warning to the Thessalonians is clear: "*For when they shall say, Peace and safety; then sudden destruction cometh upon them...*" (1 Thess. 5:3). While the false prophet and the false Messiah are offering and implementing the greatest and most enchanting world economic system, the two witness will have withdrawn to the wilderness with the 144,000.

> *And his power shall be mighty, but not by his own power: and he shall destroy wonderfully, and shall prosper, and practise, and shall destroy the mighty and the holy people. And through his policy also he shall cause craft to prosper in his hand; and he shall magnify himself in his heart, and by peace shall destroy many: he shall also stand up against the Prince of princes; but he shall be broken without hand* (Daniel 8:24-25).

> *And the woman fled into the wilderness, where she hath a place prepared of God, that they* [the two witnesses] *should feed her there a thousand two hundred and threescore days* [42 lunar months or 3 and 1/2 years] ... *And to the woman were given two wings of a great eagle, that she might fly into the wilderness ...from the face of the serpent* [satan] (Revelation 12:6,14).

The witnesses will be laboring during the first half of the tribulation period to inform the 144,000 of the truth of God's Word and the Second Coming of the Lord Jesus Christ. At the same time the witnesses will direct divine judgments upon an unrepentant and deceived world, which will be succumbing to the great delusions of the beast. The world will refuse to receive the love of the truth, that they might be saved, and instead they will choose the pleasures of unrighteousness that the first beast offers.

> *And with all deceivableness of unrighteousness in them that perish; because they received not the love of the truth, that they might be saved. And for this cause God shall send them strong delusion, that they should believe a lie* (2 Thessalonians 2:10-11).

The world will be at peace, but a battle will be raging in the heavens between satan, his angels, and the faithful angels of God (Rev. 12:7). Israel will be at peace with her Arab neighbors and everything would be great, if it were not for those two renegade Jews and their following who refuse to capitulate. These will refuse to compromise and accept this great world leader, believed by some to be the long-awaited Messiah, and the new peace agreement.

The two witnesses will know his true identity. Many professing Christians, who were left behind when the Rapture took place, will be convinced by the two witnesses that they must trust in the Lord Jesus Christ with all their heart. They must proclaim His name even as they are faced with death. This is the fiery tribulation promised to the Laodicean Church in Revelation 3:14-22.

These are the ones who thought they were Christians, but the Rapture and the ministry of the two witnesses will open their eyes and reveal their poverty and their nakedness before God. They will be convinced that they must totally surrender their lives to the Lord. This might eventually cost them their lives as they refuse to submit and worship the beast. Jesus will stand at the door of death and wait for them to enter. As they are tried and tested and found faithful unto death, they will enter into their reward. Henceforth, they will find rest from the agony, torture, and pain that will exist on earth at that time.

> *Here is the patience of the saints: here are they that keep the commandments of God, and the faith of Jesus. And I heard a voice from heaven saying unto me, Write, Blessed are the dead which die in the Lord from henceforth…* (Revelation 14:12-13).

The focus of the first four trumpet judgments in Revelation 8 are the gods of polytheistic religions and paganism. "The Egyptians, the Babylonians, and the Canaanites all had many gods, most of them manifested in the material world. These gods, though appearing in the form of familiar physical entities—rivers, seas, mountains, storms, earth, moon, sun and stars—were presumed to be personal and powerful."[9]

With the first four trumpet judgments, one-third of the earth (trees and grass) are burnt up, one-third of the seas become as blood, one-third of the rivers and fountains are poisoned, and one-third of the sun, moon, and stars are darkened (Rev. 8:1-12).

In Revelation 12:4 we learn that one-third of the stars were attracted by the tail of the dragon and cast to the earth. The portions account for that which belongs to the dragon and this is why it is being judged.

After the four trumpets are accomplished, an angel, flying in the midst of Heaven, announces three impending woes upon the *inhabitants of the earth.* The first woe is the fifth trumpet, which announces the arrival of satan who will have been forever banished from Heaven (Rev. 9:12-11).

The same events are recorded in Revelation 12:9,12, but from a heavenly perspective. They are followed by the same announcement to the *inhabitants of the earth*, "*Woe*"!

The World Wants Peace

The talk of peace today in Israel is a clear indicator that the start of the tribulation period is near, and therefore the Rapture as well, which will announce and initiate the new age. According to Scripture, the peace offered to Israel is only a pretense to get Israel to let down its guard and open itself up to military destruction. This is the motivation behind today's peace initiative in the Middle East.

A summary of an article written by Norman Frantz that appeared in *Current Thoughts and Trends*, January 1994, Volume 10, No.1, pages 29-30, but originally appeared in *Monetary & Economic Review*, reveals the true intent of the PLO in today's peace negotiations.

After phase one of today's peace plan is in place, which requires Israel to give up the Gaza Strip, Jericho, and parts of the Golon Heights, the question becomes: What will be the next step?

> "PLO spokesmen have indicated that once they have established a Palestinian state, *they will live there in peace, just long enough to strengthen their positions.* Then phase three will kick in—a general military initiative to wipe out Israel. The PNC has stated that it will strive to bring about a union of Syria, Jordan, Iraq, and Libya in order to annihilate Israel and reclaim all Palestinian territory." (Emphasis added.)

The article goes on to cite statements from Arafat, since the accord was signed in September of 1993, which " ...indicate that the *PLO plans to take Jerusalem after a peace treaty is negotiated and signed.*" (Emphasis added.)

The PLO does not know it, but they are helping to fulfill Bible prophecy right before our eyes. Furthermore, they are setting the stage for antichrist to come to power. Just as Antiochus IV (Epiphanes), a type of antichrist from earlier Maccabean Jewish history, came from Syria, the future antichrist (the beast) may come out of Syria with a promise of peace in his hand.

Many leading Jews are excited about the new age of redemption that appears to be dawning for Israel. Some see the promise of a new golden age of peace and prosperity. It is the potential prosperity within a united global economy that is fueling the world's pursuit of a one-world government and economy. But realization of this goal will require a united religious community as well; thus we have a growing ecumenical movement.

In 1994 religious leaders from all over the world gathered in Israel with leading Jewish religious leaders to emphasize their common points of interest and faith at an international conference of faith. It was the first of its kind and has planted the foundation for a uniting of the three major faiths, Christian, Jewish, and Muslim.

I strongly encourage Israel not to deal with Syria or any of the Arab nations, but what God has said must, in fact, be fulfilled. There will be no stopping the fulfillment of prophecy, for God's Word must be fulfilled. Just as Daniel 8:11-15 prophesied that Antiochus Epiphanes would come and desecrate the temple, and was fulfilled exactly, so will the prophecies of Daniel 8:23-25; 9:27, which warn us about the deceptive peace covenant of the coming antichrist, be fulfilled.

Israel and the world will come to know that Jesus Christ is Lord because Jesus will come in judgment and deliver Israel out of the hands of antichrist. He will then set up His Kingdom on earth. What time is it? The signs of His coming are all around us.

The World Rejects Truth

The struggle between the two witnesses of God and the beast will come to a head at the middle of the tribulation period. The two witnesses will be blamed by the world for the fiery judgments of the first four trumpet judgments.

> *And they that dwell upon the earth shall rejoice over them* [the deaths of the two witnesses], *and make merry, and shall send gifts one to another; because these two prophets tormented them that dwelt on the earth* (Revelation 11:10).

The reaction by the world toward them will be the same as it has always been for God's prophets: doubt and ridicule (2 Kings 1:9-15). The story of Elijah typifies the animosity that exists between those who serve the gods of the world versus those who serve the true God of Heaven.

These events in Revelation remind us of Elijah's ministry. Elijah also called fire down from Heaven when King Ahaziah sent out his captains with 50 men three times. After the second time the captain of the third group of 50 begs for mercy and Elijah goes down with him, and tells the king he will die because he trusted in the god of Ekron. Shortly after this Elijah was taken up to Heaven in a chariot of fire (2 Kings 2:11).

Many commentators believe that the identity of one of the two witnesses could be Elijah fulfilling the prophecies of Malachi 4:5, which promises to send the great prophet Elijah *before the coming of the great "Day of the Lord.*" This means that if one of the two witnesses is Elijah, then their ministry best fits into the first half of the tribulation and not the second because he comes "*before*" the coming of the great "Day of the Lord."

However, the confrontation between God's two witnesses and the antichrist will have a different ending than Elijah's encounter with King Ahaziah. The beast will come after the two witnesses at the end of the first half of Daniel's Seventieth Week and kill them (Rev. 11:7-9; Dan. 9:27).

The identity of the second witness is believed by some to be Moses or Enoch. There are many reasons why this may or may not be so, but their identity has been sufficiently debated in other works. Therefore I will not pursue this issue any further.

The earth will rejoice at the death of these two witnesses because they will think their problems are over (Rev. 11:10). Their world leader will appear to have temporarily proven himself stronger than the two witnesses by overcoming them. As a result of his attack on them, he himself will appear to be mortally wounded, but miraculously recovers. "*And his deadly wound was healed: and all the world wondered after the beast*" (Rev. 13:3).

This will elevate his appeal to the masses and cause many to believe it is futile to oppose someone who cannot be killed, "*Who is like unto the beast? who is able to make war with him?*" (Rev. 13:4) He will be wounded because God promised that whosoever hurts His two witnesses or kills them, must be killed also in the same manner (Rev. 11:5).

Chapter 8 of Revelation ends with a solemn warning that the first four trumpet judgments were not as bad as the next three. Up until this time, satan has also been battling to stay in Heaven. At the same time the ministry of the two witnesses is ending. Satan will lose the battle in Heaven and he will be cast out, knowing that his time is short (Rev. 12:7-12).

The woe of Revelation 12:12 is the same woe as Revelation 8:13, which is the fifth trumpet judgment of Revelation 9:1-12. This event takes place just prior to the middle of the tribulation. Then satan will be revealed when the peace covenant is broken and the Abomination of Desolation takes place in the reconstructed temple in Israel (Dan. 8:25; 9:27; Mt. 24:15).

With the ministry of the two witnesses, Israel and the world will have been given one last opportunity to repent and receive Jesus Christ as Lord and Savior before the outpouring of God's supreme wrath. The world's rejection of the two witnesses will add another opportunity to the parable that is recorded in Mark 12:1-11.

Just as they took Jesus, the Son of the Lord of the vineyard, and crucified Him, so too will Israel and the world reject God's last two witnesses. In Mark 12:9 the question is asked: "*What shall therefore the lord of the vineyard do? he will come and destroy the husbandmen, and will give the vineyard unto others.*"

In A.D. 70 God did just that. He destroyed Israel, the nation to whom Jesus came and was rejected. After the opportunities of the first half of the tribulation are offered and squandered by Israel and the world, God will cast satan out of Heaven, relegate him to the earth, and deliver both him and the world into judgment.

The Beginning of Great Tribulation

Chapter 9 of Revelation now identifies the fifth trumpet and the first woe as one falling as a star from Heaven. "*I beheld Satan as lightning fall from heaven*" (Lk. 10:18). "*And the great dragon was cast out...*" (Rev. 12:9).

This fallen angel will have the key to the bottomless pit and upon his arrival he will open the pit and free the imprisoned demons. These demons are the fallen angels that have been held captive for at least three-and-one-half years and longer. As a result of the battle in Heaven, one-third of the stars of Heaven (angels who follow lucifer, satan, that great red dragon) are cast out of Heaven and reserved for that appointed time when God will allow them to be loosed for a season (Rev. 12:3-4,9).

It is possible, however, that the battle taking place in Heaven as addressed in Revelation 12:7 has been going on ever since Christ ascended to Heaven. It is clear from the context of Revelation chapter 9 that it is satan, lucifer himself, the great destroyer of this world, who will be given the keys of the bottomless pit.

> *And they had a king over them, which is the angel of the bottomless pit, whose name in the Hebrew tongue is Abaddon* [which means "destroyer"], *but in the Greek tongue hath his name Apollyon*" (Rev. 9:11; see also Is. 14:12-17).

The demons who are released from this bottomless pit will inflict much pain upon men, not the environment.

> *And it was commanded them that they should not hurt the grass of the earth, neither any green thing, neither any tree; but only those men which have not the seal of God in their foreheads*" (Revelation 9:4).

This period of grievous pain and torment will continue for five months and will be part of the beast's and satan's campaign to set himself up as the "god" to be worshiped by all.

He will establish his hold on the temple in Israel by working to overcome the fear and doubt that will have come upon the world after the two witnesses are killed and resurrected three-and-one-half days later. This resurrection may take place on what would have been Easter morning, thus paralleling our Lord's resurrection.

(See Chapter 8, "God's Two Witnesses," and Chapter 10, "3 1/2 Years + 3 1/2 Days = 'Easter' " regarding the Easter morning resurrection.)

Satan, knowing that he has but a short time, works to gain total control over the world, set up his kingdom, prepare his strategy, and gather his forces against Jesus Christ as He returns.

> *For they are the spirits of devils, working miracles, which go forth unto the kings of the earth and the whole world, to gather them to the battle of that great day of God Almighty*" (Revelation 16:14).

> *But in his estate shall he honour the God of forces...*" (Daniel 11:38).

After the killing and resurrection of the two witnesses, the antichrist will use the armies of Gog and Magog (the armies of the New World

Government, "Babylon the Great") to move against Jerusalem in an attempt to gain complete control.

"In the latter years thou shalt come into the land ...thou shalt ascend and come like a storm, thou shalt be like a cloud to cover the land..." (Ezek. 38:8-10). *"And the serpent cast out of his mouth water as a flood after the woman* [Israel]" (see Rev. 12:15-17). "[With Israel's defenses down] *I will go up to the land of unwalled villages...*" (see Ezek. 38:11-12).

With chaos and confusion surrounding Jerusalem, the advancing armies of Gog and Magog, under the protection of the beast (New World U.N. Forces or United World Forces), will surround Jerusalem.

> *When ye therefore shall see the abomination of desolation, spoken by Daniel the prophet, stand in the holy place...Then let them which be in Judea flee into the mountains* (Matthew 24:15-16).

After the Abomination of Desolation, many will attempt to flee Judea to join the 144,000, which will have already been in the wilderness for three-and-one-half years. With the beast revealed to Israel, God will use this time to convince Israel of their unbelief and that Jesus Christ is Lord. God in His fury will destroy those who come against Jerusalem with a great earthquake and will send fire upon the land of Gog and Magog. *"And I will send a fire on Magog..."* (Ezek. 39:6).

> *Therefore shall her plagues come in one day, death, and mourning, and famine; and she shall be utterly burned with fire: for strong is the Lord God who judgeth her. And the kings of the earth, who have committed fornication and lived deliciously with her, shall bewail her, and lament for her, when they shall see the smoke of her burning, standing afar off for the fear of her torment, saying, Alas, alas that great city Babylon* [Magog], *that mighty city! for in one hour is thy judgment come* (Revelation 18:8-10).

Then the 144,000 and all of Israel will fear God and know that Jesus Christ is Lord.

...all the men that are upon the face of the earth, shall shake at My presence, and the mountains shall be thrown down... (see Ezekiel 38:19-20).

And I will set My glory among the heathen, and all the heathen shall see My judgment that I have executed, and My hand that I have laid upon them (Ezekiel 39:21).

And the same hour was there a great earthquake, and the tenth part of the city fell, and in the earthquake were slain of men seven thousand: and the remnant were affrighted, and gave glory to the God of Heaven (Revelation 11:13).

See also Zechariah 12:9-11.

After the Battle of Gog and Magog

After the battle of Gog and Magog, the sixth trumpet will sound and the second woe will be introduced (Rev. 9:13-14). This woe will prepare the 200-million-man army of the kings of the East. This army will have been prepared for a specific hour in order to slay a third part of men (Rev. 9:15).

These armies will be moving independently. When the beast discovers their coalition, he moves to counter them: "*But tidings out of the east and out of the north shall trouble him...*" (Dan. 11:44). He does this by diverting them to come against the false prophet, the second and religious beast of Revelation 13:11-17. (See Chapter 9 of this book for more on this conflict.)

It is interesting to note how the Eastern nations such as North Korea, China, Vietnam, India, Syria, Jordan, Iraq, Iran, and Pakistan, as well as the nations of the former Soviet Union, which lie to the north, are developing as independent forces with very loose ties to the Western powers.

Somehow the beast will convince the kings of the East to gather in the valley of Armageddon against the Lamb (Rev. 17:14). He will probably do this by sacrificing the false prophet and the remnant of Western "Christianity." (I use the term "Christianity" loosely here.)

There have been many dark days in the history of Christendom, but the darkness that exists in the kingdom of the great whore, who sits on many waters, is the most repugnant, degenerate, and wicked of all generations. God's judgment will come at the hands of the ten (Eastern) kings who gain power with the beast for one hour (Rev. 17:12-13,16-17).

The kings of the East will move against the great whore (the one-world religion, the mystery religion of "Babylon the Great") who will be carried about by the beast (Rev. 17:7,15).

This is the destruction of the apostate one-world religion that the beast will use to gain control over the people of the Western world. The kings of the East will be primarily Muslim, Buddhist, Hindu, and other Eastern religions who hate the whore and in one hour receive power with the beast.

Their hatred for the woman will be fueled by the fact that they were, for all practical purposes, excluded from this great new economic world system. As a result of this attack, the great whore (Babylon the Great), will be reduced to rubble as the judgment of God takes place. All this is now taking form in the world in which we now live. The stage is set and the curtain is about to rise on the final chapter of world history.

End Notes

1. G.V.A. Caird, *A Commentary on the Revelation of St. John the Divine*, HNTC, (New York: Harper & Row, 1966), as cited by Thomas, *Revelation 1–7: An Exegetical Commentary*, p. 490.

2. William Lee, "The Revelation of St. John," in *The Holy Bible*, F.C. Cook, ed., (London: John Murray, 1881), as cited by Thomas, *Revelation 1–7: An Exegetical Commentary*, p. 485.

3. Thomas, *Revelation 1–7: An Exegetical Commentary*, pp. 487-488.

4. Spiros Zodhiates, *Hebrew-Greek Study Bible: Lexicon to the Old and New Testaments,* s.v. "Dexios," (Chattanooga, TN: AMG Int., 1985).

5. Ibid.

6. Thomas, *Revelation 1–7: An Exegetical Commentary*, p. 490.

7. Ibid.

8. Colin Brown, Lothar Ceonen, Erich Beyreuther, Hans Bietenhard, eds., *The New Testament Dictionary of New Testament Theology*,

Vol. 3, s.v. "Tent, Tabernacle," (Grand Rapids, MI: Zondervan Publishing, 1986), p. 813.

9. Howard J. VanTill, *The Fourth Day: What the Bible and the Heavens Are Telling Us About Creation,* (Grand Rapids, MI: Eerdmans Publishing Co., 1986), p. 41.

Chapter 8

Parenthetical Chapters

Filling in the Gaps
Revelation 10–11:14

Chapters 10 and 11 of Revelation serve as parenthetical reminders. A parenthetical section is introduced, which continues through Revelation 11:14. "It does not advance the narrative, but presents other facts, which contribute to the total prophetic scene."[1]

When I say "parenthetical," I mean it in a sense that as the vision of Revelation was revealed to John, there were many different aspects to it. John first gives us a description of what he saw and heard. Then, he revealed several numbered progressive sequences, churches, seals, trumpets, and vials.

Chapters 10 and 11 take us back to the beginning of the Book of Revelation and remind us of the divine nature of its heavenly author, the Lord Jesus Christ. Verses 1-3 of chapter 10 serve to combine the descriptions given of God the Father, the Lord Jesus Christ, and the Holy Spirit found in chapters 1, 4, and 5.

The rainbow over His head suggests that the Mighty Angel, Jesus Christ, has come from the Father's throne where John earlier saw the rainbow above the Throne of God (Rev. 4:3). At the throne of God, Jesus received the book from the Father. At that time the book was closed—but in chapter 10 the book is open. Three significant points concerning John's description of this Mighty Angel need to be considered.

1. The Angel is now clothed in a cloud, indicating the location of this Angel, who must be Jesus Christ. The fact that Jesus Christ is in the clouds fits the description of the Rapture: "*Then we which are alive and remain shall be caught up together with them in the clouds to meet the Lord in the air...*" (1 Thess. 4:17). In Acts 1:9-11 the apostles were told that Jesus would return in the same manner as He was taken, which was in a cloud. But the clearest passage that pertains to this is Mark 13:24-27.

> *But in those days, after that tribulation, the sun shall be darkened, and the moon shall not give her light, and the stars of heaven shall fall, and the powers that are in heaven shall be shaken. And then shall they see the Son of man coming in the clouds with great power and glory* [after the Rapture]. *And then shall He send His angels, and shall gather together His elect from the four winds, from the uttermost part of the earth to the uttermost part of heaven* [the sealing of the 144,00] (Mark 13:24-27).

2. Jesus is coming in the clouds with great power and glory (Rev. 10:1). His face shining as the sun indicates that John was seeing a glorified Christ as described by Matthew in the transfiguration of Christ "*and His face did shine as the sun*" (Mt. 17:2).

3. His feet are described as pillars of fire. These are pillars of a purifying fire, which means He is coming to put all things under His feet with the burning fires of purification. This is a picture of Jesus coming in the clouds after the Rapture of His Church, which will be immediately followed by the sealing of the 144,000. This understanding is consistent with Revelation chapters 6 and 7 and all three Gospel accounts of Jesus' disclosure of end-time events and His description of the Second Coming.

The Chronology of the Sixth Seal and the Gospels

Before we can understand Revelation chapter 10, we need to first consider a threefold comparison between the opening of the sixth seal in Revelation 6, key verses in Revelation chapter 7, and Mark 13:24-27. The careful reader will note the similarity of the subject matter and the chronology of the events.

> *But in those days, after that tribulation, the sun shall be darkened, and the moon shall not give her light, and the stars of heaven shall fall, and the powers that are in heaven shall be shaken. And then shall they see the Son of man coming in the clouds with great power and glory. And then shall He send His angels, and shall gather together His elect from the four winds, from the uttermost part of the earth to the uttermost part of heaven* (Mark 13:24-27).

> *And I beheld when He had opened the sixth seal, and lo, there was a great earthquake; and the sun became black as sackcloth of hair, and the moon became as blood; and the stars of heaven fell unto the earth, even as a fig tree casteth her untimely figs, when she is shaken of a mighty wind. And the heaven departed as a scroll when it is rolled together; and every mountain and island were moved out of their places* (Revelation 6:12-14).

Mark 13:24
The tribulation that is said to be over is the tribulation that came within the beginning of sorrows. This tribulation consisted of the fights, wars, famines, and diseases of the beginning of sorrows. This is the same tribulation endured by the souls over centuries who are now under the altar of the fifth seal (Rev. 6:9-11). These will continue until the sixth seal is opened.

Revelation 6:12 and Mark 13:24
When the sixth seal is opened, a great earthquake will take place and the dead in Christ will be resurrected and raptured to Heaven by the Lord, instantly followed by those who are alive and in the Lord. The earthquake will be so great that it will send tons of dust into the atmosphere, causing the sun to be darkened. The moon will be turned to blood (red), possibly describing an accompanying lunar eclipse.

Revelation 6:13 and Mark 13:25
The powers of Heaven will be shaken. Great cosmic upheaval will begin to take place and people will see things falling from the heavens, possibly meteors or the arrival of the fallen angels that have been cast out of Heaven because the Church is now there (Rev. 12:4,6-9). The fact that this is described in Revelation 6:13 as *figs falling in an untimely fashion by a mighty wind*, fits the motif of fallen angels being cast out of Heaven and to earth against their will.

Revelation 6:14
The heavens will depart as a scroll. The heavens will roll back and cause great upheaval on the earth. The rolling back of the heavens may reveal Christ's Second Coming in power and great glory.

Revelation 6:16-17 and Mark 13:26
Men of low and high estate will seek to hide from the One who has revealed Himself as sitting on the throne in Heaven and from the wrath of the Lamb, for the "Day of the Lord" will have come. At that point the world will have seen the Lord coming in the clouds, and partially revealing His power and His glory to the world by opening and executing the sixth seal.

And said to the mountains and rocks, Fall on us, and hide us from the face of Him that sitteth on the throne, and from the wrath of the Lamb: for the great day of His wrath is come; and who shall be able to stand? (Revelation 6:16-17)

And after these things I saw four angels standing on the four corners of the earth, holding the four winds of the earth, that the wind should not blow on the earth, nor on the sea, nor on any tree. And I saw another angel ascending from the east, having the seal of the living God: and he cried with a loud voice to the four angels, to whom it was given to hurt the earth and the sea, saying, Hurt not the earth, neither the sea, nor the trees, till we have sealed the servants of our God in their foreheads (Revelation 7:1-3).

Revelation 7:1-3 and Mark 13:27
Immediately after the Rapture, God will introduce a delay after the seventh seal is opened (Rev. 8:1). This delay will facilitate the gathering and the sealing of God's elect of Israel (the 144,000). They will be gathered to the two witnesses and together they will go off into the wilderness to a place prepared for them (Rev. 12:6). While there, they will learn about the Lord and will come to know Jesus Christ as Lord.

Notice how the sequence of events are exactly the same. They flow from a time of promised tribulation to great upheavals. Stars are falling from the heavens and the powers of Heaven are shaken. Men's hearts are full of fear (Lk. 21:25-27). Christ adds, "*And when these things begin to come to pass, then look up, and lift up your heads; for your redemption draweth nigh*" (Lk. 21:28).

Christ then gives the parable of the fig tree, using the same metaphor of Revelation 6:13. This is no coincidence. This is the consistency of Scripture, realizing that the first six seals are not a part of the tribulation, but they lead up to it. Revelation chapter 10 is a cosmic description of the Rapture and the glory of Christ.

The Open Book/Scroll

Chapter 10 of Revelation has some amazing parallels to chapters 4, 5, and 6 of Revelation, opening with the description of a Mighty Angel that is coming down from Heaven with an "open" book in His hand. The opened book is a very important detail that needs to be explored.

Richard Bauckham links the mighty angels of Revelation 10:1 and 5:2. He concludes that the open book of Revelation 10:2 is the same closed book of 5:2. He writes, "A major key to the correct interpretation of Revelation has been missed by almost all scholars. It is that the scroll which John sees, sealed with the seven seals, in the hand of God (5:1) is the same as the scroll which he sees open in the hands of an angel in (10:2)."[2] (For a detailed discussion on the hard exegetical evidence for this conclusion, please read *The Climax of Prophecy* by Richard Bauckham, pages 243-267.)

Interestingly, as the vision in chapter 10 continues to unfold, John's flow is interrupted by a command for John not to reveal what the seven thunders had said to him.

> *And when the seven thunders had uttered their voices, I was about to write: and I heard a voice from heaven saying unto me, Seal up those things which the seven thunders uttered, and write them not* (Revelation 10:4).

Some writers have suggested that there is no need for John to write concerning the mystery because it has already been revealed to the prophets of old (Rev. 10:7). It is suggested that John may have heard what was already declared to the prophets.[3]

This intimates that there would be no need for it to be revealed again. A similar description is found in Daniel 12:5-7 of one standing upon the waters of the river with both hands lifted up to Heaven, swearing by Him who lives forever, and saying that "*it shall be for a time, times, and an half; and when he shall have accomplished to scatter the power of the holy people, all these things shall be finished.*"

Revelation 10:5-7 clearly alludes to Daniel 12:7. The angel of Revelation 10 announces that at last the period that leads immediately to the end of a godless world history has arrived (the period predicted in Daniel 12:7 as "*a time, times, and an half a times*").[4] Daniel heard the words of the angel, but he understood them not. When Daniel inquired further, he was told that the meaning of these words were sealed up until the time of the end (Dan. 12:9).

It would not be until John symbolically ate the book that the prophecy concerning the very end would be revealed. It was already revealed to Daniel that in the days of the fourth kingdom, God would begin to establish an everlasting Kingdom (Dan. 2:44-45). But God did not reveal to Daniel *when* this Kingdom would be consummated.

Much dispute has been occasioned over the different Greek words used to describe "the book" in Revelation 5:1 and 10:2; respectively, *bibliov* and *biblaridov*, the latter being translated "little book." Although Bauckham and others do an excellent job of eliminating the significance of any difference between the two words in question, the difference may be deliberately calling attention to the diminished size of the book and that as a result of the seals being removed and their decrees fulfilled.

Revelation is a book with a very long introduction. "The progressive opening of the scroll is a literary device that John used in order to narrate material, which prepares us for and is presupposed by the contents of the scroll itself."[5]

The "little book" does not include the decrees of the seven seals, but only what remains after the seventh seal has been removed. The first event encountered with the seventh seal removed is a delay and this delay is also found in Revelation 10:6. The introduction to the seventh seal covers at least 1,900 years of history because the first six seals relate to Church history, the beginning of sorrows. Therefore, to refer to the unsealed scroll as a "little book" does not preclude it from being the same book of Revelation 5:1.

When the seventh angel sounds the seventh seal, the delay associated with it will be complete and the seven years of Daniel's Seventieth Week will begin to manifest itself.

The Mighty Angel of Revelation 10:1

The Mighty Angel of 10:1 and the seventh angel who sounds the opening of the seventh seal are related in number. Revelation 6:1 identifies the first thunder and Revelation 10:7 identifies the last thunder associated with the seven seals.

The fact that seven thunders sound in Revelation 10:3, as compared to the general noise of thunder in Revelation 6:1, indicates the cumulative or compounding nature of the seven seals over time. They grow with intensity as the pangs of birth. Therefore, the conclusion is that the "open book" of Revelation 10 is the same as the "sealed book" of Revelation 5.

Revelation 6–9 overlap Revelation 10:1–11:13. The thunder of 6:1 and 10:3 are of the same grouping. A thunderous voice was heard when the first seal was opened by the Lamb (Rev. 6:1). With all seven seals opened, all seven thunders utter their voices collectively. These seven call for the sounding of the first trumpet. With the sound of the seven thunders, the Lamb of Revelation 6:1 now sounds as a thunderous roaring lion.

The description of this Mighty Angel (Rev. 10:1-3) combines the descriptions of the glorified Christ and the Father (Rev. 4:3; 1:14). The description of Revelation 1:14 is clearly a glorified Christ and God the Father (Rev. 4:3), the One who sits on the throne in Heaven. It is a picture of Jesus sharing the glory that He had always had with His Father (Jn. 17:5).

In Revelation 5:5, we find that Jesus Christ is the only One worthy to open the book by removing the seals.

> *And one of the elders saith unto me, Weep not: behold, the Lion of the tribe of Juda, the Root of David, hath prevailed to open the book, and to loose the seven seals thereof* (Revelation 5:5).

What follows in Revelation 5:6-14 is a description of the Lamb going forth with the book in His hand. The multitude of angels in Heaven includes the 4 beasts and the 24 elders breaking out in song, saying specifically (according to the Greek):

> *...Thou art worthy to take the book, and to open the seals thereof: for Thou wast slain, and hast redeemed to God by Thy blood out of every kindred, and tongue, and people, and nation; and hast made them* [*autous*] *unto our God kings and priests: and they shall reign* [*basileusousiv* is a third person, plural, present, active, indicative verb form] *on the earth* (Revelation 5:9-10, author's translation).

The rejoicing in Heaven was because the Kingdom of God could now be inaugurated on earth with those who have trusted in the Lamb, who reigned on earth as kings and priests within the Kingdom of God. This fact is confirmed early in the Book of Revelation (Rev. 1:6), when John identifies Jesus Christ as the One who "*hath made us* [*epoihsev hmas*] *kings and priests unto our God and His Father.*"

The elders were rejoicing because Jesus could now open the first seal and send the Holy Spirit into the world to inaugurate the building of His Church, and the gates of hell would not prevail against it.

To those who receive the Spirit of God, through a meaningful and true profession of faith in Jesus Christ, Jesus also offers the keys to the Kingdom of God. In other words, He offers a ruling position in His Kingdom and a priestly office. "*Thou art the Christ, the Son of the living God ...*

And I will give unto thee the keys of the kingdom of heaven..." (Mt. 16:16,19).

Those who believe and trust in Jesus Christ alone by faith are kings. Therefore, Jesus is rightfully called the King of kings (1 Tim. 6:15; Rev. 19:16). Jesus has also made us priests, now! "*But ye are a chosen generation, a royal priesthood...*" (see 1 Pet. 2:5-9). Jesus came preaching the gospel, the good news of the Kingdom of Heaven (Mk. 1:14-15) with the opening of the sealed book in His hand. It can be said that the Kingdom of Heaven was consummated on earth. Jesus was found worthy to receive the sealed book from the Father, remove the seals thereof, and initiate the first phase of the Kingdom of Heaven, the Church.

In response to the Pharisees' question of when the Kingdom of God should come, Jesus answered, "*The kingdom of God cometh not with observation: neither shall they say, Lo here! or, lo there! for, behold, the kingdom of God is within you*" (Lk. 17:20-21). The Kingdom of God, like the Spirit, is to be received. "*Whosoever shall not receive the kingdom of God as a little child shall in no wise enter therein*" (Lk. 18:17; see also Heb. 12:28).

These passages serve as a warning to all those who seek an answer to all their vain and troubling questions before they willingly commit their lives to Christ. ***Come as an innocent trusting child or not at all.*** The rejoicing in Heaven by the 4 beasts and the 24 elders in Revelation was because the long wait for the inauguration of the Kingdom of God on earth was over (Lk. 23:51).

Before Jesus ascended into Heaven, He spoke to the disciples concerning "*the things pertaining to the kingdom of God* " (Acts 1:3). When He arrived in Heaven, Jesus went to the Father, received the book, and began to loosen the seals, which sent forth the Holy Spirit into the world to conquer or defeat unbelief in the world, to the praise and glory of God, the Father and the Lamb.

This is why the multitude in heaven, including the 4 beasts and the 24 elders, responded with this:

> *...Worthy is the Lamb that was slain to receive power, and riches, and wisdom, and strength, and honour, and glory and blessing. And every creature which is in heaven, and on the earth, and under the earth, and such as are in the sea, and all that are in them,*

heard I saying, Blessing, and honour, and glory, and power, be unto Him that sitteth upon the throne, and unto the Lamb for ever and ever (Revelation 5:12-13).

Since the beginning of the Church on the Day of Pentecost, God has been working through believers with His Holy Spirit to bring honor and glory and power to Himself and His Son, while gathering the constituency of His Kingdom. God accomplishes this goal through those who accept Jesus Christ as their Lord and Savior. Until the coming of the "Day of the Lord," there will be time to serve Him. Then the Church will be raptured and the 144,000 will be sealed.

When does this time run out? When does it come to the point that it is no longer possible to avoid the wrath of God? It comes when the Lion has roared His voice and the seven thunders have uttered their voices (Rev. 10:3). The seven thunders are the voices of the Spirit of God, the Lion of Judah, when Jesus began to open the seven seals of Revelation 6:1. The decrees within the seals are working in the world to bring repentance through the ministry of the Holy Spirit, the first seal.

It is important to note that John was told not to write what the seven thunders said, but in the opening of the seals, John was told to come and see and then record what he saw. Thus, chapter 10 of Revelation is a picture of Jesus Christ standing upon the sea and on the earth, in place to rapture His Church. With the sixth seal open, this Mighty Angel lifting up His arm to Heaven is significant (Rev. 10:5; Dan. 12:5-7).

The lifting of the arm is the Rapture of the Church. The Church is the arm of the Lord in the world. The seven Spirits are the seven stars sent to the seven churches, which are in the hand of the One standing in the midst of the candlesticks (Rev. 1:20; 3:1). Lifting His arm lifts the Spirit of God, and lifting the Spirit of God symbolizes the snatching away of the Church.

The swearing by the Mighty Angel could be Jesus professing the names of believers who have confessed His name before men. The swearing is before the eternal throne of God for their admittance into Heaven. "*Whosoever therefore shall confess Me before men, him will I confess also before My Father which is in Heaven*" (Mt. 10:32). "*Because thou hast kept the word of My patience, I also will keep thee from the hour of temptation, which shall come upon all the world...*" (Rev. 3:10).

The attributes of the Mighty Angel are unparalleled to anything previously recorded in Scripture concerning the appearance of angels (Rev. 10). "This angel appears with cosmic stature, towering into the sky as his legs bestride land and sea. He is associated with all three divisions of created reality, as in Revelation 10:6: Heaven from which He comes (10:1) and the sea and the land on which He stands (10:2)."[6]

The cosmic stature appearance of this Mighty Angel parallels the cosmic disturbance of the sixth seal. When Jesus Christ returns for His Bride, mountains will be moved out of their place, seas will roar, the stars of heaven will fall, and the heavens will be rolled back. The vision of Revelation 10:1-2 portrays the One who has the authority to inflict the cosmic chaos of the sixth seal.

The Seven Thunders

The command not to reveal what the seven thunders uttered also parallels the opening of the seven seals. A review of the seals will reveal the correlation. Of the first seal it says, "*and I heard, as it were the noise of thunder, one of the four beasts saying, Come and see*" (Rev. 6:1). Of the second seal it says, "*I heard the second beasts say, Come and see*" (Rev. 6:3). For the third seal it says, "*I heard the third beast say, Come and see*" (Rev. 6:5). For the fourth seal it says, "*I heard the voice of the fourth beast say, Come and see*" (Rev 6:7).

In each case of the first four seals John heard the voice of a beast and he recorded what they said to him. But the noise or voice [*phoné*] of the thunder of seal one is not revealed. In this way it is similar to the seven thunders of Revelation 10:3. The voice of the seven thunders represents the commands of Jesus, the Lamb and the Lion, to open the seven seals and to send them into the world. But John is never allowed to reveal anything to us about what was said by the thundering voice (Rev. 4:5, 6:1, 8:5, 10:3, 11:19).

John tells us what he saw and heard the beast say, and of the cries of those under the altar, slain for the Word of God in the fifth seal. These voices are crying out "*How long, O Lord?*" until He judges and avenges their blood. John does reveal what was done for them and what was said to them (Rev. 6:9-11). John reveals to us what he saw when the sixth seal was opened. With the opening of the seventh seal there is only silence in Heaven (Rev. 8:1).

When reviewing the opening of the seven seals, note that John only revealed what he saw and nothing of what was said by the voices that thundered. The words of each beast are not the words of the thunder. The thundering voice always implies the voice of God (Rev. 4:5; 8:5; 11:19). The only words that John records are those that the beasts (living ones) speak to him: "Come and see." He was forbidden to write what he had heard the voice of thunder say (Rev. 6:1; 10:3).

John was told not to write what the seven thunders uttered because to do so would have revealed something the Lord wanted to be kept a mystery. What could this be? We can only speculate, but it is clear that a question the Lord has continually kept man from answering is "When?"

"*What shall be the end of these things*?" (see Dan. 12:8-9). "*When shall these things be*?" (Mt. 24:3). "*But of that day and hour knoweth no man*" (Mt. 24:36). "*But of the times and the seasons, brethren, ye have no need that I write unto you*" (1 Thess. 5:1).

When will the end come and how much time is left before the start of the tribulation period? To reveal these times back in A.D. 30–93 would have been devastating to the hope of believers because they would have known that the coming of the Kingdom of God would not be realized in their physical life span. Daniel knew that he would not live to see the coming of the physical Kingdom of God because he was told that he would stand in his "lot" at the end of days, signifying his resurrection.

John may have heard something that did reveal "when" the end would come, but was forbidden to record it or reveal the information to us. This is supported by this verse: "*But in the days of the voice of the seventh angel,* ***when*** *he shall begin to sound, the mystery of God should be finished, as He hath declared to His servants the prophets*" (Rev. 10:7).

The days of the seventh angel have not yet come because the mystery remains. But rest assured, when he begins to sound, the mystery will be over and the world will know that the day of the Lord's judgment has come. "*For the great day of His wrath is come*" (Rev. 6:17).

The sound of the voice of the seventh angel is the voice of the angel to the seventh church and the seventh seal, which contains the seven trumpets and the seven vials (the seventh trumpet contains the seven vials).

Therefore, there is a time coming when there will be "time no longer" for the things that are created in Heaven and in earth, whether they are things in the earth or in the sea, to maintain the mystery of God. God will reveal Himself to the world in the judgments of the tribulation period.

For seven years God will convince the world that Jesus Christ is the true Creator of the heavens, the earth, and the seas. The fact that this proclamation is made by a Great Angel from Heaven with an open book in His hand, indicates that the time of this judgment and revelation will begin when all the seals have been removed. The removal of the seals will make it possible to open the book and commence with phase "two" of the Kingdom of God, which will be, at first, to convince the world of its lack of righteousness.

Then phase three will bring the final judgment upon the world. This final judgment will be unlike the judgments of the seals and the first six trumpets because they were still mixed with the mercy of God. Phase "one" of the Kingdom of God was to convince the world of its sin, that all might see their need for Christ. But the day is coming when God will pour out His wrath upon the world, unmixed, meaning without mercy (Rev. 14:10).

Phase "one" of the Kingdom of God is in effect now and involves the opening of seals one through five and will end with the opening of the sixth seal. Phase "two" will commence immediately after seal six, then continue with the opening of the seventh seal and the trumpet judgments. Phase "three" will be the final phase of judgments that will involve the blowing of the seventh trumpet and the pouring out of the seven last plagues contained in the seven vial judgments.

Chapter 10 of Revelation makes it clear that the seals are not part of the tribulation period because the mystery declared unto the prophets is not revealed until the seventh angel begins to sound. *The seals represent God's program for the implementation of the Kingdom of God on earth.* The seals are part of the Church Age. This is why the opening of the seals immediately follows Christ's entrance into Heaven.

Revelation chapter 6 and the opening of the first six seals lies between the announcement of the Lamb being worthy to open the book (Rev. 5:5), and the announcement that the "Day of the Lord's Wrath" has come (Rev. 6:17). It is the Lion of Judah that is worthy to open the book (Rev. 5:5) and it is the Lion roaring with the book open (Rev. 10:2-3), speaking to John. What could be plainer? The book is open. The seals are removed.

The measuring of the temple in chapter 11 means that the book is opened. Therefore the seals have been removed as the seventh kingdom arrives. This truth has been overlooked until now because it has been thought that the first seal started the tribulation period. But, as we can clearly see, it makes sense to conclude that the sixth seal includes the Rapture of the Church, while the sixth seal ends the Church Age period. The seventh seal initiates the final seven years of tribulation in the world. This is because it is not until the seventh seal is removed that the seventh angel will be able to begin to sound or speak that which is contained in the opened book.

The waiting will be over because then time will be no longer and the "Day of the Lord's Wrath" will have come. The Church, the kings, and priests of God are in Heaven with the Lamb, "*Therefore rejoice, ye heavens, and ye that dwell in them...*" (see Rev. 12:10-12).

An Urgent Warning to Believers and Unbelievers

We must remember that God has commissioned us to labor as citizens of the Kingdom of God even though we may suffer occasionally. This is exactly what the seven letters to the churches are all about. The seven letters to the seven churches warn the Body of Christ about the trials that will face the Church as it draws closer to the opening of the sixth and seventh seals. We are in the final phase, the Philadelphian stage and the sixth stage, that will see the opening of the sixth seal and the Rapture.

The Church of Philadelphia was promised that it would be kept from the tribulation that was coming upon the whole world (Rev. 3:8-10). A most urgent warning is necessary:

1. Do not deny the name of Jesus Christ. There is salvation only in Him. We live in a world that finds this message intolerable. The world usually responds with such sarcastic phrases as "You can't judge other people" or "You think your way is the only way." Jesus Christ is the only way and that is why all must trust in Him alone. Jesus said that He was

"the way, the truth, and the life: no man cometh unto the Father, but by Me" (Jn. 14:6). All need to be trusting in Christ alone.

2. We need to keep His Word. Many churches have abandoned the faithful preaching of God's Word. In its place, humanistic philosophies and a socially adjusted gospel message is preached, which is a message of temporal social good that only leads to eternal damnation. But to those who overcome these trials, God promises eternal riches, a crown of glory and a guaranteed appointment with the Rapture to escape the coming judgment.

The Spirit of God was sent into the world to help believers overcome the spirit of darkness and doubt that permeates the world. God sent the Holy Spirit into the world to conquer the world for Him and recompense tribulation to them that trouble believers (Jn. 16:7-11).

> *...for your patience and faith in all your persecutions and tribulations that ye endure: which is a manifest token of the righteous judgment of God, that ye may be counted worthy of the kingdom of God, for which ye also suffer: seeing it is a righteous thing with God to recompense tribulation to them that trouble you* (2 Thessalonians 1:4-6).

God opened seals two, three, and four and sent them into the world with the Holy Spirit to convince the world of its sin, its lack of righteousness, and of the coming judgment. The pattern is one that will first take away peace and security. The rider of the horse of the second seal will take away peace from the earth. This will cause people to fight among themselves and cause a dearth of godly leadership.

The next phase will cause the disobedient and those that oppose the children of God to experience famine in the land. But those who have the Spirit of God in them will be protected. This is why the third rider is told not to hurt the oil and the wine (Rev. 6:6). The third phase will bring death and destruction by the sword, by famine, and by war. These riders will be directed by the Holy Spirit to protect and promote obedience to the truth of the gospel. Judgment is always the result of willful disobedience. God will not bless those who do not honor the Son, consequently excluding them from the Kingdom of God.

Hollywood, California, is experiencing tribulation because of repetitive "natural" disaster. This has caused much unrest. People will eventually begin to fight among themselves as the time of the recovery drags on and as money and materials become scarce. If the Hollywood elite continues to belittle the Word of God, and portray Bible believers as intolerant goofs, and if Washington does not change its immoral and godless course, famines will follow.

If famines do not get their attention, then war and death will come. As bad as these are, they are only judgments of warning. The second and third seals result in great hardships, sparing lives, but breaking the back of pride and self-reliance. Israel continued to reject the warnings of its prophets of Jeremiah and Isaiah and as a result saw their nation destroyed by divisions, famine, and finally war and exile.

If anyone thinks it can't happen to America, think again! We are already under the tribulations of the second seal with the third one looming on the horizon. Wake up, America! God wants you to repent and be saved!

Understanding the Overlaps

Revelation 8:1–11:14 takes us to the middle of the tribulation period and then passes us on into the second half of the tribulation, the dominant reign of the beast. The beast, who is empowered by satan himself, will be allowed to rule for nearly three-and-one-half years (Rev. 13:2). He will play a dominant part of the "New World Order," the seventh and final kingdom. The beast will also lead the eighth kingdom after he recovers from his fatal head wound and, as a result, displace this short-lived kingdom of the "New World Order" with his own.

John is told to eat the book that is now "open." It is the open book without the seals from which John will now prophesy. Could it be that John will be sent as one of the two witnesses in the future, prophesying to the nation of Israel and world during the first half of the tribulation period?

This may seem to be an amazing assertion, but in chapter 11 John himself is given a reed like a rod, and told to go forth and measure the temple and the people within, but not to measure that which is outside the temple. This measuring of the temple is a clear indicator that the seventh and final kingdom has begun and the sixth kingdom has fallen to the same fate as the previous five kingdoms: "*And there are seven kings: five are fallen, and one is...*" (see Rev. 17:10-12). The building, destruction, and desolation of the temple is a key to understanding each of these kingdoms.

The fall of all worldly empires came about to allow the building of the first temple by Solomon.

> *...David...could not build an house unto the name of the Lord his God for the wars which were about him on every side...But now the Lord my God hath given me rest on every side...* (1 Kings 5:3-4).

Peace is coming to Israel today ***for the same reason***!

(See chart on page 226.)

Chart #2

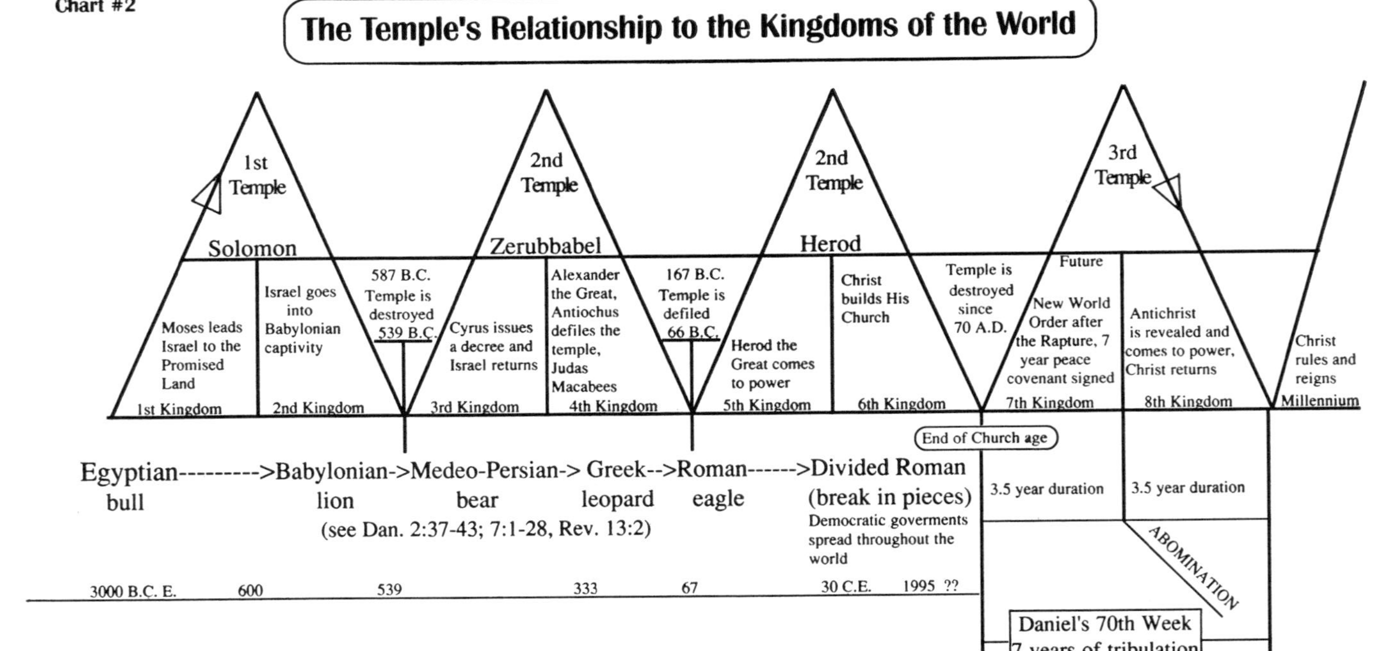

The above chart demonstrates how the construction of the temple fits in with the rise and fall of the prophesied kingdoms of the world. The book of Revelation was written during the days of the sixth kingdom. The "New World Order " will mark the end of the sixth kingdom, the end of the church age and the arrival of the seventh kingdom. The seventh kingdom will see the temple rebuilt by Israel (see Rev. 11:1-3; 17:9-11). The middle of the tribulation period marks the end of the seventh kingdom which continues for only a "short space". The temple will be defiled by the antichrist, this marks the beginning of the eighth kingdom. The eighth kingdom will see the return of Christ.

Therefore, this is also when the tribulation period will begin. If God places His two witnesses into the world just prior to the start of the final seven-year period, we could then expect them to be very active and very influential in the rebuilding of what the Jews call the "Third Temple." Jesus was incarnated and in the world at least 29 years before He officially began His "public" ministry. With the measuring of the temple, we see God focusing once again on the nation of Israel.

God will no longer be focused on the Gentiles because at this time He will be working to redeem and bless His chosen (elect) people, Israel. It is possible that John will prophesy again in the spirit of Elijah as did John the Baptist (Mt. 11:12-14). Maybe God will send another prophet that will prophesy again in the spirit of both the prophet Elijah and John.

It appears from Scripture that John the Baptist fulfilled the prophecies concerning the coming of the prophet Elijah, while denying that he was that prophet (Jn. 1:21). In truth, there is really very little difference because when a true prophet speaks, it is not the prophet but God Himself speaking through that prophet. Whether it is John or someone in the same spirit as John, the prophecy will be spoken again before the nations of the world in Israel before the "Day of the Lord's Wrath."

"*Behold, I will send you Elijah the prophet before the coming of the great and dreadful day of the Lord*" (Mal. 4:5). Concerning John the Baptist it is said, "*And he shall go before Him in the spirit and power of Elias* [Elijah]..." (Lk. 1:17).

In the days of the seventh angel God will speak to the world through the judgments that are contained in the scroll. In essence, the spirit of Elijah that prophesied was the Spirit of God speaking through Elijah. John's prophecy will speak in another time before many peoples, nations, tongues, and kings, when all of it will be fulfilled in the seventh and final kingdom as prophesied by Daniel and John:

> *For the vision is yet for an appointed time, but at the end it shall speak, and not lie: though it tarry, wait for it; because it will surely come, it will not tarry* [forever] (Habakkuk 2:3).

In the days of the seventh church, Laodicea, the seventh seal will be opened and the seventh angel will speak to a world in the days of the seventh king(dom).

Revelation 10:1–11:14 is entirely a parenthetical section, one that fills in missing details that are very important for us to understand. These events contained in this section of the Book of Revelation unfold primarily in the first half of the tribulation period. Chapter 10 reviews the events that fulfill the sixth kingdom and brings it to a close when all the seals are removed and the book is opened.

Chapter 11 introduces the coming of the seventh kingdom with the building of the temple and the start of the ministry of God's two witnesses. Chapter 11 also reveals the length of their ministry, how they are killed, and when they will resurrect. The chapter concludes with the temple of God open in Heaven and the seven vial judgments being introduced.

But it is not until we get to Revelation chapter 13 that we find ourselves clearly considering the dreadful and terrible details of the events and the ungodly characters of the second half of the tribulation period. The wrath of God is poured out upon satan, the beast, the dragon, and the unrepentant world. This is the period of Great Tribulation that will see God's wrath poured out without mixture (Rev. 14:10).

In chapter 10 John heard a voice from Heaven when he was about to write what he heard. The voice told him to seal up and not write what the seven thunders had uttered, which is the voice of Jesus, the Lion. Then John heard the angel standing on the sea and the land swearing by the One who has created everything, "*that there should be time no longer*" or no more delay (Rev. 10:6).

John was told that the mystery of God would be fulfilled exactly as it was told to the prophets of God. It will be fulfilled when the seventh angel begins to sound his first of seven trumpets. In the day that God has appointed for this angel to sound, then everything will be finished just as God had said, without further delay.

This angel that is standing on the sea and the earth is very similar to the vision that we find in Daniel 12:5-7. In that vision, however, Daniel sees *two other figures standing on opposite shores of the river* while another (the Lord) is standing on the river. It is possible that these two are the two witnesses of God "*that stand by the Lord of the whole earth*" (Zech. 4:14; see also Dan. 12:5).

Prior to this, Daniel was given a rather extensive vision and received understanding from the angel Gabriel (Dan. 9:21-22), and later the most spectacular prophecy of the seventy weeks is explained (Dan. 9:24-27). The visions given to Daniel in chapter 11 were to be fulfilled after many days, in the latter days.

The word for "days," *achariyth* means "end days." It is taken from the root word *achar*, meaning "hind end or portion." Gabriel tells Daniel about the help and the position of Michael, who stands strong with Gabriel against the princes of Persia and Grecia. In the context, then, we find these two great archangels, Gabriel and Michael, fighting on behalf of the Lord.

We also find a focus on time. When will these events occur and what significance does it have? Time is part of Daniel's primary concern (Dan. 12:8). Daniel is told twice in chapter 12 to close up, to seal up the vision until the time of the end. At the time of the end this vision will be revealed.

When is the time of the end? It is when the seventh angel of the seventh seal begins to call forth the seven angels of the seven trumpets and they begin to sound the wrath of God. It is a time when the seventh church, Laodicea, finds itself in the tribulation.

The full meaning of what Daniel foresaw with regard to the last days of history before the end remained a mystery to Daniel. Only now, to John, will the scroll of God's purpose for the coming of His Kingdom, now unsealed, be revealed.[7]

One of the men in Daniel's vision asked when the end of these wonders would be. The one on the waters indicated that it would be confined to a specific three-and-one-half-year period (Dan. 12:6-7). It would be the time when the power (Hebrew, *yad*) or the will of the people will be passed over into the hands of someone else.

This someone else is the beast of Revelation, the great horn of Daniel, the antichrist himself. He will rise to power with his true identity concealed during the first half of the tribulation. During the second half he will rule autocratically for three-and-one-half years.

"*And I...saw a beast rise up out of the sea...*" (see Rev. 13:1-2). At the end of that time, the kingdoms of this world will "*become the kingdoms of our Lord*" (Rev. 11:15) as they were during the first temple period when God gave Israel rest from all her enemies. Since Israel's entrance into the land, God has desired to be the King of Israel.

But the nation of Israel rejected God and lamented for an earthly king to rule over them. They wanted to be like other nations, so God gave them Saul, then David, and then Solomon, who finally built the first great temple in Israel.

> *And the Lord said unto Samuel, Hearken unto the voice of the people in all that they say unto thee: for they have not rejected thee, but have rejected Me, that I should not reign over them* (1 Samuel 8:7).

It is this golden period of Israel's history that Israel again longs for and will soon have, but the Kingdom that is coming will far exceed anything that Israel enjoyed in Solomon's reign. Consider Solomon's charge to the nation of Israel as he dedicated the first temple:

> *Blessed be the Lord, that hath* ***given rest unto His people Israel,*** *according to all that He promised: there hath not failed one word of all His good promise, which He promised by the hand of Moses His servant. The Lord our God be with us, as He was with our fathers: let Him not leave us, nor forsake us: that He may incline our hearts unto Him, to walk in all His ways, and to keep His commandments, and His statutes, and His judgments, which He commanded our fathers. And let these my words, wherewith I have made supplication before the Lord, be nigh unto the Lord our God day and night, that He maintain the cause of His servant, and the cause of His people Israel at all times, as the matter shall require:* ***that all the people of the earth may know that the Lord is God, and that there is none else.*** *Let your heart therefore be perfect with the Lord our God, to walk in His statutes, and to keep His commandments, as at this day* (1 Kings 8:56-61).

When Christ returns to set up His Kingdom as the rightful heir to David's throne, it will be a glorious eternal Kingdom that will never fall. It will also be a time when the world will finally know that the God of Heaven and the Lord Jesus Christ are one and the same.

Solomon's kingdom was a kingdom that fell to corruption and decay. "*And Solomon did evil in the sight of the Lord, and went not fully after the Lord, as did David his father*" (1 Kings 11:6). Solomon's kingdom was captured by satan and he ruled it in the end. Eventually, the collapse of this kingdom ended with the destruction of Solomon's temple by Nebuchadnezzar of Babylon in 586/7 B.C. Babylon was the first of the great world empires, but it was the second in the numbering of the kingdoms because Eqypt and Assyria preceded it.

From the very beginning, satan has worked to undermine God ruling in the lives of men (Gen. 3:4-5). There is a time coming when this will no longer be the case. The Kingdom of God is at hand. Jesus will crush the head of satan and "*gather together in one all things in Christ*" (Eph. 1:10). When all enemies are under His feet (His reign), He will deliver everything to the Father, so that God can be all in all.

> *But every man in his own order: Christ the firstfruits; afterward they that are Christ's at His coming. Then cometh the end, when He shall have delivered up the kingdom to God, even the Father; when He shall have put down all rule and all authority and power. For He must reign, till He hath put all enemies under His feet. The last enemy that shall be destroyed is death. For He hath put all things under His feet. But when He saith all things are put under Him, it is manifest that He is excepted, which did put all things under Him. And when all things shall be subdued unto Him, then shall the Son also Himself be subject unto Him that put all things under Him, that God may be all in all* (1 Corinthians 15:23-28).

God deals a deadly blow to satan every time a Christian says "no" to the temptations of this world and says "yes" to God instead. "*And the God of peace shall bruise Satan under your feet shortly*" (Rom. 16:20a).

There is something that we need to recall here about the feet of Jesus as described in the Book of Revelation. Jesus' feet are as a polished brass, literally a refining fire (Rev. 1:15; 2:18). They are like pillars of fire (Rev. 10:1). The change in description between Revelation 1:15 and 2:18 to

Revelation 10:1 gives the impression that the feet of Jesus are "stoked up," beginning the refining work of the first half of the tribulation period (Rev. 3:18).

In the first half of the tribulation, the first four trumpet judgments are designed to refine and warn, while the last three trumpets, with the seven vial judgments, will literally consume the earth in the second half of the tribulation period.

When the seventh angel begins to speak and to sound the seven trumpet judgments, the mystery and the waiting will be over. (The seventh angel of Revelation 10:7 is the angel of the seventh seal, while the seventh angel of Revelation 11:15 is the seventh angel of the seventh trumpet judgment, which calls forth the seven last plagues.) Note in Revelation 10:7 that it says "*But in the days of the voice of the seventh angel, when he shall begin to sound, the mystery of God....*"

The seventh seal contains the sound of all seven trumpets and it is the seventh seal that will begin to sound the mystery of God. At that time those on earth will begin to understand the mysteries that were sealed up by Daniel through the revelation of judgment. However, it may be too late for many, for they will know when the full force of God's wrath is upon them. Like those who stay to ride out a storm and choose to ignore the warnings, it will be too late to seek a rescue.

This is the way it will be once the world comes to the time when the seventh angel of the seventh seal announces that "time is no longer" and there is no more delay because the seventh seal contains the seven trumpet judgments and the seventh trumpet contains the seven vial judgments of God. The delay will begin when the seventh seal is first opened, which is necessary for the sealing of the 144,000.

"*And when He had opened the seventh seal, there was silence in heaven about the space of half an hour*" (Rev. 8:1). The trumpet judgments are precursors to the final vial judgments. The judgments increase in scope and magnitude, escalating from the first four warning judgments within the ministry of God's two witnesses to the progressively worsening woes of one, two, and three.

Finally is the rapid fire of the vial judgments, which is the seventh trumpet and the third woe. The vial judgments will purge the earth of all its wickedness and reduce the existing "One World" political, economic, and religious systems to a smoking cinder. (See Figure 1 on page 2.)

Seal one is the sending of the Overcomer, the Holy Spirit, to indwell believers.

Seals two, three, and four accompany the ministry of Holy Spirit and are used to convince the world of its sin, unrighteousness, and the coming judgment.

Seal five provides ministry to believers who died in Christ, unto the resurrection and the Rapture.

Seal six is the beginning of birth pangs and the end of a long period known as the beginning of sorrows that culminates with the Rapture. Signs appear in the heavens; a blood red lunar eclipse takes place.

Seal seven opens the book. A pause is introduced; the 144,000 are sealed and the seventh angel begins to reveal the mystery of God in judgment. The temple is already in place and upon its first dedication or its implementation on Yom Kippur the two witnesses begin their ministry and the 144,000 of Revelation 7 go into the wilderness. With the seventh seal opened and the temple in place or initiated, the seventh kingdom that must continue a short space has arrived.

The first four trumpet judgments parallel the ministry of the two witnesses. Between trumpets four and five, the two witnesses are killed. The next three trumpets are within the second half of the seven-year tribulation and are the same as the three woes!

With the "first woe," trumpet five, satan is cast out of Heaven near the middle of the tribulation. The battle of Gog and Magog takes place shortly after this.

With the "second woe," trumpet six, the eastern armies are prepared and move to destroy the spiritual whore (Rev. 17).

With the "third woe," trumpet seven the seven angels with vials are called forth and all seven are poured out upon the earth. Then Christ returns with the armies of Heaven to secure His Kingdom on earth.

The parenthetical text of chapters 10 and 11 are inserted after the blowing of the sixth trumpet, coming just after the middle of the tribulation period, after the ministry of the two witnesses. The sixth trumpet only prepares the massive 200-million-man army for use later with the sixth vial judgment. It is with this judgment and its massive army that the false prophet and the "Great Whore" are destroyed (Rev. 16:12-13; 17:1-18).

Therefore, John stops the vision before he proceeds further into the second half of the vision and reveals some important details about the characters (the main players) of the first part of his vision. After the two witnesses are killed, the world begins to gather for war. This gathering indicates that war itself is the overriding distinguishing mark of the second half of the tribulation period because the seven-year treaty has been broken and the identity of the beast revealed to those Jews who understand the Abomination of Desolation (Dan. 9:27; 12:11).

God's Two Witnesses

John is told to measure Jews and not to measure Gentiles that are not allowed inside the temple area, which could parallel the time of the sealing of the 144,000 (Rev. 7:4-8; 11:1). If the Abomination of Desolation had already taken place, then there would be no need to measure the temple or the Jews using it because the temple would be defiled. We know that the Jews will have access to the temple for three-and-one-half years because the Gentiles have control of the Holy City and the court outside the temple, while the Jews have control of the temple.

This will probably be a condition of the peace treaty that will be signed by Israel as the world enters the time of the seventh kingdom, a "New World Order" (watch for this in the news). A division is already developing in Israel. Three leading rabbis have ordered IDF soldiers not to obey government orders to remove Jews from the occupied territories. Leaders are concerned about dividing the country and might be forced to push for a concession from the Arabs that would allow the rebuilding of the temple.

The peace treaty will reverse the situation existing today. The Arabs presently control the temple mount and the Jews control Jerusalem. Somehow Arabs must agree to the rebuilding of the temple and this may indicate how a peace covenant will be made possible. Israel will forfeit strategic lands such as the Golon Heights and Jericho in exchange for the right to rebuild its temple.

Today it is the religious fundamental orthodox Jew that must be convinced to give up God's land. For the chance to rebuild the temple and reinstate temple worship as the only element missing from Israel's glorious ancient past, they will concede the land. Currently, Judaism is centered around the local synagogues but this must and will change.

It is interesting that the recent peace negotiations between the PLO and Israel are focused on a discussion as to who will control Jerusalem. Israel says "never" but the PLO say they must give up some of Jerusalem. Israel may give up Jerusalem to international control, such as to the United Nations, after another bloody war that seems to be in the making.

In exchange, Israel may ask for the right to rebuild the temple and will be granted permission to do so as part of a seven-year peace covenant between Israel and their enemies. This covenant would make Jerusalem the peace and religious capital of the world, with both Jews and Gentiles having access to the temple mount area.

In this scenario, however, we once again find evidence for the two witnesses in the first half of the tribulation period, not the second. If the two witnesses come after the Abomination of Desolation, then the temple will already be defiled and they will be killed at the very end of the seven-year period by the beast . There will not be any room for their resurrection, which comes three-and-a-half days later. This would place their resurrection after the Battle of Armageddon and the seventh trumpet, and the seven vial judgments which take place near the end of the seven years.

This cannot be correct because it places these events beyond the seven-year period (Rev. 11:12-14). If the Lord cuts the seven-year time period short, then the killing of the two witnesses after the battle of Armageddon makes absolutely no sense. David Hunt agrees with this conclusion when he says "There can be no doubt that these two witnesses will have the attention of the entire world! Their message will be a declaration to all nations on this earth to repent and to acknowledge that Jesus Christ is the world's rightful ruler. The three and a half years of their compelling preaching would seem to coincide with the first half of Daniel's seventieth week."[8]

The two witnesses will be here to prophesy (Rev. 11:3), and they will lead the 144,000 into the wilderness and teach them as the Lord taught the disciples for about the same period of time. The two witnesses will have a three-and-one-half-year ministry and will see their ministry end after satan is cast to the earth, which is the fifth trumpet and the first woe. The fifth trumpet and the casting out of satan are one and the same.

Satan has the keys to the bottomless pit and he will resurrect the beast and release the demons to torment those who dwell on the earth for five months. It is probably during this five-month period that the beast will seek to implement his mark upon the rest of mankind, but he cannot hurt the 144,000 that are sealed at the beginning of the tribulation period (Rev. 9:4).

It is the beast who will ascend out of the bottomless pit, kill the two witnesses, and then take his seat in the temple of God after the witnesses are dead. Therefore, the Abomination of Desolation will take place in conjunction with the death of the two witnesses, and the world will celebrate their death because they caused much pain and sorrow with their fiery speech and fiery judgments (Rev. 11:6-7,10).

It is at this point that some of those dwelling in Judea will "*flee into the mountains*" (Mt. 24:16). It is also at this point that the Battle of Gog and Magog will be initiated against Israel. Three days after the death of the two witnesses, they will be resurrected and this will cause a great fear to overtake those who witness this resurrection. God will make sure that their enemies will see them ascend into the clouds (Rev. 11:12).

There will be little doubt at this time as to the divine authority of the two witnesses, for their resurrection authenticates their message much in the same way that Paul was convinced when he saw the resurrected Lord on the road to Damascus.

Concluding the First Parenthetical Section

With the parenthetical thought now completed, John announces that the *second woe* has passed, which began with the sounding of the sixth trumpet and has concluded with the events of the second half well underway. The second woe included the destruction of the great whore. Before this time God also intervened on behalf of Israel and consumed the armies of Gog and Magog (Ezek. 38).

This miraculous deliverance will cause the remnant of Israel to fear God. This remnant was not killed by the earthquake that God used to destroy the armies of Gog and Magog. As a result, they will finally give God the glory and recognize Jesus Christ as their King (Rev. 11:13; Ezek. 38:19-20).

Chapter 11 concludes with a final section, taking us to the very precipice of God's angels pouring out the vial judgments. John's vision is then interrupted by another overlap section of characters and events with Revelation chapter 12. After chapter 12, there are two introductory chapters that give us some very important details about the close of the first half of the tribulation and the way the world powers are arranged for the second half.

Chapter 11 ends with the blowing of the seventh trumpet, which contains the seven vial judgments. The announcement is made that the kingdoms of this world are claimed by God. It is the time of God's judgment by rewarding the faithful and rebuking them that destroy the world. The chapter closes with the temple of God being opened in Heaven.

> *And the temple of God was opened in heaven, and there was seen in His temple the ark of His testament: and there were lightnings, and voices, and thunderings, and an earthquake, and great hail* (Revelation 11:19).

When the gaps are filled in and important details introduced, the vision then continues to unfold in Revelation 15:5.[9] Chapter 15 opens with the angels of the seven last plagues coming forward to deliver God's most severe judgments. Up until this time, there was time to repent and trust in the Lord—but not now! It is too late, for God's judgments are made manifest (Rev. 15:4).

This is why it is fitting for John to reveal the faith of all those who faithfully trusted in God and feared Him just before the vials are poured out. These faithful that are mentioned (Rev. 15:2-4) make up the Laodicean Church that will have been tried by the purging trials of the first six trumpet judgments and the trials of a godless world system (Rev. 3:18-21).

They are described as ones standing before God on "*a sea of glass mingled with fire*" for they overcame the beast in death. They are singing praises to God because they got the victory over the beast, paying with their lives (Rev. 14:13; 15:1-3). Now, the last of the faithful are gathered in Heaven as a secondary reaping takes place (Rev. 14:14-16) and the faithful ones who died in Christ are gathered to God.

Those who were raptured are the first fruits taken in a pretribulational Rapture. Those who trusted in the Lord Jesus Christ during the first half of the tribulation (and slightly beyond) are harvested from the earth just before the final judgment, the seventh trumpet of God (Rev. 14:14-16). With all the believers safely in Heaven, the final judgments of God can be poured out upon the earth. In Heaven, at this time, preparations are being made for "*the marriage supper of the Lamb*" (Rev. 19:5-10).

Going back to Revelation 15:5, we see the same declaration being made as we did in Revelation 11:19, that "*the temple of the tabernacle of the testimony in heaven was opened.*" Within the pouring out of the seven plagues (Rev. 16) we see "every" element of Revelation 11:19 expanded upon. The voices (Rev. 16:1), the thunderings and lightnings, the great earthquake (Rev. 16:18), and finally the great hail (Rev. 16:21).

There can be no doubt that Revelation 11:14-19 is an introduction to what awaits the world once the seventh angel sounds his trumpet. The seventh trumpet is, in fact, the last seven plagues of God. The announcement is that the third woe is coming very quickly after the second woe is fulfilled (Rev. 11:14).

Before the visions move forward, John gives us an absolutely critical chapter to contemplate, for within it is the one-text proof for everything that has been said thus far. It also contains the one-text proof of a pretribulational Rapture that Mr. Rosenthal has challenged "Pretribers" to produce.[10]

Introduction to Revelation 12

Therefore, chapter 12 is another parenthetical chapter that takes us back to broaden our understanding of what has been described. John describes what he saw and heard and then gives a progressive sequence of revelation. This sequence includes churches, seals, trumpets, and vials.

For example, he utilizes some of the descriptions already revealed to us. Next, John reveals some signs and symbols, which are sometimes described or explained later. Once all the pieces of the mosaic are laid out in their proper and interlocking order, we will be able to step back and get the big picture of Revelation. Revelation is, in a very real way, a picture puzzle. Just as we understand where the piece of a puzzle fits by contrasting the piece to a picture or comparing one piece to another, and by proceeding piece by piece, we begin to put the puzzle or mosaic together. As we get near the end it should become easier and easier to fit the remaining pieces into the puzzle. This analogy best illustrates how any "conclusive" study of Revelation should progress.

Scripture has revealed that the middle of the tribulation will be unquestionably marked by the Abomination of Desolation (Dan. 9:27; 12:11; Mt. 24:15; Mk. 13:14). After this piece is identified, every event or vision can be compared to it with one simple question: Does this piece best fit into the section that comes *before* or *after* the Abomination of Desolation?

Just as with a puzzle, there are pieces that are easily pieced together, while others remain unclear, as with certain events in the Book of Revelation. These pieces require closer scrutiny and deeper exegetical investigation. The Old Testament prophecies, especially Daniel, function as the border of our prophetic puzzle.

The visions of Revelation need to be pieced together within the borders of Daniel's prophecy, and by comparing all the different elements of each individual piece, the picture begins to take form. The mosaic will make a consistent whole that will yield a beautiful prophetic portrait, one that articulates volumes of confirmed truth.

Revelation ends as it began, an ending that wonderfully mates what was said in the beginning of the book: the Alpha and Omega, the beginning and end. The worlds that were created by the Word of God will be judged according to the Word of God. Therefore, just as a perfect circle drawn must end where it began, Revelation presents us with one beautiful self-contained word picture. It is a word picture made up of pieces that had their genesis in the constellations of the stars—the shapes of the letters patterned after the stars.

After a brief introduction and conclusion, the book is found to form one giant *inclusio* with the words of Alpha and Omega (Rev. 1:8; 22:13). Like the message recorded in the circle of stars in the witness of the zodiac, John recorded the events of an age that ran from the ascension of Christ to the day when God will deliver us into His eternal Kingdom. The picture is not partial. It is complete. ***It is a whole, and it is "time" for us to understand its message.***

Revelation chapter 12 can be seen as a summary of the events that have already taken place within the seven seals and the first six trumpet judgments. We must remember that the first six seals are prior to the start of the tribulation while the seventh seal moves it forward with the trumpet judgments. The fifth trumpet delivers satan to the earth and the sixth moves the world toward war and chaos.

In chapter 11 a heavenly proclamation is given, declaring that now the kingdoms of the world belong to Jesus Christ and He will rule over them. The scene then shifts to the 24 elders worshiping God and giving thanks because He has taken to Himself great power to rule and reign over the kingdoms of the world.

The response to the seventh trumpet by the 24 elders is positive, and then another shift takes place in the text. The response of the nations to this is negative. The nations become very angry because they know that the time of God's wrath has come and they have passed into a period of even greater tribulation, without a chance of escape. The panic can be likened to a world learning that a giant meteor is going to impact the earth and there is no place to hide.

The seventh trumpet is the approaching final woe, which contains the seven last plagues as introduced at the end of chapter 11. Once again, John stops our progress with another parenthetical section and reveals more details, more pieces of the puzzle.

John interrupts the flow by telling us about two signs that appeared in the heavens. These signs hold some unique descriptions. The interpretation of Revelation chapter 12 has always been and will always be one of the most critical, if not the most critical chapter, for any expositor. It holds the keys that unlocks the whole Book of Revelation. No matter what position one holds, the final interpretation of Revelation 12 must link events that precede it to the sections that follow. The information that is contained in Revelation 12 is, without a doubt, absolutely amazing.

End Notes

1. Walvoord, *The Revelation of Jesus Christ*, p. 169.
2. Bauckham, *The Climax of Prophecy*, p. 243; "The Genre of the Book of Revelation From a Source, Cultural Perspective" D.Z.M.W. Vol. 54, (Berlin, NY: deGroyter, 1989), pp. 265-279.
3. Walvoord, *The Revelation of Jesus Christ,* p. 172.
4. Bauckham, *The Climax of Prophecy*, p. 252.
5. Ibid., p. 250.
6. Ibid., p. 253.
7. Ibid., p. 261.
8. Hunt, *How Close Are We?* pp. 297-298.
9. Bauckham, *The Climax of Prophecy*, p. 16.
10. Rosenthal, *The Pre-Wrath Rapture of the Church*, p. 280.

Chapter 9

The Mystery of Revelation 12 Is Solved!

Proof of a Pretribulation Rapture and More!

The purpose of this chapter is to show how critical Revelation chapter 12 is and, therefore, is a key chapter in understanding the chronology of the whole Book of Revelation and the unfolding sequence of prophesied apocalyptic events. Revelation 12 takes us from the end of the "beginning of sorrows," the start of the seventh earthly kingdom (Rev. 17:10), to the battle of Gog and Magog and into the events of the second half of the tribulation period, and the start of the eighth and final world kingdom.

In essence, Revelation chapter 12 covers the three-and-one-half years of time when the seventh kingdom rises to power with a peace treaty and falls into the domain of antichrist until the arrival of satan himself to earth (Rev. 12:9; 2 Thess. 2:3-9).

"Most attempts to discern the structure of Revelation have found it particularly difficult to see how chapters 12–14 fit into the overall structure. The beginning of chapter 12 seems an uncharacteristically abrupt fresh start, devoid of literary links with anything that precedes."[1]

A fresh start is required because the narrative begins to review and reveal the main characters of the events that have already been disclosed up to this point in the Revelation. Prior to this study, I believed that Revelation 12:1-5 referred to the conflict between the woman and the serpent (Gen. 3:15) and Israel to the birth of Christ. I also believed that what followed the vision referred to events in the second half of the tribulation.

However, after some intense work, spanning more than four years, I no longer believe that the first five verses of Revelation chapter 12 have anything to do with the first coming of the Lord Jesus Christ! Instead, I now believe and have proven that Revelation chapter 12 has everything to do with the beginning of the final seven years of Daniel's Seventieth Week. In fact, chapter 12, when properly understood, locks in the following:

1. The pretribulation Rapture of the Church, just before or at the very beginning of the Seventieth Week.
2. The two witnesses have their three-and-one-half-year ministry in the first half of the Seventieth Week.
3. The 144,000 are in the wilderness with the two witnesses for the first half from the beginning of the Seventieth Week.
4. The tribulation period will begin in the month of Tishri or Marchesvan, September–October. (This will be proven.)
5. Satan will be cast out of Heaven at the middle of the Seventieth Week.
6. The casting out of satan, the first woe, and the fifth trumpet are the same event.
7. The woman is Israel coming into her time of trouble and the time of her great consummation (Dan. 9:27).
8. The man-child of Revelation 12:5, with a rod of iron, is Christ at the Second Coming.
9. The child caught up (raptured) to the throne is the raptured Body of Christ with Christ as the Head of His Body.
10. The flood that the devil sends out of his mouth after the woman is the battle of Gog and Mag Gog (Ezek. 38).
11. Revelation 12 reviews events from Revelation 6:12–11:14, reveals the main characters and events of the first half of the Seventieth Week, and introduces and sets the stage for the second half of the

Seventieth Week, which is also when the beast rises to power right after or with the Abomination of Desolation.

To support this, the current pretribulation, premillennial, and dispensational views need to be considered first. As a result of my studies I am convinced that the dispensational, pretribulation, premillennial position is the only biblical position that anyone should hold to because the Scriptures overwhelmingly support it. During my study I saw no need to abandon the pretribulation position, as some have suggested. However, the evidence that I now cite to support this position is different and more consistent with the whole body of scriptural evidence.

Dr. Walvoord, a man I greatly respect, states that the man-child of Revelation 12:5 (*hyion arsen*) and the child (*tekna*) refers to Jesus Christ, and Christ only, because to regard the child of verse 5 as the Church is to confuse metaphors. He writes, "If the identification of the twenty-four elders is properly to be regarded as the church in heaven, it would seem to mix metaphors to have the church represented as a male child, especially when the church is regarded in chapter 19 as the wife and the [bride]." He goes on to say, "There is no good reason for not identifying the man-child as Christ and interpreting the drama of verse 5 as the panorama of His birth, life, and ascension."[2]

It is assumed that there is nothing implied by John's use of *hyion arsen*, male-child, and *tekna*. The text does not read: "and the male-child was caught up unto to the throne of God."[3] (See endnote for more detailed information.)

John deliberately switches back to a term that he consistently used in his other writings to refer to the Church, but never used for Christ alone.[4] (See endnote for usage of [*tekna*] in the New Testament and by John.)

Why? I believe it is because the child being caught up to God just at the start of the Seventieth Week is the Rapture (*harpazo*) of the Body of Christ. The position by Walvoord is based on assumptions and he minimizes the context and the genre of the text with his interpretation. This assumption has further demanded that Walvoord and other dispensationalists assume a tremendous time gap (1,900-plus years) between verses 5 and 6 of Revelation 12 to make this assumption work. Walvoord says this time gap is obvious, but it is neither obvious nor necessary.

The evidence offered to support this view is time gaps found in other passages referring to the First and Second Coming of Christ. This is true, but it proves nothing. It is then assumed that the 1,260 days of verse 6 is referring to the second half of the tribulation.[5] All this is to prevent the Church from appearing in Revelation again until chapter 19.

By doing so, Walvoord and others are attempting to protect one of the main evidences for a pretribulational Rapture of the Church, which is usually stated something like: "Because we last see the Church on earth mentioned in Revelation chapter 3 and do not see the Church referred to again until Revelation 19 and returning with the Lord, then we must conclude that the Church was raptured before the events of chapter 6," which has been thought to be the beginning of the tribulation period, when the first seal was opened. This is not only wrong, but it is also totally unnecessary. By not being afraid to question traditional ideas about prophecy, I have sacrificed esteem and comfort, and gained rock solid truth.

The assumptions made by some dispensationalists have been primarily threefold: (a) it is assumed early on in the study of Revelation that the 24 elders represent the Church and (b) it is assumed that this passage is referring to the First Coming of Christ and not His Second Coming. The dragon represents the persecution of Jesus Christ by Herod, and (c) it is assumed that the male-child and the *tekna* child are one in the same and cannot be Christ and His Raptured Church.

Karleen states, "The total of anything can be no better than the quality of each of its components. If parts of the chain are wrong, the conclusion is false, since the argumentation toward the main conclusion proceeds by adding up subconclusions."[6]

If we were to apply this same test that Karleen applies to Rosenthal's prewrath position, pretribulationism also fails because some of the subconclusions are wrong. Even Karleen admits that "pretribulationalism [has] work to do on its position."[7] It is this work that I have endeavored to undertake for myself and now share.

In response to the three listed assertions, I offer the following:

a. It is believed by most scholars today that the 24 elders are angels.[8]

b. "The dragon standing before the woman cannot parallel Herod's plot to kill Jesus because the slaughter of the innocents was not accompanied by Jesus' ascension into Heaven. Further, the innocents do not play a part in the Johannine tradition; also the devil does not appear at the beginning of the Savior's earthly life, but at the beginning of his public ministry. In the fourth Gospel satan comes to the fore as Christ approaches His passion."[9]

c. Israel did bring forth the Christ, but she also brought forth the Church. The proper relationship then, between Israel and the Church, in metaphor, is that of a mother and her daughter, which fits nicely with the Church being the wife and the Bride of Christ, the Son of God being married to the daughter of Israel (Rev. 19:1-10).

Israel and the Church

The Church did not replace Israel in God's covenant promise. In other words, God is not going to fulfill His promises of land to Abraham through the Church. The relationship of Israel and the Church is likened to that of a mother and daughter. They are related, but separate and unique in God's plan. The Church is part of the family of God, but so is the faithful of Israel.

Those who trust in God can only be saved by faith. Jesus said "*Ye believe in God, believe also in Me*" (Jn. 14:1b). To trust that God will provide for salvation and to trust in Jesus Christ is the same measure of faith. Today, however, Israel is the unfaithful wife of God the Father and the unfaithful mother of the Church. The Church owes its birth to the faithful remnant of Israel and to those who formed the Church of Jerusalem—destined to be the Bride of the Son (Rev. 21:9-10). This makes the Church the daughter of Israel or the offspring of the Jerusalem Church (Acts 15:2).

The Church is the child or the children of "thy people" of Israel (Dan. 12:1). This verse addresses two groups of people "*the children of thy people*" and "*thy people.*" The first group could be a reference to those belonging to the spiritual seed of Abraham that would come to believe in Christ—the Church. The second group addressed are the physical Jews of Israel.

Michael, the archangel, will stand up to defend the Church, and this will happen at the Rapture (Rev. 12:5-12). Isaiah 54:1-10 clearly reveals this relationship between the unfaithful wife and the barren, desolate Gentiles that are borne by Israel (Is. 66:11-13).

In addition to this, John himself frequently referred to the Church as his children (1 Jn. 2:1,18; 3:18; 4:4; 2 Jn. 1; 3 Jn. 4). The Church is the offspring of the faithful remnant of Israel that began in Jerusalem at Pentecost and progressed to and through the seven churches of Revelation chapters 2 and 3. (To see how these birth pangs refer to the seals, see Chapter 4, "The Purging of the Church.")

All the assumptions made by the dispensationalists and those of the Reformed Covenant position (and others) concerning the beginning of the tribulation, have worked to produce a veil of confusion over the context of Revelation chapter 12, which has resulted in poor exegesis, driven partly by positional biases. Consider the following proofs.

First Proof
Consider the Genre

First consider that the *genre* of the chapter is clearly apocalyptic. A woman is in birth pangs. Birth pangs are clearly associated with the coming of the "Day of the Lord," the Second Coming of Christ, and not His First Coming (Is. 13:6-9; Mt. 24:8; Mk. 13:8; 1 Thess. 2:1-5).

J. Massyngberde Ford, in his discussion on the history and meaning of birth pangs, concludes, "Taken altogether these phrases depict the birth pangs, that is, the sufferings, which would precede the coming of the Messiah and the new *era*.... The image of the woman in childbirth is frequently used in the OT prophetic literature.... cf. Isa. 21:3; Jer. 4:31; 30:6."[10] (Emphasis added.)

"The implications of verse 2 is that the references are to the sufferings of Israel as a nation rather than to the historic birth of Christ. It may refer to the sufferings of the nation in general over its entire troublesome history."[11]

Israel will be relieved of her sorrows in and after the anguish of the Seventieth Week of Daniel. The First Coming of Christ was before Israel's travail, but the *rebirth* of the nation will be with travail. "*Before she travailed, she brought forth; before her pain came, she was delivered of a man child*" (Is. 66:7). The man-child is clearly Jesus Christ. Israel is the unfaithful married wife of the Lord God, whose seed shall inherit the Gentile nations (Is. 54:1-3).

This is being fulfilled today through the Gentiles who come to Christ and are of the faithful seed of Abraham and, thus, are related to Israel as a daughter is to a mother. In no way does the Church replace Israel, but instead the Church must be seen as initially dependent upon her for her begotten life (Is. 66:10-12).

The Church is deeply rooted and owes its existence to the faithful seed of Israel—the apostles and first century Jews who believed and preached the "good news" of the gospel. For it is as Christ said, "*salvation is of the Jews*" (Jn. 4:22), and we would do well to remember that God is not finished with Israel. She will be restored as God has promised and will inherit the land promised to her.

The Church does not inherit any land, but will be joint heirs with Christ upon returning glorified and married to Christ. Israel has suffered greatly since A.D. 30 and has borne the brunt of sorrows through the ages because she has borne the shame of the Gentiles. That burden was placed on Israel by God because she rejected and crucified her Messiah King.

But the whole world is guilty of Jesus' death because all have sinned. God used Israel to fulfill His will and to bring redemption to a pagan world. God not only sacrificed His Son, but laid a tremendous burden upon Israel as well (the prophesied crucifixion, Mk. 14:21), which they carried out with the aid of the Romans. This burden of shame will be lifted, however (Ezek. 34:29; 36:6-7).

Second Proof
Consider the Context

The context of Revelation 12 gives a description of the woman as clothed with the sun, the moon at her feet, and with a crown of 12 stars. It is often cited as "an allusion to Genesis 37:9-11." The sun and moon are Jacob and Rachel, while the 12 stars are the tribes of Israel.[12] (See Figures 4 and 6 on pages 5 and 7 respectively.)

The allusion is incomplete, however, because neither a woman or a dragon are in the Genesis passage. The woman with child is clearly Israel at the time of Daniel's Seventieth Week and identifies the time of the fulfilling of the Abrahamic covenant. The crowned heads of the dragon represent the seventh world kingdom, which immediately precedes the return of Jesus Christ. The seven heads, ten horns, and seven crowns upon the "seven" heads parallel the vision of Daniel 7:7-28. The ten horns of Daniel represent the final stages of the fourth beast, which is the revived Roman empire coming to power with the beast in the second half of the tribulation (Rev. 17:12-13).

In the original vision of Nebuchadnezzar, these ten horns were represented by the ten toes of clay and iron. Clearly, the ten toes represent the end of these worldly kingdoms, just as the head represents the beginning of the great Babylonian empire.

This is further evidenced by the fact that it is during the reign of these ten kings that Christ returns and destroys this image, which represents great Babylon, and sets up His eternal Kingdom. "*And in the days of these kings shall the God of heaven set up a kingdom, which shall never be destroyed...*" (see Dan. 2:44-45). Note that it says "*in the days*" and not "at the end of the days."

The Church is the first phase of the Kingdom of God being set up during the days of the sixth earthly king(dom). "*These* [ten horns] *shall make war with the Lamb, and the Lamb shall overcome them: for He is Lord of lords...*" (Rev. 17:14).

The seventh kingdom is the kingdom that ushers in the Seventieth Week of Daniel. It begins with a peace treaty, and the building of the "Third Temple" is a part of this treaty. This seventh kingdom will give way to the eighth kingdom, which was part of the seventh, but uses the ten horns to destroy the woman (Rev. 17:1-8,12-18).

The signs that John saw in the heavens indicate or mark out the arrival of the time or age when this seventh kingdom will rise to power and will be destroyed by Christ. This is why Christ, the "man-child," is holding a rod of iron in His hand (Rev. 12:5a). He is going to smash these kingdoms of the world upon His return. First He raptures His Church (the "child") to the throne of God (Rev. 12:5b). The Church is one with Christ. Christ is the Head of the Body and the Church is the Body of Christ. With this understanding, "every" verse of Revelation 12 can be neatly pieced to Old Testament prophecy, New Testament prophecy, and the rest of Revelation. It presents one unified mosaic.

Dwight D. Pentecost clearly ties Daniel 7 to Revelation 13:1-3 and 17:8-14, and also links Revelation 13:3 to the final world empire that is yet future.[13] It is also necessary to note that of the seven heads and ten horns, only the heads have crowns (Rev. 12:3). Later in Revelation 13:1, we find the tens horns with ten crowns. This indicates that at the time of the vision, seven heads are under the domain of the dragon with power to rule over nations and people. The tens horns, under the control of the dragon, have not been given any ruling power. They have not yet received their crowns and power. This does not happen until Revelation 17:12 when the beast, who is actually part of the seventh kingdom and is the eighth, uses the ten horns to destroy the false prophet and the Western religious dominion, which is part of the seventh kingdom.

This seventh kingdom, which is coming, is now being called "The New World Order." *Wake up!* "The Day of the Lord" is drawing near.

In order to understand the seven heads, John was told that seven heads were seven mountains and in Revelation 17:10 that they are seven kings. These seven kings are believed to be "seven successive forms of kingdoms."[14] I believe these kingdoms proceeded from the time when Solomon ruled and built the first temple—followed by the Babylonians, the Medes and the Persians, the Greeks, and the Romans.

A History of the Kingdoms

The Roman kingdom was divided and became diverse, it broke into pieces and consumed the whole earth, developing into what we know today as the modern world. The fifth kingdom fell with the destruction of the temple in A.D. 70 at the hands of the Roman General Titus. A new Rome had emerged out of its own civil wars in A.D. 69. This was a time when Rome had "four emperors." Out of the civil war Vespasian emerged victorious (Dan. 2:40-41; 7:19).[15]

Looking back, it is important to note how the history of the temple parallels the rise and fall of the dominating seven world kingdoms. The first kingdom began with the call of Abraham and God's promise of this kingdom. This hope and promise continued through Israel's 400 years of captivity until the time of Moses when God began to fulfill His promises to Abraham and to Moses to deliver the nation of Israel to the "promised land."

Abraham looked for the city whose builder was God (Heb. 11:10). It wasn't until the reign of David that Israel began to enjoy again, as they did with Joshua and Moses, the manifold blessings of God. David was a godly man, a man after God's own heart. David's son, Solomon, succeeded him to the throne and God continued to bless and protect Israel as long as Solomon fully served and obeyed God as his father did. (1 Kings 3:14). The crowning achievement by Solomon was the building of the temple.

Today this is called the first temple period. It is also the period of the first kingdom after Noah's flood, when God's chosen, set apart people, occupied and governed their own land as a nation. But satan filled the heart of Solomon with lust and idolatry and caused him to sin against God. As a result, God raised up the enemies of Israel. The nation was divided after Solomon's reign into the northern nation of Israel and the southern nation of Judah. Satan, as any good general, first attempts to divide and then conquer.

God first brought judgment against Israel at the hands of Syria in 722 B.C. Later, in a period from 607 to 586 B.C., God brought judgment upon the southern kingdom of Judah and Jerusalem. In 587/6 B.C., in the third attack by Nebuchadnezzar of Babylon, Jerusalem was plundered and the temple was destroyed. The destruction of the first temple marked the end of the first kingdom and the start of the second kingdom known as Great Babylon. The head of gold represented Babylon in the king's dream (Dan. 2:38). God allowed Babylon to bring judgment upon His disobedient people. (See Chart 2 on page 226.)

Ever since then satan has been allowed to rule the earth and control the kingdoms of the world. Satan offered these kingdoms to Jesus Christ in His temptation (Mt. 4:8-9). When Babylon was destroyed by the Medes and the Persians in 536 B.C., this marked the beginning of the third kingdom since Solomon and the second kingdom of Nebuchadezzar's dream (Dan. 2). It was during this third kingdom that the orders were given by Cyrus to rebuild the temple somewhere between 520 to 516 B.C. This period continued until 433 B.C. when another decree went out to rebuild the walls of Jerusalem.

It was during this time that the prophecies of Daniel were being fulfilled and a countdown of 483 years was to be completed before the coming of Messiah (Dan. 9:24-27). This prophecy is known as the "Seventy Weeks Prophecy" (Dan. 9:24-27). These seventy weeks translate into a period of 490 years. Christ came exactly as was predicted at the end of 483 years. Since that time, we have been waiting the time of this final phase of this kingdom—a period of seven years.

This period is the seventh kingdom (Rev. 17:9-11). By 333 B.C. the temple and Israel were back in place when Alexander the Great rose to power and conquered the Persian empire. His reign did not last long because he died in 323 B.C. and eventually his kingdom was divided between his four generals. This division later resulted in a power struggle between the Ptolemy empire in the South, centered in Egypt, and the Seleucid empire to the North, centered in Syria. Out of the Seleucid dynasty came Antiochus IV, Epiphanes (174-164 B.C.). It was on December 25, 167 B.C. that Antiochus Epiphanes marched into Jerusalem and desecrated the temple. Antiochus Epiphanes was only a type of antichrist.

This marked the beginning of the Maccabean era of Israel's history and the beginning of what Israel had hoped would be a return to glory and self-rule. It was a glorious time for Israel, with Messianic hopes and proclamations everywhere, but it was short-lived. This period also marked the rise of the fifth great world kingdom that would prove to be diverse from all others. This kingdom was the fourth kingdom of Daniel 2 and 7, but the fifth kingdom to rise since Solomon's. This fifth kingdom was the rise of the great Roman empire. Roman dominance over the land of Israel and Jerusalem itself began in 67 B.C. After the death and decline of the Maccabees, Pompey, a Roman general, invaded Jerusalem and attacked the Jews who were holed up in the temple with the high priest John Hyrcanus, who received the reign of the Maccabean dynasty from Alexander Janneus.

Pompey took Jerusalem in 63 B.C. and the stage was just about set for the first coming of the Messiah, the Lord Jesus Christ. Later Herod the Great, who was only half Jew, came to power with the aid of Rome. Herod was a great builder and a shrewd leader. He knew how to control the Jews, and by expanding the temple mount area he appeased and controlled the religious leaders, who in turn controlled the people. As long as Herod could control the people, keep order, and collect taxes, Rome was happy.

This fifth kingdom continued up to the breakout of civil wars in Rome in A.D. 69 and the destruction of the temple in A.D. 70. This civil war and the destruction of the temple marked the end of the fifth kingdom and the beginning of the sixth. At the end of the fifth kingdom Judaism began to reshape itself into the synagogue-centered religion it is today.

"The academy at Jamnia became the administrative seat of Jewish life. Its council, bet-din (lit., 'house of judgment'), became a successor to the Sanhedrin at Jerusalem. Under Johanan and Gamaliel II, grandson of Paul's teacher, post destruction Judaism took shape. The Jamnia period marks the beginning of the change from a temple-oriented Judaism comprising a variety of sects, to a more united Judaism centered around local synagogues."[16]

During this sixth kingdom, Rome was divided and fell. As it broke into pieces, it spread its influence and its principles of government and rule throughout the world. This kingdom or "world order" continues to evolve today. The sixth kingdom will continue right up to the start of the seven years of Israel's trouble, Daniel's Seventieth Week.

Each period or kingdom was distinguished by the destruction or the building of the temple. The building of the third temple indicates the passing of a kingdom and the rise of a new one. "*Rise, and measure the temple of God, and the altar, and them that worship therein*" (Rev. 11:1).

Prior to May 14, 1948, Israel was a "religion of the synagogue and law, divorced from the temple and land."[17] Today, however, Israel is once again a nation. She still does not have her temple worship; but she will—she must—because God's Word has prophesied that it will happen.

John lived in the sixth kingdom. This accounts for the fact that John was also told in his day that five had fallen, one is, and one is not yet. The sixth kingdom was contemporary in John's lifetime.[18] Evidently the Roman empire was already beginning to fragment into the sixth kingdom, according to God's perspective of history.

It was this new emerging kingdom that crushed to pieces the nation of Israel in A.D. 70. The vision that John saw in Revelation 12 indicated that the sixth kingdom was past and the seventh was in place and crowned.

Therefore, the vision that John saw of the dragon standing before the woman was in a future time reference because John was living during the time of the sixth king. "*And there are seven kings: five are fallen, and one is, and the other is not yet come...*" (Rev.17:10).

With this understanding there is no way that this vision could be referring to the First Coming of Christ because Christ came at a time when the fifth kingdom was ending and the sixth was dawning.

There is still more relative evidence to consider. Revelation 17:10 goes on to say that when this seventh king comes, "*he must continue a short space.*" What does John mean? What he means is that a new kingdom will be introduced after the sixth, for a short period of time, and then will be terminated and replaced by the eighth kingdom, which is the beast himself or one of the seven.

Putting this all together fits only one conclusion. The sixth kingdom will continue until the start of the seven-year tribulation period and the building of the temple. Both of these mark the arrival of the seventh kingdom, the start of the Seventieth Week of Daniel and the initiation of the seven-year peace treaty. The beast will be part of the seventh kingdom, but he will not be revealed until he is revealed with the Abomination of Desolation. The seventh kingdom will continue for only three-and-one-half years, "a short space," and up to the point when the fatal head wound is inflicted upon the seventh king of the seventh kingdom.

The seventh king is probably the one who is responsible for killing the two witnesses at the middle of the tribulation period. As a result, he himself is killed as promised in Revelation 11:5 and 7. Upon his miraculous recovery from the mortal head wound, the world will be led to worship this beast. He will cause the Abomination of Desolation to take place and will reveal himself as the beast empowered by the dragon (Rev. 13:8, 12-14).

This king will be the eighth and he will be part of the seventh as well. But with the power and support that he receives from the dragon and the false prophet, he will seek to subdue all the world for himself and set himself up as "god" (Is. 14:12; Rev. 13:3-5; 17:11). He is the antichrist whose mark or number is 666, and he is already living somewhere on earth.

The context of Revelation 12:1-4 is not talking about the beginning of the Roman empire when Herod sought to destroy Christ at His birth, but instead is for that period of time that the world will produce the seventh world kingdom and the final ten-nation confederacy led by the little horn (Dan. 7:8,20).

The wonders appearing in the heavens indicate the arrival of the seventh kingdom. This confederacy will be led by the first beast who came out of the bottomless pit and stood on the sands of the sea after rising out of the sea (Rev. 13:1).

Therefore the context of the Revelation 12:1-4 with the seven heads, ten horns, and seven crowns on seven heads, symbolizes the final stages of the worldly kingdoms that will receive the judgment of God as satan moves them against Israel (Rev. 12:13-17).

The context of the vision then proves that the sign John is giving us in Revelation 12:1-5 is of the days of the Second Coming of Christ because at the First Coming of Christ the Roman empire was still united. Herod ruled during the closing days of the fifth kingdom. This period is highlighted by Herod's temple mount project, which expanded and magnified the temple's appearance. The destruction of this temple marked a new era and the arrival of the sixth kingdom.

Before Christ returns, a seventh kingdom must arise, the temple must be rebuilt, and a seven-year peace treaty implemented. Once again the temple marks out and plays a critical role in God's plan of the ages.

Signs of the Seventh Kingdom

Today Israel is in her land, the world is talking about a New World Order, and Israel is negotiating for peace. On May 4, 1994, Prime Minister Rabin signed an agreement that called for the removal of Israeli troops from Jericho and Gaza. The agreement calls for more comprehensive steps to be taken in "under two years." I believe these more comprehensive steps will lead to the seven-year covenant with antichrist. (Keep your eyes on Egypt; they are rearming their military to the teeth.)[19]

We learn from Daniel that the final division of a revived Roman empire will be destroyed by Christ at His Second Coming. This revived empire is the New World Order that is ready to take center stage. How much more proof do we need to present in order to convince the doubters that the season of the seventh kingdom is near? More, you say? We will give more proof before we leave this topic.

The world today is moving to institute a "New World Order." One would have to be comatose not to be recognize this fact. If John was a contemporary of the sixth kingdom and if the sixth kingdom is the diverse kingdom of today's modern world, then the "New World Order" is the seventh kingdom that must contain the person who will be revealed a short time later as antichrist or the beast.

Consider this: Right now plans are being implemented to rebuild the temple. There is also a book entitled, *The Odyssey of the Third Temple.* This book is periodically advertised in the *Jerusalem Post.* In Issue #1732, January 15, 1994, an advertisement states the following: The book "...emphasizes the *central role* which the Holy Temple occupies in the life of the Jewish people *and all mankind.* Clearly demonstrates how *the commandment of God to build the Temple is a central theme in Judaism and that it is alive and well in Jerusalem...waiting to be fulfilled by the Jewish people.*" (Emphasis added.)

This means that we are very close to the Second Coming of the Lord Jesus Christ. There can be no other conclusion. As the world is standing on the threshold of a "New World Order," it is also on the verge of the seven-year peace treaty, the rebuilding of the temple, the Rapture, and the start of Daniel's seven years of tribulation.

In addition to what is happening in Judaism, the rest of the world has been edging closer and closer toward a global economy, a unified social/political order, and a one-world religion (Dan. 7; Rev. 17:3-5).

The recent GATT and NAFTA agreements are only the tip of the iceberg. The move toward a global unity will be greatly facilitated by the chaos that will result in the world from the tribulations of the period that the Bible calls "the beginning of sorrows" (Mt. 24:8). When the dragon sees these "sorrows" begin to intensify, he will position himself in an attempt to hinder Christ's "Rapture" of the Church. But neither satan, nor we know the exact day of the Rapture, which is a comforting thought.

However, just as we can predict, with relative success, when a woman will give birth, so we should also be able to predict, within a reasonable time frame, when the Rapture might take place. This sounds like good news, but the downside of this is, if we can be reasonably sure that the

Rapture is close at hand, so can satan. Just as the day of birth is often just an estimation, so will be any attempt to pin down the Rapture and the beginning of the "Day of the Lord." The Lord might deliver the Church earlier or later than we anticipate. This uncertainty prevents us and the devil from knowing the day and hour of the Rapture.

But the Lord only needs a twinkling of an eye to safely deliver His Church to His throne. This is the interpretation of the vision that John gives us in Revelation 12:5.

Third Proof
The Man-Child and the Child of Revelation

The man-child who is to rule (future time reference) with a rod of iron is also clearly referring to the Second Coming of Christ and not His First Coming (Rev. 19:15). Christ will rule the nations with this rod of iron. This is something that is clearly part of His Second Coming (Zech. 9:10).

It is unreasonable for anyone to insist that this passage is picturing anything but the beginning of Daniel's Seventieth Week and the characters and events already discussed in the preceding chapters of Revelation.

The child being caught up to the throne of God could be the Church, and it is consistent with earlier references (Rev. 7:9; 15). If the multitude before the throne of God in Revelation 7:9-17 is believed (by some pretribulationalists) to be the raptured Church, then why is it so hard to believe that the "child" in Revelation 12:5b (not the "man-child") is the raptured Church? This becomes especially clear when we consider the passive form of the verb *harpazo* that is used in Revelation 12:5 just as it is in First Thessalonians 4:17. "The verb (*harpazo*) is never used in any context regarding the ascension of Jesus."[20] "The verbs used for the ascension of Jesus are *analambano*, 'received up,' and *anaphero*, 'carried up.' But the idea of being 'caught up' like Paul in 2 Corinthians 12:2 is at variance with what is known of Jesus' life."[21]

When all of these facts are analyzed and assembled, one of the definitive results is a one-text proof of a pretribulation Rapture. This proof has been overlooked previously because it has been assumed that the tribulation starts with the opening of the first seal when, in fact, it commences with the sixth seal. The Rapture takes place and the tribulation continues to advance with the opening of the seventh seal. As I have said earlier, another assumption that has helped to conceal the true significance of the seals was the assumption that the 24 elders represent the Raptured Church in Heaven. It has also been assumed by dispensationalists and others that Revelation 12:1-5 symbolizes the first coming of Christ, when in fact it does not.

I say "assumed" because what has been offered as proof with previous interpretations has been tenuous at best. Christ is the Head of the Church and the Head of the Body of believers. Christ will gather believers to Himself (Jn. 14:3; Eph. 1:10), and Revelation 12:5 is a very clear reference to the Church being raptured unto the throne of God as (just before) the seven years of tribulation begin as indicated by verse 6, which itself indicates the first three-and-one-half years of the tribulation.

The Church is the offspring or the child of the faithful remnant of Israel. Before Israel's trouble or travail, she was delivered of a man-child. This man-child was the birth of Jesus Christ at His First Coming. "*Before she travailed, she brought forth: before her pain came, she was delivered of a man child*" (Is. 66:7). But Isaiah goes on to talk about those who also rejoice in Jerusalem and how Zion would bring forth her children, "*For as soon as Zion travailed, she brought forth her children*" (Is. 66:8).

Those who rejoice with Jerusalem will be those who are dependent upon the mother of Zion (Is. 66:10).

> *That ye may suck, and be satisfied with the breasts of her consolations; that ye may milk out, and be delighted with the abundance of her glory. For thus saith the Lord, Behold, I will extend peace to her like a river, and the glory of the Gentiles like a flowing stream: then shall ye suck, ye shall be borne upon her sides, and be dandled upon her knees* (Is. 66:11-12).

The context of this prophecy is clearly apocalyptic because of the travailing in birth portrayal. This understanding of the Church's relationship is one of dependence upon the faithful of Israel as is also borne out by the text of Romans 11.

> *For if the firstfruit be holy, the lump is also holy: and if the root be holy, so are the branches. And if some of the branches be broken*

> *off* [some of Israel], *and thou, being a wild olive tree wert grafted in among them* [the Gentiles], *and with them partakest of the root* [Jesus Christ a Jew] *and the fatness of the olive tree; boast not against the branches. But if thou boast, thou bearest not the root, but the root thee* (Romans 11:16-18).

The Gentile Church was borne by the faithful root of Zion, which had its beginnings in the Jerusalem Church that spread to Antioch and throughout Asia. The mother (Israel), daughter (Church) metaphor is clearly supported by Scripture. The child in Revelation 12:5b is the Raptured Church at the throne of God with Jesus Christ, the man-child. The Church will be raptured at the end of the "beginning of sorrows," just prior to the woman or the 144,000 going into the wilderness with the two witnesses of God (Rev. 12:6).

This first three-and-one-half-year period is the first half of the tribulation. Therefore, the Rapture takes place before the start of the trumpet judgments—at the very beginning of the tribulation period before the full wrath of God is poured out. ***This is a one-text proof of the pretribulation Rapture.***

Comparing Matthew 24:29, Revelation 6:12, and Revelation 12:5

This timing is supported when we compare some parallel passages. If Revelation 12:5b is referring to the Rapture of the Church, then we should find some connection in the verses before it that link it to the sixth seal. (I will paraphrase some sections with italics.)

Immediately after the tribulation of those *final* days *before the Rapture*, the sun will be darkened and the moon will not give her light, the stars of heaven will begin to fall, the powers of Heaven will be shaken. *This is where the Rapture takes place and the Lord will roll back the heavens and snatch His Church away to Heaven* (see Mt. 24:29).

The events in verse 30 are "after" the Rapture. The mourning of all the tribes of the *earth* is parallel to Revelation 6:15-16. The phrase "the tribes of the earth" clearly prevents us from concluding that this is only Israel. The Lord will cover the Rapture of the Church with a great diversion that will conceal the fact that millions are missing. Communications will be interrupted and the world will reel to and fro from the force of this cosmic upheaval. Every mountain will be moved out of its place because the earth itself will be moved.

> *Therefore I will shake the heavens, and the earth shall* ***remove out of her place****, in the wrath of the Lord of hosts, and in the day of His fierce anger* (Isaiah 13:13).

> [Now consider,] *And the stars of heaven fell unto the earth, even as a fig tree casteth her untimely figs, when she is shaken of a mighty wind. And the heaven departed as a scroll when it is rolled together* [Rapture takes place here]*; and every mountain and island were moved out of their places* (Revelation 6:13-14).

> [Finally,] *And his tail drew the third part of the stars of heaven, and did cast them to the earth: and the dragon stood before the woman which was ready to be delivered, for to devour her child as soon as it was born. And she brought forth a man child, who was to rule* [future] *all nations with a rod of iron: and her child* [the Church] *was caught up* [Rapture takes place here] *unto God, and to His throne* (Revelation 12:4-5).

These passages parallel each other. They are talking about a time when the world enters into a new era. This era will see things revealed that men have been only dreaming and reading about for centuries. The question has been asked by many an agnostic, "If there is a God, then why doesn't He show Himself?" The answer is because in the "Day" that God has appointed to reveal Himself, He knows no flesh will be able to stand (Rev. 6:17). The day when the Lord's mercies run full course is a day that unbelieving men will regret. Yet, it is for them that God patiently waits until the cup of indignation, man's sins, is full.

Is the Cup of Judgment Full?

God perceives man's sins as fruit ripening on a tree. When it is ripe, God will pluck it clean. A clear indication of a world ripe for judgment is the sin of homosexuality. No, I am not "homophobic." I am not afraid of the homosexual. Instead, I care enough about them to tell them the truth in love (Eph. 4:15).

Homosexuality is a most grievous sin and though every man may "tolerate" it, a holy and righteous God can never tolerate such behavior. In the day that God would do so, without first requiring confession and repentance, is the day that God would cease to be holy. It would also be a day that God would owe Sodom and Gomorrah an apology, and of course these things can never be. When God judged Judah and Jerusalem with the overthrow by Babylon in 587/6 B.C., we learned something about how God perceived the sins of Jerusalem and Judah and the sins of Sodom. We also learned why He was moved to judge them both.

> *The shew of their countenance doth witness against them; and they declare their sin as Sodom, **they hide it not**. Woe unto their soul! for they have rewarded evil unto themselves* (Isaiah 3:9).

Both Sodom and Judah made the mistake of bragging about their sins. They refused to recognize their sin and instead openly proclaimed their sins into the public square as being something totally acceptable. The result of such blatant openness leaves God with no choice but to pronounce an impending judgment of death. The gay community, with public support of an absolutely evil government administration that came to power in 1992, and assisted by the prestige and pomp of Hollywood, is now parading its sins in the public square, demanding special protection status under the law and bringing judgment on themselves.

They demand that their behavior be publicly recognized as being acceptable, protected, and defined as just another alternate but "normal" life style. America and the world are openly declaring their sin as Sodom and Israel did, and provide more evidence that both are indeed "*ripe*" for judgment.

On November 2, 1993, "...homosexual and lesbian appointees within the Clinton Administration held a "*coming-out* breakfast" for the press. The original goal, they said, was to secure five gay appointments by the White House. So far, they have obtained 22, and more are expected. Bruce Lehman of the Gay and Lesbian Victory Fund said, 'for the first time in the history of mankind, a president has sought to break this barrier, this taboo. For that Bill Clinton is going down in History.' "[22] (Emphasis added.)

Bill Clinton's name may be going down in history, but I sincerely doubt that one will find his name in God's book of life without him first repenting of these so-called, "historical" works of perversion. True Christians can never accept such a decree, but a liberal, lost, and love-professing Christianity is promoting just such a decree. Those who refuse to stand against open sin are the ones who are really "homophobic" because they are the ones who are afraid to take a stand for what they should know is eternally right (Rom. 1:18-32; 2 Tim. 3:1-5). Woe unto them that call good evil and evil good! (Is. 5:20) "*If the foundations be destroyed, what can the righteous do*?" (Ps. 11:3)

The answer is "nothing, but wait on the Lord for His deliverance, the Rapture, and His judgment upon a world ripe for judgment, which is Daniel's Seventieth Week" (Rev. 14:17-20). And it is quickly coming!

Immediately after the Rapture, the seventh seal will be opened (Rev. 8:1). A silence will be announced in heaven (Rev. 8:1). At this time, the 144,000 elect of the 12 tribes of Israel will be gathered to receive the seal of God (Mt. 24:31; Mk. 13:27; Rev. 7:1-8; 12:6). Then God will declare to His holy angels who are gathered for this great (as in memorable) day, "Let the judgment begin."

> *And after these things* [the cosmic disturbance of the sixth seal] *I saw four angels standing on the four corners of the earth, holding the four winds of the earth, that the wind should not blow on the earth, nor on the sea, nor on any tree. And I saw another angel ascending from the east, having the seal of the living God: and he cried with a loud voice to the four angels, to whom it was given to hurt the earth and the sea* [first four trumpet judgments], *saying, Hurt not the earth, neither the sea, nor the trees, till we have sealed the servants of our God in their foreheads. And I heard the number of them which were sealed...a hundred and forty and four thousand...* (Revelation 7:1-4).

And when He had opened the seventh seal, there was silence in heaven about the space of half an hour (Revelation 8:1).

And He shall send His angels with a great sound of a trumpet [seventh seal—the seven trumpet judgments], *and they shall gather His elect from the four winds, from one end of heaven to the other* (Matthew 24:31; see also Luke 13:27).

It is possible that the trumpet sound that will cause these angels to position themselves is the same trumpet blast which will sound the Rapture (1 Cor. 15:52; 1 Thess. 4:16). The angels will be sent forth with this great blast of the final trump of God. The Rapture will take place in the twinkling of an eye. There will be no need for another trumpet blast to be sounded.

As the angel is dispatched to gather and seal the 144,000, the seventh seal will already be opened, but will be paused until the sealing is completed. Once this sealing has been completed, the scene in Heaven will find seven angels standing before God with their seven trumpets ready to sound (Rev. 8:2).

Another angel will come and stand at the altar. This could be the same angel that had the seal of the living God, returning with the censer containing incense (Rev. 7:2; 8:3). With the burnt ash in the censer, he may have placed a mark or a seal on the foreheads of the 144,000, the elect of God.

A similar ritual is practiced by Roman Catholics on Ash Wednesday during the Easter celebration. "Incense is a common feature of Old Testament ritual. Incense was a costly offering and a sign essentially for the acknowledgment of deity.[23] Thus, the ash or mark would indicate that these elect belong to God and are therefore divinely protected.

The angel entering the throne room of God, with smoking incense, is similar to what the high priest would do on the Day of Atonement, "Yom Kippur." "On the Day of Atonement [the priest] entered into the holy of holies, carrying the burning incense. [The smoke with its] fumes...provided an atonement (Hebrew *kpar* meaning 'covering') for him as he approached the mercyseat of God (Lev. 16:12-13; cf. Num. 16:46). The rising incense smoke symbolized praise (Is. 60:6), prayer (Ps. 141:2), and worship fragrant to God."[24]

The angel offering the smoking incense up to God with the prayers of the saints will mark an end to the waiting by God because at the end of this offering, the angel will fill the censer with coals of fire and cast it to the earth. The casting of this coal into the earth will announce the beginning of the purging of a sin-infested world (Ezek. 10:2). Let the judgments begin!

The Year of Jubilee

On the fiftieth year, the year of Jubilee, which marks the completion of seven groups of seven-year sabbaths or 49 years, Israel was to sound the trumpet marking this event on the Day of Atonement. It is on this day that the "Trumpet of Jubilee" is sounded. Interestingly, the trumpet of Jubilee could parallel the final trumpet that marks the Rapture as well as the same trumpet that sets the captives free of their earthly bonds.

Maybe this sealing of the 144,00 will take place on some future day in the land of Israel with the temple rebuilt and a multitude of Jews gathered outside the temple as the priest goes into the holy of holies to offer an atonement for the sins of Israel. As the priest goes inside, the crowds will be praying outside. While inside the temple, this angel will appear before the high priest and begin the process of sealing the 144,000. This scenario is not without some precedent:

> *And it came to pass, that while he executed the priest's office before God in the order of His course, according to the custom of the priest's office, his lot was to burn incense when he went into the temple of the Lord. And the whole multitude of the people were praying without at the time of incense. And there appeared unto him an angel of the Lord standing on the right side of the altar of incense* (Luke 1:8-11).

The angel announced the coming birth of John the Baptist to Zacharias, but when the "Day of the Lord" begins perhaps the angel will announce the coming or the identity of God's two witnesses, one of which could be the prophet Elijah. Like John the Baptist, God's two witnesses will be preparing the way of the coming of the Lord, and they too will choose to reside in the wilderness with their followers. It all corresponds with the Scriptures.

Fourth Proof
The Two Witnesses in the First 3 1/2 Years

First proof: The genre of the chapter is clearly apocalyptic. A woman is in birth pangs. Birth pangs are associated with the coming of the "Day of the Lord."

Second proof: The context of Revelation 12 gives a description of the woman as clothed with the sun, the moon at her feet, and with a crown of 12 stars. The crowned dragon standing before the woman indicates the arrival of the seventh kingdom.

Third proof: The man-child who is to rule with a rod of iron is clearly referring to the Second Coming of Christ.

Fourth proof: The two witnesses have their ministry in the first half of the tribulation. If we do not force a view on the text, Revelation 12:5-6 can be clearly understood to parallel the events of Revelation 6:13–17:7. When the sixth seal is opened, global cataclysmic events will begin to unfold. The Church will be raptured when the sky rolls back like a scroll. As the seventh seal is opened, a pause is introduced to facilitate the sealing of the 144,000 from the nation of Israel. At this point, they go into the wilderness with the two witnesses of God in their midst. Revelation 12:6 also tells us that the woman goes into the wilderness so that "*they should feed her.*" Who is "they"?

I contend that it is the two witnesses. Verse 14 also reveals that the woman was given "*two wings of a great eagle, that she might fly into the wilderness.*" These two wings indicate the ministry of God's two witnesses.

The cosmic disturbances of the sixth seal are associated with the Rapture, the earthquake, stars falling from heaven, sun as sackcloth, moon becoming as blood, and the stars falling from heaven (Rev. 6:12; 12:1-2). These passages are talking about two events consisting of lunar and solar eclipses.

Between these two events something significant is going to take place. I believe that the Rapture may take place sometime just before these eclipses and that the days that follow will start Daniel's Seventieth Week. (The way that this corresponds with these two eclipses will be discussed in Chapter 10, "The Sun and the Moon in Prophecy.")

The heavens departing like a scroll (Rev. 6:14) could be necessary for the Rapture to take place. This rolling back of the heavens will be like a door opening "in the heavens" like it did for John (Rev. 4:1). It will be a kind of "gateway" to the heavenly presence of God. The earthquake associated with this event could very well indicate the resurrection of the dead in Christ (Mt. 28:2, Rev. 11:11-13).

By associating the two witnesses with the first half and not the second half of the tribulation, the Book of Revelation unfolds beautifully and without vague assumptions. A key part of this unfolding takes place in Revelation chapter 12. Schuyler English writes:

> "There is thought-provoking logic in the argument that their testimony (the two witnesses) will be given during the first half of Daniel's prophetic week, and that their martyrdom will be the first persecuting act of the beast, after he breaks his covenant with the Jews (Dan. 9:27). Their ministry will be attended with power over their enemies, whereas, according to Daniel 7:21, the 'little horn' (who is the beast) will make war with the saints and prevail against them, and this will be in the last half of the week."[25]

Revelation 12:6 to 12:14 form an *inclusio*, "a confined unit of thought." The *inclusio* functions as a set of brackets marking out the start and finish of a thought or event (Latin, "a shutting off, confinement").[26] Verse 6 notes the beginning of the three-and-one-half years, while verse 14 suggests the end of it. The events in Revelation 12:15-17 happen after the two witnesses are killed. It appears that satan attacks those who dwell in Jerusalem first. After this attack fails he then focuses his attack on the 144,000 and those who have the testimony of Jesus Christ or those saved in the tribulation.

This first attack is the battle of Gog and Magog (Ezek. 38). Satan is cast out of Heaven at the middle of the tribulation and this marks the end of the ministry of the two witnesses. At the Abomination of Desolation, the man of sin will be revealed (Mt. 24:15; 2 Thess. 2:3-4) and literally all hell will break loose on earth. *The fourth trumpet announces the overthrow of satan and his kingdom* (Ezek. 32:7; Rev. 8:12). *The fifth trumpet is the first woe and will continue for five months.*

The Casting Out of Satan

The central thought of Revelation chapter 12 is the casting out of satan from Heaven. It is clearly stated that "*neither was their place found*" (Rev. 12:8) for satan and his angels in Heaven. Could this be because the Church is now in Heaven? I believe it is, which would then indicate that this battle in Heaven could rage on for nearly three-and-a-half years. While concentrating all his efforts in Heaven, satan will not be able to focus his attention on earth. As a result, peace will break out and prosperity will seem to erupt around the world as a result of the new global economic order.

However, this false paradise will be interrupted by the three-and-one-half-year ministries of the two witnesses who call the world to repentance and call down judgment from Heaven against all ungodliness. Undoubtedly this will continue until satan is cast out of Heaven. This will explain why the world rejoices over their deaths (Rev. 11:10).

The battle in the heavens may be that which will also cause "*men's hearts failing them for fear, and for looking after those things which are coming on the earth: for the powers of heaven shall be shaken*" (Lk. 21:26). Interestingly, prior to this passage in Luke, we are told, "*And there shall be signs in the sun, and in the moon, and in the stars; and upon the earth distress of nations, with perplexity; the sea and the waves roaring*" (Lk. 21:25). The roaring of the waves could indicate great earthquakes and the resulting tidal activity. The signs will not only consist of events that are happening on the earth but of cosmic events as well. Such is the testimony of the sixth seal.

The Sign of the Son of Man

As seen in Chapter 4, we said the sign of the Son of Man would appear some time shortly after the Rapture of the Church, but before or with the start of the Seventieth Week of Daniel.

A.J.B. Higgins makes a point of this when he says, "the sign of the parousia of Jesus, the Son of man, is the sign of the Son of man. *The sign precedes the actual parousia of the Son of man.*" Higgins offers two supporting considerations. "The order of the testimony texts from Zechariah [12:10ff] and Daniel [7:13]..., as compared with the reverse order in Rev. 1:7, suggests that Matthew deliberately intended to convey the impression that the tribes [of all the earth] will mourn not at the coming of the Son of Man but at the preceding manifestation of his sign. Secondly the very omission of [epi auton, (upon him)] also points in the same direction [Matt. 24:30]. The Son of man has not yet been seen, only his sign."[27] (Emphasis added.)

But what is the sign? Higgins concludes that because Matthew replaces the "piercing of the Son of man" of Zechariah 12:10ff with the "sign of the Son of man," then "the sign of the Son of man is the cross." He believed that Matthew adapted an earlier apocalyptic motif. "He calls the sign of *the Son of man* because he is about to use that title in introducing the testimony in (Daniel 7:13)."[28] "The sign of the son of man then is an [cryptic] allusion to the cross." This sign or portent then will appear in the heavens and cause the tribes of the earth to mourn, "because it is the premonitory sign of the advent of the Son of man, the judge."[29] This brings us to our final point.

With the understanding that Revelation 12:5b references the Raptured Church in Heaven at the beginning of the seven-year tribulation period, we can now begin to understand this battle that takes place in the heavens. For centuries, the devil has tried to frustrate the work of the Church. One by one he has lost control over people's lives. With the Raptured Church in Heaven, he is permanently banished. One by one his angels, the ones who follow him, making up a third part of the heavenly host, are rounded up, cast to earth, and secured in the bottomless pit until the "great" day of judgment (Rev. 9:1-4; 12:4).

> *And the angels which kept not their first estate, but left their own habitation, He hath reserved in everlasting chains under darkness unto the judgment of the great day* (Jude 6).

With the Church in Heaven, the angels and all those who dwell therein rejoice once again when satan and all his angels are removed. For centuries, satan has accused believers before God day and night, but this too will end. The Church overcame the devil by the blood of the Lamb and by the word of their testimony, which is their faith in the Word of God (Rev. 12:11).

This is why all seven churches are admonished to be overcomers in chapters 2 and 3 of Revelation. While those residing in the heavens are rejoicing, the earth is warned of the first impending woe. The warning is that: (a) the devil is come down to earth; and (b) he has great wrath because he knows that his time is short. He has less than three-and-one-half years and he knows it. He has had centuries of one evil deed after another, but now this "galactic dog" is nearing his day.

Every verse of Revelation chapter 12 fits beautifully with the chronology of events that have unfolded throughout this study of Revelation. I am satisfied with the correspondence to the known facts, the language, the context, the logic, and the biblical support that this study has revealed. However, there are some other questions to consider concerning the sign of the Son of man.

End Notes

1. Bauckham, *The Climax of Prophecy*, p. 15.

2. Walvoord, *The Revelation of Jesus Christ,* pp. 190-191.

3. D.A. Carson, *Gospel of John,* (Leicester, England: Intervarsity Press; Grand Rapids, MI: Eerdman's Publishing, 1991), p. 350. In his commentary on John 8:35-36, he identifies Jesus' use of the phrase "Son of God," saying: "The genuine son in this context is not the Christian, but Christ himself (Gk. word for 'son' is [HO HYIOS], always used in John for Jesus Christ; believers are [TA TEKNA TOU THEOU], the 'Children of God.')" p. 350.

4. John never uses *tekna* to refer to Christ and not the Church. If so, this would be the first and last time and this is unlikely (Jn. 1:2; 8:39; 11:52; 1 Jn:1:2; 3:10; 5:2; 2 Jn 4,13; 3 Jn. 4).

See also Romans 8:16-17, which shows the *tekna* of God as joint heirs with Christ, and Revelation 2:27 as Jesus promises to believers in the Church of Thyatira a position of rule over the nations with Him and wielding a rod of iron.

Of the 99 times that *tekna* is used in 91 verses of the New Testament, only once is it used for Jesus, and that as a child (Lk. 2:48). Eighteen times it refers directly or indirectly to Israel's children; 31 times to sons, daughters, and children in general; 30 times to the sons of God, children of God, light or believers or the Church in general; and 11 times by Paul to refer to his spiritual sons in Christ.

5. Walvoord, *The Revelation of Jesus Christ*, p. 191.

6. Karleen, *The Pre-Wrath Rapture of the Church, Is It Biblical?* p. 13.

7. Ibid., p. 12.

8. Walvoord, *The Revelation of Jesus Christ*, p. 118. See also his discussion on the text of Revelation 5:9-10 by N.B. Stonehouse, "Paul Before the Areopagus," pp. 95-101.

9. A. Feuillet, *Recherches des Sciences Religieuses*, Vol. 49 (1961), p. 261, as cited by J. Massyngberde Ford, *Revelation, The Anchor Bible*, (New York: Doubleday & Co., Inc., 1975), p. 191.

10. Ford, *Revelation, The Anchor Bible*, p. 198.

11. Walvoord, *The Revelation of Jesus Christ*, p. 188.

12. Ibid.

13. Pentecost, *Things to Come*, pp. 320-322. See also page 286 where Pentecost clearly links Revelation 12:3 to what the beast possesses in chapters 13 and 17.

14. Walvoord, *The Revelation of Jesus Christ*, p. 251.

15. Everett Ferguson, *Backgrounds of Early Christianity*, (Grand Rapids, MI: Eerdmans Publishing Co., 1989), p. 336.

16. Ibid.

17. Ibid., p. 340.

18. Walvoord, *The Revelation of Jesus Christ*, p. 251.

19. Steve Rodan, "Battle for Parity," *Jerusalem Post*, No. 1742, (March 26, 1994), p. 9.

20. Ford, *Revelation, The Anchor Bible*, p. 200. See his discussion on the use of the verb *harpazo*.

21. Ibid., p. 191.

22. Dr. James Dobson, "1993 in Review," *Focus on the Family*, (Colorado Springs, CO., 1994) p. 4.

23. "Incense," *The Illustrated Bible Dictionary*, Part 2, (Cambridge, MA: Tyndale House Publishers, Intervarsity Press, 1980), p. 689.

24. Colin Brown, ed., *The New International Dictionary of New Testament Theology*, Vol. 2, (Grand Rapids, MI: Zondervan Publishing House, 1986), p. 294.

25. Schuyler English, *The Two Witnesses, Our Hope*, 47:665, (April, 1941), p. 671.

26. Richard N. Soulen, *Handbook of Biblical Criticism*, 2nd ed., s.v. "Inclusio," (Atlanta, GA: John Knox Press), p. 94.

27. A.J.B. Higgins, "The Sign of the Son of Man," *New Testament Studies,* Vol. 9 (1963), pp. 381-382.
28. Ibid., p. 382.
29. Ibid.

Part III

Signs in the Heavens

Chapter 10

The Sign of a New World Order

Consider the Data

What are the signs of Christ's coming in the heavens (Lk. 21:25; Mt. 24:3,30)? These signs are clearly associated with the coming of the prophetic Seventieth Week of Daniel. I believe that Revelation 12:1-4 is also a prophetic passage detailing the signs of the season that will usher in the beginning of Daniel's Seventieth Week, the seventh kingdom (Rev. 17:10).

However, the interpretation of the signs immediately follows the vision (Rev. 12:5-17). The interpretation of the wonders of Revelation 12 has caused much confusion because there is no historical symbolic representation whereby both these wonders can be perfectly cross-referenced.

There is, however, a literal one: the constellations Virgo and Hydra with the sun and moon at her feet in the ecliptic. Long before Genesis was written, God placed the stars in the heavens and named them (Ps. 147:4). E.W. Bullinger writes:

> "For more than two thousand five hundred years the world was without a written revelation from God. The question is, Did God

> leave Himself without a witness? The question is answered very positively by the written Word that He did not. In Rom. 1:19 it is declared that, 'That which may be known of God is manifest in them; for God hath showed it unto them. For the invisible things of Him from creation of the world are clearly seen, being understood by the things that are made, even His eternal power and Godhead; so that they are without excuse.' But how was God known? How were His 'invisible things,' i.e., His plans, His purpose, and His counsels, known since the creation of the world? We are told by the Holy Spirit in Rom. 10:18. Having stated in v.17 that 'Faith cometh by hearing and hearing by the Word (***rema***, *the thing spoken, sayings*) of God,' He asks, 'But I say, Have they not heard? Yes verily.' And we may ask, How have they heard? The answer follows—'Their sound went into all the earth (***gen***) and their words (***remata***, *their teaching, message, instruction*) unto the ends of the world (***oikoumene***).' What words? What instruction? Whose message? Whose teaching? There is only one answer and that is, **THE HEAVENS!** This is settled by the fact that the passage is quoted from Psa. 19, the first part of which is occupied with the Revelation of God written in the *Heavens*, and the latter part with the Revelation of God written in the Word.' "[1]

God recorded the promise of Israel's redemption in the names of the stars. The appearance of this alignment could mark the arrival of the age in which God will fulfill the Abrahamic covenant, which is also the Seventieth Week of Daniel. Therefore, the signs in the heavens could be a very perfect and precise astronomical description of a solar eclipse—a darkening of the sun that will take place when the sun and the new moon are in the constellation Virgo located specifically at the feet of Virgo at sunrise. The woman and the dragon are part of one vision. "These are not two separate visions, but two major figures in a single vision."[2] I believe that John has recorded a sign in the heavens that may indicate the season of the seventh kingdom. At least it is the sign of a new age that is to dawn. It is an age in which Jesus, the Righteous Judge, will appear.

> "It need occasion no surprise that we should find imagery used by St. John in his prophecy already set forth in the constellations

nearly 3,000 years before he wrote. Just as, in this same book, St. John repeated Daniel's vision of the fourth beast, and Ezekiel's vision of the living creatures, as he used the well-known details of the Jewish Temple, the candlesticks....**so he used a group of stellar figures perfectly well known at the time when he wrote**. In so doing the beloved disciple only followed the example which his Master had already set him. For the imagery in the parables of our Lord is always drawn from scenes and objects known and familiar to men."[3] (Emphasis added.)

This alignment has nothing to do with juridical astrology-divination. The alignment does not cause the events to happen. They have simply been appointed by God to accompany prophesied events. They are the hands of God's great cosmic clock. They may be the signs by which we can determine the season of Christ's Second Coming. It is not these alignments alone that indicate the Second Coming of Christ, but rather the way that these alignments line up with *everything else* that is taking place in the world. In other words, the appearance of *this very specific cosmic alignment* in Virgo, plus the fulfillment of prophesied world events, are the signs of the Second Coming of Christ.

The Sun and Moon in Prophecy

We have already discussed the importance of the new and full moons to Israel (see Chapter 1, "Israel and the Zodiac"). The moon is an indicator of months, days, and certain feasts. The sun, moon, and stars are also for seasons and signs (Gen. 1:14).

Paul M. Steidl writes, "Signs in the moon as given in the Bible are always something far out of the ordinary, either in appearance or in behavior. We find no other kind of sign given for the moon. Its signs are reserved for the last days." Steidl, while considering Joel 2:31 and Matthew 24:29, continues with, "The first possibility that comes to mind is that of eclipses...In every case, however, the two signs are described as taking place simultaneously. This is impossible if we are to explain them on the basis of eclipses, since the moon is on opposite sides of the earth during the two types of eclipse. Further, eclipses of this sort have been going on for thousands of years and have not ushered in the Day of the Lord as yet."[4] But Steidl's conclusions are premature because he fails to note the placement of each of the passages in its context and its chronology. Further, when all these passages are considered corporately they portray a composite picture with amazing detail. It is true that eclipses are very common, but the eclipses that are portrayed in these Scriptures, both solar and lunar, have never taken place. Therefore it is not just an eclipse that we are to look for, but a series of eclipses at a particular time and place in the cosmos. The alignment of all the facts point to a specific time in the not too distant future.

There are several passages that clearly portray solar and lunar eclipses. In Scripture there seems to be at least four types of darkenings associated with the last days.

1. A solar eclipse—when a new moon passes between the earth and the sun.
2. A lunar eclipse—when the earth passes between the sun and a full moon.
3. A darkening of the sun and the moon from dark volcanic soot or fires in the atmosphere—sackcloth.
4. Supernatural judgments of God.

Lunar Eclipse

> *And I will shew wonders in the heavens and in the earth, blood, and fire, and pillars of smoke. The sun shall be turned into darkness, and the moon into blood, before the great and the terrible day of the Lord come* (Joel 2:30-31).

> *And I will shew wonders in heaven above, and signs in the earth beneath; blood, and fire, and vapour of smoke: the sun shall be turned into darkness, and the moon into blood, before that great and notable day of the Lord come* (Acts 2:19-20).

> *And I beheld when He had opened the sixth seal, and, lo, there was a great earthquake; and the sun became black as sackcloth of hair, and the moon became as blood* (Revelation 6:12).

The first set of passages talk about a lunar eclipse that takes place before the great and notable "Day of the Lord." This eclipse is preceded by volcanic activity, which sends tons of dust particles into the upper atmosphere. This will darken the sun like sackcloth and cause the eclipsed moon to turn to a copper to blood-red color as it passes through the earth's shadow.[5]

Both conditions are met when we combine a lunar eclipse with volcanic activity, which is exactly what the Scripture teaches. The beginning of sorrows is terminated by the Rapture just as the birth pangs are terminated *immediately* after the birth of a child.

Solar Eclipses

> *Behold, the day of the Lord cometh.... For the stars of heaven and the constellations thereof shall not give their light: the sun shall be darkened in his going forth, and the moon shall not cause her light to shine* (Isaiah 13:9-10).

> ***Immediately*** *after the tribulation* [the beginning of sorrows] *of those days shall the sun be darkened, and the moon shall not give her light, and the stars shall fall from heaven, and the powers of the heavens shall be shaken* (Matthew 24:29).

> *But in those days, after that tribulation, the sun shall be darkened, and the moon shall not give her light* (Mark 13:24).

> *And there appeared a great wonder in heaven; a woman clothed with the sun, and the moon under her feet, and upon her head a crown of twelve stars: ... And there appeared another wonder in heaven; and behold a great red dragon, having seven heads and ten horns, and seven crowns upon his heads. ... and the dragon stood before the woman...* (Revelation 12:1,3-4).

This solar eclipse arrives with the judgments of the "Day of the Lord" at exactly sunrise. The sun is darkened when the moon passes between the earth and the sun. This can only happen when there is a new moon that gives no light. The only time the sun and moon can be together (in this case in Virgo) is when there is a new moon.

The fact that the dragon (the constellation Hydra, the crooked serpent; Job 26:13; Rev. 12:15) is said to be red also indicates the presence of volcanic activity in the atmosphere, or may indicate that Mars, the red planet, is present. This indicates that, although this eclipse is separate from the lunar eclipse before the "Day of the Lord," it must follow shortly after the volcanic activity associated with it. (See this chapter's "Coordinating the Signs in the Heavens and Earth" for greater detail.)

Dark Clouds Darken the Sun, Moon, and Stars

> *A day of darkness and of gloominess, a day of clouds and of thick darkness, as the morning spread upon the mountains: a great people and a strong; there hath not been ever the like, neither shall be any more after it, even to the years of many generations* (Joel 2:2).

> *And when I shall put thee out, I will cover the heaven, and make the stars thereof dark; I will cover the sun with a cloud, and the moon shall not give her light* (Ezekiel 32:7).

Both of these passages are speaking about a time at the middle of the tribulation when the fourth trumpet judgment is completed. God darkens satan's kingdom—He puts his lights out! In the Old Testament, the title "Pharaoh of Egypt" is used to personify satan. "*Speak, and say, Thus saith the Lord God; Behold, I am against thee, Pharaoh king of Egypt, the great dragon that lieth in the midst of his rivers, which hath said, My river is mine own, and I have made it for myself*"(Ezek. 29:3). The destruction of Egypt by Babylon foreshadows God's destruction of Egypt by Gog and Magog and eventually the overthrow of satan himself—end-time events (Ezek. 38:2-6, Dan. 11:42-43).

Volcanic Activity and Great Fires Darken Sun, Moon, and Stars

> *And the fourth angel sounded, and the third part of the sun was smitten, and the third part of the moon, and the third part of the stars; so as the third part of them was darkened, and the day shone not for a third part of it, and the night likewise* (Revelation 8:12).

And he opened the bottomless pit; and there arose a smoke out of the pit, as the smoke of a great furnace; and the sun and the air were darkened by reason of the smoke of the pit (Revelation 9:2).

These events seem to parallel each other and occur at the middle of the tribulation. The events of the first four trumpet judgments and the opening of the smoking pit with the fifth trumpet will blot out at least one-third of the light from the sun, moon, and stars. By combining the circumstances associated with natural events, the conditions required to fulfill Scripture are easily met. Eclipses are part of the signs of the coming of the "Day of the Lord."

Coordinating the Signs in the Heavens and Earth

In addition to the contemporary events taking place in the world, if we coordinate the building of the temple, the signing of a peace treaty resulting in the official declaration of a "New World Order" of peace, the growing disturbances in the cosmos, along with the appearance of the "exact" sign that John is giving us in Revelation 12:1-4, would the doubters then begin to believe that the "Day of the Lord" is at hand?

Understanding the significance of the signs or constellations of the zodiac is very important. Israel was no stranger to the zodiac. "Astronomy was a popular science because of its importance in agriculture and sailing."[6]

"Astrological ideas and symbolism were so pervasive that Judaism, although generally resistant to astrological beliefs, was yet influenced by imagery drawn from astrology."[7] "The presence of the zodiac and the representation of the sun god in his chariot in synagogue floor mosaics from early Byzantine times (as at Hammath Tiberias and Beth Alpha) reflects an openness to astrology symbols in some circles, if only to the extent of affirming the subordination of the stars and the natural order to God and His law."[8] Since Jews "regarded the temple as a symbol of the universe, the presence of such cosmic symbols agrees with the many temple motifs in synagogues."[9]

It is also very clear that the apostle Paul was familiar with the constellations because he made reference to a poem by Aratus designed to help memorize astronomical information (Acts 17:22-28). Aratus put a textbook of astronomy into verse, *Phaenomena.* Simple astronomy took the place of calendars for everyone in that time outside of urban and court life. (The preoccupation with astronomy in ancient authors was a simple matter of knowing the days and seasons, which was essential for agriculture and sailing.) Aratus' poem became a textbook in schools:

> "To the God above we dedicate our song;
> To leave Him unadored, we never dare;
> For He is present in each busy throng,
> In every solemn gathering He is there.
> The sea is His; and His each crowded port;
> In every place our need of Him we feel;
> For *we His offspring are.*"[10] (Emphasis added.)

Therefore John's use of the constellations in Revelation 12:1-4 is John's calendar and God's way of pointing to the season of when Israel will be raised to rule and reign with God. It is the time when God will put all nations and people under her feet (1 Kings 5:3; Ps. 8:6; Ps. 47:3; Is. 14:19). The sun and the moon under the woman's feet pictures the time when Israel will once again bear center stage of God's program (the Church will have been raptured to Heaven).

Clear evidence of the significance of astronomy in the first-century writings is found in the recent studies of the Roman Mithraic mystery religion. It has been believed by scholars (for the past 70 years) to be a religion based on an old Iranian god, Mithra. "Since, no writings of this secret religion are extant, it is impossible to verify or refute this claim. What has survived, however, are icons depicting a caped figure slaying a bull with the zodiac above his head and a dog, a snake, a raven, and a scorpion below his feet."[11]

Stars are also clearly visible in the icon. Studies of this icon, coupled with an understanding of modern and ancient astronomy, have revealed that these icons represent an astronomical star map. The Mithraic mystery religion, which began in the first century, the same time that Christianity was born, worshiped a god that they believed moved the sun from the background constellation Taurus (the bull) to Aries (the ram) on the first day of spring.

It was taught that any god who could move the cosmos was superior to all the gods. However, this religion was based on a false understanding of astronomy because the movement was caused by what is called "precession" and in turn is caused by the wobble of the earth on its polar axis.

In the first century man believed that the earth was the center of the universe and that the sun, planets, and stars rotated around the earth at different speeds. The alignment of the sun in Taurus marked the coming of spring for centuries, so its movement was a significant event in the life of the first-century observer.

The point of all this is that it proves first century man's awareness and preoccupation with the stars, constellations, and the passage of the sun and moon through them. Therefore, John's use of the constellations of Virgo and Hydra in Revelation 12 would have had a profound impact upon first-century believers and nonbelievers. What did it mean to them?

When the moon passes between the sun and the earth, this causes a solar eclipse. (See Figure 3 on page 4.) The description contained in Revelation 12:1-4 is too accurate to be a mere coincidence. Those who understand astronomy can confirm the significance of these alignments. E.W. Maunder demonstrates the historical background for understanding John's imagery as a solar eclipse, when he writes concerning the constellations of dragons or serpents:

> "The positions held by these three serpents or dragons (Draco in Hercules, Hydra and Cetus) have given rise to a significant set of astronomical terms. The dragon marked the poles of both ecliptic and equator; the Watersnake [Hydra] marked the Equator almost from node to node; the serpent marked the equator at one of the nodes. The 'Dragon's Head' and the 'Dragon's Tail' therefore have been taken as astronomical symbols of the ascending and descending nodes of the sun's apparent path—the points above the equator in the spring, and to descend below it again in the autumn [SEPTEMBER/OCTOBER].
>
> "The moon's orbit likewise intersects the apparent path of the sun in two points, its two nodes; and the interval of time between its passage through one of these nodes and its return to that same node again is called a Draconic month, a month of the dragon.

> The same symbols are applied by analogy to the moon's nodes. [See Figure 4 on page 5.]
>
> 'Indeed the Dragon's Head,' is the general sign for ascending node of any orbit, whether of moon, planet or comet, and the 'Dragon's Tail,' for the descending node. We only use these signs in astronomical works today, but the latter sign frequently occurs, figured exactly as we figure it now, on Babylonian boundary stones 3000 years ago. [See Figure 7 on page 8.]
>
> "But an eclipse either of the sun or of the moon can only take place when the latter is near one of its two nodes—is in the 'Dragon's Head' or in the 'Dragon's Tail.' This relation might be briefly expressed by saying that the dragon—that is of the nodes—causes the eclipse. Hence the numerous myths, found in so many nations, which relate how '*a dragon devours* the sun (or moon)' at the time of an eclipse."[12] (Emphasis added.)

Applying these facts to the signs in Revelation 12:1-4 lead to an understanding that the dragon who stands before the woman waiting to devour her child is pointing to a solar eclipse when the sun and moon are in the node of the "Dragon's Tail" at the feet of Virgo.

A complete understanding of the signs might conclude that the woman represents Israel and the sun represents Christ, the "Sun of Righteousness," and the moon, not showing its light, is the Church. The Body of the Church, having no righteousness of its own, is to reflect the righteousness of Christ into the world.

> "God in the beginning set two great lights in the firmament for signs and seasons; and the prophets throughout use the relations of sun and moon as types of spiritual relations. The Messiah was the Sun of Righteousness; the chosen people, the Church, was as the moon which derives her light from Him. The 'signs of heaven' were symbols of great events, not omens of mundane disasters."[13]

The dragon stands ready to devour Jesus Christ and the Church when Jesus comes to rapture His Church to the throne of God. Just as the dragon is set in the constellations of the sky to devour the sun and moon during a solar eclipse, satan is set waiting for that faithful day. When the Rapture takes place, he will know that his time is short.

> "The myth of the Dragon, whose head and tail cause eclipses, must have been derived from a corruption and misunderstanding of a very early astronomical achievement. The myth is evidence of knowledge lost, of science on the down-grade."[14]

John and other prophets used these ancient symbols and signs to indicate the coming of the "Day of the Lord" as a day of darkness. *Therefore, the child that the woman brings forth is represented as the sun and the moon. The man-child and the child represent the Second Coming of Christ and the Raptured Church respectively* (Rev. 12:5).

The first half of the tribulation is a time when Christ will begin to convince the world of its deficient righteousness. The second half will be a time of impending and final judgment when the woman flees from the "face" of the serpent.

(The face or head of the serpent is the other node of the ecliptic where solar and lunar eclipses can take place. Therefore, a series of possible future lunar and solar eclipses might include a solar eclipse that follows three-and-one-half years after the first in the node in the "Tail of the Dragon shifting to the dragon's head.")

> *For, behold, the day cometh* [the Day of the Lord], *that shall burn as an oven; and all the proud, yea, and all that do wickedly, shall be stubble: and the day that cometh shall burn them up, saith the Lord of hosts, that it shall leave them neither root nor branch. But unto you that fear My name shall the Sun of righteousness arise with healing in his wings; and ye shall go forth,* [the 144,000 go into the wilderness] *and grow up as calves of the stall* (Malachi 4:1-2).

This passage in Malachi references the coming of the "Day of the Lord" when the 144,000 of Israel are sealed and led into the wilderness with the two witnesses or "*two wings of a great eagle, that she might...*[be] *nourished for a time, and times, and half of time, from the face of the serpent*" (Rev. 12:14). It is also a time when He shall make the wicked as ashes under their feet (Mal. 4:3). The phrase "Sun of righteousness" points to the appointed day that Christ will appear as the righteous judge to first rapture His Church and then judge the world with the fiery trumpet judgments and restore Israel, thus fulfilling the Abrahamic covenant. (See Figure 5 on page 6.)

Earlier I referred to Paul's reference to an astronomical poem by Aratus, but what is interesting is that Paul continues by warning his fellow Romans that God has appointed a judgment day.

> *Because He hath appointed a day, in the which He will judge the world in righteousness by that man whom He hath ordained; whereof He hath given assurance unto all men, in that He hath raised Him from the dead* (Acts 17:31).

The Second Coming of Christ will also mark the day that Christ begins to convince the world of its lack of righteousness because they failed to be convinced of their sin during the Church Age. The Rapture is a judgment that separates the righteous (those convinced of their sin and justified by Christ) from the unrighteous, the wheat and tares judgment.

> *Henceforth there is laid up for me a crown of righteousness, which the Lord, the righteous judge, shall give me at that day: and not to me only, but unto all them also that love His appearing* (2 Timothy 4:8; see also 1 Corinthians 15:22-25).

The passage in Malachi 4:2-3 clearly points to an ancient astronomical description of a solar eclipse when the appointed day of God's restoration would begin.

In describing a solar eclipse, Maunder writes;

> "There it shines, pure, lovely, serene, radiant with light like molten silver, wreathing the darkened sun with halo like that round a saintly head in some noble altar-piece; so that while in some cases the dreadful shadow has awed a laughing and frivolous crowd into silence, in others the radiance halo has brought spectators to their knees with an involuntary exclamation, 'The Glory!' as if God Himself had made known His presence in the moment of the sun's eclipse.

> "And this, indeed, seems to have been the thought of both the Babylonians and Egyptians of old. Both nations had a specially sacred symbol to set the Divine Presence—The Egyptians, a disc with long outstretched wings; The Babylonians, a ring with wings. The latter symbol on Assyrian monuments is always shown as floating over the head of the king, and designed to indicate the presence and protection of the Deity... Sometimes...the corona shows itself in a striking and simple form—when sun-spots are few in number, it spreads itself out in two great equatorial streamers."[15]

At the eclipse of Algiers in 1900, "...one observer who watched the eclipse from the sea, said, 'The sky was blue all around the sun, and the effects of the silvery corona projected on it was beyond any one to describe. I can only say it seemed to me what angels' wings will be like.' "[16] (See Figure 5 and 6 on pages 6 and 7.)

"It seems exceedingly probable that the symbol of the ring with wings owes its origin to a total eclipse of the sun with a corona of minimum type."[17] Perhaps the prophet Malachi makes reference to this characteristic of the eclipsed sun, with its corona like "angels' wings....But, if this is so, it must be borne in mind that the prophet uses the corona as a simile only. No more than the sun itself, is it the Deity, or the manifestation of the Deity."[18] Worship of the sun is strictly forbidden in the Bible (Deut.4:19; 2 Kings 23:5; Job 31:25-27; Ezek. 8:16). (See Figure 4 on page 5.)

The Woman Is Virgo

The fact that the woman in Revelation 12:1-2 is clothed with the sun indicates that she is hidden—exactly what happens when the sun is in the constellation Virgo. When the sun is in Virgo you cannot see the stars that make up the constellation. Furthermore, that the sun and moon are together clearly indicates that John is describing a new moon. The only time the sun and the moon can be together is when there is a new moon, just as the only time a lunar eclipse can take place is with a full moon.

A new moon always marks the beginning of a new month on the Jewish calendar. Because the sun is in Virgo, the month must be Tishri/ Marchesvan, which is our September/October. When the full moon is at the head of Virgo, without the sun, it is Nisan and Passover. Therefore, John is being very specific with his descriptions of the signs.

The Lord has given us a sign that indicates that Israel's trouble (pain of labor) is about to begin somewhere around the month of some future September/October when the sun and moon are in the constellation Virgo. The precise location of the solar eclipse is at Virgo's feet in the ecliptic path of the sun and moon in the "Tail of the Dragon." Understanding God's great cosmic clock will alert us. It is *time* to look up, for our salvation is drawing nigh when we see all these things—"*signs in the heavens.*" (See Figures 3, 4, and 6 on pages 4, 5, and 7.)

Solar Eclipses

God's cosmic clock is mathematically precise and scientifically predictable. Today, with the aid of computers, we can calculate the position of the sun, moon, planets, constellations, and stars and reproduce them on our computer monitors and printers. "We can reproduce cosmic alignments from our ancient past and we can forecast with great accuracy lunar and solar eclipses, as well as other cosmic alignments of the future."[19]

The sun moves along an ecliptic through the zodiac. An eclipse repeats itself roughly about every 18 years, 10 and 1/3 days, but "never" at exactly the same time and the same place. (See Figure 4 on page 5.) Are all these astronomical inferences pointing to a very specific series of eclipses? I believe they are.

> "Solar eclipses can be quite spectacular and marshal a religious response from even the most arduous of disbelievers. What happens during the last few seconds before totality commences is spectacular in the extreme. The lunar shadow can be seen racing in the west with frightful velocity."[20]

> "The line of the crescent suddenly breaks up into discrete beads of intense light ('Baily's Beads'), shining through the clefts in the lunar limb, while darkness falls like a pall dropped suddenly over everything. During the total phase the corona, the outer atmosphere of the sun, casts only a feeble glow (no brighter than moonlight), while several of the brightest stars become visible. For example, at the total eclipse of 136 B.C., Babylonian astronomers saw Venus, Mercury, Jupiter, and Saturn as well as the brighter stars."[21]

> "Long before totality commences, Venus is usually visible, except in rare instances it is doubtful whether any other planet or star can be discerned until the crescent vanishes. The other pronounced effect that accompanies a large eclipse is the fall in temperature, typically about 5 degrees centigrade, which occasionally causes dew to form. Only those who have personally witnessed a total solar eclipse are in a position to judge the impact on early observers...vivid accounts from ancient and medieval world prove that a total solar eclipse was universally regarded with awe."[22]

John and Isaiah both describe a sunrise solar eclipse being associated with the beginning of the "Day of the Lord." They did this at a time when the science of astronomy was largely undeveloped and computers were thousands of years into the future. How did they do this if it was not by divine guidance and inspiration?

The Bible is the Word of God. John's description of the wonders that appeared in the heavens are too detailed for us to just dismiss as coincidence. Coupling John's description to the collaborative passages of Isaiah 13:10, Joel 2:1-2, Malachi 4:1-2, and Revelation 12 warrants careful deliberation. What do these prophecies mean? If eclipses are predictable, can we use our computers to look into the future and find these alignments? The answers are yes, and we have.

When the sun is in Virgo with the new moon it is always late September or October. This fact is absolutely reliable. When we look up at the stars at night and if we were able to see the constellation Virgo in the early morning hours (in Israel) we would note how the constellation Hydra (dragon or serpent) stands before it in the heavens in late September and October. Hydra and Virgo always appear together with the sun in the months of late September through October. During these months they always appear in the "*morning hours*" with Virgo standing straight up and Hydra standing before her.

As the day progresses, these two constellations rotate clockwise from a vertical position to a horizontal position and then to an inverted position. This rotation is caused by the spin of the earth on its North and South axis. It is always late September/October when the sun is in Virgo, in Israel, or anywhere on earth for that matter. See Figure 3 on page 4 to understand what I mean when I say that the "sun is in Virgo."

John describes these two constellations with absolute precision for a reason (Rev. 12:1-4). Isaiah 13:10 tells us that the "Day of the Lord" will come when the constellations will not give their light and at a time when the sun is darkened at exactly sunrise and the moon is unable to shine.

Why? Why mention the constellations and the sun and the moon in relationship to the coming of the "Day of the Lord"? Were these given so that those who study prophecy and are looking for the "Day of the Lord" could know that the season of the Lord's coming is upon them and thereby sound the warning? Are these the signs in the heavens that we are to be looking for? Maybe this is why eclipses were so feared in ancient days. Could it be that the ancients knew that the judgment of God would come with a darkening of the sun and, not knowing "which eclipse," the ancients sought to appease the God of Heaven with their pagan sacrifices at every occurrence of an eclipse?

This fear and ignorance of the cosmos and God's Word led to the perversion of the heavenly signs, thus the warning was given to Jeremiah not to be dismayed as the heathen were at the signs in the heavens (Jer. 10:2). Wolfram von Soden, who has spent his life studying Assyriology, writes:

> "The sun, moon, planets, and fixed stars were even more carefully observed in the first millennium, and the high temples were often used in this endeavor as observatories. In Assyria, whose kings had bestowed upon astronomy a quite unique position after the ninth century B.C., the royal residence-city Calah was the center of astronomical observations. The new capital cities of Dur-Sharrukin and especially Nineveh, with their observatories, came later. We know a great many astronomers by name from letters and from the numerous astronomic-astrological reports of the period after 700. Drawings of noteworthy phenomena in the heavens were already being made at an early date; according to Ptolemy, lists of eclipses were kept after 747 with absolute precision. An initial result of this practice was that lunar eclipses could be reckoned with approximate accuracy after 700; **previously these had been seen as signs of the wrath of the gods.** The same was also true with the much rarer solar eclipses, as in

> the case of the total solar eclipse of June 15, 763. Nevertheless, the astrological texts often mention 'untimely' eclipses that took place before they were expected. Thales of Meletus, however, was able to predict accurately the momentous solar eclipse of May 28, 585 B.C. on the basis of Babylonian series of observations."[23]

The temple in Jerusalem was destroyed in 586 B.C. Clearly described in Scripture, the Day of the Lord comes with the moon being turned to blood (red) before the "Day of the Lord" (Joel 2:31; Acts 2:19-20) and with the sun, moon, and stars not showing their light (Is. 13:10). An interesting point for us to note here is that the date of the writing of Isaiah 13:10 is also between 750 to 700 B.C. This is the same period of time that the observation of solar and lunar eclipse observations were being predicted with greater accuracy.

Is this just a coincidence or is it because the ancients knew that the coming of the wrath of God would be indicated by a sunrise solar eclipse in the now ancient Near East? **Therefore every solar and lunar eclipse is at least a reminder to mankind that the "Day of the Lord" will arrive. According to Scripture the wrath of God will begin with a darkening of the heavenly luminaries.** He will either accomplish this with appointed predictable eclipses or by supernatural cause and effect. We can observe the heavenly bodies and wait to see what events God coordinates with them.

It is becoming increasingly clear that the ancients were very keen and precise observers "of the rising and setting of the sun, moon, and stars. The famous Stonehenge on Salisbury Plain in England is now recognized as a primitive astronomical observatory" and has been dated back to 2000 B.C. by archaeologists.[24]

Scientific Confirmation

Further contemporary proof that John is describing the constellation Virgo and Hydra in Revelation 12:1-4 is evidenced by the description used by John in the second half of the sign that he describes in the heavens. Indeed the constellation Hydra, sometimes called "Hydra the Serpent or the Dragon" stands before the constellation in the early morning hours in Israel in the months of September/October (see Job 26:13; Ps. 75:14; and Is. 27:1). Here John also describes how a third of the stars of the heavens are drawn by the tail of the dragon and cast to the earth.

Is this just a meaningless bit of information or was John given some insight to the powers and design of the cosmos? In the July 1993 issue of *Astronomy Magazine* there is an article entitled, "Cosmic Tug of War" by David Burstein and Peter L. Manly. In the article, they describe this hidden force found in the constellation Centarus. They call it "The Great Attractor." This "Great Attractor" of hidden dark matter is located in and at the very tail of "Hydra the Serpent or the Dragon." (See Figures 3 and 6 on pages 4 and 7.) But what is most interesting is how they describe just what this "Great Attractor" is attracting or drawing to it. I quote:

> "Whereas galaxy clusters contain many galaxies in a small region, the Great Attractor has its many galaxies spread over an enormous volume of space. As we see it, over five thousand galaxies in the Great Attractor splay across 60 degrees of the sky, covering *one-third of the southern hemisphere.*"[25] (Emphasis added.)

This truth about the "Great Attractor" was not officially discovered and released by scientists until 1987, but John describes this sign in the heavens the same way—exactly 1900 years earlier (Rev. 12:1-4). "Our local group of galaxies, which consist of our galaxy, Andromeda, and some 30 smaller galaxies is moving at about 630 km per second towards this Great Attractor."[26] That is about 391.5 miles per second or about 23,488.25 miles per hour.

We are being drawn toward the constellation Centarus at the tail of Hydra, which is also toward the southern Crux (The Cross). As the seven discoverers of this Great Attractor have concluded, "we will not stop falling into Virgo Supercluster and the enormous mass of the Great Attractor will increasingly draw us towards it."[27] As we get closer and closer to the Great Attractor, it will increase its pull upon the earth. The earth and the local group that it is part of, will be caught up in this celestial tug of war. The powers that are at work in our universe are absolutely awesome.

Jesus used a fig tree to illustrate the coming of the "Day of the Lord." The fig tree was real. It began to bloom as spring drew near and then bloomed in its season. This is why it was such an effective illustration and teaching tool. Jesus also used the constellations of Hydra and Virgo. Jesus was well aware that one-third of the stars were being drawn by the tail of the Hydra or the dragon (serpent) and that is why He used it.

He also knew that scientists would be allowed to discover this someday. To John, it may not have meant much, but to us today, with our growing understanding of the stars, the cosmos, and the Bible, it is a very effective sign and teaching tool.

"*We have also a more sure word of prophecy*" (2 Pet. 1:19). John was indeed describing the constellation Virgo and Hydra. I am convinced that the Lord, through John, is using this conjunction to signify the nearness of the "Day of the Lord."

The "Day of the Lord" Is Close

This awareness of the closeness of the "Day of the Lord" is only because we see so many prophetic events being played out on the center stage of world news. God may be revealing so much to us now because we are too close to the season of fulfillment to affect imminency. In fact, it is the imminent potential fulfillment of so many events that has Christians so stimulated and, therefore, talking much about the Lord's imminent return. Recent fascination with end-time events grows out of the proliferation in recent years of threats to human survival.

> "Following the use of the atomic bomb in World War II, humankind has been increasingly haunted by the specter of nuclear extinction. Meanwhile, other menaces have kept pyramiding: the population explosion, famine and hunger, disease, pollution, economic injustices, the energy crisis, the diminishing of natural resources, festering alienation in the human community, increasing crime and violence, war, terrorism, natural calamities and the like [greatly increasing in frequency]. Cults feed on humankind's fears and uncertainties. Astrologies thrive. Satan worship is blatant and open. By any test, along with other similar periods in human history, these are indeed apocalyptic times."[28]

An issue that will be much more important, as the final days draw close, will be for us who understand and see these signs, to raise the warning call of the watchman (Ezek. 33). God does not take pleasure in the death of the wicked. Although many have tried in vain to calculate when the "Day of the Lord" might arrive through convoluted systems of numbering and symbolic interpretations, we must be reminded that Jesus said to watch for the signs of things that would come *in their season.*

Jesus did not tell us to calculate and compare things of the past. He has told us to watch for things that are coming. When they come, they will all fit and explain what God has revealed to us beforehand. God chose, however, to link the appearance of the earthly signs to the heavenly signs within His universal solar clock.

The use of eclipses to date historical events is not without precedent. The astronomer, F.R. Stephenson, gives evidence of the accuracy to dating events by past solar events. "The subject is one of few instances in academic research where the physical scientist (astronomer) and the literary scholar (e.g. historian) can make definite contributions to one another. It is a fact that the discovery by the latter of a definite eclipse record becomes vital data for the former. Solutions based on these observations are very valuable in astronomy, physics, and even cosmology, at the same time providing the historian (in full circle) with precise dating events."[29] In other words, if the astronomer can look to ancient literature that records the detailed event of a solar eclipse, then he can date the event with an absolute precise date.

The same is true with a "*future*" eclipse. If the Bible predicts, in detail, future solar and lunar eclipses associated with the coming of the "Day of the Lord," then we should be able to pinpoint these events ahead of time. The only question then becomes: What do they mean? Does the prophesied event mean the day of the Rapture? Does it mean the sealing of the 144,000? Does it mean the beginning of the first trumpet judgment? Perhaps it just means that the world has entered a new age and a season of heightened awareness or expectancy?

Let us say, for the sake of argumentation, that we are able to locate future solar eclipses and lunar eclipses that fulfill, to the letter, every detail of Revelation 12, Isaiah 13, Joel 2, and Acts 2. As a result, we warn the world and tell them what it could possibly mean. Many will believe it to be possible and true and as a result some may get saved. Many others will not. Many scoffers will rise up and say that for decades and longer people have been predicting the return of Christ and nothing has happened.

"*Where is the promise of His coming?*" (2 Pet. 3:4) Then the predicted events take place. Along with the predicted eclipses, the world is thrown into convulsions. Millions of people mysteriously disappear and one-third of all the people on the planet are killed because of worldwide and cosmic upheaval.

The recent collision of the comet Shoemaker-Levy 9 with Jupiter leaves little doubt that such an event on Earth would have devastating effects. The destructive force of much smaller meteorites have already left their devastating mark on Earth. The Tugusta meteorite that fell in Siberia on June 30, 1908, burned everything within an 11-mile radius and all the trees within a 25-mile radius were laid flat. No crater was ever found because it is now believed that the meteor exploded in the atmosphere due to the intense pressure that built up in front of it as it entered our atmosphere.

This pressure causes a vacuum to form behind the meteor. The resultant explosion causes a tremendous amount of destructive blast, from meteors as small as three to five meters in diameter, to be released. Had the Siberian meteor or comet hit an inhabited area, the loss of life would have been devastating.[30]

An asteroid just 300 meters in diameter would pack an explosive force greater than all the nuclear weapons on earth. Some scientists believe that we can expect to cross the path of a half-mile-wide asteroid once every 10,000 years. We are now due for this encounter. In fact, this may be exactly what Scripture is describing in the first four trumpet judgments of Revelation 8 and Isaiah 47:11-15.

In 1989 the earth came close to being smashed by a large asteroid. The asteroid came within 690,000 miles of Earth, which is just a little over twice the distance to the moon. But NASA scientists became really concerned when in 1991 an asteroid passed Earth within 106,000 miles. That is less than half the distance to the moon. On December 9, one came within 10,000 miles of Earth—less than one-third of the distance to the moon. This has caused so much concern among scientists that they are now proposing to build an early warning system that would alert us of potential impacts because these two of these three "Near Earthers" were only found two months before they would have intersected the path of Earth's orbit around the sun. The last one, which was the size of a house, was not seen until it streaked past our planet.

Scientist know that, in astronomical terms, these were near "hits" and they are stepping up plans to colonize other planets because they feel that it is "only a matter of time." They feel that the colonization of other planets would help to preserve the human race should such a disastrous encounter take place (see Is. 47:12-13).

Even Carl Sagan considers the impacts on Jupiter to be a warning. Some asteroids, like Series, are over 600 miles across, but this asteroid does not concern scientists because it is too far away to be a threat. But the orbits of a group of asteroids called "Near Earthers" does concern scientists. There are three main groups of these "Near Earthers": Aten, Apollo, and Amor. The Aten group orbits between Venus and Earth, the Apollo group primarily between Earth and Mars, and the Amor group orbits strictly between Earth and Mars. Scientists know of about 150 such "Near Earthers," but are adding to this list every year. They suspect that there may be thousands more that they have not yet discovered. Two points of interest for us are: (a) NASA never said anything about their concern until "after" the asteroids had passed without incident because they knew that just the slightest change in speed or course would have meant disaster for planet Earth; and (b) why are we now becoming aware of the real dangers of impacts from asteroids or comets? These could all be part of the signs in the heavens that the Lord has told us to look for.

> *And there shall be signs in the sun, and in the moon, and in the stars... men's hearts failing them for fear, and for looking after those things which are coming on the earth: for the powers of heaven shall be shaken* (Lk. 21:25-26).

It is time to take seriously and literally what the Bible has prophesied!

Returning to our scenario; suppose that with the predicted eclipse, eyewitnesses and pictures reveal that at totality the grouping of the star Spica (a first magnitude star) above the eclipsed sun and the Morning Star Venus produce what appears to be a "*cross*" in the heavens or the "*wings*" of an eagle (Mt. 24:30; Rev. 1:7; 22:16).

This cross or wings in the morning sky may be part of the sign of the coming of the Son of Man. If in conjunction with this eclipse man also becomes aware of coming meteor storms or imminent destructive meteor impacts, the conclusion would be that the Day of the Lord's Wrath has come. The formulation would be this: The prophecies + belief + warning signs + fulfillment of unprecedented upheavals = The realization that the Day of the Lamb's Wrath has come for those left behind (Rev. 6:17).

These beginning events are part of a transitional period from the Lord's First Coming as a Lamb to take away the sins of the world, to a time when He speaks as a roaring Lion in judgment. The wrath of the Lamb is designed to reveal sin and bring sinners to repentance during the period labeled as the "beginning of sorrows." The sixth seal is the last judgment of that period. After these events Jesus is identified as a Lion, roaring in righteous judgment upon a self-righteous world (Rev. 10:3).

He will cause the world to consider its lack of true righteousness, short of declaring all-out war. Jesus will come as the Faithful and True, King of kings, and Lord of lords to make war against those gathered against Him (Rev. 19:11-16,19). The descriptions of Christ parallel His role in judgment.

1. The Lamb who comes to take away sin.
2. The Lamb of wrath who comes to reveal sin.
3. The Lion who roars in judgment.
4. The One who comes to rule and reign as King with a smashing rod of iron.

The unbelieving world does not recognize Jesus Christ as the Messiah because they do not understand the precision of the prophecies surrounding Christ's First and Second Coming. Some who lived in the first century did understand. The wise men of the East understood and came to Christ.

What Did the Wise Men Know?

Many have speculated as to what star or conjunction of stars and planets were in the heavens at the time of Christ's birth. Some believe that the "star" may have been a comet, but comets were portents of doom—not glad tidings. Perhaps it was a supernova that has since dissipated.

I believe, however, that the answer may be much more complex than any of these. The complex combination of events coming together, all at the same time, bore a message to the minds and hearts of the wise men. At the same time this complexity concealed its significance from those who were ignorant of the witness in both the Word of God and the heavens.

I also believe that there are sufficient clues in the Bible and ancient astronomy to piece together a good portion of the puzzle. We might be able to conclude that the sign was a combination of the "star Spica" (meaning "the seed" or "the branch") in the constellation Virgo—the Virgin and the occulation of that star by Mercury, followed by the "morning/evening star Venus" traveling out of the heel of the constellation Leo/Judah the Lion. Spica and Venus, converging on Tishri 1, could then be the "Star of Bethlehem." The appearance of Venus, the morning and evening star in a particular group of constellations, at a particular time of the year, and at a particular place of Daniel's Seventy Weeks prophecy (see Dan. 9:24-27), could have indicated to the wise men that the Messiah was about to be born. It would be the birth of deity, the King of the Jews.

The ancient prophecy of Balaam says:

> *I shall see him, but not now: I shall behold him, but not nigh: there shall come a Star out* [lit. tread] *of Jacob, and a Sceptre shall rise out of Israel, and shall smite the corners of Moab, and destroy all the children of Sheth* (Numbers 24:17).

The information contained in this prophecy is a major key to the puzzle. To solve it, we need to understand the astronomical relevance of the Star and the Sceptre and their symbolic usage in ancient times.

The prophecy clearly predicts two comings, which relate to the First and Second Comings of Christ. The Second Coming is with a "rod" and is recorded in Revelation 12:1-5a. There the sign appears in the constellation of Virgo also. According to the prophecy of Balaam, the coming "Star" was to tread or follow out of the heel being supplanted. The name *Jacob* means "heel holder." Therefore, the wise men may have been looking for a star holding the place of the heel in the Lion, moving into Virgo, and converging with the star Spica. The wise men were led by the star, which means it moved among the stars. Therefore, the guiding star may have been the morning/evening star, Venus.

Venus represented beauty, love, and fertility to the ancients. Christ was of the seed and offspring of David, who came out of the Lion of Judah (Rev. 5:5); He also said that He was the bright and Morning Star (Rev. 22:16). That simply meant that He was the Son of God.

The Romans believed that a descedent of Venus was a claim of deity. Thus, Caesar Augustus claimed to be a descendent of Eros, or the family of Venus. So Venus treading out from the heel of the Lion into the constellation of Virgo, the Virgin, then merging with the star Spica (the seed) 20 degrees above the western horizon on September 8, 5 B.C., may be the star that the wise men followed to Bethlehem from the east to the west. The morning star, Venus, became the evening star that appeared, disappeared, and reappeared each evening to guide the wise men to the place of Christ's birth.

Many living today, however, do not recognize the precision contained in some of the prophecies of Christ's Second Coming. Will you, dear reader? My prayer is that you have or you will convince yourself to accept God's Word and turn to Jesus for salvation before it is too late. Jesus is the only "Way" of escape.

3 1/2 Years + 3 1/2 Days = "Easter"

A most interesting observation about this unchangeable solar clock or sign that the Lord has given to us (Is. 13:10; Rev. 12:1-4), is this: Putting all the information together indicates that September/October or the seventh month of Tishri is when "something" is going to happen. If we calculate three-and-one-half years (3 years + 180 days) from the "Day of Yom Kippur" (fifth day of Tishri), which precedes the new and full moons in the month of October, our calculations will take us exactly to Passover. (See Figures 1 and 2 on pages 2 and 3.)

If the two witnesses have their ministry in the first half of the tribulation, as I believe they will, then that means they will probably be killed on the Lord's Passover. Their ministry will be instituted with the cosmic disturbance of the sixth seal and this will be the beginning of the judgments of the nations for persecuting Israel, God's elect, through the centuries.

> *And I beheld when He had opened the sixth seal, and, lo, there was a great earthquake; and the sun became as sackcloth of hair, and the moon became as blood; and the stars of heaven fell unto the earth, even as a fig tree casteth her untimely figs, when she is shaken of a mighty wind* (Revelation 6:12-13).

> *Come near, ye nations, to hear; and hearken, ye people: let the earth hear, and all that is therein; the world, and all things that come forth of it. For the indignation of the Lord is upon all nations, and His fury upon all their armies: He hath utterly destroyed them, He hath delivered them to the slaughter...And all the host of heaven shall be dissolved, and the heavens shall be rolled together as a scroll: and all their host shall fall down, as the leaf falleth off from the vine, and as a falling fig from the fig tree. ... For it is the day of the Lord's vengeance, and the year of recompenses for the controversy* [defense or pleading] *of Zion* (Isaiah 34:1-4,8).

When these prophesied events take place, there will be no doubt that the Day of the Lord has come. Maybe the comet collision with Jupiter (the ancient god of war) and the fulfillment of the prophesied sunrise solar eclipse of Isaiah 13:10 and Revelation 12:1-4 in the Near East are God's last physical warnings to mankind.

As these events unfold, the two witnesses will take the 144,000 into the wilderness where God will protect and provide for them.

> *And the woman fled into the wilderness, where she hath a place prepared of God... And to the woman were given two wings of a great eagle, that she might fly into the wilderness, into her place, where she is nourished* [for three-and-one-half years]... (Revelation 12:6,14).

> *But they that wait upon the Lord shall renew their strength; they shall mount up with wings as eagles...* (Isaiah 40:31; see also Isaiah 35).

The *araba* (Hebrew for desert), which is located in the wilderness between the southern end of the Dead Sea and the northern end of the Gulf of Elat or Aqaba, has begun to blossom in recent years. Could this be in preparation of receiving God's elect—the 144,000 of Revelation chapter 7? This blossoming in the wilderness is in fulfillment of Isaiah 35 and 41:18-20. "*I will make the wilderness a pool of water, and the dry land springs of water*" (Is. 41:18b).

After three-and-one-half years in this wilderness, the two witnesses will be killed and their resurrection, three-and-one-half days later, could take place on an Easter Sunday morning. "Easter day is always the first Sunday after the full moon which happens upon, or next after, the 21st day of March (the vernal equinox); and if the full moon happens on a Sunday, Easter day is the Sunday after."[31]

This would then parallel the crucifixion and the resurrection of Jesus Christ and act as a very powerful announcement of God's imminent and ultimate wrath, which begins with the sounding of the fifth trumpet and culminates with the seventh (Rev. 8:13; 9:1; 11:15).

Imagine an unbelieving world that has rejected Christ and the Word of God when the two bodies, that have been lying in the streets for three-and-one-half days, suddenly stand up and ascend into Heaven. Fear will sweep over the world. Imagine this happening before the cameras of CBS or CNN News, which is owned and operated by the self-professed atheist Ted Tuner. Every knee will begin to bow at the name of Jesus! (Phil. 2:10)

Isaiah 13–14 and Revelation 12

An ominous warning! Isaiah 13:6-9, as we have said, corresponds to our passage in Revelation 12:1-4 with the same birth pang metaphors and a very clear apocalyptic genre concerning the coming of the "Day of the Lord." It is interesting to note that Isaiah 13:10 clearly details that the "Day of the Lord" will be when the stars of heaven and the constellations will not give their light (during daylight), the sun will be darkened at exactly sunrise, and the moon will not give her light either. As stated, this passage indicates a solar eclipse taking place in conjunction with the coming of the "Day of the Lord" at exactly sunrise. Is it just another coincidence, or has the Lord revealed to us a sign in His great cosmic clock that *time* is near, even at the doors? (See Figures 3 and 6 on pages 4 and 7.)

Another interesting point to ponder is the chapter that follows Isaiah 13, which concerns the fall of lucifer, *son of the morning* (Is. 14:12-20). This is what happens after the Battle of Armageddon. Satan and his followers are cast alive into a lake of fire. Isaiah 14 talks about the time when satan is cast into the pit. The pit of Revelation 20:2-3, "*And cast him* [satan, serpent, dragon, the devil] *into the bottomless pit*" parallels these events of Isaiah 14:15, "*Yet thou shalt be brought down to hell, to the sides of the pit.*"

Both of these passages are talking about the same event, since satan has yet to be defeated. The events of Isaiah 13 are also of the same events that precede and lead up to this final day of judgment for satan and his followers, just as Revelation 12:1-4 precedes 12:8-9, the casting out of satan. To ignore these passages and their continuity would be irresponsible. Therefore, it is very fitting that the "Day of the Lord" should begin at exactly sunrise because it is a time when lucifer (meaning the "son of the morning") begins to get his due punishment.

Consider also the parallels between Revelation 12:15-16 and the battle of Gog and Magog (Ezek. 38:18-19). It has been suggested by some biblical scholars that the term Gog and Magog is a code word for Babylon or, specifically, Babel and the king of Babel. Because Ezekiel 38 was written during the time of Babylonian captivity Ezekiel would have to be very careful when writing about the destruction of Babylon.

It is believed that the Hebrew letters that followed each consonant contained in the name were substituted. Thus B = G and L = M. The pointing of the vowels would not appear. The "M" could serve to code the "L" of the Hebrew and/or indicate the first later of "*melek*," the Hebrew word for king. The meaning of Gog and Magog could be Babel and the king of Babel or Babylon and the king of Babylon.

In Ezekiel, the army that comes up against Jerusalem is like a cloud that covers the land and is defeated by a supernatural earthquake. In Revelation 12:15 we are told something very similar: the serpent casts a flood out of his mouth after the woman, which is Israel or Jerusalem, and then the earth helps the woman (see also Zech. 14:1-4; Rev. 11:13;14:1).

The destruction of Gog by God in the land of Israel could be the beginning of the destruction of Babylon the Great that sought to invade Israel (Ezek. 38:18-19; Rev. 12:15-16). After destroying the armies of Gog in the land of Israel with an earthquake (Ezek. 38:19), God will send a fire of destruction upon the land of Magog or the seat of beast (Ezek. 39:6). While in its weakened state, the kings of the East will come against the remnants of the North and this will be the tidings that the beast hears coming from the North and the East (Dan. 11:44).

The beast will intervene and form a coalition with the armies of the "ten horns" of the East and destroy the false prophet and the Mother of Harlots (Rev. 17:12-18; 18:1-19). The invasion will destroy the Mystery of Babylon—the final remnants of the seventh world empire and religion. With the western and northern forces destroyed, all that remains is to destroy Israel and keep God from fulfilling His promises to Israel. If satan were to succeed, he would succeed in dethroning God, which is his ultimate goal.

Of course, he cannot and will not be successful. As he gathers the remaining armies of the world together to do battle against Israel and Jesus Christ Himself, satan and the armies of the world will be destroyed (Ezek. 39:11-20; Dan. 11:45; Rev. 19:19-21).

Building a Scenario

If, for example, the two witnesses should begin their ministry on or near Yom Kippur (October 4, 1995), followed by the first full moon on October 8 and then followed with the new moon of October 24, 1995, three-and-one-half years later takes us to the start of Passover, 6:00 p.m., and would allow the two witnesses to be resurrected three-and-one-half days later on Easter morning. For example, from Yom Kippur 1995 to Yom Kippur 1996 equals one year. Then Yom Kippur 1998 would equal three years. From Yom Kippur 1998 to March 31, 1999, the first day of Passover, is one day short of 180 days. But *Thursday, April 1, 1999*, would be exactly three-and-one-half years from Yom Kippur of October 4, 1995. Three-and-one-half days later would be April 4, 1999, Easter Sunday morning.

The deaths of the two witnesses is part of the fifth trumpet. The fifth trumpet lasts for five months (Rev. 9:5). Five months after the new moon of Nisan takes us to the new moon of August 11, 1999, in which there will be another solar eclipse beginning at noon in the "Head of the Dragon," Hydra. (See Figures 2, 4, and 6 on pages 3, 5, and 7.)

Revelation 12:1-4 points to the beginning of the seventh king(dom). This kingdom comes into power *after* the cosmic disturbance of the Rapture and after the 144,000 are sealed. The sequence of events, according to Revelation 12:5b-6, must include the Rapture, the introduction of the two witnesses, and the sealing of the 144,000 of Israel. With the 144,000 sealed, the two witnesses take them into the wilderness to escape the influence of the New World Order and its antichrist.

> *Woe be unto the pastors that destroy and scatter the sheep of My pasture! saith the Lord. Therefore thus saith the Lord God of Israel against the pastors that feed My people; Ye have scattered My flock, and driven them away, and have not visited them: behold, I will visit upon you the evil of your doings, saith the Lord.* ***And I will gather the remnant of My flock out of all countries whither I have driven them, and will bring them again to their folds; and they shall be fruitful and increase.*** [Israel returns to Zion in 1948.] ***And I will set up shepherds over them which shall feed them: and they shall fear no more, nor be dismayed, neither shall they be lacking****, saith the Lord.* [The two witnesses come and take a faithful sealed remnant into the wilderness (Rev. 7:1-8; 11:3-11; 12:6,14).] *Behold, the days come, saith the Lord, that I will raise unto* ***David a righteous Branch****, and a King shall reign and prosper, and shall execute judgment and justice in the earth.* [Jesus Christ is the offspring of David that will return at the end of the tribulation to set up His everlasting kingdom (Rev. 22:16).] *In His days Judah shall be saved, and Israel shall dwell safely: and this is His name whereby He shall be called,* ***THE LORD OUR RIGHTEOUSNESS. Therefore, behold, the days come, saith the Lord, that they shall no more say, The Lord liveth, which brought up the children of Israel out of the land of Egypt; but, The Lord liveth, which brought up and which led the seed of the house of Israel out of the north country, and from all countries whither I had driven them; and they shall dwell in their own land*** (Jeremiah 23:1-8).

> *Behold, the days come, saith the Lord, that I* ***will perform that good thing which I have promised unto the house of Israel and to the house of Judah. In those days, and at that time, will I cause the Branch of righteousness to grow up unto David****; and He shall execute judgment and righteousness in the land.* ***In those days*** *shall Judah be saved, and Jerusalem shall dwell*

> *safely: and this is the name wherewith she shall be called, The Lord our righteousness* (Jeremiah 33:14-16).
>
> *And in that day seven women shall take hold of one man, saying, We will eat our own bread, and wear our own apparel: only let us be called by thy name, to take away our reproach. In that day shall the branch of the Lord be beautiful and glorious, and the fruit of the earth shall be excellent and comely for them that are escaped of Israel. And it shall come to pass, that he that is left in Zion, and* ***he that remaineth in Jerusalem, shall be called holy, even every one that is written among the living in Jerusalem*** ["whosoever was not found written in the book of life was cast into the lake of fire" (Rev. 20:15)]: *when the Lord shall have washed away the filth of the daughters of Zion, and shall have purged the blood of Jerusalem from the midst thereof by the spirit of judgment, and by the spirit of burning* [the spirit of judgment is the tribulation period with the angels of the first six trumpets, while the spirit of burning takes place with the outpouring of the vials] (Isaiah 4:1-4).

We are told in Joel 2:30-31 and Acts 2:19-20 that there will be wonders (*teras*) in the heavens and signs (*simeion*) in the earth beneath, vapor of smoke. The sun shall be turned into darkness, and the moon into blood, before that great and notable "Day of the Lord" comes.

Now if we are right to think that the judgments associated with the great and notable day of the Lord could come by October 24, 1995, and that the Rapture of the Church takes place during the month of Tishri, late September/October 1995, and that the sealing of the 144,000 takes place in a ten-day period just after Yom Kippur, then there should be a lunar eclipse sometime after the Rapture and before the coming of the "Great Day of the Lord."

The moon is turned to blood red when a lunar eclipse takes place after volcanic activity on earth. The opening of the sixth seal provides more than enough disturbance to fill the upper atmosphere with dust and smoke. "*And the sun became black as sackcloth...*"(Rev. 6:12b). Light filtering through the earth's atmosphere and onto the moon will make it appear blood red as the moon passes through the earth's shadow.

"Is there going to be a lunar eclipse sometime between Yom Kippur, October 4, 1995, and October 24, 1995?" ***Yes!*** On October 8, at 1800 hours, or 6:00 p.m. Israel's time, right at the beginning of the Feast of Sukkoth, there will be a lunar eclipse that will cover one-third of the moon in Israel, but the moon will be in the *penumbra* and part of the *umbra* of the earth's shadow, turning it to blood red for at least three hours. Consider Acts 2:19-20 very carefully: "*vapor of smoke.*"

Now we know from the science of astronomy that on October 8, 1995, at exactly 6:00 p.m. (Israel time), Israel and the world will experience a lunar eclipse, which is also the first hour of the first day of Sukkoth, the celebration of the Feast of Tabernacles. Coincidence? Maybe, but again maybe not. This eclipse could potentially fulfill the prophecies of Joel and Acts if the solar eclipse at sunrise on October 24, 1995, is used by God to fulfill the singular prophecy of Isaiah 13:8-11 and Revelation 12:1-4.

One point that I need to clarify in our scenario is that, although the opening of the seventh seal would have been accomplished before the twenty-fourth of October (on October 4, Yom Kippur), a delay would have been introduced to accomplish the sealing of the 144,000. This delay then may be a total of 20 days. If I am right, I believe that the ministry of the two witnesses of God will begin on Yom Kippur, the "Day of Atonement." The trumpet judgments and the seven-year countdown will proceed forth with the new moon on the first day of the Jewish eighth month, Marchesvan. In 1995, the first of Marchesvan is October 24.

Interestingly, because I believe that the two witnesses have their ministry in the first half of the tribulation period and not the second, I counted three-and-one-half years from Yom Kippur and came to March 31, 1999—Passover. This is a Wednesday, which means that if the two witness are killed after three-and-one-half years and are then resurrected three-and-one-half days later, they will be resurrected on Easter Sunday morning, April 4, 1999. This would parallel the resurrection of Jesus Christ.

Is it just coincidence that three-and-one-half years plus three-and-one-half days takes us to Passover and then Easter Sunday in 1999? I do not think so. Even if I am wrong to suspect that October 1995 is the start of the Day of the Lord, this scenario does prove, at least, that if the two witnesses begin their ministry on or near the Feast of Tabernacles, it is absolutely logical and scripturally supportable to put their ministry in the first half of the tribulation and not the latter half. But wait, I still have more!

Consider Revelation 2:10. The message to the Church is that it will have ten days of tribulation at the hands of the devil, but believers are to be faithful unto death (Rev. 6:9-11). There are ten days before Yom Kippur after the New Year begins, and Hoshana Rabba comes ten days after Yom Kippur. These first ten days are known as the ten "Awesome Days" that require all to search their hearts before God while singing the great Hallel of Psalms 113–118. It is the Feast of Ingathering.

This could be when the 144,000 are gathered and sealed, while the ten days before Yom Kippur could be ten days of testing for the Church. Ten days may simply indicate the length of time that believers have to endure severe persecution just before the Rapture (Dan. 1:14-15).

Is it just coincidence that January 1, 1995, was also a day of a new moon? This means that January 1, 1995, also began a new month for the Jewish calendar. Counting the months from January 1 to October 4, 1995, we have a few days over nine months. The ideal gestation period for a woman with child is 277-278 days. Counting the days to October 4, 1995, back to January 1, 1995, we get 277 days. This, I believe, could begin a period of great trouble on the earth, but this is a period that is only the final stages of the "beginning of sorrows." It is a period that is for the purpose of warning God's people that the time of the Lord's return is coming. *Watch, when you "begin" to see these things happen.*

Another interesting point of fact is that the Feast of Tabernacles is celebrated during September/October. It is a time when Israel is to remember its "wilderness" wanderings. This would seem to be a perfect time for the 144,000 to be taken into the wilderness. The celebration of Sukkoth is completed with the great Hoshana Rabba on the seventh day. This is the great day of salvation where Jewish tradition has it that the skies will open up and any wish made will be answered. It is also a time when the Jews celebrate their Thanksgiving. The celebration includes the use of palm branches. It is said to be a time of happy "harvest." In conjunction to this, it is interesting to note that Revelation 7:9 finds the Raptured Church in Heaven with palm branches in their hands. Why? They are also giving blessing of "thanksgiving" (Rev. 7:12). Why? They are also singing songs of great salvation (Rev. 7:10). Why? The offering of incense by the angel just before the start of the trumpet judgments parallels the offering of incense on the Day of Atonement, Yom Kippur. Why? Why are all these elements found in Revelation 7:9-17; 8:1-5; and 12:12 and, therefore, are consistent with a Church raptured and in Heaven near the Feast of Tabernacles?

This Rapture would have to take place sometime just before Yom Kippur. Why is the Feast of Tabernacles continued during the Lord's reign on earth (Zech. 14:16)? I believe the answer to all this is because it is the season when we should expect to see it all begin to happen—the Rapture, the peace covenant, the construction of the third temple, and the sealing of the 144,000.

Maybe the great day of Hoshana Rabba, October 15, 1995, is the day that the two witnesses begin their ministry in Israel. Maybe it is on this day that the Lord will reveal Himself from Heaven and all the tribes of the earth will begin to mourn as they see the Lord in the clouds with all His glory. Then they will know that the Day of the Lord's Wrath has come (Rev. 6:15-17; Mt. 24:30-31).

Please note the added detailed information of Revelation that is unfolding. Three-and-one-half years, plus three-and-one-half days, points to an Easter Sunday resurrection if the two witnesses begin their ministry on Yom Kippur. Note the consistency, note the logic, and most of all, note the Scriptural continuity. The pretribulation Rapture is rock solid!

Why So Much Now?

Why now? Why are we beginning to understand so much of Revelation now? It is the time of the end. "*For the words are closed up and sealed till the time of the end*" (Dan. 12:9). The signs coming in the heavens do fit perfectly into the timing and portrait of events recorded in Scripture. Can this just be coincidence for all these factors to line up in the month of Tishri of 1995?

That's right, in 1995. The signs given to us by John in Revelation 12 and Isaiah 13 will come together in the heavens in the month of October, or Tishri 5756. There are many who believed that the year 1994 would be a significant year because on September 6, Rosh Hashanah, the Jewish new year of 5755, began a new sabbatical cycle. This cycle of sabbaths has been correlated to the destruction of the second temple in A.D. 70 as marking the end of a sabbatical cycle by Rabbi Maimonides, A.D. 1175. Each cycle is seven years long.

As a result, some have believed that the year 2000–2001 may mark the end of this age and the dawning of a new millennium with Christ ruling. They also thought that the tribulation period might begin in September of 1994 because it marked the beginning of a new seven-year cycle. But of course it didn't happen.

Rabbi Wacholder disagrees with the conclusion of Rabbi Maimonides. He believes the temple was destroyed before the sabbatical year commenced. For some, this would make September/October of 1995 the next prime candidate for the tribulation to begin. This is also the time that the signs in the heavens described in Revelation 12:1-4 are also indicating. But no one can know for sure.

All we can do is work for, watch for, and wait for the coming of the "Day of the Lord." As we get closer to that fateful day, the signs will be even more apparent to those who believe. The Spirit of God will make it plain to those He indwells.

On October 24, 1995, the tail of the dragon will appear to devour the sun just as Revelation 12:4 describes. Three-and-one-half years plus the five months of the fifth trumpet judgment (Rev. 9:5) would take us to August 11 of 1999. There we find another solar eclipse predicted for just after noon in Israel, in the head or face of the dragon.

> *And to the woman were given two wings of a great eagle, that she might fly into the wilderness...from the face of the serpent* (Revelation 12:14).

> *And it shall come to pass in that day, saith the Lord God, that I will cause the sun to go down at noon, and I will darken the earth in the clear day* (Amos 8:9).

I cannot unequivocally convince myself that the alignment of all these events are just a coincidence. These signs in the heavens could be the prophesied signs of the end. It is time for some to get serious about God. It is time to get saved if you are not saved. It is time to start serving the Lord and it is time to stop giving lip service to good intentions and start living and looking for the Lord. Do not be like the poor unfortunate virgins who did not have oil (representing the Holy Spirit) in their lamps when the Lord comes to take away His Church in the Rapture (Mt. 25:1-13).

Only those who are truly saved will be taken in the Rapture. Many people who call themselves "Christian" may be left behind and will find a closed door that can only be breached through death (Mt. 25:10; Rev. 3:20). After the Rapture those who begin to trust in the Lord alone and claim *Jesus as their righteousness* will, at that time, suffer tribulation for their testimony.

We may not have much time left. Those who are left behind will have an opportunity to be saved out of the Church of Laodicea. Those who faithfully follow the Lord will be tried for their faith and persecuted by Babylon the Great, the Mother of Harlots (Rev. 3:15-19; 14:13; 15:2-4; 17:5-6; 20:4). This Mystery Babylon is the new one-world religious system of the "New World Order." Christians who come to trust in the Lord after the Rapture must refuse to give into unifying with this one-world religion.

Today, pastors receive pressure from other churches to attend ecumenical meetings or conferences that overlook major doctrinal differences for the sake of unity. If they refuse to unite, they are accused of being unloving or judgmental. We must choose to stand with and for the Lord and upon His Word first (Rev. 3:8-10). The Word of God is not ours to compromise. If others want to join us, all they have to do is agree to preach, teach, and obey *all* of Scripture, and unity will take care of itself.

As We Begin to See These Things!

In addition to all that I have already stated, there has been another sign in the heavens. It is interesting to note, that between July 16 and 22, 1994, scientists witnessed the predicted event of a comet impact on the planet Jupiter. This comet, Shoemaker Levy-9, was broken up into

21, 1-kilometer meteorite pieces (about 3,281 feet across) by the gravitational fields of Jupiter. This happened the last time Shoemaker Levy-9 had a close encounter with the planet less than two years ago. Each piece of this comet was expected to pack a punch 250,000 times greater than a 1-megaton hydrogen bomb, and it did that and more.

The entire astronomical science community was focused on Jupiter because this was a very unusual "observable" event, with the outcome and significance very uncertain. Scientists will be studying the data for a long time, but the questions are already coming. Could it happen to Earth? The answer from the science community is "yes" and the answer from Scripture is that "some day it will."

"*And the stars of heaven fell unto the earth...*" (Rev. 6:13); "*a great mountain burning with fire was cast into the sea...and there fell a great star from heaven*" (see Rev. 8:1-12); "*And there fell upon men a great hail out of heaven...*" (Rev. 16:21).

However, the most interesting thing to me is *where* Jupiter was when the impacts took place. Jupiter was in almost exactly the same celestial location, "in Virgo," as the eclipse that will follow it in October of 1995. With the eyes of the world focused on Jupiter, and therefore Virgo, is God calling the world's attention to a sign that He has prepared and prophesied about long ago? (See Figures 3 and 6 on pages 4 and 7.)

It may also indicate that our solar system is entering an age when meteor impacts might become more frequent and more deadly for Earth.

The message in the heavens and the Word of God agree in witness that the second coming of the Messiah is close, but are we wise enough to interpret the warning in the signs in heaven and earth? Do they indicate the coming of the Messiah and of God's judgment?

> *Yea, the stork in the heaven knoweth her appointed times; and the turtle and the crane and the swallow observe the time of their coming; but My people know not the judgment of the Lord* (Jeremiah 8:7).

> *...When it is evening, ye say, It will be fair weather: for the sky is red. And in the morning, It will be foul weather to day: for the sky is red and lowering. O ye hypocrites, ye can discern the face of*

the sky; but can ye not discern the signs of the times? (Matthew 16:2-4)

The Pharisees were looking for a sign to believe in Jesus and His teachings. Jesus ridiculed them because they could not recognize all the prophecies concerning His first coming—fulfilled before their very eyes. They failed to receive their King because they failed to understand the signs of His coming in the books of the prophets.

But I do not need signs to believe in Jesus Christ. I have already believed His words and trusted in Jesus Christ as my Savior. Believers need to be looking for the prophecies of Christ's Second Coming to be fulfilled and I affirm that I do see them appearing. With this affirmation I, therefore, believe that the day of the Rapture and the Day of the Lord's Wrath is very near.

If we believe this to be true, then we must warn as many as we can before it is too late. This is the greatest purpose of this book, whether it happens in 1995, 2001, or 2020! Someday the Lord will return. Are you ready for that day?

This is a possible sequence of events (*if and when*) the signs in the heavens recorded in Revelation 12:1-4 parallel other prophesied events (i.e., rebuilding of the temple, peace treaty, one-world government, increased earthquakes, wars, and famines).

1. January 1, 1995, was also a new moon. This means that January 1 also began a new month for Israel. This could also mark the beginning of the final phase of the "beginning of sorrows," a nine-month period of intensified calamities before the coming of the two witnesses and the events of the sixth seal. If 1995 turns out to be a bad year globally and gets worse and worse as the year progresses, then that will make October 1995 much more plausible. This is the time of birth pangs before the coming of the "Day of the Lord," a 277- or 278-day gestation period.

2. As the sixth seal is opened and fulfilled, worldwide chaos and destruction results. The sun and skies are darkened as a result of global upheavals (Joel 2:31; Rev. 6:12-17). Rapture occurs and the Church is before the throne of God. This must take place sometime before October 4, 1995?? (The Rapture is veiled by the chaos.)

3. On Yom Kippur, the two witnesses begin their ministry, October 4, 1995, and reveal themselves at the end of the Feast of Tabernacles to the 144,000.

4. On October 8, an eclipsed full moon turns to blood red before the coming of the wrath of the "Day of the Lord" (Joel 2:31; Acts 2:19-20). This is also the first day of the Feast of Tabernacles. The lunar eclipse begins at precisely the same hour of the Feast of Tabernacles (6:00 p.m.).

5. The 144,000 are sealed and taken into the wilderness by the two witnesses after or during the Feast of Tabernacles. The Rapture must take place before this event. (Remember, the opening of the seventh seal has a delay associated with it. The delay could be from one full moon to the next new moon in October.)

6. The world consolidates and the "New World Order" is finally ratified. A new order comes out of the chaos. The antichrist is part of this New World Order, but he conceals his true identity from the world. (The U.N. has scheduled a world conference in March 1995 in Copenhagen to discuss global governance.)

7. On October 24, the first trumpet of the "Day of the Lord" sounds. Israel wakes up to a sunrise solar eclipse located at the feet of the constellation Virgo as the "New Moon" passes between the sun and the Earth on the ecliptic in the tail of the Dragon Hydra. This solar eclipse, combined with the already darkened skies, will make this a day of darkness (Joel 2:31; Is. 13:1-10). The Day of the Lord's Wrath has come!

8. Three-and-one-half years plus five months after the beginning of the "Day of the Lord" on August 11, 1999, there will be another solar eclipse beginning just after noon and reaching totality at 1:00 p.m. in the head of the dragon in Israel. This darkening of the sun will fulfill Amos 8:9 and marks the sounding of the sixth trumpet.

Time to Consider the Possibilities

The careful reader should make a note that on October 24, 1995, while the sun is in constellation Virgo and the moon at her feet, there will be a total eclipse of the sun in the Near East, which begins at exactly sunrise in the land of Israel. Venus will be under the sun and the moon and the star Spica; a first magnitude star will be above. Spica is also known as "*The Branch*" in ancient star charts.

> "Spica, the bright star in Virgo's left hand, has the ancient meaning of '*The Branch*' and marks the ear of wheat (the seed) that she holds.
>
> "Thus, the personal identity of Him who was to be the seed of the woman is connected with the prophecies of the Branch and is none other than the Lord Jesus Christ. He was to be the seed of the woman that would bruise the head of the serpent while Himself being bruised (Gen. 3:15)."[32]

The very star that represents Jesus Christ will be visible in areas where the October 24, 1995, eclipse is total. Could this be the sign of the coming of the Son of man (Rev. 22:16)? This fourfold conjunction of an eclipsed sun, Spica, Mercury, and Venus could produce the sign of the cross—the sign "*of the Son of man in the heaven*" (Mt. 24:30). Christ was born in September; therefore, Virgo is His sign.

As I have put the pieces of this mosaic puzzle together, it has been easy to see piece after piece interlocking with the next. Together, we can step back and begin to see that the time is upon us. There are still more startling cosmic details that prove the accuracy and the certainty that John's signs are, in fact, pointing to the constellations Virgo and Hydra and to a solar eclipse that will take place in the days of the seventh king(dom) (Rev. 12:1-4).

A review is now in order.

1. The woman is the constellation Virgo and the dragon is the constellation Hydra, which stands before the woman in the heavens. (See Figures 1, 2, 3, and 4 on pages 2, 3, 4, and 5.)

2. The time of this constellation is when the sun is clothing the woman, which simply means it is when the sun appears to be in the constellation Virgo, which is always the months of September/October. Please note also that there is a ring of 12 stars (with a magnitude of four to five or greater) that surround the head of the constellation Virgo. The lower the number is, the brighter the star. Magnitude five stars are visible with the naked eye. Magnitude one stars, like Spica, are very bright.

3. Because the moon is also present with the sun, it means that it is a new moon, since this is the only time that we can have the sun and the moon together.

4. The location within the constellations are very precise; the moon is at the feet of the "woman." John may be describing a particular solar eclipse that happens at a point when the sun and moon are together in the constellation Virgo in the months of September/October in Israel. (See Figures 3 and 6 on pages 4 and 7, and note the October 24, 1995, eclipse.)

5. This interpretation is further evidenced by the description used by John in the second sign that he describes in the heavens. Indeed the constellation Hydra, sometimes called "Hydra the Dragon," stands before the constellation in the early morning hours in Israel in the months of September/October. But John also describes how a third of the stars of the heavens are drawn by the tail of the dragon and cast to the earth. In the July 1993's issue of "*Astronomy Magazine*" the article, "Cosmic Tug of War" by David Burstein and Peter L. Manly confirms this description.

6. In Isaiah 13:10 we saw another reference to the constellations and the sun and moon. In this passage we are told several things. The "Day of the Lord" will come when the constellations will not give their light and when the sun is darkened when it goes forth. Because the moon is also referenced with it not showing its light either, it is then very easy to conclude that what Isaiah is describing is a solar eclipse at exactly sunrise (see Is. 13:10).

7. The context and the genre of Isaiah 13 and Revelation 12 are the same. Both passages have a woman in birth pangs ready to be delivered, and I believe that both passages are telling us that when the "Day of the Lord" comes, it will come at a very precise and appointed time when the sun and moon are in Virgo and at its feet in the ecliptic orbit of the sun and moon through the background of the zodiac (Is. 34:16; Hab. 2:2-4).

This is the time of harvest. Harvest time is the time that we should expect deliverance and salvation (Jer. 8:6-11, 20). This is when God will send the angels to bind and separate. This is the season when the Rapture will take place (Mt. 13:37-43; Rev. 14:14-16). This is when the first fruits will be gathered (Rev. 14:4), which is the Church at the throne of God. In other words, John is telling us that the "Day of the Lord" begins when the woman (Israel) comes through the beginning of sorrows, and it will be indicated (not caused) by signs in the heavens and signs on the earth. The sign is a solar eclipse that will take place at exactly sunrise in the Middle East, in the month of October at the feet of the constellation Virgo. *On October 24, 1995, the Middle East will experience a solar eclipse at exactly sunrise while the sun and moon are found at the feet of the constellation Virgo.* Venus, the morning star, which could be the star that guided the wise men to the birth of Christ, will also become visible in the east at the time of totality (Rev. 2:28; 22:16).

8. The name of the star, Spica, is also known by the ancients who knew of the sign of the first coming of Christ. This, in conjunction with the planet Venus, could form the sign of the cross or the prophesied sign of the coming of the Son of Man. The solar system is God's universal clock and these signs are like the hands of a great clock. The problem is, we have forgotten how to read the signs of the times. We have forgotten how to tell time. There is too much here for coincidence. The mathematical odds of these prophecies coming together all at once, with this eclipse, in Virgo, within the seventh month and the seventh feast, are against one concluding complete coincidence.

The Signs Are All Around Us!

If our scenario with these prophecies is right, then 1994 was the pivotal year, in that God slowly began to increasingly convince mankind of the coming judgment. Watch for horrendous destructive storms, growing famine, wars, social upheavals, and the increased threat of war. God has dealt Hollywood several severe warnings because of its role in undermining and ridiculing His Word and true believers, while promoting and advocating perversion and lies. Still with all the unrest, floods, fires, storms, mud slides, blizzards, and earthquakes, many are not yet convinced of their need to repent. No one is telling them that judgment is indeed knocking at their door. The mainline media did not report that the earthquake of 1994 in California hit the heart of the pornographic industry, wiping most of it out. Since the January 1995 earthquake in Japan, to the date of this writing, the world has experienced one eathquake per week of 5.5 to 7.5 magnitude. According to the U.S. Geological Survey's National Earthquake Information Center, there were 10,493 eearthquakes recorded in 1984 while 21, 476 were recorded in 1993.

The year 1995 may see the spread of worldwide famine and disease. The warnings are already going out. The *Baltimore Sun*, February 20, 1994, on page 24A, had an article entitled "Mutant Strains of Common Bacteria Pose Increasing Threat, Researcher Warns." In the article Alexander Tomasz of Rockefeller University of New York City says that, "in the post-antibiotic world, the simplest infections could quickly escalate into fatal illnesses. Most people think it will happen…it's unpredictable when." And the consequences? "No one knows." The article ends with, "If you get the infection…you are in the Almighty's hands."

We will also see Russia hit by famine and unrest. We will see Russia return to threats of expansionism and we will see a dramatic increase in earthquakes and volcanic activity in 1995.

The year of 1995 will be a year of sorrows. It will be a year of growing unrest between nations and a nuclear threat will again plague the world's security. It will be a year that will get progressively worse from month to month until we get to October. By the way, it is also interesting that October 1995 is the date set by the Clinton administration to have the armed forces reach their mandated reductions in size and strength. Why?

As a result, we predict that Christians who stand by a "literal" interpretation of the Word of God will be persecuted for their warnings of impending judgment. They might even be blamed for the chaos. All this will come to pass if October 1995 delivers the world to the "Day of the Lord." Without these signs, the "Day of the Lord" will not come. To us it will clearly indicate that seals two, three, four, and five are opened and the sixth seal will be the convincer. In it the sky will be rolled back, the Church will be raptured, and the world will know that the Day of the Lord's Wrath has come (Rev. 6:17).

This pattern of God's progressive warning is consistent with the pattern in Old Testament judgments. Therefore, as for me and my house, we will continue to keep a vigilant watch for the coming of the Lord and will serve Him and His people from harvest to harvest until the Lord takes us home or returns for His Church (Josh. 24:15; Jer. 8:20).

Chapters 9 and 10 Summary

To summarize then, this study thus far shows how and why Daniel's prophetic week cannot begin until after the opening of sixth seal and will proceed with the seventh seal removed. The first six seals are associated with the beginning of sorrows and are part of the age of the Church. The seal judgments were first manifested in the destruction of Jerusalem in A.D. 70. Once opened, the seals continue to impact our world during this dispensation of grace and continue into the first half of Daniel's prophetic week.

The seventh seal opens the scroll, and the week begins only after the 144,000 are sealed and make their way into the wilderness with the two witnesses. The first four trumpet judgments are within the first half of the week and are part of the ministry of the two witnesses. The two witnesses are killed by the beast. This gives rise to the eighth king(dom) and the beast overthrows the remaining powers of the seventh king(dom) (Rev. 17). The middle of the tribulation is marked with the fifth trumpet and by the Abomination of Desolation (Dan. 9:27). The five months of the fifth trumpet see the armies of Gog and Magog (Babylon the Great) coming against Israel but God destroys them. This upsets the beast. The sixth trumpet sounds shortly thereafter. The armies of the ten horns are gathered against what remains of the seventh king(dom), which continues only for a short time (three-and-one-half to four years). With the Harlot and Western powers destroyed, and with now no threat of anyone coming to Israel's aid, the beast rallies the armies of the world against Israel. They will then be gathered into the valley of Armageddon, set for the blowing of the seventh trumpet judgment and the final battle—the Second Coming of the Lord Jesus Christ.

The sounding of the seventh trumpet will commence the pouring out of the vial judgments, which will end only when the seven vials are fully poured out. Following these judgments, Christ Himself will return to fight the final battle in the valley of Armageddon (Rev. 19:11-21).

Revelation chapter 12 is a dynamic chapter that needs to be fully considered, applied, and related to the chapters that precede it in order to understand that it separates the first half events of Revelation and Daniel's prophetic week from the second half. It also introduces the contrast between the fates of those who will trust and follow the Lord versus those who will follow and worship the beast.

In chapter 13 we see the destiny of those who follow and worship the beast, while in chapter 14 we see the hope of those who trusted and followed the Lord. Chapter 12, when properly understood, locks in the chronology of the pretribulation Rapture.

The sealing of the 144,000 takes place and they go into the wilderness with the two witnesses (two wings of an eagle) for three-and-one-half years in the first half of the tribulation.

After three-and-one-half years, the fifth trumpet sounds and the first woe, which is the casting out of satan from Heaven, takes place. This is also the time when the Abomination of Desolation takes place and when the two witnesses are killed. Finally, the battle of Gog and Magog, followed by the final assault against the land of Israel in the Battle of Armageddon, is indicated by the last verse of chapter 12. Satan will gather the nations against the believing remnant of Israel and against Christ for the final war in world history (Rev. 19:11-19).

It is clear to me now that the "Day of the Lord" may potentially come in October of 1995. In October of 1995 the signs that John describes in Revelation 12:1-4 and those of the prophet in Isaiah 13:10 will appear in the heavens in Israel at exactly sunrise on October 24. The way that this eclipse also fits in with the Jewish feasts, the lunar eclipse on October 8 and the solar eclipse of August 11, 1999, says that this is too much to just dismiss as coincidence or as insignificant.

I believe it would be irresponsible to dismiss these facts. This happening, when considered in conjunction with everything else, demands some very special consideration. For those who would scoff at such a consideration, I have one question. Do you choose to stand up and tell me that the "Day of the Lord," in light of the evidence presented, cannot begin in October of 1995? If the rapture is imminent, then why not October 1995 or shortly before these signs take place?

What evidence do you present? I would rather sound the warning and be wrong, than maintain my silence and my contemporary standing and be right. *As a watchman for the "Day of the Lord," I am sounding the alarm that the time we have remaining before the coming of the "Day of the Lord" appears to be running out.*

I have reviewed the data over and over. I have even considered the possibilities of the significance for this alignment in John's day. On September 14, A.D. 93, for example, Virgo was clothed with the sun and the moon appeared under her feet, marking the new moon of the seventh month. But, because of the precession of the stars over time, this alignment now marks the eighth month. This simple alignment occurs many times, but the description of Revelation 12:1-4 also notes that the dragon stood ready to devour, which, when coupled with other Scripture and historic data, indicates a solar eclipse in the "Tail of the Dragon."

The fact is that only October 24, 1995, fits with total and absolute accuracy the description of all the passages that reference the coming of the "Day of the Lord" at sunrise and in the constellation of Virgo. Perhaps the feast has nothing to do with the coming of the "Day of the Lord." The feasts vary with the precession of our planet through the stars. I only know that the timing and location of the October 8 and October 24 eclipses of 1995, coupled with the new moon of January 1, 1995, and the August 11, 1999, eclipse, are a very interesting family of events.

The uniqueness is most convincing because I believe that the eclipses of October 8 and 24, 1995, may be the prophesied signs understood by few, just like the star of Bethlehem, which indicated to a few the birth of the Messiah.

End Notes

1. E.W. Bullinger, *The Witness of the Stars,* (Grand Rapids, MI: Kregel Publications, 1967), p. 1.

2. Bauckham, *The Climax of Prophecy*, p. 17.

3. Maunder, *The Astronomy of the Bible*, (New York: Mitchell Kennerley, 1908), p. 208.

4. Paul Steidl, *The Earth, the Stars, and the Bible,* (Phillipsburg, NJ: Presbyterian and Reformed Publishing Co., 1979), p. 65. Note: Steidl thinks that the signs in the sun, stars, and moon must be more than just eclipses because, as such, they would be too predictive. However, noting the detail in Scripture, the commands to watch for signs of the end and the promises by our Lord to give signs in the heavens, Scripture then singles these signs out as being very uniquely associated with the "Day of the Lord." Understanding will arrive with the signs. (See page 81 for his argument.)

5. Ibid.

6. Ferguson, *Backgrounds of Early Christianity*, p. 188.

7. James H. Charlesworth, *Jewish Astrology in the Talmud, Pseudepigrapha, the Dead Sea Scrolls, and Early Palestinian Synagogues,* HTR 70, (1977), pp. 183-200.

8. Rachel Hachilili, "The Zodiac in Ancient Jewish Art," *Bulletin of American Schools of Oriental Research,* 228, (1977), pp. 61-77.

9. Ferguson, *Backgrounds of Early Christianity,* p. 189.

10. Ibid., pp. 282-283.

11. David Ulansey, "Solving The Mithraic Mysteries," *Biblical Archeological Review,* (September/October, 1994), pp. 41-53.

12. E.W. Maunder, *The Astronomy of the Bible,* pp. 198-199.

13. Ibid., p. 123.

14. Ibid., p. 202.

15. Ibid., p. 126.

16. *The Total Solar Eclipse of May, 1900*, p. 22, as cited by Maunder, *The Astronomy of the Bible*, p. 129.

17. Ibid., p. 129.

18. Ibid.

19. For more information on solar eclipses, see F.K. Ginzel, *Spezieller der Sonnen-und Mondfinsternisse*, (Berlin, 1899); J.F. Schroeter, *Spezieller Kannon der zentralen Sonnen-und Mondfinsternisse*, (Kristianna, 1930); M. Kundlek and E.H. Mickler, *Solar and Lunar Eclipses of the Ancient Near East From 3000 B.C. to 0 With Maps*, (Neukirchen-Vluyn, 1971).

20. The statements are taken from the exhaustive compilation of nineteenth century eclipse observations by A.C. Ranyard, "Observations Made During Total Eclipses," *Memoirs of the Royal Astronomical Society*, (1879), p. 41.

21. F.R. Stephenson, "Astronomical Verification and Dating of Old Testament Passages Referring to Solar Eclipses," *Palestine Quarterly,* (1975), p. 108.

22. Ibid.

23. Wolfram von Soden, *The Ancient Orient: An Introduction to the Study of the Ancient Near East*, Geiorgio Buccellati, ed., (Grand Rapids, MI: Eerdmans Publishing Co., 1994), p. 170.

24. Stewart Custer, *The Stars Speak, Astronomy in the Bible*, (Greenville, SC: Bob Jones University Press, 1977), p. 18.

25. David Burstein and Peter L. Manly, "The Great Attractor," *Astronomy,* (Waukesha, WI: Kalmbach Publishing Co., July 1993), p. 42.

26. Alan Kogut, as quoted in "COBE Shows Motion of Local Group," *Astronomy,* (April 1994), p. 20.

27. Ibid., p. 45.

28. Boyd Hunt, *Redeemed! Eschatological Redemption and the Kingdom of God*, (Nashville, TN: Broadman & Holman Publishers), p. 275.

29. F.R. Stephenson, "Astronomical Verification and Dating of Old Testament Passages Referring to Solar Eclipses," *Palestine Quarterly,* (1975), p. 120.

30. Sharon Begley, "The Science of Doom," *Newsweek*, (November 23, 1992) p. 59.

31. Maunder, *The Astronomy of the Bible*, p. 298.

32. Custer, *The Stars Speak, Astronomy in the Bible,* p. 132.

Chapter 11

Possibilities

When the Day of the Lord Comes!

Several realities make it probable that the feasts of the seventh month may introduce the world to the "Day of the Lord"! The last day of the Feast of Tabernacles, Hoshana Rabba, appears very fitting for such an inauguration. Predicting a precise date will, of course, always prove pointless. Attempting to predict the arrival of the "Day of the Lord" is, however, much like predicting the birth of a child, only much more complex. We cannot be absolutely certain, but we can know by the pangs that the birth is imminent and within a certain time frame. Likewise, we cannot precisely predict the travail of Israel's trouble and the Rapture of the Church that will precede it. This is good.

As we begin to see increased signs of sorrows, we should be warned. If, when referencing that "day," Isaiah 13:10, Malachi 4:2, and Revelation 12:1-4 together signify a sunrise eclipse in Virgo, in the Middle to Southeast Asia, then the "Day of the Lord" may arrive somewhere near October 24, 1995. This is the only time in the near future when all these alignments will be fulfilled perfectly. Certainly, it will be the first time since Israel regained its sovereignty.

If, however, Revelation 12:1-5 is simply indicating the first day of Marchesvan (the eighth month of Israel's calendar), then the only conclusion that may be drawn is that some future October will see the arrival of the "Day of the Lord."

In addition to the evidence of Revelation 12:1-5, which clearly indicates astronomically that the "Day of the Lord" begins in the month of October, we must also consider other passages that reference a solar eclipse. I have clearly tied these passages together. As a result of this timely discovery, other passages reveal their hidden manna that have helped to give evidence supporting my thesis.

Now I would like to consider, in greater detail, the correlation between these cosmic events and the Feast of Tabernacles. Hoshana Rabba is the seventh day of the seventh feast of the Jewish religious calendar for the year. It means the "Day of Great Salvation." It is believed by some that, at midnight on this day, the skies will open and anything that one wishes for will come true. The wish associated with this day is the desire or a prayer to be saved.

One very important and significant ritual of the Feast of Tabernacles, in biblical times, was the pouring of water in the temple. This ceremony lasted seven days. The last day was called *Hosha'na Rabba*, meaning "Day of the Great Hosanna." All this was done as the priests blew trumpets. With the waving of their *lulav* (palm branches), the Levities and all the people sang the Great Hallel (Psalms 113 through 118). Toward the end of the Hallel are these words: "*Save now, I beseech Thee, O Lord...*" (Ps. 118:25). [1]

Tabernacles, Modern Observance

Today, "in the commemoration of God's mighty deliverance of His people from Egypt and their 40 years of wilderness wandering [and dwelling] in tents and tabernacles, Jewish people erect booths. [These booths are] erect[ed] in the yards of many homes and adjoining synagogues. ...During Succoth, meals are eaten in the booth (succah). In the synagogues, Succoth is observed in a ritual featuring the *lulav* (palm branch), the *esrog* (citron), *shannas* (willow twigs), and *hadassah* (myrtle). The *lulav* and *esrog*, held in the hands of the worshipers, are gently swayed in the direction of the four corners of the earth during a recital of the Hosanna hymns" (Mt. 24:31; Rev. 7:1-2).[2]

The following is taken from a 1976 Jewish calendar:

> "Five days after Yom Kippur, the holiest day of the Jewish year, comes **Sukkoth**, a happy harvest festival that the Bible names the Feast of Booths. It is the Jewish Thanksgiving, celebrated in Israel with renewed importance and joy. Among its many traditions—such as the building of the sukkah, a booth of twigs decorated with fruit and flowers, is that of Hoshanna Rabba, the seventh day of **Sukkoth.** *At midnight, it is said, the skies open, and any wish made then will undoubtedly come true!*" (Emphasis added.)

Coulson Shepherd says that the Feast of Tabernacles typifies or foretells of God's marvelous planned redemption for the nation of Israel. Not only is it the redemption of the Jewish nation, but through them, eventually, a period of peace.

> "The number seven is very prominent in the Feast of Tabernacles. It is the seventh feast, observed in the seventh month, and was to last seven days. Seven is the biblical number of completion. It was on the seventh day that God rested from all of His work (Gen. 2:2)....This feast points very definitely to the Millennium, considered by many Bible scholars as the seventh dispensation."[3]

In the days of the seventh angel, when the seventh seal is opened, a delay will be introduced for the sealing of the 144,000 Jews (Rev. 7:1-8; 8:1). It will also be a time when the seventh angel speaks to the seventh church of Laodicea that has entered Daniel's "Seventieth Week" (seven years of tribulation) and the seventh kingdom that must continue for a short space (Rev. 17:10).

God has a wonderful future in store for a redeemed Israel who will obey and worship Him with sincerity of heart. Of that day, Zechariah tells us:

> *Thus saith the Lord of hosts; In those days it shall come to pass, that ten men shall take hold out of all languages of the nations, even shall take hold of the skirt of him that is a Jew, saying, We will go with you: for we have heard that God is with you* (Zechariah 8:23).

Everything Agrees

1. We have consistently said that Revelation 7:9-17 is a view of the raptured saints in Heaven just after the Rapture. From our studies in Revelation 12, we have concluded that the "Day of the Lord" must begin somewhere during the months of September/October because this is the only time when the sun can be found to be in the constellation Virgo.

It is fitting, then, for us to anticipate the seventh king(dom) to come of age and, therefore, that the Rapture must take place sometime before the beginning of the "Day of the Lord." The Rapture will help to mark the beginning of the seventh king(dom). Someday, if this conclusion is correct, while celebrating or preparing for the Feast of Tabernacles, Jews will see the clouds roll back and hear the trumpet of the Lord sounding—the last trumpet announcing an end of the seventh and final feast of the Jewish year.

2. It is no accident that we find the raptured saints standing before the Lamb's throne wearing white robes signifying redemption, and with palm branches in their hands. These palm branches may indicate that the time of the Rapture is near the time of the Feast of Tabernacles (Rev. 7:9). The angel of Revelation 8:1-4 appearing at the altar of God also parallels the offering of incense on the Day of Atonement, Yom Kippur. The angel appears there after the opening of the seventh seal, with the seven angels of the seven trumpets, ready to sound.

Therefore, if this scene in Heaven does parallel the events of the Day of Atonement, then the scene of Revelation 7:9-17 could be the Church in Heaven after the sealing of the 144,000 has taken place, and could be on the days between Yom Kippur and the Feast of Tabernacles.

With the sealing of the 144,000 accomplished, the Feast of Tabernacles is celebrated both in Heaven and on earth with the 144,000 going into the wilderness with the two witnesses to a place prepared for them by God (Rev. 12:6,14).

3. The last day of Sukkoth is Hosana Rabba, "The Great Day of Hosanna" or "The Great Day of Salvation. Maybe this is why we find the Raptured Church singing "*Salvation to our God which sitteth upon the throne, and unto the Lamb*" (Rev. 7:10).

4. The Feast of Tabernacles is the Jewish Thanksgiving in Revelation 7:12, where we have the angels, and the elders, the four living ones about the throne, falling on their faces, worshiping God, and saying "*Blessing,*

and glory, and wisdom, and thanksgiving, and honour, and power, and might, be unto our God for ever and ever" (Rev. 7:12). This is like the reciting of the Great Hallel (the reciting of Psalms 113–118) in Heaven. This is the only time that we find thanksgiving being mentioned in the Book of Revelation. This may be the time of the Feast of Tabernacles when the "Day of the Lord" has arrived (Rev. 7:11-12). The feast on earth, like the temple parallel, is the heavenly pattern (Heb. 9:23-24).

5. It is a time of the harvest moon (Mt. 24:39-41). The end of this godless world system comes with a harvesting of the first fruits to God (Rev. 14:4).

6. I have also said that the "Day of the Lord" comes with the opening of the sixth seal, with earthquakes, hail from Heaven, and mountains being moved out of their place. The heavens will roll back like a scroll, which could be the fulfillment of expected prayer associated with the seventh day of Sukkoth, known as Hoshana Rabba. This is when the skies will open and those who have trusted in the Lord will be greatly saved.

Maybe the Lord is going to reveal Himself to the world several days or weeks after the Rapture takes place. This would make sense, since the Rapture comes as a thief in the night. Only after the Church is secure in Heaven and the 144,000 are sealed, does the Lord reveal Himself and His glory in the heavens (Mt. 24:29-31; Lk. 21:27; Rev. 6:16-17).

7. On October 14, 1995, Hoshana Rabba will be celebrated. Ten days later, at exactly sunrise, a solar eclipse will take place exactly as it was described by John almost 2,000 years ago (Rev. 12:1-4); by the prophet Isaiah over 2,600 years ago (Is. 13:9-10); by the prophet Joel (2:1-3) over 2,700 years ago; and in the Gospels almost 2,000 years ago. "*And then shall appear the sign of the Son of man in heaven...*" (Mt. 24:30). The blowing of the trumpet (Joel 2:1) *could be* the final trump (1 Thess. 4:16; 1 Cor. 15:51-52).

Just One Possibility

Wednesday, October 4, 1995, Yom Kippur, the Day of Atonement and the holiest day of the year for Israel, may mark the beginning of the ministry of God's two witnesses. Imagine this as a time when Israel is dedicating its rebuilt temple and the two witnesses begin their ministry. Three-and-one-half years, after the two witnesses have completed their ministry, they will be killed by the antichrist at Passover.

It is impossible for us to point to any particular day as the day of the Rapture. But, if we are right to project that October 1995 holds some ominous warning, as indicated by this very precise solar eclipse and the preceding lunar eclipse, then we can at least be certain that the Rapture must take place sometime before *the 144,000 go into the wilderness* (Rev. 12:5-6) and before the onset of the Lord's wrath (Rev. 8:1-4).

Yom Kippur is on the tenth day of Tishri. Sometime during this ten-day period, the Church could be raptured. Although it is impossible to be dogmatic about *which day* the Rapture will occur, satan has already started to set up his diversions.

Notice how much we are starting to hear about "prophets" like Nostradamus, Edgar Cacye, the appearances of the "Virgin Mary," and the New Age UFO's. These are all the work of that prophetess Jezebel (Rev. 2:20). Satan is working to short-circuit the warnings going out from Christians.

For example, a program that aired on television, March 1, 1994, entitled "Ancient Prophecies" (produced by Greystone International, a Coast to Coast Production), was completely void of any hope of salvation in Jesus Christ. The message of this two-hour program was "New Age" rhetoric. The only way for the world to avoid the coming judgment, according to this production, is found in protecting the environment. "Man must change his ways. Man must stop abusing the planet before it is too late."

Yet, it is amazing how the prophecies in this program paralleled Bible prophecies. The program revealed that the 15th century "prophet" Nostradamus predicted the coming of a third antichrist named "Mabus" in the month of October 1995. This may be more that just a coincidence, as it coincides with the eclipse of October 1995 and John's precise descriptions of a heavenly alignment. He also predicted the arrival of the "King of Terror" in relationship to an August 1999 solar eclipse.

I myself am without an explanation for Nostradamus ability to predict or see into the future. This program had just enough truth to deceive the untrained. Christians will not be fooled because we know the *truth* of God's Word. We know there is hope. We know there is a judgment coming. We also know the Rapture is really going to happen and we know that we have nothing to fear.

The Rapture may come at some time after the "Ten Awesome Days" that fall between Rosh Hashanah, the first of Tishri, and Yom Kippur, the tenth of Tishri, or on Hoshana Rabba (the Day of Great Salvation), the last day of Succoth. Maybe these ten days before Yom Kippur have some significance in explaining the ten days of Revelation 2:10.

> *Fear none of those things which thou shalt suffer: behold, the devil shall cast some of you into prison, that ye may be tried; and ye shall have tribulation ten days...* (Revelation 2:10).

It could be that the Church is raptured out of the first week of the tribulation as it arrives. This is why it can be said that "*These are they which came out of great tribulation*" (Rev. 7:14). After only ten days of the beginning of the tribulation, God will save His people from that hour of great temptation (Rev. 3:10).

Will this be sometime in September/October of 1995? October 1995 appears to be a season of time that holds some rather ominous significance, but no one will know until that day arrives. Rosh Hashanah, the New Year of the Jewish people, "ushers in the Days of Judgment for all mankind."[4]

> "Jewish tradition teaches that, in the course of these ten days, God examines the lives of all human beings....Then He determines their fate for the coming year. In the words of a familiar prayer, 'On Rosh Hashanah, it is written, and on Yom Kippur, it is sealed.' "[5]

This seems to be an ideal time to rapture the Church, whose faith is sealed by the Holy Spirit of promise (Eph. 1:13), and to seal the 144,000 Jewish remnant at the very beginning of the "Seventieth Week" of Daniel (Rev. 7). As I have already noted, other scholars have also indicated that the seventh month, with the Feast of Trumpets and the Feast of Tabernacles, could hold some significance for the timing of the Lord's return.

What I have written and interpreted about Revelation chapters 7 and 12 only support this view. The Church may go through ten days of tribulation at the end of the "beginning of sorrows," but the tribulation to the Church will be caused by the devil who stands before the woman (Rev. 12:4). "*Immediately after the tribulation of those days shall the sun be darkened, and the moon shall not give her light...*" (Mt. 24:29). Satan is waiting for her child to be brought forth, which is with Christ at the Rapture of the Church (Rev. 12:5).

For ten days the Church may have to endure tribulation, and she must remain faithful at that time because the Lord will rescue her (Rev. 2:10; 3:10; 7:14). It will be a time of separating the wheat from the tares and a time of great apostasy. The letter to the Church of Smyrna gives indication that the purpose for the suffering by that faithful soul was to serve as an opportunity for testing. Thus, it could be a reference to a ten-day period of testing for believers (Dan. 1:14-15).

In other words, God will not allow the devil to persecute believers more than ten days. Thus, these ten days could be fulfilled just before or after Yom Kippur or Hoshana Rabba. The ten days before Yom Kippur are known as the "Awesome Days" of purging.

Coulson writes, "The ten days between Rosh Hoshanna and Yom Kippur are known as 'The Awesome Days.' They are ten days of repentance when Jewish people are commanded to search their hearts and afflict their souls. In Biblical times the emphasis on this was so strong, that anyone who did not afflict his soul would suffer death. Hear again the pronouncement: For whatsoever soul it be that shall not be afflicted in that same day, he shall be cut off from among his people" (Lev. 23:29).[6]

During these ten days any one of the following is possible:

1. The Church is raptured in the ten days that precede Yom Kippur.
2. The Church is raptured sometime before these ten days and during this time the 144,000 are sealed.
3. The Church is raptured on some future Yom Kippur and the 144,000 are sealed in the ten days that follow.
4. The Church is raptured sometime even earlier than Tishri 1, which is the seventh month, and begins with the Feast of Trumpets. Or, the Rapture may occur on the last day of the Feast of Trumpets when the final trump is sounded.

Of these four I choose the third as the most favorable, but two and four are just as plausible. I do not know how God's Word will be fulfilled, but I have shown "how" and when it could be fulfilled, using very natural cosmic phenomena to do so.

The days between Yom Kippur and Rosh Hoshanna may be awesome days indeed, if they are ten days of pretribulation testing. Either way, in light of the feast and their prophetic significance, *only a pretribulation Rapture fits the prophetic timing within the feast of the seventh month.*

Those who have an ear will hear the Lord speaking at that time, possibly through the words of the two witnesses. The two witnesses will be telling the 144,000 to get ready to follow them into the wilderness to escape the coming trials and tribulations of the "Day of the Lord." The Church will be in Heaven and then the Lord will work to bring Israel and the world to acknowledge Him as Lord, through the ministry of the two witnesses and the 144,000.

The period of silence associated with the seventh seal and after the opening of the sixth seal, may be one and the same, or it may point to the heavenly awe commonly associated with a solar eclipse as the sign of the Son of Man appears in the heavens (Rev. 12:1-4). Just prior to this time, the 144,000 Jews will be sealed by God and the two witnesses will gather them up, take them into the wilderness, protect them, and teach them.

Their ministry will continue for three-and-one-half years. They will begin their ministry on or near Yom Kippur. The first of seven trumpet judgments will begin to sound after the 144,000 elected Jews are sealed. The judgments of God will greatly intensify what was decreed in the opening of the seventh seal, days later.

There will be no more delay when the Lord's wrath arrives, marked by a sunrise solar eclipse in Israel, literally fulfilling the prophecies (Is. 13:9-10; Mt. 24:29; Mk. 13:24; Lk. 21:25; Rev. 12:1-4). The lunar eclipse that precedes the coming of the "Day of the Lord" on October 8, 1995, could fulfill Joel 2:30-31, Acts 2:19-20, and Revelation 6:12.

Time will see God's Word fulfilled exactly as it has been written. It is impossible to be absolute sure whether or not October 1995 is the fulfillment. I have listed some very interesting parallels that are found in the Word of God and future cosmic alignments that appear to fulfill these conditions.

I simply ask you to consider the possibilities and to watch and pray. Many believe that the season of the Lord's return is upon us. One of the scenarios that I have presented may be totally right or partially right. Or, they may be all totally wrong. I do not claim to be a prophet, only one who is prayerfully watching and studying God's Word. I have reported what I have seen and what I believe it could mean. Everyone will have to read the Scriptures for themselves and determine whether or not what I have written is potentially true and accurate or just a coincidence and without any prophetic significance.

One of the biggest obstacles to overcome that I face is people's unfamiliarity with the astronomical data. I will continue to serve the Lord with each and every day by adding as many souls as I can to the Body of Christ. I will plan and build for the future (should I be wrong) if the Lord chooses to tarry for many years. This we must do because, as mere mortals, it is the most prudent action for us.

Not "knowing" if the Lord is really coming in 1995 or 1996, 1997, etc., we must continue to watch, hope, and serve until we "are" with the Lord. The signs seem to indicate 1995, but men will continue to learn more and more relative truth about the Second Coming as it draws closer with each passing day. The "Day of the Lord" will come and the Rapture will precede it at the Lord's appointed time.

I am reasonably certain that the sixth seal includes the Rapture, that the "Day of the Lord" commences with the seventh seal, and that the two witnesses have their ministry in the first half of the tribulation. The only thing I am really uncertain about is "*when*," but I am very comfortable with this uncertainty.

The Rapture is coming and when it comes, then and only then will we "know" when the "Day of the Lord" has come. For those who know and have accepted Christ as their personal Savior, they will be with Him at His throne in Heaven and will truly "know" and understand. Until that day comes, we must continue to watch and serve.

A Final Warning

Luke offers us some good advice.

> *And take heed to yourselves, lest at any time your hearts be overcharged with surfeiting, and drunkenness, and cares of this life, and so that day come upon you unawares. For as a snare shall it come on all them that dwell on the face of the whole earth. Watch*

ye therefore, and pray always, that ye may be accounted worthy to escape all these things that shall come to pass, and stand to before the Son of man" (Luke 21:34-36).

Each of us needs to look at ourselves and ask, "Am I truly ready for the Lord to return?" If we find ourselves totally ignorant of the signs around us, perhaps fearfully hoping that the Lord might delay His return so we can enjoy the things of this world, then we care too much for worldly pleasures. We cannot allow the sweet-sounding rhetoric of this world to intoxicate us to the point that the signs of the Lord's coming remain obscure.

The truth is concealed from ears and eyes that have been dulled by the empty promises of a world feasting in a quagmire of self-love. The "Day of the Lord" will come as a thief to those who are totally unaware of the events taking place in the world. They will be the ones left behind with the other unbelievers and hypocrites (Mt. 24:45-51; Lk. 12:42-46).

The Rapture is coming as a thief, but the ruling reign of Christ will be well announced. The Abomination of Desolation and all the events of the trumpet and the vial judgments will leave little doubt as to the Second Coming of Christ and the arrival of the Kingdom of God. Just as the First Coming of Christ had two parts, so will the second.

First, Christ came to provide salvation through His atoning death, burial, and resurrection. Many did not recognize Jesus as the Messiah because they were looking for the setting up of the Kingdom of God wherein they would jointly rule over the kingdoms of the world with the Messiah as their King.

David Hunt does a great job of explaining this in his book, *How Close Are We?* I agree with him when he says, "Failure to understand that the Rapture and the second coming are two different events separated by seven years lies at the heart of this confusion."[7]

Therefore, do not be confused and do not allow the world to weight you down and preoccupy your time. Preoccupation with this passing world will only blind you to the message contained in *The Signs in the Heavens* and the Word of God. There are numerous indications of the Lord's Second Coming. Watch while praying, that you may be accounted worthy to escape *all* these things that are coming upon the world and *stand* before the Son of Man.

The last section of Luke 21:36 is most interesting. Who will be able to stand on that day when the Lord shakes the whole earth, when every mountain is moved out of its place, the skies are rolled back, and the earth is moved out of its place? Only those who are standing before the throne of God, with the Lamb in the midst of them, can stand (Rev. 7:15; 12:5).

Only those who have had their sins washed away by trusting in the shed blood of the Lord Jesus Christ will be raptured from the face of the earth and therefore able to stand. Just consider the following passage:

> *And said to the mountains and rocks, Fall on us, and hide us from the face of Him that sitteth on the throne, and from the wrath of the Lamb: for the great day of His wrath is come; and who shall be able to stand?* (Revelation 6:16-17)

Why ask this question in this context? This is the day that the Lord will come as a thief. This is the day that the Lord will shake the heavens and the earth and will rapture His Church. Those taken will be found standing before Christ in Heaven:

> *After this I beheld, and, lo, a great multitude, which no man could number, of all nations, and kindreds, and people, and tongues,* ***stood*** *before the throne, and before the Lamb, clothed with white robes, and palms in their hands* (Revelation 7:9).

The Greek verb "to stand" used in all three cases is *histemi.* In the same case in Luke 21:36 and Revelation 6:17, the verb is an aorist (past tense) passive infinitive. These infinitives are used as adjuncts to the subjects of the verbs "you" and "who" respectively of these verses. The aspect of these verbs is that it applies to an indefinite action relative to time. It simply asks, "Who will be able to stand?"

This is a simple event without relationship to time or duration. Time is inferred as from the context. When that day, the "Day of the Lord," arrives with the sudden snatching away of the Church, "Who will be able to stand?" The passive indicates that the standing is something done to the subject of the infinitive. "Who will the Lord leave standing?"

The answer is, "Those who are actively standing (perfect, active participle) before His throne" (Rev. 7:9). In Revelation 6:17, the verb literally means "to stand firm or to hold one's ground in battle." Those who are left behind after the pretribulation Rapture will not be left standing because the Lord is going to shake the whole earth.

No one on earth will be left standing on that day; "*every knee shall bow*" (see Phil. 2:9-11). This day recalls something that happened on a much smaller scale when the Pharisees, Sadducees, scribes with Judas, and the temple soldiers came for Christ in the Garden of Gethsemane. "*As soon as He had said unto them, I am He, they went backward, and fell to the ground*" (Jn. 18:6).

On that glorious day when Jesus Christ first comes to rapture the Church, when that trumpet blast roars, and all the saints (dead and alive in Christ) are gathered to stand before His throne, they will have been judged acceptable in that "Great Day of the Lord." They will be found standing with the Lord. They will be standing with the Lord because they have not denied His name and they have kept His Word (Rev. 3:8-10).

The world will be left trembling and those who professed to be Christians (but were not) will have had their nakedness revealed. Their religion and their accumulated works for salvation will have been judged worthless and found insufficient in the coming of the "Day of the Lord." They will falter and be snared with the unbelieving world. They will be empty vessels. They were lukewarm and unpalatable to the Lord. To believe in God's existence is not enough.

All must repent of their sin and trust in Jesus Christ alone, by faith, calling upon the name of the Lord Jesus Christ for salvation! It must be now, for tomorrow may be too late. As it is literally said within the great Hebrew "Hos-an-na": "Save us now," Lord Jesus! Get saved today and begin to serve the Lord because the time is short.

The Philippian jailer asked the apostle Paul, "*What must I do to be saved?*" Paul and the others with him replied, "*Believe on the Lord Jesus Christ, and thou shalt be saved, and thy house*" (Acts 16:30-31).

Your religion will not save you! I do not care how good you are or how little you have sinned, you are still a sinner in need of Jesus the Savior. He is one with the Father and is the only One who can save you. The

Bible clearly tells us that there are *none* righteous before God. *All* have sinned and *all* have come short of the glory of God (Rom. 3:10,23). Not by works of righteousness which we have done, but according to His mercy He saved us, by the washing of regeneration, and renewing (work) of the Holy Spirit (Tit. 3:5).

This happens when a person is truly born again. God sends the Holy Spirit to anoint and seal the believer. This sealing and anointing is God's claim on that person forever. At that point God begins to teach and change the thinking and the nature of the individual through the ministry of the Word of God. "*Faith cometh by hearing, and hearing by the word of God*" (Rom. 10:17). "*For whosoever shall call upon the name of the Lord shall be saved*" (Rom. 10:13). Those who sincerely repent of their sins and give up trying to earn their way to Heaven through religious works (Jewish, "Christian," or otherwise) and call upon the name of the Lord, Jesus Christ, will be saved.

Paul was one of the most religious men who ever lived, but he labeled all his religious works as dung or as worthless. He gave up trusting in what he was doing and instead trusted in *who* God sent and what Jesus Christ has done. Jesus paid for the sins of the world and it is now up to every man, woman, and child either to accept God's gift of salvation or prepare to have his works judged on the final day of judgment. But be warned, on that final day, no one, and I mean no one, left behind will stand. Everyone attempting to justify themselves before God by their good works will be unable to stand in the day of the Rapture (Rev. 6:17) and in the day of the final White Throne Judgment (Rev. 20:11-15).

> *And I saw a great white throne, and Him that sat on it, from whose face the earth and the heaven fled away; and there was found no place for them. And I saw the dead, small and great, stand before God; and the books were opened: and another book was opened, which is the book of life: and the dead were judged out of those things which were written in the books, according to their works. And the sea gave up the dead which were in it; and death and hell delivered up the dead which were in them: and they were judged every man according to their works. And death and hell were cast into the lake of fire. This is the second death.*

And whosoever was not found written in the book of life was cast into the lake of fire (Revelation 20:11-15).

Pride is the only reason anyone chooses to work for something that God has already paid for. He has offered salvation as a free gift to all. Religion has confused salvation by obligating people to earn their way to Heaven. No one will earn the right to have his name written into the "Book of Life" or earn his way to Heaven because God wants all to praise Jesus Christ for what He has done.

No one will be able to boast of themselves (Eph. 2:8-9; 1 Cor. 1:29-30). If Jesus does not write your name in the "Book of Life" for you, then it will not be found there. The *only* way that God will save anyone is through trust in Christ *alone*, without the works of the law (Rom. 3).

We must choose the way to God that He has provided. This is why Jesus said, "*I am the way, the truth, and the life:* ***no man cometh unto the Father, but by Me***" (Jn. 14:6). It is not by works, not by a particular religion, but by a particular person—the Lord Jesus Christ.

Christians do good to their fellow man and obey God because they are saved. Knowing this truth sets men free to serve others. Most religions teach men to do good for the purpose of meriting salvation. This is contrary to the Word of God. We show our faith and our assurance of salvation by our works. Faith that does not manifest itself in works is dead. Dead faith does not have the power to transform or save (Jas. 2:14-26).

But to everyone who is truly "born again," who truly believes on His name, He gives the power to become the sons of God (Jn. 1:12). Faith without the evidence of the fruit of the Spirit will not save anyone (Jas. 2:17; Gal. 5:22-25).

Dear friend, do not allow your religion, your pride, or the cares of this world to keep you from the greatest and the only salvation available. The Rapture is coming soon. All those who are writing today about the return of Jesus Christ, regardless of theological positions, are saying the same thing—His return is soon!

I have labored to sound the warning that the "Day of the Lord" is at hand. For those who read this book I simply say, "It is entirely your choice to accept or reject what I have disclosed."

My duty is simply to sound the warning—to go and tell. Whether or not those hearing this warning will heed the call is not my problem, but it will always be one of my greatest concerns. *The wheat is white unto harvest, but the laborers are truly few.*

May God bless all who read this book with a greater understanding of His Word of prophecy and His will for all men to be saved—for it is time for Jesus to come again and it is time for us to understand the *Signs in the Heavens*. This is because what we are beginning to see and hear about, concerning what is coming in the heavens, is aligning itself with the Word of God. **The message that pours into my heart from God's "handywork" is one reaffirming "I am"** (see Ps. 119).

First He will Rapture His Church, and then He will reign on earth as the King of kings and the Lord of lords with the faithful of Israel and His Church at His side. Let God be true, but every man a liar. In light of the "*signs*" appearing in our time, it is time to sound the warning for all to take heed. It is time, for our world "*is near, even at the doors*" of fulfillment (Mt. 24:33).

End Notes

1. Coulson Shepherd, *Jewish Holy Days,* (Loizeaux Brothers, 1961), p. 75.
2. Ibid., pp. 74-75.
3. Ibid., p. 76.
4. Ruth W. Gregory, *Anniversaries & Holidays,* 4th ed., (Chicago, IL: American Library Association, 1983), p. 171.
5. Eric A. Kimmel, *Days of Awe*, (New York: Penguin Books USA, Inc., 1991), p. 12.
6. Shepherd, *Jewish Holy Days,* p. 75.
7. Hunt, *How Close Are We?*, p. 204.

Afterword

In Hebrews 10:25, the writer tells us that believers should not forsake the assembling together, but to exhort or edify one another "*so much the more, as* [we] *see the day approaching.*" We need to prepare the ground, plant in the spring, and labor in the summer. Then, we will reap in the time of harvest.

When we reach the harvest, we should earnestly look for the Lord of the Harvest, and as the Lord continues to tarry, we may respond as Jeremiah the prophet did so many harvests ago: "*The harvest is past, the summer is ended, and we are not saved*" (Jer. 8:20).

With this realization, may we continue, from harvest to harvest, truly serving the Lord Jesus Christ in all earnestness, fully expecting His return, but never giving into despair and complacency, for no man knows "for sure" the very day the Lord Jesus will return.

Astronomical Glossary

Asteroid—A small planet. It is thought of as a very small "planet" because it is in orbit around the sun. Most are in an asteroid belt between Jupiter and Mars. Some known as the Apollo group do intersect the earth's orbit and pose a potential threat to our planet's survival.

Astrology—The archaic term that was used to describe the study of the stars. It was perverted by juridical astrology, which believes that the planets and the stars, in their courses, control or influence human events. The term *astronomy* is now used to distinguish between the scientific and the superstitious practices of astrology.

Astronomy—Science which studies the stars or things outside the earth's atmosphere.

Autumn Equinox—This is when the sun crosses the celestial equator as it passes southward along the ecliptic. See also "Ecliptic."

Comet—A celestial object that usually consists of a bright nucleus and is trapped in a highly eccentric orbit around the sun. Solar winds cause the comet to appear with a tail, which seems to emanate from the central body. The tail is made up of ice water and other gases that break away from the comet as it travels through our solar system.

Conjunction—The alignment of two or more heavenly objects along the same line of right ascension. An object's ascension is traced across the sky as the earth rotates on its polar axis.

Contact—During a solar eclipse, this is when the leading edge of the moon appears to make contact with the orb of the sun as it passes in front of it. During a lunar eclipse the earth's shadow makes contact with the lunar surface when the earth passes between the sun and moon.

Corona—The outermost layer of the sun and the other stars faintly visible as a halo of super hot gases. The sun's corona becomes very visible during a solar eclipse at the moments of totality. The ancients have recorded such solar coronas that appeared as "eagle's wings." In 1991 such a solar corona was photographed.

Eclipse—The passage of one celestial body between the sun and another celestial body. A partial eclipse is when the disk is only partially covered. See also "contact."

Ecliptic—An imaginary line that traces out the path of the sun through the 12 background constellations of the zodiac during the course of one complete solar cycle, 365.24 days.

Equinox—The place where the sun's ecliptic path intercepts the celestial equator. The times of the year when the sun is at those points are known as the vernal, autumnal equinox. At this time the intervals of day and night are equal.

Full moon—This is when the moon, which faces the earth, is completely illuminated. It marks the middle of the lunar, Jewish month. Lunar eclipses can only take place at full moons. A full moon will rise at exactly sunset and is exactly opposite the sun.

Lunar Eclipse—Occurs when the moon passes throughout the earth's shadow. When it passes through the "umbra," it is usually a total eclipse but at times it can turn "blood red" when excessive pollutants in the earth's atmosphere reflect a copper-red light off the darkened moon's surface.

Magnitude—The brightness of a celestial object. A change of 5 magnitude indicates a brightness increase or decrease by a factor of 100.

The brighter the object is, the smaller the number. The sun's magnitude exceeds -27 while the lowest magnitude star visible with the unaided human eye is about +5, and this under dark sky conditions. Some of the brightest stars have a magnitude -1, 0 and 1.

Meridian—An imaginary circle on the celestial sphere that passes through the poles and the zenith relative to the latitude of the observer. Someone living at 40 degrees north latitude will trace out a celestial meridian of 50 degrees while facing south.

Meteorite—A small chunk of rock, metal, or ice that does not vaporize as it passes through the earth's atmosphere and strikes the earth.

Meteor—A small chunk of rock, metal, or ice that completely vaporizes in the earth's atmosphere.

New Moon—This is when the surface of the moon, which faces the earth, is completely dark. It is located with the sun in the celestial equator and marks the beginning of a new lunar cycle. It also begins a new lunar month or Jewish month. Solar eclipses can only take place when the moon is new. A new moon rises and sets with the sun.

Penumbra—During an eclipse, the area of partial shadow surrounding the darker umbra shadow. It is a shadow where the illuminating body is not completely hidden. See also "Umbra."

Precession—The slow wobble in the earth's axis and its effect on the location of celestial objects relative to the earth. This is why Passover is no longer celebrated with the sun, in the spring, while in constellation of Aries as it was 2,000 years ago. This is because it has moved to the background stars of Pisces.

Solar Eclipse—This is when the new moon passes directly between the earth and the sun. A total eclipse occurs when the disk of the moon completely covers the sun's disk relative to a specific location on earth.

Spring Equinox—See "vernal equinox."

Umbra—During an eclipse, that part of the earth or moon's shadow where the solar disk is completely covered. This is the darkest part to the disk's shadow over the celestial object.

Vernal Equinox—This is when the sun crosses the equator on its journey to the north about March 21. Because of precession it continues to move against the background stars of the zodiac. In A.D. 30 the sun was in the constellation Aries when it crossed the equator, but today is in Aries. The spring equinox occurs when the sun is in Aries. This is when day and night are equal.

Zodiac—A group of constellations that trace out the course of the sun as the earth orbits the sun. Known in the Bible as "Mazzeroth."

Zodiac, Lunar—The 28 major constellations that the moon passes through during its transition through its monthly phases from one new moon to the next.

Theological Glossary of Terms

144,000—A group of Jews, 12,000 from 12 different tribes of Israel, that are selected by God to receive a special seal upon their foreheads. This seal will protect this select group from the powers of satan. They are sealed during a parenthetical period of time between the sixth and seventh seals.

Abomination of Desolation—A very important prophetic event. It refers to the future defilement of the temple in Israel. In order to be fulfilled, the temple must be rebuilt. The defilement of the temple by Antiochus in 167 B.C. prefigures the defilement of the future antichrist. The prophecy marks the middle of the coming seven-year tribulation period. It marks the breaking of the peace covenant by the antichrist in Daniel 9:27. Matthew 24:15, Mark 13:14, and Revelation 13 testify to the central significance of this prophecy.

Amillennial—A theology based on the belief that there will not be a literal 1,000-year reign of Christ.

Armageddon—The biblical name for the final battle between the returning armies of Christ and the armies of satan in the valley of Jezreel in Israel. (See Rev. 16:16; 19:17-21; Dan. 2:35.)

Antichrist—One who will come as a false Messiah. He represents the embodiment of satan and performs satan's will in the tribulation period. He will introduce the false peace covenant and commit the abomination of desolation in the reconstructed temple of God. He will rise to power during the seven years of tribulation and will deceive the world through the miracles of the false prophet, who will cause the world to believe and accept the antichrist as their political and spiritual leader. His number is 666.

Beginning of Sorrows—A term used to describe that period of Church history which that include wars, famines, pestilence, earthquakes, and other natural disasters (Mt. 24:2-8). The significance of this term is found in the fact that both Old and New Testament prophecy that concern the coming of the "Day of the Lord," the beginning of the seven year-tribulation period, incorporate terms that symbolize the birth of a child. Thus, the period before the birth is the "**beginning** of sorrows" while the actual arrival of the "Day of the Lord" is the actual birth or final birth pangs. The implications are such that these sorrows will increase in scope, magnitude, and frequency as the "Day of the Lord" draws near. As we near the end of the days of the Church on earth, all these sorrows will increase dramatically and announce the imminent and expectant return of Christ to first, rapture His Church, and then begin the final seven-year countdown of Daniel's Seventieth Week.

Birth Pangs—The actual arrival of the Day of the Lord. It is believed by this author that the cosmic and worldwide chaos of the sixth seal of Revelation 6:12-14 is in fact the final birth pangs that raptures the Church and introduces the world to the wrath of the Lamb.

Born Again—Those who have come to Christ knowing that they are sinners, but believing that their salvation has become a reality based solely on the atoning and substitutionary death of Jesus Christ. They have experienced the "new birth," which gives them a totally new spiritual perspective of themselves, God, and the world. They are those who have declared themselves dead to this world and alive to and for God. They are the only true Christians in God's eyes. Jesus said, "You must be born again" (Jn. 3:7).

Day of Atonement (Yom Kippur)—When the high priest would enter into the "Holy of Holies" within the temple of God, where he would make a once-a-year atonement for the sins of Israel. The ten days before Yom Kippur are known as the ten "awesome days" in which all Israel are to prepare their hearts before God. This is in preparation for Yom Kippur.

Day of the Lord—A term used in the Bible that relates to a time when God reveals Himself to mankind in judgment. There have been previous periods of Israel's history where Scripture refers to the past judgment of God as the Day of the Lord. (See "Seven Years of Tribulation.")

Dispensations—Taken from a Greek word meaning "stewardship, oversight, administration, or management." It refers to a specific period of time in which man is tested in respect to his obedience to some specific revelation of God's will. Dispensationalist divide the Bible into different dispensations that help to show the progress of man's fall and God's work and plan to redeem the faithful.

Feast of Tabernacles (Sukkoth)—Feast of the Jews that begins on the fifteenth day of Tishri with the full moon. Celebrates Israel's wandering in the wilderness for 40 years. During this time, the observers dwell in booths or tents to recall the days of their wilderness wanderings. It is a time of final harvesting.

Great Tribulation Period—(See "Seven Years of Tribulation.")

Hoshana Rabba—Literally means the great day of salvation. It is the eighth day after the Feast of Tabernacles in which Jewish tradition teaches that the skies will open and prayers will be answered.

Midtribulation—Marks the 3-1/2-year point of the tribulation period. (See "Abomination of Desolation.")

Nisan—The first month of the Jewish religious calendar. On the fourteenth day of Nisan, Israel celebrates Passover.

Posttribulation—Belief that the Rapture will take place at or near the end of the seven years of tribulation.

Premillennial—Belief that Christ will return to earth before the millennial kingdom can begin.

Pretribulation—Belief that the Church, all truly born-again Christians, will be raptured before the start of the seven years of tribulation.

Prewrath—Belief that the Church will go through about four or more years of the tribulation period for testing and purification. It is a view propagated by Marvin Rosenthal, who makes subtle distinctions between the wrath of God and references to the tribulation and the great tribulation period. This position teaches that only the final segment of the tribulation period is the "Day of the Lord."

Rapture—A term taken from the Latin word *raptus*, meaning to snatch or steal away. It is used to translate the Greek word *harpazo*. A belief that God will supernaturally steal away the Church before He begins to judge the world. (See Gen. 5:21-24; 1 Cor. 15:51-53; 1 Thess. 4:13-18).

Seven Seals—These seals are removed from a scroll held by Jesus Christ that have been believed to symbolize the beginning judgments of the tribulation period. But, this author believes that the judgments of seals 1 through 6 coincide with the beginning of the Church, Pentecost, the intervening "beginning of sorrows" period, and concluding with the Rapture of the Church. The seventh seal marks the beginning of the seven-year-tribulation period.

Seven Trumpets—The seventh seal contains the seven trumpet judgments. These trumpet judgments announce and dispense the judgments of God throughout the seven years of tribulation. The first four trumpets are part of the first 3 1/2 years of Daniel's Seventieth Week. The last three trumpets are part of the second 3 1/2 years and are called "woes." The last trumpet contains the seven vial or bowl judgments.

Seven Vials (Bowls)—The seven last and devastatingly final judgments of God upon an unrepentant world and satan's armies.

Seven Years of Tribulation—The length of the final tribulation period. These are part of a prophecy contained in Daniel 9:23-27. The prophecy predicted that God had determined a special 70 group of sevens or weeks for the nation of Israel and against the kingdoms of the world. The prophecy is tied to the return of the Jews with the prophet Nehemiah in 445 B.C. and "the rebuilding of the wall." The time period is divided into two basic groups of 69 and one group of sevens. Each seven represents seven years, thus the total prophecy was for 490 years. Daniel predicted that the Messiah would come, but would be "cut off" after 69 weeks or 483 years. This first part was fulfilled completely by Jesus Christ. Ever since His ascension, the Church has been waiting for His return and the resumption of this prophecy for Israel and the world. This final unfulfilled group of sevens of Daniel's prophecy will be a period of great tribulation, thus the terms "The Seven Year Tribulation Period"; "The Great Tribulation"; and "The Day of the Lord."

Seventieth Week of Daniel—Seven years of yet unfulfilled, worldwide tribulation that will restore Israel as the leader of nations with the Messiah ruling from the throne of David. (See "Seven Years of Tribulation.")

Tishri—Seventh month of the Jewish religious calendar. The first of Tishri marks the beginning of the Jewish secular year, "Rosh Hashanah." It coincides with late September, early October.

Tribulation Period—(See "Seven Years of Tribulation.")

Two Witnesses—Revelation 11:1-14 clearly teaches that these two future witnesses of God will have a 3 1/2 year ministry and be killed within the tribulation period. They will resurrect after 3 1/2 days. They will warn the world of God's coming, all-out judgment, and lead the 144,000 sealed Jews of Revelation 7 into the wilderness where they will teach them about God and lead them to accepting Jesus Christ as their true Messiah. Their ministry is in the first half of the tribulation period. Many believe they may actually be the prophesied prophet Elijah with Moses or Enoch.

General Topical Index

S

People Index

Place Index

Scripture Index

Mark

Order Information For:
SIGNS IN THE HEAVENS Biblical Prophecy and Astronomy

Cost per book is $15.99. Bookstores and book distributors, please call 410-208-0839 for quantity discount prices.

Send orders with payment to:

Signs in the Heavens
6519 Ocean Pines
Berlin, MD 21811 U.S.A.

Over 400 Pages:

Number of Copies	Cost	Shipping/Postage		MD Tax		Total
1 copy	$15.99	+ Shipping/Postage	=	$18.99 + $ .80	=	$ 19.79
2 copies		+ Shipping/Postage	=	$37.99 + $1.59	=	$ 39.58
3 copies		+ Shipping/Postage	=	$55.99 + $2.39	=	$ 58.38
4 copies		+ Shipping/Postage	=	$71.99 + $3.20	=	$ 75.19
5 copies		+ Shipping/Postage	=	$86.99 + $4.00	=	$ 90.99
6 copies		+ Shipping/Postage	=	$99.99 + $4.80	=	$104.79

For orders greater than six books, please send $16.70 per copy. This includes shipping and postage.

For orders of 20 or more copies, please send $16.50 per copy. This includes shipping and postage.

Sales tax applies to Maryland residents ONLY. Please add 5% sales tax to orders.

Copies also may be ordered through Destiny Image Publishers, Inc., P.O. Box 310, Shippensburg, PA 17257. Their handling charges may differ. Call 1-800-722-6774.